THE HUMAN TOLL

The Human Toll

*Taxation and Slavery
in Colonial America*

Anthony C. Infanti

NEW YORK UNIVERSITY PRESS

New York

NEW YORK UNIVERSITY PRESS
New York
www.nyupress.org

© 2025 by New York University

Please contact the Library of Congress for Cataloging-in-Publication data.

ISBN: 9781479829866 (hardback)
ISBN: 9781479829880 (library ebook)
ISBN: 9781479829873 (consumer ebook)

This book is printed on acid-free paper, and its binding materials are chosen for strength and durability. We strive to use environmentally responsible suppliers and materials to the greatest extent possible in publishing our books.

The manufacturer's authorized representative in the EU for product safety is Mare Nostrum Group B.V., Mauritskade 21D, 1091 GC Amsterdam, The Netherlands. Email: gpsr@mare-nostrum.co.uk.

Manufactured in the United States of America

10 9 8 7 6 5 4 3 2 1

Also available as an ebook

For Hien and Rose Mai

CONTENTS

LIST OF BOXES, FIGURES, AND TABLES

TABLES

Introduction

Can taxation be *evil*? Despite making only a cameo appearance in the academic literature on law and evil,[1] taxation is often called a necessary evil[2] or even a matter of choosing the lesser evil.[3] Others, however, have moved beyond the occasional rhetorical flourish to label taxation *evil* with the more serious aim of undermining the integrity of the tax system. For instance, in the 1950s, the libertarian Frank Chodorov published a small volume titled *The Income Tax: Root of All Evil*, in which he asserted that the income tax "is an instrument that has the potentiality of destroying a society of humans."[4] Chodorov condemned the income tax as a form of robbery and a path to slavery that reduces human beings to the status of yoked animals.[5] More recently, libertarian academics such as Robert Nozick and Murray Rothbard, the libertarian tax lawyer and historian Charles Adams, and political actors such as US Senator Rand Paul and the conservative antitax activist and president of Americans for Tax Reform Grover Norquist have all likened taxation to theft or slavery.[6] But make no mistake, this is no recent phenomenon—likening taxation to theft or slavery has been a recurring feature of resistance to progressive taxation since the Civil War.[7]

Such antitax rhetoric purposefully (however misguidedly) taps into legitimate concerns about abuse of the taxing power and, when referring to slavery, evokes the centuries-long suffering of enslaved Black people to garner sympathy for the cause of undermining the tax system. At times, that implicit connection with human suffering has been made explicit, as when it has been baldly asserted that "it's better to be a chattel slave than a tax slave."[8] But more than just bombastic and dismissive of the plight of enslaved persons, this antitax rhetoric is profoundly ahistorical because it ignores the important role that taxation played in entrenching and perpetuating *actual* theft and slavery during the American colonial period. Redirecting attention toward this "deceitful flow from the heart of an impenetrable darkness" lurking within taxation, this book examines and documents how the thirteen colonies that later became the United States of America used the power to tax in service of the real evils of racism, White supremacy, and slavery.[9]

Acknowledging Taxation's Power to Destroy

While the power to tax can uplift by fostering a people's shared life together in ways that permit both individuals and the community to flourish, there is also the potential in any form of taxation for its power to be turned to evil ends. Indeed, the Janus-faced nature of the power to tax has long been recognized. In the early nineteenth century, US Supreme Court Chief Justice John Marshall matter-of-factly observed in the landmark case of *McCulloch v. Maryland*, "That the power to tax involves the power to destroy; that the power to destroy may defeat and render useless the power to create . . . are propositions not to be denied."[10]

Given the long-standing awareness that the power to tax is equally capable of creation and destruction, it is perplexing that legal academic discourse espouses a sanitized view of tax law as a quasi-scientific sub-discipline of economics concerned only with raising the revenue that is the lifeblood of society's existence and government's proper functioning.[11] In this rosy view of taxation that starkly contrasts with the stygian view of people seeking to undermine the tax system, tax policy need be concerned only with identifying an appropriate tax base (e.g., income, property, or wealth), establishing the economically sound parameters of that base, and collecting revenue from taxpayers as fairly and efficiently as possible. Social concerns and value judgments are relevant only when determining whether departures from the "ideal" tax base are required to administer the tax law effectively.[12] Closely related to this view of taxation as economic "science" is the notion that tax law is "exceptional"—that is to say, "special" or "'other' in the sense of being a unique and different area of the law, and often one that is seen as elevated, above the fray, or somehow on a higher plane."[13] From this vantage point, societal evils like systemic racism have no place in discussions of "neutral" and "objective" tax questions because, unlike other areas of the law, tax is above the need to acknowledge (let alone grapple with) the invidious discrimination present in society.[14]

But as the contrarian group of scholars who take a critical approach to tax law have shown—and as a growing number of "mainstream" tax academics are coming to acknowledge—taxation *is* deeply embedded in the fabric of society and, through choices regarding what, whom, and how to tax, sends messages about those whom society values and validates as well as about those whom society marginalizes and oppresses.[15] This book expands on the insights and analyses of critical tax scholars as part of a larger project examining the relationship between tax law and society. The book illustrates how taxation was embedded in slavery and a broader tapestry of racism and oppression, furnishing financial incentives and disincentives to shape behavior in the service of evil.[16] In this regard, tax law was not "exceptional." The racism that permeated the colonial law of property, contracts, torts, successions, domestic relations, and criminal punishment was equally present in colonial tax law.[17] This book thus contributes to an important vein of critical tax scholarship by demonstrating that, contrary to widely held views among tax scholars, tax law is deeply connected with society and, far from being above the fray, was no different from other areas of the law that were used to protect and promote slavery. By transporting the critical tax literature into the distant past, the book also anchors the need for, and importance of, critical perspectives in the long history of taxation being used as a tool for oppressing subordinated groups.

At the same time, this book excavates and documents fiscal history that, until now, has garnered little notice from historians. Past historical work has shown in detail how nontax aspects of the colonial legal regime supported and entrenched the institution of slavery.[18] In contrast, the role of taxation in supporting and promoting slavery has merited little more than passing mention.[19] This book endeavors to fill that gap by undertaking a detailed examination of the ways in which taxation protected and promoted slavery, providing a completer and more accurate picture of just how widely entrenched systemic legal supports for slavery were in the colonial period. Given the amount of primary source material relied on here as well as the insights brought by viewing this material from a tax law scholar's perspective, this comprehensive portrait of the links between taxation and slavery in colonial America will hopefully serve as a resource for historians, allowing them better to take account of taxation in their own work.

Taxation and Slavery

Part 1 of this book consists of three chapters examining in detail the relationship between taxation and slavery in colonial South Carolina. Chapter 1 begins with the colony's early legislative experimentation with forging ties between taxation and slavery. Chapter 2 then proceeds to the crystallization of the legal regime of closely intertwined tax and nontax measures that exerted ever-tighter control over South Carolina's enslaved population. Chapter 3 concludes with the legislature's refinement and routinization of that regime in the late colonial period. South Carolina is uniquely suited for this extended study because it was the only American colony that was a slave society from its founding and that had a White minority ruling over an enslaved Black majority for much of the colonial period. With slavery so central to its society for so long, South Carolina became the epitome of the tax imagination turned to evil ends.

The centrality of slavery to life in South Carolina was directly reflected in the colony's tax laws. Most obviously, taxation marked the enslaved as property—and, therefore, as appropriate *objects of* taxation rather than as human beings *subject to* taxation—but its role in reinforcing and perpetuating the institution of slavery went far beyond that. Taxation quickly became a key component of the system of oppressive control that White South Carolinians maintained over the lives of the colony's enslaved Black majority, facilitating the cooperation of slaveholders with the most draconian punishments under the colony's slave codes and serving as a tool to manipulate the racial balance of the population with the aim of cementing White domination.

Taxation was bound up tightly with South Carolina's oppressive slave codes, which controlled important aspects of daily life for the enslaved and mandated harsh punishments for offenses criminalized under those codes. Corporal punishment was the only viable option for transgressions by enslaved persons because fines and imprisonment either were not feasible or ran counter to slaveholders' interests. Among a horrifying list of prescribed corporal punishments, death was the ultimate punishment used to maintain the enslaved in subjugation. But like fines and imprisonment, putting enslaved persons to death was against slaveholders' financial interests, and during the colonial period, government takings of property did not give rise to a right to compensation as they do today.[20] Paying compensation to the holders of executed enslaved persons thus became a political question, and the choices that colonial legislatures—including South Carolina's—made regarding the scope and source of funding for that compensation revealed much about the role of slavery in society.

Beginning early in South Carolina's history, its legislature experimented with a variety of different tax mechanisms to provide compensation to slaveholders upon the execution or killing of enslaved persons who transgressed the slave codes. Eventually, the legislature settled on a broadly redistributive funding scheme that centralized the vetting and processing of slaveholder compensation claims in the annual tax legislative drafting process. Taxation was thus used to grease the wheels of the institution of slavery when it greased the palms of South Carolina's slaveholders to secure their cooperation in a legalized system of subjugation, bondage, and killing. More than simply reflecting the centrality of slavery to South Carolina society, however, the legislature's gravitation toward a centralized practice of vetting slaveholder compensation claims as part of the annual tax legislative drafting process opens a window onto South Carolina's slave society, providing glimpses throughout chapters 1 through 3 not only of the mindset of colonial legislators but also of the lives of slaveholders and the enslaved.

Taxation likewise served as a tool to manipulate the colony's racial balance. Because South Carolina was the only American colony with a majority Black population, there were recurring fears of uprisings against the ruling White minority. To assuage these fears, the legislature used taxes on the importation of enslaved persons as a lever to shape the colony's racial balance. On several occasions, import taxes were raised to prohibitively high levels to deter and suppress the importation of enslaved Blacks. At the same time, the legislature repeatedly took steps to encourage White migration to South Carolina to achieve a racial balance that would better ensure control of the enslaved—eventually dedicating the revenue raised from import taxes on enslaved Blacks to providing bounties to encourage and ease the arrival of Whites.

Although South Carolina might have been the epitome of the tax imagination turned to evil ends, it was by no means alone in forging connections between taxation and slavery. Part 2 explores the links that other American colonies established between taxation and slavery, with three chapters devoted to separate geographic regions (i.e., the northern, middle, and southern colonies). In chapters 4 through 6, echoes of the South Carolina experience are encountered in other colonies' use of taxation to (1) mark the enslaved as a dehumanized form of property, (2) facilitate slaveholder cooperation with enforcement of slave codes by redistributing their economic losses among taxpayers, and (3) control the flow of enslaved persons into the colonies. Nevertheless, these chapters make clear that the American colonies were far from monolithic in how and when they chose to establish ties between taxation and slavery.

Because slavery was an important feature of all the American colonies—in both the South *and* the North—it is only natural that tax law mirrored the importance and centrality of slavery to these societies. The degree and extent to which taxation was used to support and protect slavery in the American colonies varied widely based on local experience and local conditions—and it shifted over time, especially in the years leading up to the American Revolution, when prohibitive taxation was used in some colonies to curtail or end the slave trade. Chapters 4 through 6 thus directly advance this book's aim to excavate and document fiscal history while demonstrating the deep connections between tax law and society, as differing levels of connection to slavery and the slave trade influenced the nature and intensity of the connections that different colonies forged between taxation and slavery.

As these chapters unfold, tax history will vividly illustrate how overblown rhetoric likening taxation to slavery or theft ignores the ways in which taxation can be—and has been—bound up with systemic racism and *actual* slavery and theft. At the same time, illuminating the dark side of the tax imagination, this book strips off academics' rose-colored glasses by starkly demonstrating how taxation can contribute to the destruction of lives and livelihoods even when those who are singled out as targets are not taxpayers at all or the taxes imposed are not intended to be collected. With this history in mind, the book's conclusion underscores the importance of subjecting today's tax rules to a critical gaze, because we must always remain alert to the lurking potential for the power of taxation to be used in service of societal evils—whether it be the racism encountered here or the sexism, homophobia, transphobia, or other forms of invidious discrimination present in US society today.

Connecting this deeper understanding of the tax past with the present, the conclusion also considers how this study might inform contemporary movements for reparations for slavery and the deeply entrenched systems of racial discrimination established in the wake of its abolition. In doing so, the conclusion highlights the stark contrast between, on the one hand, the significant legal constraints that the modern federal judiciary has imposed on reparations advocates and, on the other hand, the nearly unfettered experimentation and high degree of imagination that colonial legislators exhibited as they fashioned tax and other legal systems to support and promote slavery. On the basis of this stark contrast between a highly imaginative tax past and an intellectually stunted tax present, the conclusion suggests that reparations advocates shift tactics and work for changes to the composition of the US Supreme Court with an eye toward removing artificial constitutional impediments to reparations programs. Reparations advocates would then be able to unfetter their own legal imaginations and craft meaningful reparations proposals, just as colonial legislators were able to let loose their imaginations when laying the legal foundations for the systems of slavery and racial discrimination that underpin reparations claims.

*　*　*

Given my general approach of seeing tax law "in" society, this book moves beyond legislative text and taps into tax legislative history and contemporary news accounts, as well as petitions, pardons, letters, and other historical documents. To situate tax law in its larger historical, social, and political context, numerous quotations from these documents are interspersed throughout the chapters of this book. As a project documenting racism, White supremacy, and slavery, it is worth noting early on that this language might shock the reader at times—whether because of the choice of words, the tenor of the language, the context in which the words were written or uttered, or some combination of these and other factors. However painful the reading experience might be, the aim here is to avoid whitewashing history (a deliberate choice of words given the subject of this book). If we are to learn from the past and apply those lessons to the present, we cannot avert our gaze from these horrors any more than we can or should avert our gaze from the horrors occurring around us in the present or bury our heads in the sand when considering the possibility of horrors being visited by or upon us in the future.

In keeping with this focus, I have chosen to capitalize "Black" and "White" when referring to racial groups in this book. With the present-day reader in mind, it has been argued to be "important to call attention to White as a race as a way to understand and give voice to how White-ness functions in our social and political institutions and our communi-ties."[21] This argument only grows in strength in the context of a study exploring the legal and historical underpinnings of the racial categories that continue to form the basis for both discrimination and privilege in US society today. This choice may jar some readers, but shaking up pre-conceptions about race and tax is one of the goals of this book.

With these cautionary words in mind, let us now begin our journey into the tax past by traveling back to colonial South Carolina to witness how taxation was employed to shape, entrench, and reinforce the subju-gation of that colony's enslaved Black majority.

PART I

Taxation and Slavery in Colonial South Carolina

1

Early Experimentation

This chapter, in tandem with chapters 2 and 3, explores how taxation shaped the institution of slavery in colonial South Carolina.[1] Because slavery was central to life in colonial South Carolina, these three chapters chart the tightly intertwined relationship among (1) slave codes that were designed to protect and preserve the institution of slavery, (2) tax legislation that compensated slaveholders to ensure the smooth operation of those codes, and (3) taxing measures that, in conjunction with the slave codes and other legislation, marked the enslaved as property and endeavored to manipulate the racial balance of the colony to dampen the threat of rebellion and resistance from the enslaved population. Taken together, chapters 1 through 3 demonstrate how colonial South Carolina's ruling White minority used the power of taxation in service of evil, integrating taxation into their racist designs to oppress and subjugate—and, when it advanced their project, to destroy—Black lives held in bondage.

Due to the length of time covered by this study and the deeply entrenched relationship between taxation and slavery in South Carolina, this chapter concerns only the colony's early years—from settlement in 1670 to the 1730s. The chapter first briefly describes the advent of slavery in South Carolina and the rise of an enslaved Black majority in the colony.[2] It next describes the legislature's enactment of slave codes both to control the lives of enslaved persons and to ensure that Whites enforced and cooperated with those controls. In relation to the latter aim, the chapter then delves into the legislature's experimentation with a variety of tax mechanisms to provide the financial compensation required to secure slaveholder cooperation when the threat of the slave codes' most draconian punishment—the death penalty—loomed large. In addition to demonstrating how tax law reflected the centrality of slavery in colonial South Carolina, this discussion of taxation's role in providing slaveholder compensation opens a window onto life in South Carolina's slave society that chapters 2 and 3 explore further. This chapter then closes by examining the legislature's complementary experimentation with a combination of tax and other measures designed to manipulate the colony's racial balance to enhance White control over the enslaved population and thereby protect and preserve the institution of slavery.

Overall, the early colonial period in South Carolina was marked by a high degree of legislative experimentation aimed at calibrating and optimizing the operation of the tax and nontax measures that served as the legal underpinning of the institution of slavery. Chapters 2 and 3 cover the period from the 1739 Stono Rebellion to the American Revolution, when the relationship between taxation and slavery in South Carolina coalesced and became routinized.

Slavery in South Carolina

Though Europeans and Africans had "mingled with the Indians over the years, no overseas visitors were able to sustain a separate settlement upon South Carolina shores until 1670."[3] Unlike other North American colonial settlements, South Carolina has been described as the "colony of a colony" because many of its early settler-colonialists came not from Europe but from Barbados.[4] In Barbados, first settled by the English in 1627, "whites had predominated during the first generation of settlement, blacks became a majority during the second, and their numerical dominance in Barbados continued to grow" due to the sharply rising labor demands of the sugar industry.[5] Barbados thus became "the first English colonial society to change from a society with slaves into a slave society, a world in which the master-slave relation was the central pivot of the entire social order."[6]

In contrast, South Carolina "was a slave society from the very first."[7] The first enslaved person was brought to South Carolina in 1670,[8] and "in the earliest years, between one fourth and one third of the colony's newcomers were Negroes."[9] To lure settlers, South Carolina established a headright system for granting land to new arrivals that rewarded slaveholding—at its most generous, this system allotted 150 acres for each imported enslaved man.[10] Ultimately, however, it was the cultivation of rice that coincided with increased reliance on enslaved labor.[11] Indeed, it has been said that "South Carolina planters were least doubtful of the

value of slavery to the economy, claiming that without Negroes rice production would be simply impossible."[12] By 1695, South Carolina's Black
population had risen to approximately two thousand, "making the percentage of blacks in this colony higher than that in any other American
colony."[13] During the following two decades, "when rice production
took permanent hold in South Carolina, the African portion of the population drew equal to, and then surpassed, the European portion."[14] By
1708, enslaved Blacks outnumbered Whites.[15]

Although the population of enslaved Native Americans likewise
grew rapidly in the first decade of the eighteenth century, "this was a
short-term trend that contributed directly to the frontier wars of the
ensuing decade, after which the Indian presence would diminish rapidly."[16] Aside from potential negative effects on security and trade, the
colonists learned that enslaved Native Americans were more valuable
if exported to faraway places where they were less likely to attempt escape.[17] Notwithstanding a sharp decline in the trade after the Yamasee
War of 1715, the colonial government still found it politically useful—
and profitable—to continue trading in enslaved Native Americans, as
did individual colonists.[18] Within the colony, however, "natural demographic forces and attrition steadily reduced the number of Indian slaves
already working on Carolina plantations until, by the 1730s, they had
become a rarity."[19] Enslaved Black labor appears to have been preferred
because it offered the advantage of avoiding "the serious diplomatic and
strategic questions posed by Indian labor."[20]

Over the dozen or so years after Blacks became a majority, "the white
population rose by scarcely 2,500 ... while the Negro population added
over 4,000 by natural increase and above 3,600 more through imports."[21]
By 1720, it is estimated that enslaved persons constituted 65 percent of
South Carolina's population.[22] During the 1720s, the trend continued,
with the enslaved population nearly doubling while the White population increased by only about half.[23] Thus, "the early eighteenth century
in South Carolina was characterized demographically by the emergence
of a clear-cut black majority."[24] In fact, in 1737, a new arrival from Switzerland remarked in a letter home that "Carolina looks more like a negro
country than like a country settled by white people."[25]

In South Carolina's low country, the Black majority only continued to
grow: "In 1740 the ratio of blacks to whites ... was two to one; by 1770,

the ratio had climbed to three-and-a-half to one. In 1780 . . . the region contained nearly four blacks for every white person."[26] South Carolina's backcountry was settled much later and was not as densely populated with enslaved persons during the colonial period; nevertheless, by the 1760s, the number of enslaved there "was growing rapidly."[27] In short, "South Carolina was unique among the American colonies in becoming at [an] early date, and in remaining so throughout the colonial period, the only colony where blacks were a majority of the population."[28]

Slave Codes: Controlling the Black Majority

The legislature governing the area that later became the province of South Carolina first regulated slavery approximately twenty years after settlement.[29] Unsurprisingly, as a colony of a colony, South Carolina's early slave codes were modeled on those of Barbados.[30] Within a short time, the jump-start provided by the combination of "the development of rice plantations and the Barbadian example . . . yield[ed] in South Carolina the most rigorous deprivation of freedom to exist in institutionalized form anywhere in the English continental colonies."[31]

South Carolina, through its slave codes, constrained and controlled the enslaved population by circumscribing freedom in daily life and prescribing harsh punishments for criminalized transgressions of the codes.[32] At the same time, the slave codes alternated between punishing Whites for failing to enforce the codes and rewarding them for compliance.[33] The 1712 Slave Code was the first to include a detailed preamble explaining the rationale for the colony's increasingly elaborate legal regime regulating slavery:

> WHEREAS, the plantations and estates of this Province cannot be well and sufficiently managed and brought into use, without the labor and service of negroes and other slaves; and forasmuch as the said negroes and other slaves brought unto the people of this Province for that purpose, are of barbarous, wild, savage natures, and such as renders them wholly unqualified to be governed by the laws, customs, and practices of this Province; but that it is absolutely necessary, that such other constitutions, laws and orders, should in this Province be made and enacted, for

the good regulating and ordering of them, as may restrain the disorders, rapines and inhumanity, to which they are naturally prone and inclined; and may also tend to the safety and security of the people of this Province and their estates; to which purpose, . . . *Be it therefore enacted* . . .[34]

Much like present-day legislation, "the South Carolina slave laws . . . set formal standards which were not always rigidly enforced. But the statutes do reflect the felt necessities of the chief slaveowners who sat in the colonial assembly and composed the laws. Their expectations, fears, and anxieties are closely woven together in the statutes."[35]

Tellingly, South Carolina's slave codes gave voice to White fears and anxieties by punishing a wide variety of criminalized transgressions with death. For instance, under the 1722/3 Slave Code, capital punishment became mandatory for conviction of "heinous or grievous" crimes (e.g., murder, burglary, robbery, and arson), while lesser crimes were subject to escalating punishments that ranged from branding all the way to death.[36] Notably, however, the 1722/3 slave code acknowledged that "negroes and other slaves, under pretence of hunger, do frequently break open corn-houses and rice-houses, and steal from thence corn and rice," impelling the legislature to downgrade what had previously been classified as burglary (i.e., a capital offense) by punishing it with branding and whipping for the first and second offenses and imposing capital punishment only for a third offense.[37]

Beginning with the 1712 Slave Code, enslaved persons who were engaged in or preparing for rebellion were punished with death or such other punishment as the court might deem fit.[38] Under the 1712 Slave Code, escapees who intended to leave South Carolina were subject to a mandatory death sentence, while those who did not intend to leave the colony were subject to escalating punishments that culminated in death.[39] The 1722/3 and 1735 Slave Codes focused their attention solely on escapees who intended to leave South Carolina. Under the 1722/3 Slave Code, those escapees continued to be punished with death.[40] If several escaped together—and advertisements for "runaways" suggest that escaping in groups was fairly common[41]—then "one, or two, at most, of them, who shall . . . be thought to be the most notorious offenders, shall suffer death."[42] The 1735 Slave Code took a slightly different approach. It eliminated the death penalty for those who escaped on their own and reserved that punishment for the "greatest offenders" among groups of escapees.[43]

Under the earliest slave codes, physical violence against Whites was punishable by whipping for a first offense, whipping and mutilation for a second offense, and whatever punishment the court saw fit—up to and including death—for a third offense.[44] If, however, the White person were "maimed and disabled," then the crime was automatically treated as a third offense.[45] In 1714, the punishment of "any slave or slaves that shall strike, beat or maim their respective masters, mistresses or overseers, (being white persons,) or any other white person" was left to the discretion of the court, effectively making capital punishment "discretionary even for the first offense."[46] The 1722/3 Slave Code reinstated corporal punishment for a first offense and, on a second offense, opened the way for the court to "inflict any punishment according to their discretion, death excepted"—but a death sentence was mandatory if the White person was "bruised, wounded, maimed or disabled."[47]

In all these cases, capital punishment was meted out not by the regular South Carolina courts but more summarily by ad hoc slave courts consisting of two justices of the peace and three freeholders.[48] Under some circumstances, however, the slave code legally authorized Whites to kill enslaved persons without even going through this summary judicial process. For instance, a "ticket" system controlled the movement of enslaved persons in South Carolina even before enactment of the colony's first slave code.[49] Under that system, enslaved persons were required to be punished by whipping if found away from the slaveholder's property without written permission.[50] In the name of protecting the people enforcing the ticket system, it was early on "declared Lawful for any white Person to beat maim and assault and if such Slave cannot otherwise be taken to kill any Negro or Slave that shall refuse to show his Tickett either by running away or resistance endeavour to avoid being apprehended or taken."[51] The slave codes similarly authorized the extrajudicial killing of enslaved persons who were caught stealing and who resisted apprehension.[52]

In addition to legally authorizing courts to inflict capital punishment and individual Whites to kill enslaved persons under color of law, the slave codes granted slaveholders wide latitude when punishing their own enslaved persons. For instance, the 1712 Slave Code specified that there would be no legal repercussions if an enslaved person were to "suffer in life or member" as a result of punishment ordered by the slaveholder.[53] A slaveholder would be punished only if, "of wantonness, or only of bloody-mindedness, or cruel intention," he were to "violently kill a negro or other slave of his own"—but even then, punishment was only a fine.[54]

Taxation and the Slave Codes: Compensating Slaveholders

In South Carolina, capital punishment was "surprisingly common, given the fact that each slave represented a considerable investment to the whites."[55] The colony's slave codes thus gave rise to "a constant conflict between protecting the property interest of the master and assuring that crimes by slaves were punished and deterred."[56] Slaveholders had little incentive to cooperate with enforcement of the slave codes because conviction and punishment for one of the growing number of capital crimes would harm them economically by destroying their human "property." The alternative to cooperation was either concealing enslaved persons' transgressions or selling them outside the province so that slaveholders might rid themselves of troublemakers while minimizing their economic losses or even making a profit. To avoid such economically self-interested behavior, penalties for concealing criminals and financial compensation for executed enslaved persons became early and enduring features of South Carolina's slave codes.[57]

During the early colonial period, the legislature repeatedly tinkered with the slave code's compensation scheme, each time grappling with the question of how best to defray the cost of slaveholder compensation. Naturally, answering that question implicated the core functions of taxation: raising revenue, redistributing income and wealth, and shaping taxpayer behavior with financial incentives and disincentives. The legislature did not, however, settle immediately on a single approach to funding slaveholder compensation; rather, the legislature engaged in a decades-long experiment with a mix of tax measures, repeatedly changing course in its view of the appropriate relationship between taxation and slavery. Nonetheless, as it haltingly moved toward the taxing scheme that would fund slaveholder compensation during the remainder of the colonial period, the South Carolina legislature forged ever-tighter links between taxation and slavery.

Redistributive Scheme

Under the earliest South Carolina slave codes, slaveholder compensation was generally to be paid by the colony's public treasurer upon receipt of a certificate issued by designated authorities (e.g., a court or other public official). For instance, the 1695/6 Slave Code provided that, "for the Better encouragement of all owners of Slaves to putt in Execution, all the penall Clauses in this Act," the public treasurer was to pay £20 for each enslaved person who was executed or who died following punishment by castration—so long as the slaveholder showed "to two Justices of the peace that his Slave dyed as aforesaid And that not for want of Care."[58] The 1712 Slave Code explained the motivation behind this redistributive scheme when the availability of compensation was expanded and earlier monetary caps were removed:

> Now, forasmuch as the loss of the negroes and other slaves that shall suffer death, or be killed, by this Act, would prove too heavy for the owners of them to bear, and that the owners of negroes and slaves may not be discouraged to detect and discover the offences of their negroes and slaves, and that the loss may be borne by the public, whose safety, by such punishments, is hereby provided for and intended, *Be it therefore enacted* . . . That in all cases whatsoever, where any negro or other slave, by the appointment and provision of this Act, shall suffer death, then [the court] who adjudged such negro or other slave to suffer death, immediately after return thereof given, shall inquire, by the best means they are able, of the full and true value of such negro or slave, and make certificate thereof to the public receiver for the time being, therein requiring him to pay out of the public treasury the full value of the said negro or slave, to the owner thereof, who is hereby required to pay the same accordingly.[59]

Parallel provisions were included for assessing the value of enslaved persons killed under color of law (i.e., by individual Whites for violating the ticket system or when caught stealing), with the public treasurer again being required to pay compensation upon receipt of a duly issued certificate.[60] In either case, if the public treasurer failed to pay the authorized compensation, then "the party injured shall have an action of debt upon such certificate . . . against the public receiver, in any court of common pleas in this Province."[61] Additionally, the 1712 Slave Code authorized compensation from the public treasury for enslaved persons who died of punishment by castration.[62] It likewise required the public treasury to cover any shortfall when only a few members of a group engaged in rebellion were executed as an example, because the compensation required to be paid directly by the holders of those spared to the holders of the executed was capped at one-sixth the value of those spared.[63]

In 1714, South Carolina revisited its slaveholder compensation scheme because "the public treasury hath been very much exhausted by the extraordinary sums that have been allowed for criminal slaves of all sorts, without distinction."[64] To stem the drain on the public treasury, the legislature took two steps: First, a £50 cap was imposed on compensation for executed enslaved persons.[65] Second, to avoid the "great charge and expense to the public" of executing enslaved persons for "felonies of a smaller nature," the public treasurer was required to deport those who were convicted of capital crimes (other than murder) "to any other of his Majesty's plantations, or other foreign part, where he shall think fitting to send them for the use of the public"—that is to say, for sale there with the aim of "ridding the colony of convicted Negroes while still salvaging a profit"—and then to pay compensation to the slaveholder from the public treasury equal to the enslaved person's appraised value.[66]

Up to this point, the cost of slaveholder compensation was largely defrayed using general revenues held in the public treasury. The cost of compensation was spread broadly, on the theory that slaveholder compensation provided a public benefit by encouraging slaveholders to cooperate with enforcement of the slave code. Without publicly funded compensation, slaveholders might either (1) cover up enslaved persons' capital crimes or (2) ship them out of the province for sale elsewhere if their continued presence could no longer be countenanced—all to avoid the loss of previously invested capital and/or the funds necessary to purchase a new enslaved person to take their place. To avoid such economically self-interested behavior, the loss occasioned by the execution or killing of enslaved persons was generally not borne by the individual slaveholder but instead spread among all the colony's taxpayers, whose income was taken through taxation and given to affected slaveholders to induce their cooperation in enforcing the slave code's most draconian punishments.

Internalizing the Costs of Slavery

Just three years after the 1714 changes to the compensation scheme, the legislature again bemoaned the burden of reimbursing slaveholders for the value of enslaved persons who had been killed or executed.[67] To address this concern, the legislature repealed the portion of the 1714 act that required deportation of enslaved persons convicted of lesser felonies.[68] Illustrating the dangers associated with sale outside the province as either a private or public solution for resistance to bondage, the legislature observed that the switch from execution to deportation had only "encouraged negroes and other slaves to commit great numbers of robberies, burglaries and other felonies, well knowing they were to suffer no other punishment for their crimes, but transportation, which to them was rather an encouragement to pursue their villanies."[69]

In place of deportation, the 1717 legislation reverted to the punishment prescribed by the 1712 Slave Code—namely, death.[70] At the same time, the 1717 legislation radically altered the slaveholder compensation scheme that had prevailed for more than two decades. Aside from enslaved persons convicted of murder, whose execution gave rise to no compensation whatsoever, the 1717 legislation provided that slaveholders would be paid the "full value" of enslaved persons executed or killed under color of law—but payment would no longer come from a public treasury that "hath been very much exhausted by the extraordinary sums of money that have been paid for criminal slaves of all sorts without distinction."[71] Instead, the assessed value of the enslaved person was to be transmitted "to the constable of the parish where such negro or slave that was condemned or killed, did commit the fact, to levy the full value of the said negro, as he shall be appraised by the [court], on all and singular the inhabitants of such parish where the fact was committed, possessing negroes or other slaves, by an assessment which shall be equally laid on the owners or possessors of negroes or slaves . . . to be rated at so much per head."[72]

The 1717 legislation represented a sea change in the legislature's view of how to distribute the burden associated with funding slaveholder compensation. Abandoning the earlier redistributive approach that spread the cost of slaveholder compensation among all South Carolina taxpayers on the basis of a public benefit theory, the legislature decided to fund slaveholder compensation through a tax imposed on only a small slice of the population: slaveholders in the parish where the enslaved person was killed or executed. By paying compensation out of a tax levied only on local slaveholders—and, in the case of murder, effectively levying the tax entirely on the holder of the executed enslaved person—the legislature now imposed the cost of compensation aimed at protecting and preserving the institution of slavery on those who exploited enslaved labor.

This shift in the legal incidence of taxation sent the message that slaveholder compensation did not benefit the public but rather was a cost of doing business with enslaved labor. Enslavement naturally led to acts of resistance by those who were held in bondage, with resistance taking forms large and small and sometimes involving crimes such as theft, arson, or even murder.[73] Slaveholding thus gave rise to harms that impacted White society as a whole and—according to repeated complaints from legislators, many of whom were slaveholders themselves[74]—required burdensome financial payments to secure slaveholder cooperation in prosecuting offenders who might be put to death. The shift in tax incidence forced slaveholders to internalize this cost of doing business with enslaved labor by requiring (1) those whose enslaved persons were convicted of murder to personally bear the economic loss associated with execution of the offender and (2) all slaveholders in the local community to bear the cost of compensating those whose enslaved persons were either convicted of other capital crimes or killed under color of law.

By requiring local slaveholders to internalize these costs, the 1717 compensation scheme also appears to have been aimed at influencing slaveholder behavior. By confining taxation to local slaveholders, the 1717 scheme created financial incentives for slaveholders to take steps to reduce forms of resistance that threatened the rest of White society— and to encourage their neighbors to do the same. By deterring capital crimes from occurring, slaveholders could lessen (or even obviate) the need for imposing the tax, thus sparing themselves direct financial burdens and sparing White society the harms associated with transgressions of the slave code. Moreover, the 1717 scheme provided each slaveholder with a personalized incentive to deter murders from occurring, because losses occasioned by executions for that crime were taxed to the slaveholder alone.

A Hybrid Approach

During the 1720s and 1730s, South Carolina continued to experiment with tax mechanisms for funding slaveholder compensation. Legislators mixed their two earlier approaches when they adopted a tax regime that required some slaveholders to internalize the cost of compensation but permitted others to benefit from spreading their economic losses through redistributive taxation. Simultaneously—but slowly—moving toward what would become the predominant approach to funding slaveholder compensation, legislators began a parallel practice of using annual property tax legislation to authorize select compensation payments to be made directly from the public treasury. This section first briefly describes the hybrid tax regime enacted in 1722/3 and then details the practice that developed during the 1720s and 1730s of authorizing slaveholder compensation payments through the annual tax legislative drafting process. In addition to demonstrating how tax law mirrored the centrality of slavery in colonial South Carolina, the latter payments provide a glimpse of life in that slave society.

1722/3 SLAVE CODE

The 1722/3 Slave Code required the holders of enslaved persons executed for escaping on their own to bear the economic loss themselves.[75] When enslaved persons escaped or rebelled in a group, however, the holders of those who were spared death were required to pay compensation to the holders of those who were executed.[76] In both cases, the 1722/3 Slave Code, like the earlier 1717 legislation, required individual slaveholders to internalize the costs of doing business with enslaved labor and provided them with a financial incentive to alter their behavior, here in ways that reduced the possibility of escape or rebellion. Indeed, the 1722/3 Slave Code acknowledged that slaveholders bore some culpability in the actions of their enslaved persons when it stated that "there is sometimes reason to suspect that slaves do run away for want of a sufficient allowance of provisions."[77] The 1722/3 Slave Code imposed fines to encourage slaveholders to provide adequate food to their enslaved persons;[78] however, given the limited ability to police violations,[79] it seems that requiring slaveholders to absorb the economic loss associated with executions provided a more powerful incentive to conform their behavior to societal expectations.

For other crimes and for extrajudicial killings, the 1722/3 Slave Code reverted to a modified and more limited form of redistribution. Resurrecting the earlier notion that compensation encouraged slaveholders to cooperate with enforcement of the slave codes, the legislature decreed that the economic loss from killing or executing enslaved persons should generally "be borne by the public, whose safety, by such punishments, is hereby provided for and intended."[80] Yet, the legislature's view of the "public" who should bear this loss was now much narrower than it had been in the past. Whereas publicly funded compensation had previously been paid from the colonial treasury, the 1722/3 Slave Code required slave courts issuing valuation certificates to send those certificates "to the judges and justices of the several counties or precincts . . . to which the said negro or slave shall belong, who shall assess any sum on the lands and negroes lying within their respective jurisdictions, not exceeding eighty pounds, current money."[81] Parallel valuation and compensation procedures were created for enslaved persons killed under color of law.[82]

Under this regional compensation scheme,[83] the legislature ceased treating slaveholder compensation as a cost of doing business with enslaved labor but, at the same time, shied away from fully embracing the redistributive power of taxation to spread the cost of compensation diffusely among all South Carolina taxpayers. The legislature instead spread the economic loss associated with the execution or killing of enslaved persons among regional landholders and slaveholders—groups that overlapped but were not identical.[84] The legislature's choices regarding what, whom, and how to tax sent the message that slaveholder compensation did not benefit the public broadly but rather benefited only property holders in the region. Nonetheless, by spreading the cost of compensation across a broader geographic area and by expanding the taxpaying population to include nonslaveholders, the legislature simultaneously dampened the financial incentives that previously existed for slaveholders to minimize the negative impacts of resistance to bondage on White society by altering the treatment of their own enslaved persons and encouraging their neighbors to do the same.

In one respect, however, the 1722/3 Slave Code did fully embrace the redistributive power of taxation. The legislature authorized payment of up to £100 from the public treasury for killings or executions carried out under earlier laws (with the exception of executions "for wilful murder").[85] This compensation was to be paid upon receipt of a court order specifying "the name of the slave killed or executed, together with his age and qualifications, as near as they can learn, the time when and the cause for which such slave was killed or executed, and by whose order."[86] By drawing these payments from the public treasury, the legislature reverted to its earlier approach of spreading the cost of compensation among all South Carolina taxpayers—that is to say, at the colonial rather than the regional or local level.

THE ANNUAL TAX-ACTS

Parallel to the 1722/3 Slave Code's hybrid regime for authorizing and funding slaveholder compensation payments, the South Carolina legislature adopted a practice of itself auditing claims for slaveholder compensation (alongside all other public claims) and authorizing the colonial treasurer to pay those claims, once it routinely began to pass annual property tax legislation.[87] While reminiscent of the colony's early redistributive schemes for funding slaveholder compensation, the legislature's new practice created a qualitatively different—and much tighter—connection between taxation and slavery. By paying slaveholder compensation out of taxes imposed at the colonial level, the legislature deployed the power of taxation to redistribute income and wealth by spreading slaveholders' economic losses broadly across South Carolina's taxpaying population, much as the early slave codes had. But this redistribution was not accomplished through payments from whatever general revenues happened to be on hand in the public treasury, as had been the case under the early slave codes. Instead, as described in box 1.1, South Carolina's Tax-Acts effectively erased the divide between taxing and spending by (1) directly tying the precise amount of revenue to be raised from the property tax each year to the sum of public claims approved by the legislature (including slaveholder compensation claims) and (2) authorizing the revenue raised under the Tax-Act to be spent on those approved claims and nothing else. By erasing the divide between taxing and spending in the annual Tax-Acts, the South Carolina legislature established an inextricable link between taxation and enforcement of the harshest punishments used by the ruling White minority to control the colony's enslaved Black majority.

Box 1.1. South Carolina's Annual Tax-Acts: Erasing the Divide between Taxing and Spending

In contrast to the present-day United States, where sharp distinctions between taxing and spending have been the subject of sustained scholarly debate and ineffectual congressional action aimed at curtailing government spending through the nation's tax laws, the wall between taxing and spending in colonial South Carolina was neither so rigid nor formalistic. Beginning in 1715, South Carolina embarked on a practice of enacting annual property tax legislation that became the "centerpiece" of its tax system (with some notable gaps, particularly in the late 1720s and early 1770s).[a] Robin Einhorn has nicely summarized the content of a typical Tax-Act:

> This law had two parts. One described the property tax, fixing the flat and ad valorem tax rates, naming "inquirers" and collectors for each parish, and laying out rules and deadlines. The other part, the "Schedule," was an appropriation law, a list of the people to be paid from the proceeds with the purposes and amounts of the payments. The assembly framed the Schedule by auditing claims for salaries and other payments, including slaveholders to be reimbursed because officials had executed their "criminal slaves." . . . Once the assembly completed the Schedule, it subtracted revenue from its imposts and other funds and fixed property tax rates to raise the balance.[b]

Illustrating the tight connection between taxing and spending, the 1736 Tax-Act's schedule tallied South Carolina's public expenses for the year beginning March 25, 1735, and ending March 25, 1736, at the precise figure of £31,387 3s 7d.[c] (Beginning with the 1733 Tax-Act, the schedule always covered past expenses, which is what permitted the specification of such precise amounts of revenue to be raised.) As the government already had £1,000 on hand, the legislature levied a tax of £30,387 3s 7d, with one-sixth of the tax to be paid by residents of Charles Town (now Charleston) and the remainder by those residing outside Charles Town (the "country tax").

---

a. ROBIN L. EINHORN, AMERICAN TAXATION, AMERICAN SLAVERY 93 (2006); see MAURICE A. CROUSE, THE PUBLIC TREASURY OF SOUTH CAROLINA 66 (1977).
b. EINHORN, *supra* note a, at 93.
c. 1736 Tax-Act, No. 608, 3 STATUTES AT LARGE OF SOUTH CAROLINA 438 (Thomas Cooper ed., 1838).

As had long been customary, the Tax-Act's core revenue-raising mechanisms were flat taxes "on all negroes and other slaves whatsoever and wheresoever within the limits of this Province" and on every one hundred acres of land outside of Charles Town. In Charles Town, tax was raised through an assessment on "real and personal estates, stocks and abilitys . . . rateably and proportionably, according to the best of [the assessors'] skill and judgement." Outside Charles Town, an ad valorem tax was imposed on the "stock and cash" of country storekeepers. Additionally, as part of a short-lived experiment, the 1736 Tax-Act imposed a poll tax on "male white persons from the age of twenty-one to sixty years," but at a higher rate than applied to enslaved persons (17s 6d vs. 12s 6d). Later Tax-Acts tinkered with the tax base by, for example, jettisoning the poll tax on Whites but instituting a poll tax on free Blacks without taxable property.[d]

These taxes aimed to include within the tax base "the labor power at the disposal of taxpayers, casting this labor as a proxy for wealth, but also using race and gender categories as proxies for the kinds of labor it was associating with wealth."[e] In the 1736 Tax-Act, the labor power of White females of all ages and of young and elderly White males was excluded from the tax base, sending the message that their labor did not generate wealth. In contrast, the labor power of working-age White men and all Blacks—men *and* women, no matter their age—was included in the property tax base. Yet, radically different, race-based assessments of wealth-generating power prevailed, with the labor power of White men taxed 1.4 times as much as the labor power of enslaved persons. Shortly after the 1736 Tax-Act, the legislature returned to carving the labor power of White men out of the tax base, leaving only the commodified labor of enslaved persons to be treated as property subject to tax. Moreover, enslaved labor was consistently taxed at flat rates (i.e., per capita), conveniently avoiding the intrusion that valuation would entail for "taxpayers who thought of themselves as the 'masters' of 'families.'"[f]

The revenue raised by the 1736 Tax-Act was to "be appropriated, applied and paid by the publick treasurer, according to the schedule or estimate hereunto annexed, and not otherwise." The list of authorized expenses included a variety of items in amounts specified down to the penny—from salaries (e.g., £300 to the captain of the garrison at Fort

---

d. *E.g.*, 1756 Tax-Act, No. 856, S165001, Box 29, S.C. Dep't of Archives & Hist.

e. EINHORN, *supra* note a, at 37.

f. *Id.* at 38.

Moore) to "house rent for the Assembly" (£200 to Miles Brewton) to "cleaning small arms" (£320 1s 2d to Philip Massey) to the cost of "running the line" between North and South Carolina (£480 to Alexander Skeen) to what may be two payments of compensation for enslaved persons killed (£80 each to Sarah West and George Chicken). Property taxes were thus a direct function of the government's approved expenses for the year and, once raised, could be used to defray only those expenses and—to borrow the words of the Tax-Act—"not otherwise."

Further illustrating the direct linkage between taxing and spending, later Tax-Acts addressed the acceptable media for paying both the government's authorized expenses and the taxes imposed by the act. Payment was authorized in South Carolina currency, British pounds sterling, and Spanish pieces of eight.[g] Because of the time required to assess and collect taxes, in the mid-1740s, the Tax-Acts began to authorize the issuance of tax certificates (i.e., written acknowledgment of a debt owed by the colony to a public creditor); however, there is evidence of the Commons House of Assembly ordering the public treasurer to issue tax certificates as early as 1736.[h] Effectively collapsing any real distinction between taxing and spending, these tax certificates could be used to pay taxes in South Carolina—as well as any other debt owed to the colonial government, not to mention private debts.[i]

---

g. *E.g.,* 1751 Tax-Act, No. 792, S165001, Box 26, S.C. Dep't of Archives & Hist.

h. 1744 Tax-Act, No. 712, S165001, Box 22, S.C. Dep't of Archives & Hist; JOURNALS OF THE COMMONS HOUSE OF ASSEMBLY: MAY 1736, at 32 (LLMC Digital).

i. *See* 1751 Tax-Act, *supra* note g; CROUSE, *supra* note a, at 78; W. ROY SMITH, SOUTH CAROLINA AS A ROYAL PROVINCE: 1719–1776, at 229, 277–78 (1903); ROBERT M. WEIR, COLONIAL SOUTH CAROLINA: A HISTORY 112 (1983); Ivan Allen Marcotte, Colonial South Carolina: A Quantity Theoretic Perspective 45–46 (1989) (PhD dissertation, University of South Carolina) (ProQuest).

TAX ~~EXCEPTIONALISM~~

South Carolina tax law was thus no different from other areas of law in how it became entwined with—and was actively used to promote and further—the racialized subjugation of enslaved human beings. This discussion of taxation's role in providing slaveholder compensation has demonstrated that South Carolina tax law was most definitely *not* "neutral" economic legislation that occupied some higher plane, allowing it to hover above the reach of the evils of racism and slavery. To the contrary, taxation was in the trenches—often embedded in the slave codes themselves in the colony's early years—providing the financial means both to secure slaveholder cooperation with enforcement of South Carolina's slave codes and to shape slaveholder behavior to reduce the potential harms to White society associated with exploiting enslaved labor. Far from being exceptional, special, or unique, taxation was a workaday component of the system of oppressive legal controls that South Carolina's ruling White minority established to govern the lives of the colony's enslaved Black majority.

Besides demonstrating the close connection between tax law and society, acknowledging the reality that colonial South Carolina's tax laws shared an intimate and sustained connection with the institution of slavery presents a unique opportunity. As described more fully in chapters 2 and 3, the legislature's practice of vetting claims from public creditors as part of the process of drafting the annual Tax-Acts eventually displaced earlier experiments in providing and funding slaveholder compensation. The legislature's embrace of this practice expanded taxation's role in protecting and preserving slavery beyond shaping slaveholder behavior and securing slaveholder cooperation in enforcement of the slave codes. As an integral part of determining the annual property tax burden, this new practice required the legislature annually to examine and approve claims for slaveholder compensation. The legislature's centralization of, and direct involvement in, the vetting of slaveholder compensation claims opens a revealing tax window onto South Carolina's slave society and its use of the threat—and, often, actual infliction—of death as a means of controlling and subjugating the colony's enslaved Black majority.

Looking through this tax window, one can do more than just tally up the dead, as others have done when mentioning in passing the number of slaveholder compensation payments included in the Tax-Acts during different periods.[88] By plumbing tax legislative history as well as contemporary news accounts and documentation of the executive petition and pardon process, one can often witness the circumstances surrounding the execution or killing of enslaved persons and even sometimes learn their names. Uncovering this contextual detail is important because in a further mark of their dehumanization—having already been classified (more than once) as a taxable form of "property"—enslaved persons who were killed or executed under color of law were, with rare exception, *not* themselves identified in the Tax-Acts, even though *their* deaths occasioned the economic losses for which slaveholders were compensated.

The possibility of documenting this history increased once the legislature's practice of vetting slaveholder compensation claims matured near the end of the period covered in this chapter. By that time, the colony's first newspaper began to be published, and the Commons House of Assembly had fully centralized the process of vetting slaveholder compensation claims by wresting control of the tax legislative drafting process from the Council and governor in the name of reposing primary control over taxing and spending measures in the hands of the colony's elected representatives.[89] Taking advantage of these developments to contextualize the slaveholder compensation payments not only allows for the creation of a more accurate historical record but also forces to the surface the deeper connections between taxation, slavery, and colonial society in South Carolina, making those connections legible and opening them to investigation.[90] Absent the legislature's expansion of the role that taxation played in providing slaveholder compensation, these insights into South Carolina's slave society would probably have been lost to history because of the "dearth of documentation for the everyday practice of slave courts [due to] their local and ad hoc nature."[91]

The next part of this chapter begins to peer through this tax window onto South Carolina's slave society by documenting the slaveholder compensation payments included in the Tax-Acts during the 1720s and 1730s. Chapters 2 and 3 continue and significantly expand on this work because they cover periods when compensation from the public treasury and centralized vetting of slaveholder compensation claims as part of the annual tax legislative drafting process became the norm. Overall, chapters 1 through 3—together with the table of compensation payments in the appendix (table A.1)—provide an exhaustive cataloging of slaveholder compensation paid through the South Carolina Tax-Acts.

Opening a Tax Window onto South Carolina's Slave Society

The first compensation payments included in the Tax-Acts were not made to identified slaveholders. The 1721 Tax-Act included a payment of £1,000 for "slaves condemned and shot."[92] These funds were to come from import and export taxes levied under separate legislation; however, if those taxes proved insufficient, the shortfall was to be paid out of property tax revenues.[93] Illustrating how the legislature became involved in approving payments that technically required only judicial certification,[94] the 1723/4 Tax-Act authorized £500 to be paid from the property taxes collected under that act for "arrears due for negroes killed."[95] This amount covered payments for five enslaved persons killed under color of law, as evidenced by the House journal's later recounting of a dispute over the failure of the public treasurer to make one such payment:

> Cap[t] Tobias Fitch laid before the house. an order of two Justices & free holders for paying M[r] Roger Sanders the sum of one hundred Pounds for a Negro killd then being run away, and Motion being made that Coll[o] Parris should be sent for, he attended the house & being askt why he had not paid the said order, he informd the house that the Law's being ambiguous he did not knô if the s[d]: Order was a sufficient Authority for him to pay the s[d] Money and being order'd to withdraw the following order was directed to be drawn
>
> Order'd
>
> That Alexand[r] Parris Esq[r]- Treasurer do pay out of the five hundred Pounds formerly raisd, and appropriated for Payment of five Negroes. killed by the Authority of former negro Acts unto M[r] Roger Sanders for a Negro man killd in takeing who was run away From the s[d] Roger Sanders. & had robbd several People, the Sum of One hundred Pounds, and that this order be sent to his Excell[cy] the Govern[r]: & his Maj[es] hon[ble]: Council for their Concurrence and that M[r] Speaker do sign the same.[96]

In 1724, the question of whether all payments for enslaved persons executed or killed under color of law should come from the public treasury resurfaced in connection with discussion of potential amendments to the 1722/3 Slave Code: "The Question was putt if the full Value of all Slaves Executed by Public Authority Should be payd for by the publick according to their appraisement—Carryed in the Affirmative."[97] The sense of the House was not, however, translated into legislative text. But even without a duly enacted amendment to the slave code, the legislature took to authorizing compensation from the public treasury in circumstances that implicated the slave code's prohibitions but that fell outside its compensation scheme:

> The Petition of Thos: Henley that by a Certificate under the hands of two Justices and three freeholders of Craven County, it appears that a Negro Man belonging to the said Hendley was killd by one Andrew Collins, at the time when the people of Winyaw were under Arms from some apprehensions they had of the Waccamaw Indians designing mischief against them for that the said Collins in the Night seeing a Man armed coming up to his house challenged him who not answering he thereupon shott him dead which proved to be the Negroe beforemention'd belonging to Mr: Hendley.
>
> The Committee [on Petitions and Accounts] are of Opinion the case of Mr: Hendley is the same with that of Collo: Fenwick Mr: Stone and others who were all paid by the Publick for Negroes kill'd by accidents of this Nature and do therefore recomend that Provision be made in the Estimate for the ensuing Year to pay the said Hendley the Sum of £100:0.0 which is the sum allowed by Law in such Occations.[98]

The reference to payments to Colonel Fenwick and others appears to be to the 1724/5 Tax-Act's blanket authorization of £2,544 16s 2d to be paid for accounts approved by the legislature.[99] As described by the Committee on Petitions and Accounts, among the authorized accounts were those of Fenwick and others whose enslaved persons were killed by Native Americans:

> Mr: William Rhett from the Com'ittee on Petitions & accounts made the following Report.
>
> Upon several matters Vizt:
>
> The Memorial of Collo. Fenwick praying payment out of the Treasury for a Negro man who run' away & was kill'd by an Indian
>
> The Petition of Madm: Margaret Johnson for payment out of the Treasury for a Negro man who ran away & was killed by Indians sent in pursuit of him, both wch: memorial & Petition your Com'ittee have examin'd & find the facts as there set forth to be true but no provision being made in the negro act for cases of this nature the Com'ittee do therefore Submitt the Consideration of them to this Honble,, house[100]

The House approved the requested compensation and directed that a payment be made "for each of their negroes out of the publick the Sum' of eighty p^{ds}: & that it be provided for in the Estimate of the Curr^t Year."[101]

In contrast, immediately after considering Hendley's petition, the Committee on Petitions and Accounts rejected William Miles's petition requesting £80 "for a Negroe of his Executed for killing another Negroe."[102] In justifying the different treatment, the committee stated that "there is Sufficient Provision made by Law for the better Governing and Ordering of Slaves for the payment of all such Negroes as should be condemned and Executed According to Law, by an assessment to be made on the Inhabitants of the Precincts where such Negroe is executed and the Com'ittee are of Opinion that there can be no Difficulty in making such an Assessment for the Precinct of Charles Town as the Petitioner setts forth but rather a failure in the Justice of the Precinct."[103] Notwithstanding its stringent treatment of Miles's petition, nine days later, the committee recommended paying £100 to William Cattell—a member of an old and wealthy South Carolina family that makes a number of appearances in the Tax-Act schedules—"for his Negro it appearing he was killed in making resistance, according to the power of the Negro Act."[104] This payment seems to fall just as squarely under the 1722/3 Slave Code's regional compensation scheme as Miles's did, not to mention that the payment should have been capped at £80 under that scheme. Nevertheless, the 1725 Tax-Act authorized £100 payments to Hendley and Cattell—but not to Miles—"for a negro killed."[105]

The 1722/3 Slave Code and its slaveholder compensation scheme lapsed at the end of the 1720s—a time when the legislature was paralyzed due to controversies over enlarging the currency and other matters.[106] Legislative action eventually resumed, with the 1722/3 Slave Code being revived in 1731 and 1733 alongside the legislature's parallel practice of vetting slaveholder compensation claims.[107] The 1733 Tax-Act included £80 compensation payments for the killing of seven enslaved persons, with one payment being designated for "an Indian woman killed," three others "for a negro killed," and the remainder simply being labeled "ditto."[108] The House journal provides some indication of the circumstances surrounding these payments, stating that Benjamin Izard was compensated for "the loss of a runaway negro man" and that both Arthur Middleton and William Creely were compensated "for a runaway negro who was killed."[109] James Rothford and Benjamin Child each received compensation "for a Negro Fellow who was shot," and John Carmichael received compensation after "complaining a negro man of his had been shot some time ago."[110] Indeed, Carmichael had placed a notice in the *South Carolina Gazette* in early February 1732/3 advertising a £5 reward for information on how his "Negro Man" had come to be "found dead, with 10 Swan Shot in his Head, about 3 or 400 Yards from his House."[111] Finally, Ann Donovan received compensation after submitting a petition "praying that she may have an allowance from the Public on account of an India man [woman?] of hers who was shot."[112]

The 1734 Tax-Act included compensation for the execution of four enslaved persons and the killing of four others.[113] The House journal provides some information regarding two of the compensation payments stemming from executions: James Thompson, a butcher, was compensated "for a negro man named Tom alias Jack apprehended and condemned for committing a Robbery on the body of Mary Coachman on the High Road," and Isaac Mazyck received compensation "for a negro man executed for a robbery on the highway."[114] Demonstrating how summarily death was meted out as punishment, the *South Carolina Gazette* reported, "On Saturday last, a Negro Fellow belonging to Mr. *Isaac Mazyck*, sen. pull'd a young Lad off his Horse, on the Broad Path, and rode away with the Horse, and Bags thereon, in which were Cloaths of Value: He was taken on Sunday, on Monday brought to Town, tried, and condemned; and the next Day, about Noon, he was hanged."[115]

The 1734 Tax-Act failed to specify the reason for one of these compensation payments; however, the House journal indicates that, "as in such cases is usual," £160 was paid to Catharine Cattell for "two negro men run away from her and in taking was wounded by some Cussoe Indians of which wounds they died."[116] The House journal similarly recounts that John Colleton was "allowed Eighty pounds as usual" for an enslaved man "who being run away was killed in taking [by] some Winyaw Indians."[117] In contrast, the House journal recounts how Thomas Fleming was denied compensation "for a negro who was executed for the murder of a white man" because, "a debate arising thereon, a Clause in the negro act was ordered to be read by which it appeared that slaves executed for wilful murder were excepted."[118] Providing further detail, the *South Carolina Gazette* reported that "a Negro Man belonging to *Thomas Fleming* of *Charlestown*, took an Opportunity, and kill'd the Overseer with an Axe. He was hang'd for the same yesterday."[119]

Finally, the 1735 Tax-Act included compensation for the killing of eight enslaved persons; however, it did not mention the reason for the payments, merely listing amounts paid and recipients.[120] Nevertheless, the House journal permits these payments to be identified and documented. A payment of "the usual allowance of £80" was made to William Elliott Sr. "for a negro man Shot by Mr Bull."[121] Similarly, Gerit Vanderheydon and Isaac Cordes were each paid £80 "for his negro that was killed."[122] Tobias Fitch was paid £80 "for a negro Man of his that was Shot," and Paul Jenys, who was then serving as Speaker of the House, was paid £160 "for two runaway Negroes killed."[123] Underscoring the importance of settled practice, the payments to Fitch and Jenys were justified on the ground that "it having been usual to make that allowance in Cases of the like nature."[124] Though not accompanied by similar justifications, payments of £80 were likewise made to James Kerr "for a Negro killed on Otter Island and who had been run away some time" and to Isaac Lessene "for a negro of his that run away & was killd."[125]

Shortly before enactment of the 1735 Tax-Act, the 1735 Slave Code replaced the 1722/3 Slave Code.[126] In contrast to earlier slave codes, the 1735 Slave Code made little mention of slaveholder compensation. It provided only that if a slave court were to decide to execute one or more enslaved persons among a group who had escaped or rebelled together, then the holders of those who had been spared death would be required to indemnify the holders of the executed.[127] With a seemingly more restrained approach to slaveholder compensation, it is unsurprising that the legislature included no payments of slaveholder compensation in the Tax-Acts during the remainder of the 1730s. But as described in chapter 2, that situation would change quickly following the 1739 Stono Rebellion.

Manipulating the Racial Balance

This chapter has thus far explored the connection between taxation and slavery in South Carolina with a focus on the legislature's repeated experimentation with tax mechanisms that (1) provided the financial inducement necessary to secure slaveholder cooperation in enforcing the colony's slave codes and (2) influenced slaveholder behavior in ways that would minimize transgressions of those slave codes. The chapter now turns to considering how the legislature engaged in closely related tax experimentation with the aim of manipulating the racial balance of South Carolina's population to keep its enslaved Black majority in check and forestall the rebellion and resistance that was punishable under the slave codes. This section first lays the groundwork for discussing this tax experimentation by briefly describing the legislature's authorization of bounties for importing White servants and its regulation of the ratio of Blacks to Whites in work areas. This section then turns to the closely intertwined use of taxation as both a carrot to encourage White immigration and a stick to discourage the importation of enslaved Blacks.

White Bounties and Regulated Racial Ratios

Concerns about the growing size of South Carolina's enslaved population surfaced early in the colony's history.[128] In 1698, out of fear that "the great number of negroes which of late have been imported into this Collony may endanger the safety thereof," South Carolina passed an act that provided "encouragement . . . for the importation of white servants" by (1) paying bounties to those who imported indentured white male servants and (2) requiring plantation owners with "six men negro slaves above sixteen years old" to be chosen by lot to accept a proportionate number of those servants.[129] This legislation aimed "to ensure distribution of white servants among plantations where slaves had become numerous enough to get the upper hand" but was repealed early because it had "already accomplished" its purpose.[130]

In 1716, the legislature again authorized bounties and, "for a further encouragement to all such persons as shall first import servants to this Province," a bonus for servants imported within two years.[131] Plantation owners were again to be chosen by lot to take the imported servants, at a ratio of one servant for every "ten slaves, young or old."[132] Although this legislation was intended to remain in force for four years, it was repealed after one year because the legislature concluded, without further explanation, that it proved to be "so far from answering the good intentions thereby designed, that it has proved the chiefest discouragement for the importation of white servants, and is in many respects impracticable and prejudicial to the Province."[133]

In tandem with these financial incentives to import White servants, the slave codes effectively mandated the hiring of Whites by regulating the ratio of enslaved persons to Whites in work areas. The early slave codes required "one or more white men" to live on "any plantation, cow pen or stock house," with violations punishable by fine.[134] The 1712 Slave Code similarly fined anyone who employed six enslaved persons at "any plantation, cow-pen or stock, that shall be six miles distant from his usual place of abode," unless there were "one or more white persons living and residing upon the same plantation."[135] The 1722/3 Slave Code raised the threshold to ten enslaved persons but applied the prohibition regardless of the distance from the slaveholder's abode.[136]

In 1726, the legislature explicitly combined its carrot and stick approaches when it altered the 1722/3 Slave Code's ratio in the name of "better securing this Province from Negro Insurrections" by creating job opportunities that would encourage "industrious labouring men" to come to South Carolina from "Great Britain and other parts."[137] To achieve the goals of balancing out and exerting control over the colony's enslaved Black majority, the 1726 legislation provided that "every owner of a plantation or cow-pen, who is possessed of any negroes or other slaves, shall be obliged to keep and maintain one white man on such plantation or cow-pen."[138] A plantation or cow-pen with twenty enslaved persons was required to have two White men present, and another White man was required for each additional ten enslaved persons.[139] The 1735 Slave Code later reverted to the 1722/3 scheme.[140] There is some question, however, about how zealously these restrictions were enforced in practice.[141]

Tax Carrots and Sticks

Paying bounties for the importation of White servants and regulating the ratio of Blacks to Whites in work areas were not the only means used to manipulate the racial balance of South Carolina's population. Complementing these measures, the legislature employed taxation both to discourage the importation of enslaved persons and to encourage White migration to the colony.

In keeping with the view of enslaved persons not as people but as a form of taxable property, South Carolina imposed a revenue-raising tax on enslaved persons imported for sale as early as 1703.[142] This tax proved to be "a large, although erratic, source of revenue."[143] In 1714, an additional £2 tax was imposed on each enslaved person twelve years or older who was imported from Africa.[144] As the legislature explained, this additional tax was not imposed to raise revenue but rather to affect the racial balance of the colony: "And *whereas*, the number of negroes do extremely increase in this Province, and through the afflicting providence of God, the white persons do not proportionably multiply, by reason whereof, the safety of the said Province is greatly endangered; for the prevention of which for the future, *Be it further enacted . . .*"[145]

The legislature again sounded the alarm in 1717 when it imposed an additional £40 tax on "all negro slaves of any age or condition whatsoever, imported or otherwise brought into this Province, from any part of the world"—just the year after it had set the revenue-raising tax on enslaved persons imported from Africa at £3 and imposed a prohibitive £30 tax on enslaved persons imported from other colonies.[146] As commonly occurred with prohibitive taxes, the 1717 tax did not take effect for eighteen months, and it remained in force for thirty months thereafter.[147] Although it has been said that this additional tax was "so high that it effectively stopped the sale of new Negroes in the colony," evidence indicates that there was a steep decline—but not a complete halt—of imports of enslaved Blacks during the early 1720s.[148] Legislation passed in 1719 would have repealed both the 1714 and 1717 taxes and enacted a £10 tax on enslaved persons imported from Africa and a £30 tax on enslaved persons imported from elsewhere; however, the colony's Proprietors disallowed that legislation along with a number of other measures.[149]

In 1722/3, when the legislature once again imposed prohibitive taxes on enslaved persons imported from other colonies, it explained that "it has proved to the detriment of some of the inhabitants of this Province, who have purchased negroes imported here from the Colonies of America, that they were either transported thence by the Courts of justice, or sent off by private persons for their ill behaviour and misdemeanours."[150] In other efforts to foster a more tractable enslaved population, the legislature placed prohibitive taxes on the importation of enslaved Native Americans beginning in 1721 and later imposed even higher taxes on "the importation of Spanish Indians, mustees, negroes, and mulattoes" because their importation "may be of dangerous consequence by inticing the slaves belonging to the inhabitants of this Province to desert with them to the Spanish settlements near us."[151]

The legislature continued to impose revenue-raising taxes on the importation of enslaved persons in the 1720s and 1730s.[152] Yet, in 1731, due to "the great discouragement of the merchants trading thither from the coast of Africa," royal instructions were circulated to all American colonies, including South Carolina, forbidding the enactment of taxes "payable by the importer, or upon slaves exported that have not been sold in the said province and continued there for the space of twelve MONTHS."[153] As described in chapter 2, South Carolina did not come into compliance with these instructions for nearly a decade, eventually doing so only because the colony's interests aligned with those of the slave traders who had complained to the Board of Trade.[154]

The legislature also added tax carrots to the mix with the aim of increasing South Carolina's White population. In 1725, to entice migrants from Europe, South Carolina offered a seven-year holiday from the payment of all taxes for those migrating in groups or as a family during the following three years.[155] After the expiration of this tax holiday, targeted property tax exemptions for new settlers became a recurring feature of the annual Tax-Acts.[156] What is more, beginning in 1735, all revenue raised from taxes on the importation of enslaved persons was dedicated "to and for the use of purchasing tools, provisions and other necessarys for poor Protestants lately arrived in this Province, or who shall come from Europe and settle in his Majesty's new Townships, laid out in this Province."[157] This dedicated stream of revenue, which by the late 1730s was significant in size, was called for because the usual appropriation for this purpose had repeatedly proved insufficient.[158] Nonetheless, it has been observed that "slaveowning assemblymen were still less than total in their commitment to offsetting black labor with white"—but that would soon change.[159]

Reflection

During the early colonial period, South Carolina experimented with a variety of legal tools for controlling and subjugating the colony's enslaved Black majority. Far from "neutral" economic legislation, tax law constituted an integral part of that continuous legislative experimentation and starkly reflected just how much South Carolina was a slave society from the start. Not only were enslaved persons marked as appropriate objects of taxation—that is to say, as a form of "property" on which tariffs and property taxes might be imposed—but tax measures were also intertwined with nontax measures (e.g., the slave codes and immigration legislation) to create a multifaceted system of social control and engineering that reinforced and perpetuated the evils of slavery in South Carolina.

South Carolina's slave codes expanded and evolved as the legislature exerted ever-tighter control over an enslaved Black majority while seeking to ensure the vital cooperation of Whites in the enforcement and operation of those restrictions. The soft power of taxation to shape behavior through the provision of financial incentives proved to be key for achieving the latter objective. Legislators were quick to recognize that slaveholders (many being among their own number) would not cooperate when the specter of the most draconian punishment under the slave code—death—threatened to harm them economically by summarily wiping out their investment in enslaved labor. To secure slaveholder cooperation in the prosecution and killing of enslaved persons, the legislature first provided compensation to slaveholders from general revenues on hand in the public treasury, allowing slaveholders' economic losses to be spread broadly across South Carolina's taxpaying populace. Later, bemoaning the crushing financial burden that these compensation payments imposed on the colony, the legislature shifted course dramatically by enacting a scheme that taxed local slaveholders only, forcing them to internalize the costs imposed on society by their exploitation of enslaved labor while simultaneously incentivizing them to alter their treatment of the enslaved in ways that would reduce transgressions of the slave code (and induce them to pressure their neighbors to do the same). Just a few years later, the legislature again shifted course when it combined its earlier experiments to create a hybrid tax regime that required some slaveholders to internalize their losses, allowed others limited redistribution of their losses, and allowed yet others broad redistribution of their losses. Alongside this hybrid tax scheme, the legislature adopted a practice of itself authorizing slaveholder compensation payments from the public treasury that were inextricably linked to the taxes imposed under the colony's annual Tax-Acts.

While South Carolina's ruling White minority was experimenting with tax mechanisms for funding slaveholder compensation, it experimented with a combination of tax and nontax measures to manipulate the colony's racial balance and enhance its control over the enslaved Black majority. Faced with an ever-expanding Black population, the legislature endeavored to increase the number of Whites in the colony by paying bounties for imported servants, establishing Black-White ratios in work settings to create job openings for White immigrants, and enacting tax holidays for new settlers. In tandem with these efforts to increase White immigration, the legislature endeavored to suppress the growth of the colony's Black population and better maintain control over it by occasionally deploying the hard power of taxation to impose prohibitive taxes aimed at deterring the importation of all enslaved Blacks—or, more often, just those who might stir up trouble (e.g., criminals from other colonies and Spanish Blacks and Native Americans who might entice others to escape south with them to Florida). Then, echoing the erasure of the divide between taxing and spending in the Tax-Acts, the legislature linked these two approaches together when it dedicated the revenue collected from taxes imposed on the importation of enslaved persons to purchasing provisions for poor White settlers who had recently arrived in the colony as a means of encouraging White immigration.

The common thread running through all this legislative experimentation is how taxation was consistently used to facilitate the subjugation—and often the outright killing—of enslaved persons in the name of maintaining a White supremacist racial order. South Carolina, through its tax system, loudly and clearly communicated the message that White livelihoods mattered more than Black lives, which could be taken for a price whenever it served White interests. There simply could be no more compelling example of the taxing power being used to destroy than this.

But more than just revealing the evil lurking at the heart of South Carolina's slave society, taxation opened a window directly onto that society once the legislature began vetting and approving slaveholder compensation claims as part of the annual tax legislative drafting process. As that practice matured, blanket authorizations of slaveholder compensation gave way to identifying individual slaveholders in the Tax-Acts and specifying the exact amount of compensation paid for the killing or execution of enslaved persons. Reflecting how the enslaved were treated as a fungible commodity, the tax legislative history did not mention an enslaved person's name until the mid-1730s—instead referring simply to "Negroes" or "Indians," with at most an accompanying mention of their gender. But even at this early stage, the tax legislative history often contained some indication of the circumstances surrounding the execution or killing of these enslaved persons. In contrast to the pattern observed in chapters 2 and 3, the Tax-Acts during the 1720s and 1730s provided compensation for a large number of killings, many of which were associated with the apprehension of escapees. Given the great risks and severe penalties associated with escape, its prevalence at this juncture—which is starkly illustrated by figure 1.1[160]—serves as a harbinger of the 1739 Stono Rebellion, which is the starting point of chapter 2.[161]

Evidence of the harshness of life under slavery in South Carolina also surfaced in Thomas Fleming's claim for compensation related to the execution of an enslaved man who murdered Fleming's overseer. That claim was denied under the exception in the slave code requiring the holders of those who were convicted of murder to bear the economic

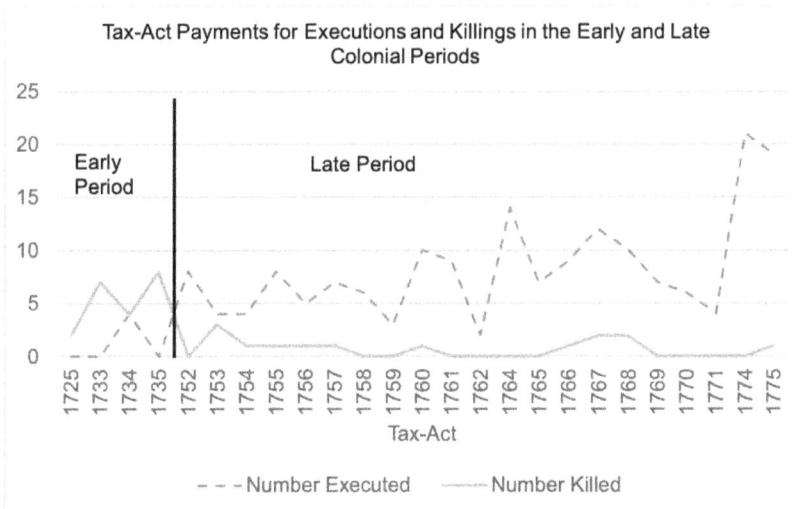

Figure 1.1. Tax-Act payments for executions and killings in the early and late colonial periods

loss themselves. When taken in the context of the broader compensation scheme, this exception effectively imposed a tax penalty on slaveholders such as Fleming that should have influenced them to alter the treatment of their enslaved persons in ways that minimized the incidence of such open forms of resistance. Given the identity of the victim, this tax penalty does not appear to have worked in Fleming's case, notwithstanding the *South Carolina Gazette*'s casual description of the incident as involving no more than the enslaved man's having taken an "opportunity" to wield an axe and kill the overseer. Notably, however, Fleming's name does not later reappear in the Tax-Act schedules.

As Fleming's case illustrates, after the *South Carolina Gazette* was established in the early 1730s, the ability to contextualize the execution or killing of enslaved persons was enhanced because details provided in the tax legislative history could be supplemented with news reporting. Indeed, the *Gazette*'s reporting on the execution for robbery of an enslaved man held by Isaac Mazyck illustrated just how quickly and summarily enslaved persons could be put to death. In that case, the crime was committed on Saturday, and the unnamed enslaved man was apprehended on Sunday, tried on Monday, and executed on Tuesday.

Tax legislative history also reveals the somewhat contradictory and conflicted thought processes of legislators as they navigated the process of vetting slaveholder compensation claims. In one remarkable example, the same group of legislators voted to pay compensation to Thomas Hendley in a situation that fell entirely outside the slaveholder compensation scheme but, with their very next vote, refused to compensate William Miles even though he pleaded his case on the basis of the failure of the compensation scheme to operate as intended. Taken together, Hendley's and Miles's claims for compensation—along with Fleming's request described earlier—confirm the legislature's oft-reiterated view that financial compensation was necessary to secure slaveholder cooperation with enforcement of the slave codes. Exhibiting a tenacity that will likewise be on display in later chapters, Hendley sought compensation even though his case fell outside the parameters of the slave code's compensation scheme, while Miles and Fleming both sought compensation in situations in which the law denied payment from the colony's public treasury. That slaveholders pursued these claims before the legislature demonstrates the importance that they placed on being able to take advantage of the colonial tax system to redistribute their losses from executions and killings perpetrated under the slave codes.

Whereas this tax window merely afforded a glimpse of life in South Carolina's slave society in this chapter, the window will be opened wider in the remainder of this part of the book. To begin, chapter 2 will take a longer, more revealing look through the tax window during the pivotal period following the 1739 Stono Rebellion. At the same time, chapter 2 will continue to examine other facets of the relationship between taxation and the evils of slavery during that period. Overall, chapter 2 will demonstrate how the regime of intertwined tax and nontax measures that, in this chapter, was constantly being refined and recalibrated to better achieve the goal of keeping South Carolina's enslaved Black majority in check crystallized into the shape that it would take for the remainder of the colonial period.

2

The Stono Rebellion and Its Aftermath

Crystallization of the Regime

This chapter continues to explore the ways in which taxation supported and reinforced the evils associated with slavery in colonial South Carolina. The focus here is on the 1739 Stono Rebellion and its aftermath—a period when the colonial legislature concluded the tax experimentation documented in chapter 1 and established tight and enduring connections between taxation and slavery. The chapter details how, in the wake of the Stono Rebellion, the legislature (1) revised South Carolina's slave code into the form that would govern long past the American Revolution, (2) secured slaveholder cooperation in enforcing that code by making publicly funded compensation provided through the colony's annual Tax-Acts the norm, and (3) endeavored to cement White control over the colony's enslaved Black majority by imposing prohibitive taxes that significantly depressed the importation of enslaved persons while dedicating the bulk of the revenue raised from those taxes to the encouragement of White migration to the colony. During the dozen years covered in this chapter, the regime of intertwined tax and nontax measures employed to control South Carolina's enslaved Black majority crystallized into the form that it would take for the remainder of the colonial period—subject only to the refinement and routinization of its operation detailed in chapter 3.

The Stono Rebellion

On a Sunday morning in September 1739, "a group of slaves struck a violent but abortive blow for liberation which resulted in the deaths of more than sixty people. Fewer than twenty-five white lives were taken, and property damage was localized, but the episode represented a new dimension in overt resistance."[1] Some of the rebels were killed on the day of the uprising; however, others escaped, and it took a month before "a correspondent in South Carolina could report that 'the Rebellious Negros are quite stopt from doing any further Mischief, many of them having been put to the most cruel Death.'"[2] Yet, "white fears were by no means allayed," as some of the fugitives were not "brought in for execution [until] the following spring, and one ringleader remained at large for three full years."[3]

In June 1740, another planned uprising was uncovered that resulted in the arrest of fifty enslaved persons who "were hanged, ten in a day, to intimidate the other negroes."[4] There were other suspected acts of resistance, including a November 1740 fire in Charles Town.[5] By then, "the implications of growing rebelliousness among slaves had already become unavoidable for the white minority,"[6] leading to the passage of the 1740 Slave Code:

> The comprehensive Negro Act, which had been in the works for several years but about which white legislators had been unable to agree in less threatening times, was passed into law and stringently enforced. This elaborate statute, which would serve as the core of South Carolina's slave code for more than a century to come, rested firmly upon prior enactments. At the same time, however, it did more than any other single piece of legislation in the colony's history to curtail *de facto* personal liberties, which slaves had been able to cling to against formidable odds during the first three generations of settlement. Freedom of movement and freedom of assembly, freedom to raise food, to earn money, to learn to read English—none of these rights had ever been assured to Negroes and most had already been legislated against, but always the open conditions of life in a young and struggling colony had kept vestiges of these meager liberties alive. Now the noose was being tightened: there would be heavier surveillance of Negro activity and stiffer fines for masters who failed to keep their slaves in line.[7]

The preamble to the 1740 Slave Code signaled this shift through its adoption of a markedly different tone from that of the 1712 preamble reproduced in chapter 1:

> WHEREAS, in his Majesty's plantations in America, slavery has been introduced and allowed, and the people commonly called negroes, Indians,

mulattoes and mustizoes, have been deemed absolute slaves, and the subjects of property in the hands of particular persons, the extent of whose
power over such slaves ought to be settled and limited by positive laws,
so that the slave may be kept in due subjection and obedience, and the
owners and other persons having the care and government of slaves may
be restrained from exercising too great rigour and cruelty over them, and
that the public peace and order of this Province may be preserved: We
pray your most sacred Majesty that it may be enacted . . .[8]

To these ends, the 1740 Slave Code mandated the death penalty for a
number of additional offenses: poisoning; "homicide of any sort, upon
any white person, except by misadventure, or in defence of his master
or other person under whose care and government such slave shall be";
raising an insurrection; "endeavor[ing] to delude or entice any slave to
run away and leave this Province"; and aiding or abetting insurrection
or enticement to escape.[9] In the case of group escape or insurrection,
however, the court was permitted to spare those "who they shall think
may deserve mercy," but only so long as at least one among the group
was "executed for example, to deter others from offending in the like
kind."[10] By 1745/6, the death penalty was thought too harsh for "every
slave who shall endeavour to delude or entice any slave to run away
and leave this Province" because "it might happen that such offender
may afterwards alter his intentions."[11] To remedy this defect, the 1745/6
legislation reserved the death penalty for those who had both enticed
another to escape and "actually prepared provisions, arms, ammunition,
or any boat, canoe or other vessel, whereby such their intentions shall be
manifested."[12] Once a death sentence was pronounced, the slave court
was required to have punishment carried out "by inflicting such manner
of death, and at such time, as the [court] shall direct, and which they
shall judge will be most effectual to deter others from offending in the
like manner."[13] For instance, death sentences for poisoning were vari-
ously carried out through burning at the stake, hanging, or gibbeting.[14]

The 1740 Slave Code also increased the punishment for physical violence against Whites. A death sentence was now mandatory for third
offenses, and "in case any such slave shall grievously wound, maim or
bruise any white person, though it be only the first offence, such slave
shall suffer death."[15] Likewise, the killing of enslaved persons was legally

authorized if they assaulted and struck any White person who apprehended them for potential violations of the ticket system.[16] Not only
did the 1740 Slave Code sanction such extrajudicial killings of enslaved
persons, but it also financially rewarded those killings under certain
circumstances. Because "many disobedient and evil minded negroes
and other slaves" had recently escaped to the Spanish colony in Florida,
where they had been promised their liberty, the 1740 Slave Code provided rewards to "any white person or persons, free Indian or Indians,"
who caught enslaved persons escaping south.[17] The reward for those
captured alive was £50 for adult males (raised to £100 if captured closer
to Florida), £25 for adult females and boys over twelve, and £5 for children under twelve.[18] A more gruesome reward was offered for those
brought back dead: "for every scalp of a grown negro slave, with the two
ears, twenty pounds" (raised to £50 for those killed closer to Florida).[19]

Furthermore, the 1740 Slave Code retroactively conferred legitimacy
on—and thus absolved the perpetrators from liability for and spared
them from being questioned about—the lynching of enslaved persons
in connection with the Stono Rebellion.[20] On the ground that "the exi-
gence and danger the inhabitants at that time were in and exposed to,
would not admit of the formality of a legal trial of such rebellious negroes, but for their own security, the said inhabitants were obliged to put
such negroes to immediate death," the 1740 Slave Code provided that "all
and every act, matter and thing, had, done, committed and executed, in
and about the suppressing and putting all and every the said negro and
negroes to death, is and are hereby declared lawful, to all intents and
purposes whatsoever, as fully and amply as if such rebellious negroes
had undergone a formal trial and condemnation, notwithstanding any
want of form or omission whatever in the trial of such negroes."[21]

Opening Wide the Tax Window onto South Carolina's Slave Society

While tightening restrictions and harshening punishments of the
enslaved, the 1740 Slave Code also revisited the scheme for compensating
the holders of executed enslaved persons—a subject that had garnered
little attention in the 1735 Slave Code. Still concerned that slaveholders
might "be tempted to conceal the crimes of their slaves to the prejudice

of the public," the 1740 Slave Code authorized slave courts to award compensation of up to £200, payable from the colony's public treasury, for enslaved persons executed for crimes other than murder or rebellion.[22] In the mid-1700s, this monetary cap approximated the average price for newly arrived enslaved persons; however, it has been observed that £200 was "insufficient compensation for a prime field hand, and some slave crime was concealed on this account."[23] Nonetheless, it is worth noting that a number of compensation payments made during this period were for amounts well below the £200 cap (see appendix table A.1). Eventually, as described in chapter 3, the legislature did create a mechanism for providing compensation above the cap for the loss of more valuable enslaved persons.

A minimum of one-half of the enslaved person's value was to be paid directly to the slaveholder; the balance was to be paid by the public treasurer "to the person injured by such offence for which such slave shall suffer death."[24] Even though a portion of the payment might end up in the hands of persons other than the slaveholder, the entire payment was still seen as redounding to the slaveholder's benefit. In fact, the House debate on the compensation provision included discussion of whether slaveholders should be held "liable to make good the Damages to the Party injured by such Slave to the Amount of one Half of the Payment they shall receive from the Public for such Slave."[25] When that question was put to a vote, it "was carried in the Affirmative."[26] Ultimately, the legislature simplified the operation of that policy by having the public treasurer pay directly to victims their share of slaveholder compensation, rather than having it pass through slaveholders' hands.

Despite the 1740 Slave Code's embrace of a broadly redistributive scheme for funding slaveholder compensation, it carved out one important exception: "Apparently, masters whose slaves committed such particularly heinous crimes [as murder and rebellion] were thought to bear some of the blame and therefore did not deserve compensation."[27] These slaveholders were required to internalize the economic losses occasioned by the execution of their enslaved persons, providing them with a clear financial incentive to alter their behavior in ways that would reduce the incidence of these forms of resistance. In contrast, the 1740 Slave Code broke with earlier practice by no longer requiring individual slaveholders to internalize the economic loss associated with the execution of escapees. When enslaved persons were "condemned to be executed for deserting out of this Province," the slave court was to determine their value prior to execution, and that amount was to "be paid by the public of this Province, the full sum and rates at which such executed slave or slaves shall be valued . . . without being a charge to any particular owner or owners."[28] In another departure from past practice, the legislature left unmentioned the subject of slaveholder compensation for extrajudicial killings of enslaved persons. That omission would not be rectified for more than a decade.

Overall, the 1740 Slave Code accompanied tighter control of the lives of the enslaved, and a concomitant harshening of punishments for transgressions, with a marked shift toward allowing slaveholders to foist the economic losses occasioned by the execution of their enslaved persons onto a diffuse public. These losses would now be shared by all payers of South Carolina property taxes, with the amount of each taxpayer's annual payment under the Tax-Acts being directly affected by slaveholder compensation payments. Simultaneously, the legislature centralized control of the slaveholder compensation process. In the 1720s and 1730s, the legislature's nascent practice of vetting and approving slaveholder compensation claims through the annual tax legislative drafting process operated parallel to the regional compensation scheme handled through the slave courts. After enactment of the 1740 Slave Code—at a time when the House was cementing its tight control over all aspects of the power of the purse[29]—House vetting of slaveholder compensation claims (alongside all other claims of public creditors) became the norm. A distinct benefit of the centralized processing of slaveholder compensation claims as part of drafting the annual Tax-Act is that it opens wide the tax window onto South Carolina's slave society that, in chapter 1, had only been left ajar. This procedural shift affords a fuller view—and, more importantly, enables a fuller accounting—of the legalized killings of enslaved persons that were facilitated by the colony's tax system to control the enslaved population and maintain it in subjugation.

Taking advantage of this development to continue in earnest the work begun in chapter 1, this section of the chapter documents slaveholder compensation payments made through South Carolina's annual Tax-Acts, providing contextualizing detail regarding the identity of executed enslaved persons and the circumstances surrounding their deaths

whenever possible. This section first documents payments made between 1740 and 1745. This section then separately documents payments
made between 1746 and 1751, after the legislature eliminated restrictions
on compensation based on the nature of the crime and ceased using tax
incentives to shape slaveholder treatment of the enslaved.

Tax-Act Payments, 1740–45

The Tax-Acts immediately following the Stono Rebellion contained no
slaveholder compensation payments—but not for a lack of executions.[30]
Indeed, in early 1740, the Commons House of Assembly considered a
petition from a group of slaveholders whose enslaved persons had been
killed in the rebellion. These slaveholders began their petition by tout-
ing how they "had always taken the best Care they possibly could for
the keeping [of their enslaved persons] in good Order and Demean-
our."[31] Tapping into the notion that slaveholder culpability had some
bearing on the availability of public compensation, the slaveholders
bemoaned their "Misfortune" and "great Sufferings," which they saw
as being due to no fault of their own but to the fact that "Negroes by
Nature are generally prone to Cruelty, Barbarity and savage Endeav-
ours."[32] The slaveholders requested whatever compensation the House
might deem proper for their enslaved persons so "that some Relief
might be given them in their present Calamity towards repairing their
respective Losses."[33] The matter was referred to a committee, which
reported back that it was "of Opinion, that the Petitioners are not inti-
tled to any Relief from the General Assembly"—an opinion that the
House unanimously affirmed.[34]

The 1740 Tax-Act did, however, include a different form of compensation arising out of the Stono Rebellion. A £1,000 payment was occasioned by the manumission of Thomas Elliott's enslaved man July, who
had fought against the rebels.[35] July had been "very early and chiefly in-
strumental in saving his Master and his Family from being destroyed by
the rebellious Negroes," having "bravely fought against the Rebels, and
killed one of them."[36] The House, with the concurrence of the Council,
decided to set July free "as a Reward for his faithful Services, and for an
Encouragement to other Slaves to follow his Example in Cases of the
like Nature."[37] July was also given "a Present of a Suit of Clothes, Shirt,

Hat, a Pair of Stockings, and a Pair of Shoes."[38] (Other enslaved persons received similar rewards for apprehending rebels but were *not* set free by the legislature.)[39] After the House informed Elliott that July was to be manumitted, it ordered an appraisal of his value, which was set at the £1,000 that Elliott was paid.[40] Though the payment to Elliott was not compensation for an execution like the other payments documented here, it is notable for two reasons: First, the compensation was five times the prevailing cap in the 1740 Slave Code, leaving one to wonder whether the valuation was inflated because White society viewed July's conduct as laudable (in contrast to the scheme for authorizing compensation above the £200 cap described in chapter 3, under which criminal behavior depressed an enslaved person's value). Second, the aim of this payment, like that of other slaveholder compensation payments, was to reinforce the systems of control established by the slave code. In this case, however, the payment went far beyond providing a financial inducement to secure slaveholder cooperation with government decisions regarding the operation of the institution of slavery. The payment to Elliott attempted to purchase enslaved persons' own cooperation in their subjugation by singling out and rewarding with freedom just one among the enslaved persons who enforced the slave code's restrictions against participants in the Stono Rebellion.

The legislature resumed providing compensation for executed enslaved persons with the 1741/2 Tax-Act. That act authorized a £150 payment to John Garnier for an enslaved person "executed for setting an House on Fire in Charles Town" and a £200 payment to John Roberts for an enslaved person executed for "wounding a White man."[41] Though not specifically denoted in the Tax-Act as compensation for the execution of an enslaved person, the House journal indicates that £178 was paid to John Skene on account of the execution of his enslaved man Isaac for robbery and £22 was paid to Edward Perry for damages suffered as the robbery victim.[42] Of these three crimes, only the house fire garnered significant attention in the *South Carolina Gazette*. The reporting there reveals (1) details regarding the circumstances surrounding a crime that threatened the entire town, (2) how the threat of death was used to elicit accusations against suspected accomplices, and (3) the gruesome punishments that were inflicted on enslaved persons as a warning of what might befall others who resisted bondage:

Thursday *Boatswain* a Negro-Man Slave belonging to Mr. *John Garnier* was burnt to Death, having been convicted on his own Confession, and the Evidence of *Kate* a Negro Woman Slave belonging to Mr. *Francis Varambaut*, of setting Fire to a House where Mrs. *Snowden* lives, with a malicious and evil Intent of burning down the remaining Part of the Town; The said *Kate* had been before convicted of the same Crime on the Evidence of *Jenny* an old Negro Woman who happened, when this wicked Act was perpetrated, to be alone in the House, and no Body had been with her but *Kate* for some Time before the People cried-out Fire; *Kate* on her Tryal would own no Accomplice, seeing the Preparation making for her Execution, and receiving a Promise of Pardon if she would confess the Person or Persons really concern'd with her, she accused this *Boatswain*; On his Tryal after much Prevarication and accusing many Negroes, who upon a strict Examination were found to be innocent, he confessed that none but he and *Kate* were concerned, That he took the Brand End from her together with a Light-Wood Junk, *Kate* had taken from behind the old Womans Box were [*sic*] it was hid, which when found in the Fire, the old Woman knew, and that he went softly upstairs and put the Fire under the shingles & that in returning he stumbled on the Stairs, and *Jenny* crying-out in a Fright who was there *Kate* answered Me, and the Fellow got out at the Back-Door, without the old Woman's ever perceiving him; He would make no Confession but died like an impudent hardened Wretch as he was; and *Kate* being positive, that there was no other Negro with them, it is probable, there was no Plot in the Case, but the Effect of his own sottish wicked Heart, especially since he looked upon every white Man he should meet as his declared Enemy.[43]

The 1743 Tax-Act included two payments for the execution of enslaved persons: £100 to Elizabeth Cheeseman and £200 to Michael Jeans.[44] In Cheeseman's case, the *South Carolina Gazette* once again illustrated "the expeditious manner in which justice could be dispensed by the slave court" when it reported that "Thursday last a Negro Fellow, belonging to Mr. *Cheesman*, was brought to Town, tried, condemn'd and hang'd, for attempting to murder a white Lad."[45] Jeans's case was more sensational—it involved a potentially wide escape plot, one plotter's escape from custody, and a few procedural twists along the way:

On Tuesday last were tried . . . two Negro Men Slaves, the one named *Sampson* belonging to Mr. *Michael Jeans,* and the other *Harry* belonging to Mr. *Samuel West,* for having *endeavoured to delude and entice several other Slaves to run-away and leave this Province*; and convicted, on the Evidence of Mr. *Rantole's Peter,* (which was confirmed by that of several others) the former as Principal, who was accordingly condemned to be hanged on Friday next . . . and the other as an Accomplice, Aider or Abettor, and was therefore ordered to be severely whip'd and pickled, on three several Days, round the Square of *Charles-Town*: Several other Slaves were likewise tried, some of whom appearing to be entirely innocent, and the others to have had the Secret hinted to them only in general Terms, were accordingly acquitted. *Peter* having first impeached *Sampson, Harry* and *Sambo* belonging to Mrs. *Toomer,* before *Thomas Drayton,* Esq; in the Country, was allowed to be Evidence for the King, with a Promise of Pardon, if he would make a full Discovery; but *Sambo* who was ordered with him, to Town for Tryal, made his Escape out of the Constable's Custody.[46]

In the next week's edition, the *Gazette* reported that Sampson had not yet been executed, "his Death Warrant being said to be left."[47] In fact, Jeans had applied to the governor for clemency for Sampson on the ground that his own incapacity prevented him from working, which meant that his family relied for its survival entirely on Sampson's labor as a trained painter and glazier.[48] Even more strikingly, Jeans argued in support of his petition

that the Crime for which the said Slave is Convicted did not upon the Tryal Appear to be Attended with any Aggravating Circumstances of Intended Mischief other than to runaway and leave the Province and to persuade some other Slaves to go with him with the Sole design of Obtaining Liberty a desire so naturally implanted in the minds of all Mankind that Seldom any Other Consideration has been found Sufficient to root it out. And as this desire of Liberty is founded on the General Law of Nature the Attempts in Slaves to Obtain it are punishable by the Laws of Particular Countries yet the Crime taken Simply has ever been deemed only an Evil prohibited and never ranked amongst those termed Evil in themselves by the best Civilians as well as Common Lawyers.[49]

Despite Jeans's obvious preference to continue to benefit from Sampson's forced labor rather than having his loss redistributed among South Carolina taxpayers—undermining the notion that enslaved persons were fungible property and that monetary compensation would be sufficient to purchase slaveholders' quiescent cooperation with enforcement of the slave code's most draconian punishments—the petition for clemency was quickly rejected.[50] But when it came time to carry out the death sentence, the constable claimed that the death warrant had been lost, which gave rise to a request for guidance from the governor and Council because the prescribed time for carrying out the sentence had passed.[51] The governor and Council advised that the court should issue a new death warrant and the constable who failed to produce the original death warrant should himself be indicted.[52] The following edition of the *South Carolina Gazette* noted, "On Saturday last Mr. *Jeanes's Sampson* was hang'd, pursuant to his Sentence."[53]

Much like the 1740 Tax-Act, the 1743 act also included a payment to compensate for the loss of an enslaved person who cooperated in enforcing the slave code. John Pagett was paid £300 "for a Negro killed in attempting to apprehend a fugitive Slave."[54] According to the House journal, "on the 22d Day of March last (in the Night Time) a runaway Negro Man named Hannibal came to the Petitioner's Plantation, when two of the Petitioner's Slaves attempted to apprehend him, but he being armed with a Knife stabbed one of your Petitioner's said Slaves (named Harry) in the Heart of which he instantly died, and maiming the other very much made his Escape."[55] The request for compensation for Harry's death was made under a provision that conferred discretion on the legislature to provide a reward to "any Person . . . maimed, wounded, or disabled in pursuing, apprehending, or taking any Slave that was run away . . . and if any such Person should be killed, his Heirs, Executors, or Administrators should receive the like Reward."[56] Even though this provision did not specifically authorize compensation for injuries to non-Whites, the House allowed Pagett £300—again far more than the general cap on slaveholder compensation—because "Petitioner hath lost a valuable young Negro Fellow."[57]

The 1745/6 Tax-Act contained a single compensation payment of £100 to Joseph Blake—a wealthy and influential slaveholder who also makes an appearance in chapter 3—which the House journal indicates

was "the appraised Value of a Negro that was executed."[58] After examining the underlying criminal offense to determine whether it
qualified for compensation, the Committee on Petitions and Accounts
remained "in some Doubt whether the Exception in the Negro Law
did not extend to the said Negro"—that is, the exception denying compensation for those convicted of murder or rebellion—which moved
the committee to refer the question to the House for consideration.[59]
Though the House journal does not indicate the nature of the crime
committed, the *South Carolina Gazette* reported, "On Wednesday last
an old Negro Man belonging to the Hon *Joseph Blake*, Esq; was hang'd
in Chains on a Gibbet near *Dorchester*, having attempted to poison his
Master, &c."[60] Two days after the committee's referral of the matter to
the House, the House journal summarily reports that the House had
"Resolved that the Sum of one hundred Pounds be allowed to the said
Joseph Blake, Esquire."[61]

Contemporaneously, the House considered "an Order drawn . . . in
Favor of Mr. Burrel Massingberd Hyrne for the Sum of four hundred
Pounds, being the appraised Value of two Negro Men, that were accused
and convicted of the Homicide of a white Person."[62] Again because of
doubt regarding whether the offense qualified for compensation, the
Committee on Petitions and Accounts was instructed to "inspect the
Act for the better ordering and governing Negroes and other Slaves to
see if the Public is liable by the said Act to pay for Slaves executed for the
Crime of which the Negroes . . . were convicted."[63] When the committee
brought the matter back to the House, it was moved that the payment
should be approved; however, the motion was opposed and, ultimately,
voted down.[64] Hyrne later petitioned the legislature for relief, but his
claim was once again rejected—this time with the grounds for denial
more clearly spelled out. Apparently, the court had determined a value
for the two enslaved men because it found them guilty of homicide and
not murder.[65] But demonstrating the legislature's independent role in
vetting slaveholder compensation claims as part of the process of drafting the annual Tax-Acts, "the House was informed that the Offence for
which the two Negroes . . . were executed was for Rebellion in tying their
Overseer up, and Murder in whipping him to Death."[66] The House then
denied Hyrne compensation under the exception for enslaved persons
found guilty of murder or rebellion.[67]

Tax-Act Payments, 1746–51

In 1745/6, the legislature amended the 1740 Slave Code's compensation scheme. Under the revised scheme, holders of enslaved persons "put to death for any crime or crimes whatever" were to be compensated by the public, effectively eliminating the exception for rebellion and murder that had served as the ground for denying Hyrne compensation.[68] The £200 compensation cap remained untouched, and at least half of the authorized compensation was still to be paid to the slaveholder, with the balance going directly to the injured person.[69]

The 1746 Tax-Act authorized Alexander Rantowl to be paid £200, "being the appraised Value of a Negro belonging to Benjamin Seabrook who was executed for maiming of John Norman."[70] Another £200 was split between Francis Gracia (£150) and William Roper (£50) in connection with the execution of an enslaved man for burglary.[71] The *South Carolina Gazette* summarily reported the circumstances surrounding the latter payments: "On Thursday last was hang'd, *Brutus*, a Negro Fellow belonging to Mr. *Gracia* of this Town, convicted of House breaking."[72]

The 1746 Tax-Act authorized a total of £180 to be split among William Walker (£118 11s 5d), Christopher Smith (£22 17s 1d), and John Pollock (£38 11s 6d), "being the Value of a Negro Wench who dyed under Condemnation."[73] The claim for this compensation had been submitted to the House in an earlier session, but the House had not acted on it.[74] The unusual circumstances surrounding the case led the public treasurer to decline payment until receiving the legislature's advice on whether compensation was legally permitted.[75] A petition was submitted to the House and the Council, with the Council providing some detail regarding the request when it referred the petition to the House for consideration.[76]

As reported by the Council, the petition stated that "a Negroe Wench named Hagar, the property of the Petitioner Elizabeth Walker's [deceased] Husband, was try'd . . . and convicted of maliciously burning a dwelling House" that belonged to Christopher Smith and was occupied by John Pollock.[77] Because Hagar "prov[ed] to be with Child," her execution was delayed so that the court might determine "how the Law in such Cases had provided and directed."[78] While the court was undertaking its legal inquiry and Hagar was in the constable's custody, "she jumped out of a Garret Window, three Story high," and was so severely injured that she died the next day.[79] In view of Hagar having been condemned to death "and her desperate attempt to escape from her Confinement and from Justice, occasioning her death," the court was persuaded "that the Owner and the other Sufferers were as justly entitled to what the Law provides in the Case of Slaves being legally put to Death, as if she had been actually executed by the proper officer."[80] The House agreed.[81]

The 1747 Tax-Act also included compensation payments of mixed vintages, some stemming from older and others from more recent executions.[82] On the basis of a claim that had been carried over from the previous legislative session, Thomas Mellichamp was paid £400 as compensation for two enslaved persons who had been executed.[83] Edward Bond was paid £155, "being the appraised Value of a Negro Man . . . that was executed."[84] Finally, Hyrne's claim for compensation that had been rejected twice before was renewed and finally succeeded, just one year after he declined to take a seat in the House that he had won in a special election.[85]

As recapitulated in the House journal, Hyrne's petition explained his claim for relief as follows:

> The Petitioner in the Year, one thousand seven hundred and forty-four, had the Misfortune to have two valuable Slaves convicted of the Homicide of a white Person, for which Offence . . . they suffered Death. . . . That, after a full Hearing and Examination of every Circumstance, [the court] determined the Offence of which the said Slaves were convicted to be Manslaughter and not Murder, and accordingly . . . appraised the said two Slaves at two hundred Pounds each, and drew an Order upon the Public Treasurer for the same. That there being no Money provided for that Use in the Treasury, the said Order was laid before a former House of Assembly, but (as the Petitioner humbly conceives) by some Mistake in the Case, was never provided for. And therefore humbly praying the House to take the same into their Consideration, and, as the Directions of the said Negro Act seem very full and particular, and the Triers appear to have been duly qualified in every Respect to carry the same into Execution, that the House will look on the said Order as a just Demand on the Public, and be pleased to make such Provision for the Payment thereof as to the House shall seem meet.[86]

A committee appointed to examine the petition found that, under the slave code, the court "had a Right to determine the Nature of the Offence" and thus recommended deferring to the court's judgment that the offense amounted to manslaughter and not murder.[87] With the claim now fully vetted, the House agreed and approved £400 as compensation to Hyrne for the execution of the two enslaved persons.[88]

The 1748 and 1749 Tax-Acts each included compensation for the execution of two enslaved persons.[89] Somewhat anomalously, the House journals provide no details regarding the circumstances surrounding these payments, aside from mentioning that one of the four was executed for burglary.[90] The *South Carolina Gazette* contained no reporting regarding these executions that might add further contextual detail.

The 1750 Tax-Act was the first to dedicate a separate section in its schedule to payments "For Criminal Slaves"—a grouping that became a standard feature of later Tax-Acts.[91] In addition to payments of constable fees relating to trials and executions, the section "For Criminal Slaves" in the 1750 Tax-Act included compensation for the execution of fourteen enslaved persons. Among these payments were the following:

- John Thompson was paid £200 "being the appraised Value of a Slave . . . that was executed for the Murder of John Chambers."[92]
- A total of £200 was paid "for a Negro Fellow executed, named Santee Jemmy": "the Committee were informed he belonged to a Gentleman in North-Carolina, and are of opinion that the Sum of thirty six Pounds . . . be paid to Mr. Thomas Fuller as Executor to his late Father for the damage sustained; and that the Balance of one hundred and sixty four Pounds, be likewise provided for, but to remain in the Treasurers Hands until a proper power be produced from the Heirs of the Gentleman whose property the said Negro was, as the Committee are informed he is since deceased."[93]
- William Cattell Jr. was paid £200 for the execution of his enslaved man Frank (the circumstances surrounding his execution are discussed later).[94]
- Josiah Parry was paid £200 for the execution of an enslaved man named Cupid.[95]
- Algernoon Wilson was paid £200 "for a Negro Man named Pharaoh that was executed."[96] Notably, in Wilson's capacity as constable, he was

likewise compensated "for Fees on the Trial and Execution of several Slaves."[97]

- A payment of £200 was authorized "in favour of Mr. William Harvey . . . for a Negro named Quamino executed" but was made to Messrs. Smith and Palmer because Harvey had assigned his compensation claim to them.[98]

- James Akin, who served as a justice of the peace and thus would have sat on the ad hoc slave courts, was paid £200 "for a Negro named Joe, executed."[99]

- A £200 payment was split equally between Walter Holman and Robert Wright, "being the appraised value of a Negro man belonging to the said Walter Holman that was condemned and executed (for the Murder of a Negro that belong'd to the said Robert Wright)"; however, Wright's share was paid over to William Walter, who held the mortgage on Duff, the murder victim.[100]

Greater information regarding Duff's murder is available because a record of the trial was included in the Council journal in connection with a clemency request submitted by the court that tried and convicted his killer, an enslaved man named John.[101] John had given Duff "one mortal wound with a Knife under the left Breast of which he immediately Died."[102] According to the testimony of Robert Wright's enslaved man Simon, John had been knocking at Duff's door early on the morning of June 25, 1749.[103] Duff eventually answered the door and told John that "he was a Fool and that he did not want to see him, to which [John] replied he was no Fool, but that [Duff] was a Scoundrel and had used him ill."[104] Simon then heard Duff running and calling after John, who did not reply, and "presently after heard Duff hollow and immediately cry out twice he was Murthered."[105] Simon woke his sister Hannah— who had fallen asleep in her clothes after returning late from working in the fields—and asked her to check on Duff because he was "a Cripple himself and not able to go out."[106] Hannah went out and met John, who told her "that Duff had beat him very much and knocked him down three times and that he did not know where he was gone."[107] When Hannah said that she believed John had killed Duff, "he answered how should he kill Duff that was as strong as an Horse."[108] But Hannah saw John holding a large butcher's knife and said that she thought that he had killed Duff with the knife—an accusation that John did not answer.[109] Hannah then searched for Duff, and after she found him dead, John fled the scene.[110]

There was testimony indicating that there had been a falling out between John and Duff and that they had spoken about possible escape from slavery.[111] According to John's testimony, Duff had attacked him with a stick when he was on his way home after they had argued, and John had no design to kill Duff but had been "blinded with Passion" after being attacked and had struck Duff with his knife with the intent only to wound him.[112] After testifying, John showed the court his injuries from the scuffle.[113]

The court was sharply split on the verdict, with two voting "not guilty" and three voting "guilty" because John's presence on Wright's plantation was itself a violation of the slave code's ticket system—and the potential plot between John and Duff to escape "a much greater" violation—which, in their eyes, made John "answerable for all the Consequences."[114] With the requisite quorum of three voting in favor of conviction, the court sentenced John "to be hanged by the Neck till he should be dead on some part of the high Road."[115] Nevertheless, execution of the sentence was delayed so that the court might submit a clemency request to the governor.[116] Along with the record of the trial, the clemency request included a brief description of John's life, which indicated that he had been born to free parents in Havana and had been a free man who worked at sea prior to being sold into slavery in South Carolina.[117] After considering the request, the governor and Council concluded "that there was nothing appeared to them in the case that could recommend the Criminal to Mercy,"[118] resulting in John's execution and the compensation payments authorized by the 1750 Tax-Act.

In addition to the payments listed earlier, Deborah and James McCree submitted a petition seeking compensation for the execution in early March 1745/6 of "four Negro Men belonging to the Estate of . . . Dougle McKerthen [who] were tried and convicted of the Murder of their Master."[119] Deborah McCree had previously been married to McKerthen's son Thomas, and she was the administrator and sole heir of Thomas's estate when the compensation claim was submitted.[120] The McCrees' petition raised thorny legal questions for the House to decide:

That though the Trial of the said Slaves was antecedent to the passing of the [1745/6 amendment to the 1740 Slave Code], yet the Execution was subsequent thereto, and would intitle the Petitioners to a Satisfaction for the said Negroes had their Value been certified by the [court], which was a Ceremony not known in that Part of the Country to be directed by Law, at the Time of trying the said Negroes; the said Appraisement was therefore not made till after the Execution of the said Negroes, which, though not strictly conformable to the said Act, yet the Petitioners hope, from the Justice of this House, and the great Loss sustained by so mournful an Accident, and as the Petitioner, Deborah, was assiduous to have the said Slaves brought to Justice, the Petitioners humbly hope, for the Encouragement of all Persons to bring such atrocious Offences to Light, and the Offenders to Justice; and as being within the Meaning, though not within the Letter, of the said Act, therefore humbly praying Relief in the Premises.[121]

A committee was appointed to consider the petition and report back to the House.[122] Before the committee reported back, William McCluer's estate petitioned for compensation for four enslaved men—Tony, Titus, Bob, and Cudjoe—who had been executed for McCluer's murder.[123] Apparently, at the time of conviction, McCluer's estate (and, seemingly, the slave court) had been unaware of the 1745/6 change to the compensation scheme, and the slave court had not appraised the value of the four men who were executed.[124] Because the two petitions raised similar legal questions, the House referred the McCluer petition to the committee considering the McCree petition.[125]

When the committee reported back, it recommended paying £600 to McCluer's estate for the four executed enslaved men but only £300 to the McCrees.[126] The committee summarily recommended the compensation for McCluer's estate because "the Law makes provision for the said Slaves," who were "not appraised by the [court] agreeable to Law."[127] The committee took a more legalistic approach to the McCree petition. The 1745/6 amendment of the slave code was passed on March 22, and "it makes provision for all Slaves hereafter to be put to death for any Crime."[128] The court convicted the four enslaved men of killing Dougle McKerthen on March 7; however, "two of the said Negroes broke out of George-town Goal, and were taken and executed some Days after the passing of the Act under which the Petitioners beg relief."[129] Because only "two of the said Slaves were executed after passing the said Act," the committee recommended only half the compensation afforded to McCluer's estate.[130] Both recommended payments were approved by the House and included in the 1750 Tax-Act.[131]

Finally, the 1751 Tax-Act included compensation for the execution of four enslaved persons.[132] William Elliott was paid £200 for "a Negro man . . . named Lymas that was tryed and condemned to be executed (for the murder of another Slave)."[133] A £200 payment was split between John Brunson, who was paid £150 for an enslaved man named Duke who had been executed for an unidentified felony, and Jeremiah Cutteneau and John Greene, who were paid £30 and £20, respectively, as compensation for damage that Duke caused.[134] Similarly, a £200 payment was split between John Ainger, who was paid £192 for an enslaved man named Robin who had been executed for an unidentified felony, and William Branford Jr. and Elizabeth Butler, who were each paid £4 for damage that Robin caused.[135]

Thomas Miles was originally to be paid £400, "being the appraised value of two Negros . . . named Kitt and Venus that were tryed for Poisoning and condemnd to be executed."[136] The victim had been Miles's wife, who "was taken so suddenly and violently ill that she immediately suspected herself to be poisoned but is now considerably better and has hopes of recovering a good State of health."[137] Kit had apparently "dropt some hints to one of his fellow Slaves which created suspicion that he might have been concerned in Administering Poison to his said Mistress."[138] Miles and his family decided "to examine in the strictest manner" Kit's fifteen-year-old wife, Venus, "in hopes of discovering sufficient Evidence to convict the said Kit and his accomplices."[139] Following "great persuasion" and "promises of safety" from Miles's sons, Venus confessed that, at Kit's instigation, she "had mixed Poison with the water of which her mistress drank."[140] She also testified that the poison had been provided by an enslaved man named Frank who was held by William Cattell Jr.[141] The court, which was not aware that Venus's testimony had been induced by pressure and promises from Miles and his family, convicted Kit, Venus, and Frank and sentenced them to death.[142] Miles promptly submitted a clemency petition on behalf of Venus on the ground that both Kit and Frank would probably have escaped punishment had it not been for Venus's testimony against them, and the governor granted a temporary stay of execution.[143] Ultimately, the petition was granted, and Venus "was afterwards sent off the Province."[144] Accordingly, the compensation to Miles was reduced from £400 to £200 to reflect that only one of his enslaved persons—namely, Kit—had been executed.[145] It is worth noting that Frank was also executed, with compensation having been earlier paid to Cattell under the 1750 Tax-Act.[146]

The 1751 Tax-Act included two additional compensation payments that related not to executions but to extrajudicial killings.[147] The Reverend John McLeod was paid only one-half of the £250 that he requested "for a run away Negro that was killed by the Patrol."[148] According to the patrol's commander, the patrol, which had been "in pursuit of fugitive Slaves," surprised "a Camp of them on the Marshes near New-Cut; and firing among them, one of the said Run-aways was killed upon the Spot; which they were then informed (by some of Mr. Grimbald's Negroes) belonged to the reverend Mr. John McLeod; and that his name was Ben."[149] Similarly, William Kelvert was paid £200 "for a Slave of his that was killed by Indians who were hunting for fugitive Slaves."[150] It appears that Kelvert's enslaved man Hector was in the wrong place at the wrong time. Escaped enslaved persons had caused a disturbance near the plantation where Hector lived, and the local militia had been called to suppress the disturbance with the help of some Native Americans who had been hired to search for escapees in the swamps.[151] Hector, "happening to go some distance from the said Plantation, and in sight of the Inhabitants thereabouts, was met by the said Indians; one of whom shot him that he dyed of his Wounds."[152] In requesting relief, Kelvert stated,

That the Petitioners said Negro was a hard working Fellow, and always behaved himself as a Slave ought to do; and the Petitioner is at a great Loss for the want of him, not being able to carry on his Plantation business.

And therefore most humbly praying his Excellency and their Honours to take the case into consideration: and that as the said Indian did kill the said Negro, who had never transgressed the Law, his Excellency and their Honrs. will be pleased to allow him such Satisfaction as the Laws, both of the Militia and the Negro Act in that case made and provided do allow.[153]

In authorizing compensation to McLeod and Kelvert, the House made clear that these were situations not covered by law and that "the granting of the said Sums to the said John McLeod and William Kelvert, was in Consideration of the Equity attending their particular Cases; and that the same ought not hereafter to be drawn into Precedent."[154] Nevertheless, immediately thereafter, the House decided to prepare an amendment to the 1740 Slave Code that, as described in chapter 3, altered the compensation scheme to once again cover situations like McLeod's and Kelvert's.[155]

Manipulating the Racial Balance

The Stono Rebellion led not only to the harshening of the slave code and expansion of its redistributive slaveholder compensation scheme but also to renewed attempts at manipulating the racial balance of South Carolina's population. In addition to continuing to embrace targeted property tax exemptions for White immigrants,[156] the legislature quickly settled on a combination of tax and nontax measures embedded in the slave code and general duty act that would endure throughout the remainder of the colonial period, subject only to the refinements described in chapter 3.

Concerned that "plantations settled with slaves without any white person thereon, may be harbours for runaways and fugitive slaves," the 1740 Slave Code imposed a fine on any person who kept "any slaves on any plantation or settlement, without having a white person on such plantation or settlement."[157] A month before enacting this mandate of White supervision over the enslaved—no matter how small their number—the legislature enacted import tax legislation that aimed to manipulate the racial cast of new arrivals to the colony in direct response to the threat posed by the Stono Rebellion:

> WHEREAS, the great importation of negroes from the coast of Africa, who are generally of a barbarous and savage disposition, may hereafter prove of very dangerous consequence to the peace and safety of this Province, and which we have now more reason to be apprehensive of from the late rising in rebellion of a great number of the negroes lately imported into this Province from the coast of Africa, in the thickest settlements of

this Province, and barbarously murdering upwards of twenty persons of his Majesty's faithful subjects of this Province, within about twenty miles from the capital of this Province; and whereas, the best way to prevent those fatal mischiefs for the future, will be to establish a method by which the importation of negroes into this Province should be made a necessary means of introducing a proportionable number of white inhabitants into the same; . . . We, his Majesty's faithful and loyal subjects . . . do humbly pray that it may be enacted . . . [158]

In what has been described as the legislature's "most dramatic move" to affect the racial balance of the colony and forestall the possibility of rebellion, the 1740 General Duty Act imposed "a prohibitive duty upon new slaves arriving from Africa and the West Indies."[159] Using height as a proxy for age (as slave traders commonly did),[160] the legislature imposed a £10 tax on newly arrived enslaved persons four feet two inches or taller, a £5 tax on those under that height but taller than three feet two inches, and a £2 10s tax on all others ("sucking children excepted").[161] After fifteen months, the tax increased tenfold to £100, £50, and £25, respectively; however, the increased tax rates applied for only three years, after which the duty reverted to the lower amounts for the remainder of the five-year period that the legislation was in force.[162] Still with an eye on keeping out potential troublemakers, an additional £50 tax was imposed on imported enslaved persons who had spent at least six months in "any of his Majesty's colonies or plantations in America."[163]

In combination with the economic impact of war and other factors, these prohibitive levels of taxation had a significant impact on the importation of enslaved persons: "While Negroes had arrived at a rate of well over one thousand per year during the 1730s, slave importations were cut to nearly one tenth this size during the 1740s. . . . Before 1750 the slave trade was resuming its previous proportions, but this interim of nearly a decade meant that newly imported slaves would never again constitute so high a proportion of the colony's total population as they had in the late 1730s."[164] As depicted in figure 2.1, evidence of the steep drop in the importation of enslaved persons can be found in the correspondingly steep drop in import taxes collected during the 1740s.[165]

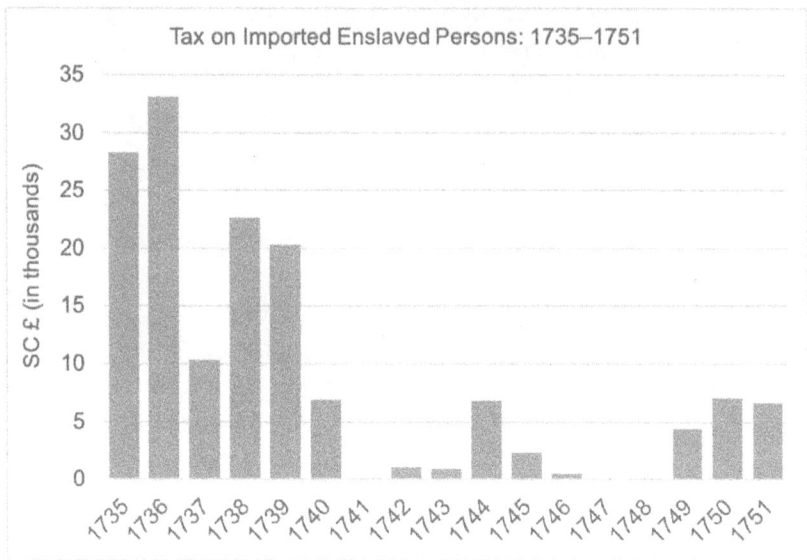

Figure 2.1. Tax on imported enslaved persons, 1735–51

Coupled with this tax disincentive that significantly diminished the importation of enslaved Blacks, the 1740 General Duty Act dedicated two-thirds of the revenue raised from the import tax to

> defraying the charge of transportation or carriage of poor protestants from Charlestown to the townships or other place where they shall settle . . . , and for purchasing tools necessary for planting and settling, and provisions for one year for each of such poor protestants, (not being upwards of fifty years of age) and also for purchasing one cow and calf over and besides such provisions, for every five persons who shall actually become settlers in any of his Majesty's townships laid out in this Province, or in any other of the frontier places of this Province, in which such poor protestants shall be from time to time directed to settle by the Governour or Commander-in-chief for the time being, by and with the advice and consent of his Majesty's Honourable Council.[166]

Accordingly, any importation of enslaved Blacks that occurred during this period was to fund—and be counterbalanced by—programs to attract White immigrants who would serve as a check on the growth of South Carolina's Black majority and the threat that it posed to the colony's White minority.

The legislature's past experimentation with such financial assistance had indicated, however, that the desired effects could be undercut when "divers poor protestants who have arrived in this Province . . . have been disappointed, and not met with that speedy supply or been so soon settled as the exigency of their case did require."[167] The promised financial assistance was slow to arrive "by reason of the length of time that . . . was given to the merchants and factors for paying unto the publick treasurer the duty imposed . . . on the importation of negroes."[168] To remedy this shortcoming, the tax was no longer imposed on the importer but on the purchaser of the enslaved person, finally complying with royal instructions that the colony had flouted for nearly a decade.[169] The purchaser was required to pay the tax "before he or they remove the said slave or slaves, or cause the same to be removed from the place where he shall buy or purchase the same"; in fact, purchasers had to show a receipt for payment from the public treasurer before enslaved persons could be released into their custody.[170]

Reflection

In the aftermath of the Stono Rebellion, the relationship between taxation and slavery in South Carolina crystallized into the shape that it would take for the remainder of the colonial period. The 1740 Slave Code simultaneously tightened control over the lives of the enslaved and provided the financial inducement necessary to ensure that slaveholders would cooperate when the specter of the code's harshest punishment— the death penalty—loomed large. The slaveholder compensation scheme was funded with property tax revenues raised under the colony's annual Tax-Acts on the theory that this compensation provided broad public benefits. As explained in chapter 1, the House-approved payments to slaveholders and other authorized expenses in the Tax-Act schedules determined, down to the penny, the amount of the property tax burden each year, creating an inextricable link between taxation and spending— and, consequently, between the power to tax and the killing of enslaved Blacks for the purpose of perpetuating the evils of slavery, racism, and White supremacy in South Carolina.

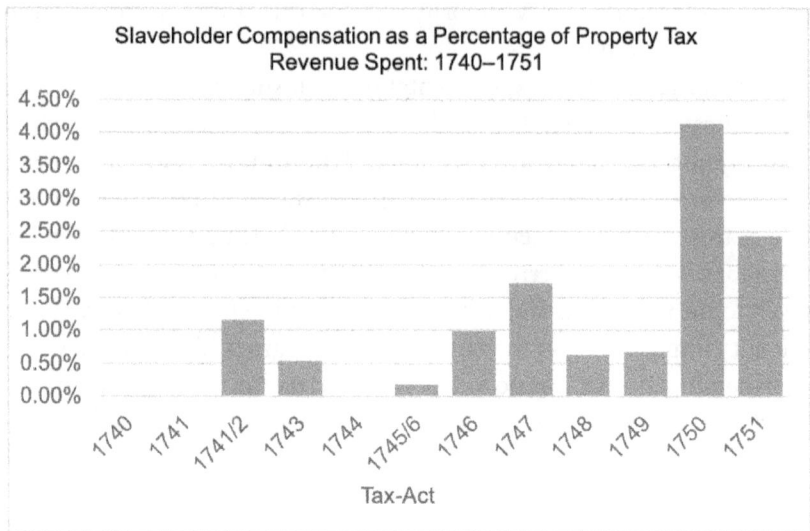

Figure 2.2. Slaveholder compensation as a percentage of property tax revenue spent, 1740–51

As indicated in figure 2.2, during the period covered by this chapter, slaveholder compensation ranged from £0 in the 1740, 1741, and 1744 Tax-Acts—a misleading figure given that the earliest of these acts covered a period when a large number of enslaved persons were killed for rebelling[171] but when requests for slaveholder compensation were flatly rejected—to a high of £2,500 in the 1750 Tax-Act (more than 4 percent of total property tax revenue spent that year). On average, total annual slaveholder compensation payments during this twelve-year period were £570. To provide some perspective, the sole payment in the 1745/6 Tax-Act—£100 compensation to Joseph Blake for an enslaved man hung in chains on a gibbet for attempting to poison Blake—was equivalent to a year's salary for "the Gunner of Broughtons Battery" or for "one years hire of the Court Room."[172] More consequentially, the £2,500 in slaveholder compensation paid in the 1750 Tax-Act amounted to more than the colony's total expenditures that year for forts (£1,448 12s 6d) but less than its expenditures for scout boats (£3,684 9s 11d).[173]

In tandem with purchasing slaveholder cooperation in exerting control over enslaved Blacks through the threat and terror of public executions, the South Carolina legislature enacted a mix of tax and nontax measures designed to manipulate the colony's racial balance to reduce the potential for repetition of the Stono Rebellion. Weeks before the 1740 Slave Code mandated White supervision of all enslaved persons in work areas, the 1740 General Duty Act attempted to shape the racial composition of new arrivals to the colony by discouraging the importation of enslaved Blacks (especially potential troublemakers from other colonies) and encouraging White immigration. Prohibitive taxes significantly depressed—and, in some years, effectively eliminated—the importation of enslaved persons to South Carolina. And in stark contrast to what the slave codes had in store for newly arrived Blacks, the legislature continued to dedicate most of the revenue raised from these taxes on trafficking in human beings to attracting and supporting new White arrivals to the colony—providing them with tools, provisions, and livestock to encourage them to migrate to South Carolina and to facilitate their successful acclimation once there. What is more, to ensure prompt payment of the tax—and, in turn, adequate and prompt assistance to newly arrived Whites—the legislature altered the method of paying taxes on the importation of enslaved persons to make the purchaser (rather than the seller) liable for payment of the tax.

Choices regarding the use of language are equally revealing of the racialized hierarchy embedded in the regime of intertwined tax and nontax measures employed to control South Carolina's enslaved Black majority. This is particularly true of the Tax-Acts, which took on greater importance in the period covered by this chapter. As the recipients of compensation for loss of their valuable "property," slaveholders were invariably identified in the Tax-Act schedules. In the period covered here, slaveholders were specifically named in all but one case: when compensation was paid following the execution of Santee Jemmy, because the exact identity of his North Carolina slaveholder was unknown (despite significant information, including the fact of the slaveholder's recent demise, having been discovered and recorded by the House). The names of the enslaved—those who had been put to death and for whom the compensation was being paid—continued to be omitted from the Tax-Acts. At most, the Tax-Acts referred to the enslaved generically as "a negro executed" or "a slave executed."

When mentioned at all, as happened more commonly near the end of the period covered by this chapter, the names of the enslaved either were tucked away in the tax legislative history or appeared more prominently in the occasional news story in the *South Carolina Gazette*. For instance, Sampson, who had attempted to orchestrate the escape of a group of enslaved persons, was able to be identified here because he was mentioned in both tax legislative history and the newspaper. Sampson's story is even more interesting for the ways in which the slaveholder Michael Jeans deliberately mixed acknowledgment of Sampson's humanity with his claims over Sampson as valuable "property." After Sampson's conviction and sentencing, Jeans made a futile request to the governor for clemency that acknowledged Sampson's humanity in pursuing the freedom that all human beings desire. Yet, at the same time, Jeans pleaded for the governor's mercy on the ground that his family relied nearly entirely on Sampson's forced artisanal labor for its livelihood, backhandedly recognizing Sampson's humanity because Sampson was a person whose skills could not easily be replaced (i.e., he was not some fungible "commodity" for which simple monetary compensation would do). Sampson's fate was also the subject of a series of stories in the *South Carolina Gazette*. The *Gazette* first reported on the intrigue associated with the trial—from the testimony by several enslaved persons against Sampson and his coconspirator Harry to other enslaved persons being tried in connection with the plot but acquitted to the escape of Sambo, another coconspirator, prior to being required to appear in court for his own trial. The *Gazette* followed up with a story regarding a further twist—the constable purportedly losing Sampson's death warrant—which made it legally impossible to put him to death when scheduled, resulting in a call for a new death warrant and for the indictment of the constable. The *Gazette* closed the case when it reported that Sampson had finally been hanged in accordance with his death sentence.

Opening the tax window onto South Carolina's slave society even wider, the legislative history underpinning the Tax-Acts demonstrates just how persistent slaveholders could be when pursuing compensation. Burrell Massingberd Hyrne petitioned on three separate occasions for compensation after the execution of two of his enslaved men who had tied up and killed an overseer. Seemingly unmoved by any of these three deaths, Hyrne made legalistic arguments to the House that his enslaved men had been convicted of homicide and not murder. These arguments ultimately succeeded in allowing Hyrne to shift his economic losses onto

South Carolina taxpayers by escaping the provision in the 1740 Slave Code that denied compensation to the holders of enslaved persons executed for murder or rebellion. Similarly, Deborah McCree pressed her own case for compensation, specifically noting how she had sought the punishment of four of her father-in-law's enslaved men for murdering him and how compensating her would encourage other slaveholders to do the same. McCree argued that she was entitled to compensation because the exception for murder had been repealed between the time when the four men were tried and when they were executed. The House, in equally legalistic fashion, afforded McCree compensation—but only for the two enslaved persons who had escaped from jail and been apprehended and executed *after* repeal of the exception and not for the two who had been executed *before* repeal. As so often happens when the focus turns to fine interpretation of the law, one can lose sight of the broader, real-world impact of the legal question at hand. Here, what all the legal players appear to have ignored are the lives of the enslaved persons that were lost, not to mention the story of the lives that they lived and what events or circumstances might have impelled them to take the life of another—the life of an overseer who was whipped to death in Hyrne's case or the life of the murdered slaveholder in McCree's case.

But what is made abundantly clear by these instances of slaveholder persistence is the importance placed on being able to take advantage of the redistributive power of taxation to force South Carolina taxpayers to share in slaveholders' economic losses. Otherwise, as described in chapter 1, slaveholders had little incentive to cooperate with enforcement of the slave codes because conviction and punishment for capital crimes would harm them financially. The alternative to cooperation was for slaveholders either to conceal enslaved persons' crimes or to rid themselves of troublemakers through a sale outside the province that mitigated their economic losses (and, depending on where the enslaved person was sent, might mean nothing more than a slower death for the offender). Buttressing the compensation scheme's financial incentives, slaveholder cooperation in enforcement of the slave codes allowed for the infliction of widespread terror on the colony's enslaved population, with the public spectacle of executions serving as a generalized means of reducing resistance to bondage. From the view through the tax window provided in this chapter, hanging seems to have been a common form of punishment, but more grisly examples surfaced as well, including Boatswain's being burned alive as punishment for arson and Joseph Blake's unnamed enslaved man being hung in chains on a gibbet as punishment for attempting to poison Blake.

The Tax-Acts not only provide insight into the slaveholder mindset but also furnish a window onto the everyday life of the enslaved in colonial South Carolina. This chapter illustrated how quarrels between the enslaved could escalate into murder—in sometimes complicated and controverted circumstances—as happened when John murdered Duff after an apparent falling out between them. John's case also provides a glimpse into the lives of others who were tangentially involved in his criminal case. Testimony revealed Simon dispatching Hannah to check on Duff after he cried out for help, even though Hannah was exhausted because she had been forced to toil until so late that she fell asleep in her clothes when she arrived home. Simon asked Hannah to do this because, for unspecified reasons, he was physically incapable of doing so himself. John's case further reveals how mercy for the enslaved seems to have been hard to come by. A plea for clemency on John's behalf proved fruitless despite its having been made not by his holder but by the sharply split slave court that tried him. The clemency plea was accompanied by sympathetic information regarding John's early life, explaining how he had been born free in the Americas, worked at sea, and only later been sold into slavery in South Carolina (with no explanation as to how or why he had been enslaved). None of that was enough, however, to spare him from being hanged.

Separately, this chapter recounted how the slaveholder Thomas Miles and his family pressured Kit's young wife, Venus, with "great persuasion" and "promises of safety"—given the nature of the crime, presumably dangling before her the choice between life and death—to secure her testimony against her husband and his other accomplices so that they might be convicted of poisoning Miles's wife. Venus acceded to the pressure, which led directly to the deaths of her husband, Kit, and an enslaved man named Frank. Venus's life was spared, but only after Miles submitted a clemency petition to the governor asking him to make good on the family's promises that Venus would not be put to death if she testified against her husband and others. The petition was granted—and the promise of being spared immediate death upheld—but Venus was deported from South Carolina to suffer an uncertain fate.

A pardon was similarly dangled before Kate after her conviction for arson and while the preparations for her execution were being made in the hope of securing her testimony against others involved in the plot. Kate accepted the offer and identified Boatswain as her accomplice. At his trial, Boatswain identified yet others, perhaps in a vain attempt to see his own life spared as Kate's had been. But all the accused were acquitted. Only then did Boatswain confess that only he and Kate had been involved in the arson. In the end, Boatswain was convicted and, as mentioned earlier, burned to death as punishment.

Venus, Kate, and Boatswain were not alone in being faced with awful life-or-death choices. Hagar, who had been convicted of arson and sentenced to death, benefited from a brief reprieve while the court determined whether a pregnant woman could legally be executed. Facing certain death—whether sooner along with her unborn child or later after she had been forced to give birth and surrender her child into a life of slavery—Hagar attempted escape. She jumped from a third-story window, only to be so severely injured that she died the next day. In another testament to the callousness of slaveholders, Elizabeth Walker pressed her legally questionable compensation claim and was rewarded with payments totaling £180 to cover both her own economic loss and the damages caused by Hagar to others. Walker's claim was allowed on the ground that it was only Hagar's attempt at escape that prevented the execution from being carried out and that, therefore, compensation should be paid as if Hagar had been executed. Analogizing to the provision in the slave code that permitted constables to press enslaved persons into service to inflict punishment on others,[174] one could just as easily see Hagar as having been pressed by the force of circumstance into service as her own executioner.

Though Hagar's imputed enforcement of the slave code's punishment was certainly not willing, a few slaveholder compensation payments examined in this chapter demonstrate how the enslaved sometimes took an active part in enforcing the slave code against others. Thomas Elliott received a large payment upon the legislature's manumission of his enslaved man July. The legislature rewarded July with his freedom in gratitude for his efforts to protect Elliott and his family and to suppress the Stono Rebellion—and as encouragement to other enslaved persons to behave likewise. John Pagett received a large but less generous compensation payment—even though that compensation appeared to fall outside the letter of the law—when his enslaved man Harry was killed in attempting to apprehend Hannibal, an escapee who stabbed Harry in the heart and injured another enslaved man who had been helping Harry.

But even enslaved persons who chose neither to resist nor to enforce the slave code could find their lives endangered because of the color of their skin. William Kelvert's enslaved man Hector had gone off Kelvert's plantation—but was still in sight—when he was shot by a group of Native Americans who were working with the patrols to capture a group of escapees. Merely being Black and outside a plantation was enough for Hector to be presumed to be an escapee whose life was at the mercy of Whites and the people working with them. Although Hector's killing was not technically compensable under the 1740 Slave Code, the legislature nonetheless authorized equitable relief in light of Kelvert's argument that his loss should be indemnified by the public because Hector's killing would prevent Kelvert from continuing to carry on his business as a planter and, while alive, Hector had toed the line just as Whites expected enslaved persons to do.

Far from hovering above the fray, taxation was tightly bound up with colonial society in South Carolina—and, more particularly, with reinforcing and perpetuating the institution of slavery that existed at that society's core from the very start. Tax law and the associated tax legislative history have provided insights into the mindset of legislators as well as snapshots from the lives of slaveholders and the enslaved alike. As explored next in chapter 3, the close relationship between taxation and slavery forged in the aftermath of the Stono Rebellion continued throughout the remainder of the colonial period, when the intertwined tax and nontax measures discussed in this chapter were refined and routinized.

3

The Late Colonial Period

Refinement and Routinization

This chapter continues to examine the legal regime of closely intertwined tax and nontax measures that South Carolina's ruling White minority created to subjugate and control the colony's enslaved Black majority. Picking up where chapter 2 left off, this chapter covers the period from 1751 to 1775. The chapter begins by describing the legislature's refinements to the 1740 Slave Code and its slaveholder compensation scheme. It then turns to documenting both the steady stream of slaveholder compensation payments in the late colonial period and the Commons House of Assembly's reduction of the processing of slaveholder compensation claims to a sinister routine. The chapter next describes the nature and impact of legislative tinkering with the combination of tax carrots and sticks designed to influence the racial composition of new arrivals to the colony. The chapter then closes with a meditation on the close connections established between taxation and slavery in colonial South Carolina, considering how, far from immune to the call to further the evils of systemic racism, taxation was an active participant in supporting and perpetuating the institution of slavery in ways that illustrate taxation's true power to destroy.

Revision of the 1740 Slave Code

In 1751, South Carolina passed an "Additional and Explanatory Act" that amended the 1740 Slave Code to refine its provisions and further restrict the lives of the enslaved.[1] Notably, the 1751 legislation gave voice to White fears stoked by a recent spate of poisonings—a surreptitious and potentially deadly form of resistance that leveraged African knowledge of plants and medicines and, as witnessed in Kit and Venus's case in chapter 2, enslaved domestics' ready access to vehicles for administering poison (i.e., food and beverages).[2] Observing that "the detestable crime of poisoning hath of late been frequently committed by many slaves in this Province, and notwithstanding the execution of several criminals for that offence, yet it has not been sufficient to deter others from being guilty of the same," the legislature extended the death penalty to all "negroes, mulattoes and mestizoes, whether free or bond," who poisoned anyone, who furnished poison to an enslaved person, or who knew of a poisoning or planned poisoning and did not report it.[3] To encourage "slaves to make discovery of the designs of others to poison any person," monetary rewards were offered for reporting planned poisonings, but only upon conviction of the offender.[4] Those who provided false information to obtain a reward suffered the same punishment as the person falsely informed against.[5]

Poisoning was so feared that any enslaved person who taught "another slave in the knowledge of any poisonous root, plant, herb, or other sort of poison whatever . . . shall . . . suffer death as a felon."[6] The punishment of the student was left to the court's discretion but could not extend "to life or limb."[7] To the same end, doctors and druggists were prohibited from employing enslaved persons "in the shops or places where they keep their medicines or drugs," and "no negroes or other slaves (commonly called doctors,)" were permitted to administer medicine to any enslaved person except "by the direction of some white person."[8]

Addressing the draconian punishments required by the slave codes, the 1751 legislation noted that "upon the trials of slaves in this Province, it hath sometimes happened, that certain circumstances have attended the facts upon such trials, as would have induced the [court] to have mitigated the punishment, but being strictly bound by the letter of the law, such slaves have suffered death."[9] Accordingly, slave courts were authorized to mitigate punishments "in all and every case where any favorable circumstance shall appear and induce them to be of opinion that such punishment ought to be mitigated."[10]

Concomitantly, the 1751 legislation reaffirmed the existing slaveholder compensation scheme and, to address cases like McLeod's and Kelvert's discussed in chapter 2, extended its coverage to include escapees killed by the patrols or militia.[11] For the first time, the 1751 legislation authorized compensation "if any such fugitive or runaway slave or slaves, shall happen to be wounded, maimed or disabled by such party."[12]

Correspondingly, a provision authorizing "any white person or persons, to apprehend any notorious fugitive slave that shall have been runaway for the space of twelve months, or upward," afforded compensation for "the damages sustained by the owner of such runaway"—damages that could extend to the death of the escapee—subject, however, to a lower monetary cap.[13]

The Tax Window onto South Carolina's Slave Society

In contrast to the period following the Stono Rebellion, every Tax-Act passed in the late colonial period contained slaveholder compensation payments. To complete the work of documenting the legalized killings of enslaved persons facilitated by South Carolina's tax system, this section first details the payments authorized in the Tax-Acts from 1752 to 1769 and then those authorized by the Commons House of Assembly from 1770 to 1775. The latter payments were never formally enacted into law due to a struggle between the House and imperial authorities over the scope of the House's spending power. Nevertheless, as described later, the House did create a mechanism to provide satisfaction to the colony's public creditors, including slaveholders seeking compensation for enslaved persons killed or executed.

Documentation of these slaveholder compensation payments continues to provide a tax window onto South Carolina's slave society, albeit in a somewhat different fashion than in previous chapters. In contrast to chapter 2, where the absence of contextualizing detail was anomalous, the House appears to have routinized the processing of slaveholder compensation claims in the late colonial period, as evidenced by the increasing number of claims dealt with in a perfunctory manner. Nonetheless, insight into South Carolina's slave society is still provided by contemporary newspaper accounts as well as through administrative details that fill some of the space left by the refinement of the tax legislative drafting process.

Tax-Act Payments, 1752–69

Consistent with the attention received by the crime in the 1751 slave code revisions, two separate slaveholder poisonings accounted for five of the eight compensation payments authorized by the 1752 Tax-Act.[14] William Waties's estate was paid £200 for the execution of Waties's enslaved man Moon, who had poisoned him.[15] A total of £680 was paid for the execution of four enslaved persons who together had poisoned Joseph Blake: Blake's estate received £400 for the execution of two of his enslaved persons, Parmenas Way received £200 for the execution of his enslaved man Primus, and William Simmons (acting on behalf of John Sumner's estate) received £80 for the execution of an enslaved woman.[16] As described in chapter 2, Blake had been the subject of an earlier attempted poisoning that gave rise to the execution of another of Blake's enslaved persons (and an associated compensation payment in the 1745/6 Tax-Act). Blake, who was first a member of the House and then, from 1740 until his death, a member of Council, was "one of the wealthiest men in South Carolina," owning nearly thirty thousand acres and operating five separate plantations that relied on the labor of some 283 enslaved persons.[17] One can only wonder what the repeated attempts on Blake's life say about the conditions experienced by the enslaved on those plantations.

Additionally, the 1752 Tax-Act authorized Alexander Hext to be paid £200 for "a Negro Man Slave . . . that was condemned & executed for the Murder of another Negro" and Samuel Wells to be paid £200 for the execution of his enslaved man Pharis for an unspecified crime.[18] Compensation for the execution of an enslaved man named Will "for a complication of Crimes" was split between the slaveholder William Brown's estate (£175) and John Brunson (£25, "for damages which he sustained by the said Negro").[19]

The 1753 Tax-Act was the first during this period to contain payments for both executions and killings under color of law.[20] Among the executed, a total of £200 was paid for an enslaved man executed for murder, with half going to the slaveholder George Somers and the other half to Benjamin Harvey, a planter, for unspecified damages.[21] Rachel Russ was paid £150 "for a Negro Man Slave of hers which was executed for poisoning."[22]

John Cattell was paid £200 "for a Slave executed for poisoning her Master."[23] Cattell's attempted poisoning may have been accomplished in 1749 by Hannah, who had also implicated her husband, Will, in the attempt and caused him to be "under Sentence of Death for being concerned with his Wife in giving [Cattell] Poison."[24] As death grew near, Hannah stated that "Will was Ignorant of any Poison that she ever gave his Master and that it was all lyes that she told upon her Husband and that she could not be Easie and that she told so many lyes upon so many People."[25] In light of Hannah's confession that she had falsely testified against Will and Will's own declaration that "he knows nothing of the matter," Cattell petitioned the governor for a pardon.[26] Though it is unclear whether Will's pardon was granted, if the payment in the 1753 Tax-Act to Cattell was delayed compensation for Hannah's execution, the inclusion of a single compensation payment lends support to the notion that the pardon was granted.[27]

A total of £80 was paid for an enslaved woman named Jinny who was executed for poisoning, with £50 going to the slaveholder Hugh Anderson and £30 to John Methringham for damages.[28] Jinny had been sentenced to death by hanging for "poisoning a Negro Girl, the property of Mr Matheringham."[29] Anderson petitioned the governor to "relieve [his] distress" in whatever way the governor deemed fit, based on "Some Circumstances favourable to the Prisoner and as the Executing the Negro will be of Great Prejudice to y^r Petitioner and his family."[30] The court that tried Jinny advised the governor that it had learned after trial that Jinny's daughter might have been intimidated into providing evidence against her mother.[31] On the Council's advice, the governor delayed Jinny's execution for ten days and ordered the court to investigate the new allegations.[32] Given the compensation payment authorized by the 1753 Tax-Act, the court's further investigation must have been to no avail in sparing Jinny's life.

The 1753 Tax-Act included compensation for the killing of three enslaved persons by the patrols—with John Cook, Joseph Elliott Jr., and Silas Miles each receiving £200.[33] Cook was compensated for "an outlawed Negro killed," and Elliott was compensated for "a fugitive Negro Man named Daniel . . . that was shot dead by a Party of the Militia in St. Pauls Parish who were in pursuit of Fugitive Slaves."[34] The House journal provides greater detail regarding the killing of Miles's enslaved man Primus. Primus had shot "his Overseers Wife, which alarmed the Neighbourhood, and some of them applied to Colonel Hyrne for authority and directions."[35] As a result, "two Partys went out to take the said Negro . . . but in the pursuit of him he got over Saltketchee River, and the Party that pursued him after calling often to him to surrender, he declared he would shoot any One that attempted to take him, upon which he was shot by the said Party and in their own defence, he going to take up his Gun, and without swimming they could not further persue him; the Shot went through his Head."[36]

The 1754 Tax-Act included compensation for the execution of four enslaved persons and the killing of another.[37] Thomas Drayton was paid £100, which was the appraised value of "a Negro Wench executed for poisoning."[38] William Main, acting on behalf of Richard Baker's estate, was paid £200 "for a Negro . . . that was executed for Murder."[39] Captain Robert Sams was paid £200 "for a Criminal Slave executed," and Mary Hughes was paid £200, "being the appraised Value of a Negro Man that was executed pursuant to the directions of the Negro Act."[40] In addition, Maurice Keating's estate was paid £200 (reduced from the £250 originally requested), being "the Value of a Negro Man named Caesar" who was "a fugitive Slave killed by a Party of the Militia."[41]

The 1755 Tax-Act included a £200 payment "for the Value of a Negro Man named Glascow belonging to James Anderson of Santee" that was split between Anderson (£150) and John Atcheson's estate (£50) because Glascow had been "executed . . . for murdering a Negro belonging to the said John Atcheson."[42] William Chicken was paid £200 "for a Slave of his that was shot" and "killed for murdering John Steel."[43] John Joiner was paid £175 "for a Negro Wench executed for poisoning her Mistress," and Richard Field was paid £150 "for a Negro Slave of his that was executed for poisoning."[44] The 1755 Tax-Act also authorized James Michie to be paid £200 "for a Negro Man Slave belonging to him that was killed by a Party of the Militia who were in pursuit of fugitive Slaves."[45] In fact, Michie had advertised in 1754 for an entire family—"*Boston*, his wife *Sue*, and child *Sib*"—who had escaped after he purchased them from Andrew Quelch;[46] however, it is unclear whether the enslaved person killed by the militia was a member of this family or another enslaved person held by Michie.

Foreshadowing what would become a marked shift in treatment by the end of the decade, the House journal provides no contextualizing detail regarding payments of £200 that were made to Joseph Edward Flower, David Godin's estate, Childermas Croft, and Charles Pinckney Jr. for executed enslaved persons.[47] Though not addressed in the House journal, the payment to Childermas Croft may have been compensation for one of his enslaved women who was burned to death. According to the *South Carolina Gazette*, she and another enslaved woman were suspected of having willfully set a fire "in an Out House at the Plantation of *Childermas Croft*, Esq; commonly known by the Name of *Fortynine*, which entirely consumed the fine Dwelling House he had there, with some of the Furniture, and all the Out-Buildings."[48] Though both women were to be executed, the other was lucky to get the benefit of "some favourable Circumstances" that earned her a reprieve.[49]

The 1756 Tax-Act authorized John Miles to be paid £400 for "two Negros . . . executed for poisoning the Infant Son of the said Miles."[50] Charles Field's estate was paid £200 "for a Negro Slave, named Plenty, convicted of causing Poison to be administered to James Field & his Wife."[51] In addition, John Edwards was paid the £50 appraised value of "a fugitive Slave, named Tony, that . . . was killed for resisting [James] White, who attempted to apprehend him."[52] Perhaps most gripping of the public imagination, however, were the circumstances surrounding the payment of £400 to Sarah Purry for two enslaved men, Jemmy and Robin, who were executed "in Chains" for murdering the slaveholder Charles Purry.[53]

Jemmy and Robin's story was the subject of a series of articles in the *South Carolina Gazette*. In late July, the newspaper first reported on Purry's death:

> Yesterday we received the following melancholy Account from *Beaufort*, that last Monday Morning the Body of Mr. *Charles Purry*, of that Town, Merchant, was found in the River, with Bags of Shot tied to each of his Wrists and Feet, a Stab in his Breast, and one of his Eyes thrusted out of his Head; supposed to have been murdered by some of his own People, two or three of which have been taken up on Suspicion. Sunday Night at 9 o'Clock (which was about the usual Time of his going to Bed) his Family left him sitting in his Piazza alone; but not coming in in half an Hour after, Mrs. *Purry* sent to inquire the Occasion of his Stay, when, to her great Surprise he was miss'd; and tho' the most diligent Inquiry and Search was immediately made for him, no Discovery was made till the next Day, when his Hat and Wig, with the Track of some bare Feet, [illegible] to the Place where his Body had been thrown and sunk.[54]

In mid-August, the *Gazette* reported that it was indeed Purry's enslaved persons who had murdered him.[55] Though only two compensation payments were made, there were actually three enslaved people involved in the incident: Jemmy and Robin, mentioned earlier, along with their sister, who "impeach'd the Fellows."[56] According to the Thursday, August 22, edition of the *Gazette*, Robin had been hung on the gibbet a week earlier, and Jemmy was soon to suffer the same punishment.[57] In the August 29 edition, it was reported,

> The Negro who was gibbetted at *Beaufort*, for the Murder of Mr. *Charles Purry*, did not die before last Thursday, and 'till within an Hour before he expired, constantly declared his Innocence; but at last confessed, that he himself had perpetrated that Murder, and at the same Time disclosed a Scene equally shocking, in which he and 8 other Negroes were to have been concerned, *i. e.* the Murder of two other Gentlemen of *Beaufort*, on the Night after Mr. *Purry*'s Death, (which only the finding of his Body had prevented;) after which they were to have taken a Schooner in the Harbour, belonging to Mr. *John Smith*, and [illegible] the best of their Way for *St. Augustine*.[58]

This report apparently refers to Robin, who experienced the ignominy of a weeklong period of public torture as part of his execution.[59]

The 1757 Tax-Act authorized £200 compensation to John McQueen, "being the apprais'd value of a Slave executed for burning his Master's Barn";[60] to Joseph Seally "for a Negro Man . . . named Pompey, executed for poisoning a Negro-man named Peter";[61] and to Thomas Hale "for the Trial & Execution of a Negro Fellow who intended to kill . . . Hale, near Amelia Township."[62] John Gordon was compensated for "the Trial & Sentence of death on John, a Negro Man, for breaking open the Cellar of John Gordon, in Beaufort, Port Royal."[63] The House journal fails, however, to specify the nature of the "Felony" that resulted in the execution of Joseph Poole's enslaved man Caesar, William Flin's enslaved man Hartford, or Thomas Waties's enslaved man Prince.[64] Additionally, the 1757 Tax-Act authorized a £200 payment for "a fugitive Slave, named Joe, the property of James McGirt, killed on resisting the Person who attempted to apprehend him."[65] Thomas Crawford had killed Joe "for resisting said Crawford, by snapping a Gun at him twice, on which, in his own defense, [Crawford] was obliged to kill him."[66]

The 1758 Tax-Act signaled the beginning of the routinization of the House's claims-vetting process, which the 1755 Tax-Act had foreshadowed. As illustrated in the appendix (table A.1), the House had already abandoned its short-lived practice of sporadically providing greater detail in the schedule regarding crimes committed by the enslaved. The 1758 Tax-Act took the quest for economical legislative drafting further by including a single payment labeled "for slaves executed"—notwithstanding that the payment compensated for only a single execution—and five payments labeled "do." (i.e., "ditto").[67] The House journal deals with these six payments in an equally perfunctory fashion, providing contextualizing detail in just one case—naming the enslaved person's crime in passing—and otherwise documenting only how the House ensured that all legal requirements had been satisfied prior to authorizing payments from the public treasury. For instance, a £200 payment was authorized to Hugh McCulchin's estate "for a Negroe Sentanced to Death . . . for Poisoning"; however, "as no notice is taken whether or not the said Negroe was Executed Conformable to his Sentance, the Committee recommend it may be allowed [on] producing a proper Certificate that he was put to death."[68] A £400 payment was authorized to William Dalton "for two Slaves Executed"; however, this payment was similarly held in abeyance and "allowed when it Shall Appear the Slaves were Executed."[69] As illustrated in figure 3.1, during the remainder of the colonial period, the House increasingly dealt with slaveholder compensation claims in a similar fashion, by eschewing factual detail in favor of documenting administrative issues relating to claims.

The House journal provides few details regarding the payments authorized by the 1759 Tax-Act for the execution of three enslaved persons.[70] Thomas Wilson was paid £200 for "a Negroe hanged" for an unnamed offense.[71] William Glen was paid £150 "for a Negroe Man named Pompey Executed," and John Sikes was paid £50 "for the Injury done him by Pompey."[72] A total of £200 was split evenly between John Cleland and Robert Weaver for the execution of "a Negroe Man named George, the Property of Mr. Weaver, for the Murder of a Negroe belonging to the said Mr. Cleland."[73]

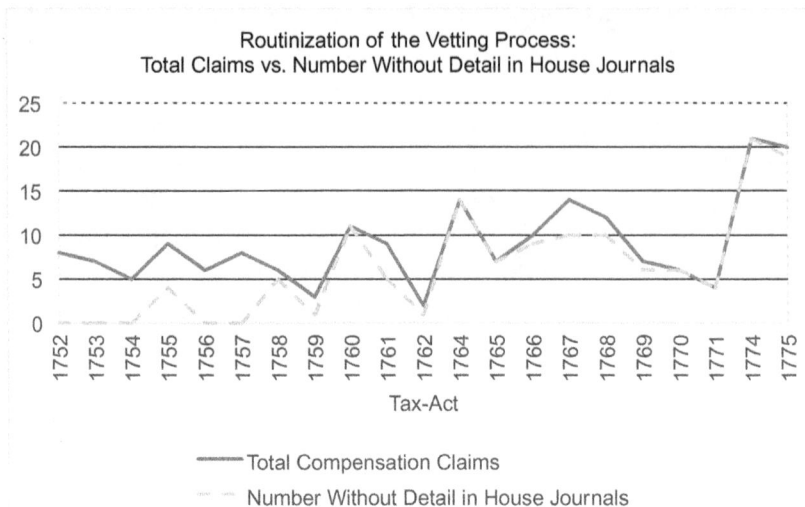

Figure 3.1. Routinization of the vetting process: total claims vs. number without detail in House journals

The House journal includes even less detail regarding the compensation payments authorized by the 1760 Tax-Act for the execution of ten enslaved persons and the killing of another.[74] Two of the payments, however, involve noteworthy side stories. The 1760 Tax-Act authorized a £200 payment to John Hamilton for an executed enslaved person, who, based on news accounts, appears to have been his enslaved man Pompey.[75] Pompey had escaped Hamilton but was captured by "one *Hooker*, who carried him to his House, and secured him, as he thought; but . . . in the Night, the Negro got loose, and laid hold of an Axe, with which he mortally wounded the said *Hooker* and his Wife, and killed one of their Children," following which he killed Martin Kooner and his two children.[76] Pompey was later captured with "an Axe, a Gun and *Dutch Knife*" and brought to the workhouse.[77] After conviction, Pompey was "hung in Chains, on Tuesday" but "escaped from his Gibbet the same Night," only to be "retaken on Thursday, and is now again gibbeted nearer this Town."[78] Interestingly, Hamilton, who was a constable, submitted a separate claim for "Disbursements on the prosecution of" Pompey; however, the committee auditing the public accounts concluded that "the Charges in this Account are unusual and neither certified, nor attested; not allowed."[79]

The 1760 Tax-Act split an additional £200 payment evenly between Thomas Bradwell (slaveholder) and Thomas Shoemaker (for damages). The missing details regarding these payments surface in the House journal—but only in connection with consideration of Shoemaker's separate claim for compensation for his enslaved man Scipio, who died while aiding in the apprehension of Bradwell's enslaved man Sandy:

> A Petition of Thomas Shoemaker setting forth, That the Petitioner had a very valuable Negro Man, named Scipio, who, on the 29th June 1759, as he was returning on an Errand, unfortunately met with a Negro Man, nam'd Sandy (a vile Offender), belonging to Thomas Bradwell; who Scipio knowing to be run away, endeavoured to persuade to return home, but intreaty failing, and believing it his duty to apprehend so great a Villain, he had recourse to Violence, and after some Blows had passed on both sides, the said Sandy seemed to submit, but, stooping down, as if to adjust something about his Boot, drew a long Knife, stabbed Scipio in the Belly, and cut one of his Guts half off, of which Wound he died. That, on the 9th July following the said Sandy was convicted of murdering the said Scipio and was executed; being first valued at Two hundred Pounds, one half whereof is order'd to be paid to the Petitioner, which Sum being three hundred Pounds less than the said Scipio's intrinsic worth, and for as much as the Petitioner has no other Remedy for his great Loss, but by applying to this House.[80]

After considering the petition, which requested whatever relief the House deemed reasonable, the committee auditing the public accounts recommended, "Tho' no provision is made in any Law for such Cases as this, yet in consideration that the said Negro, who was a very valuable Slave, lost his Life, not only in a lawful but commendable Action, the Committee are for allowing £200 to the said Shoemaker."[81] While the House had handed out compensation for executions as an unremarkable matter of course when drafting the 1760 Tax-Act, it took much-greater time and care in describing, considering, and lauding the actions of Scipio, who had taken it upon himself to enforce the slave code and for whose loss Shoemaker was, in fact, paid the recommended £200 in addition to the £100 portion of Bradwell's compensation that he had been separately awarded and that was the only compensation authorized by the slave code.[82]

The 1761 Tax-Act authorized £200 to be paid to John Fryerson on a belated petition requesting compensation for an enslaved person who had been executed *and* for the victim:

> READ also A Petition of John Frierson of Amelia–Township Setting forth—That the Petitioner resided in the said Township from his Infancy & has always behaved himself as becometh an Honest Industrious Man as appeared by the Certificate Annexed—That by his Industry he was enabled to Purchase two Negroes one of whom on the 21st of July 1759 Murdered the other & the Murderer was agreeable to Law on the 31st day of the said Month Sentenced to be Executed & suffered accordingly as Appeared from the Certificate of the Justices & Freeholders also Annexed together with a Certificate of Appraisement of the Negro who was Murdered. That the Petitioner being thus deprived of his whole Property; was soon after draughted from the Militia to go upon the Expedition to the Cherokee Nation whereby he was deprived of an Opportunity of laying his Misfortunate Case within the Time prescribed before your Hoñble House & therefore prayed that the house would take his unfortunate Case into Consideration & grant him not only the relief allowed by Law for his Negro which was Executed but such other relief for the other Negro also that was Murdered as to this House should seem meet.[83]

Fryerson's petition was referred to the committee auditing the public accounts, which "recommend[ed] that he be Allowed for a Negro Executed £200" and implicitly denied additional compensation for the murder victim.[84]

A few others among the executed merited naming in the House journal: Abel Johnson's estate was paid £200 compensation for Sabinah, Susannah Bee was paid £200 for Cirys, and John Remington was paid £200 for Quash.[85] According to an advertisement in the *South Carolina Gazette*, Quash had been arrested in 1760 for breaking into Dunbar & Young's store on Broad Street in Charles Town—the purpose of the advertisement was to offer a £20 reward for the capture of Glasgow, who was also involved in the robbery but who had escaped, despite it being "supposed [he] was wounded by the stroke of a cutlash."[86] Likewise worthy of note is the smallest (and perhaps saddest) payment included in the 1761 Tax-Act, which was for £25 to Catharine Cattell for an unnamed "Junior Negro Executed."[87]

The 1762 Tax-Act authorized £200 to be paid to Alexander McGillivery for his enslaved man Caesar for an unspecified crime.[88] The committee auditing the public accounts also authorized a £350 payment to Samuel Winburn for the execution of two enslaved persons; however, without explanation, that payment was omitted from the 1762 Tax-Act schedule.[89]

The 1764 Tax-Act, which covered two years due to a power struggle between the House and the recently departed governor,[90] contained payments of odd amounts that included both "principal"—that is to say, compensation for an executed enslaved person—and interest at a rate of 8 percent to compensate for the delayed payment. Thomas Elf was paid £205 4s (£190 principal and £15 4s interest).[91] Jacob Motte was paid £140 8s (£130 principal and £10 8s interest); this claim had been assigned to Motte by Joseph Shute, who had been entitled to £115 of the principal, and Benjamin Joy, who had been entitled to the remaining £15.[92] Charles Bedingfield (on assignment of John Bedingfield's claim), Hugh Dowse's estate, Fotheringham & McNeil, Henry Filder, the church wardens of St. George's parish, Benjamin Smith (on assignment of Anthony White's claim), Austin & Laurens (a firm that "imported more slaves between 1735 and 1775 than any other company"),[93] Micajah Williams, and Joshua Screven were each paid £216 (£200 principal and £16 interest).[94] The House journal provides no further details regarding these payments.

Likewise, the House journal provides no contextualizing detail regarding the compensation authorized by the 1765 Tax-Act for the execution of seven enslaved persons.[95] The House did, however, note that a £350 payment to the public treasurer was to cover an advance that he made at the direction of the House to John Gibbons (£200) and George Fickling (£150) because the compensation owed them had been "omitted by mistake to be incerted in the Schedule to the last Tax Act."[96] According to the *South Carolina Gazette*, the executed were "a fellow called *Abraham*, belonging to Mr. *John Gibbons*, and a wench of Mr. *George Fickling*," who together had poisoned Fickling—but "having speedy recourse to *Caesar's* antidote, he recovered."[97]

Of the ten compensation payments included in the 1766 Tax-Act, the House journal elaborates only on the £200 paid to Miles Brewton for an escapee who was killed.[98] This payment was "for a Fugitive Slaves [sic] called Wilkes, who was killed by a party in November last, going in pursuite of a Gang of Runaway Negroes."[99] Similarly, of the fourteen compensation payments included in the 1767 Tax-Act, the House journal elaborates on only a select few.[100] John Becket was paid £180 "for one half the Valuation of two Negroes executed for Poisoning a Negro the property of the said Becket";[101] however, the corresponding £180 payment to the holder of those who were executed is nowhere to be found in the schedule. Although the schedule included a £200 payment to Alexander Rantowle "for a negro executed," the House's consideration of his claim flatly contradicts that designation. According to the House journal, the House received and approved "a Certificate in favour of Alexander Rantowle for a Fugitive Slave Shot by the Patrol in pursuit of Run away Negroes £200."[102] In contrast, the House received "a Certificate in favour of Champernoon Williamson Estate for a fugitive Slave Killed by a party of the Militia in pursuit of Run away Negroes £200,"[103] and that payment was correctly reflected in the schedule as compensation "for a fugitive slave killed by the militia."[104]

Additionally, the House journal reports on Alexander Fraser's unsuccessful request for compensation:

> READ a Petition of Alexander Fraser Esquire, in the Words following. That some time the last Summer, a Stout Young Negroe Man belonging to the Petitioner did Arm himself with a Scymeter and broke into his Dwelling House. That he afterwards sent in several Impudent Messages to him, such as threatening to get a Gun, either out of the House, or by way laying a Waggon, in order to destroy some of his people, and a Defiance to take him alive; That some Nights after about twelve o Clock he came into the Plantation with a View, as he apprehends to put his Scheme into execution but being discovered, was pursued, and standing Armed upon the Defensive he was killed; Your Petitioner therefore prays that your Honors would take the Matter into their Consideration, And grant him such redress, as in your wisdom, you shall think right.[105]

The House referred the petition to the committee auditing the public accounts, which stated that it "can find no precedent to support the

Petition, and being at a Loss what Report to make thereon, they therefore beg leave to submit the same to the Determination of the House."[106] Upon consideration, the House summarily ordered "that M^r. Fraser have leave to withdraw his Petition."[107]

The House journal furnishes no details regarding the ten payments in the 1768 Tax-Act compensating for the execution of enslaved persons; however, it does elaborate on the circumstances surrounding the two extrajudicial killings for which compensation was paid.[108] John Ainslie submitted a claim for £200 "for a fugitive Slave Shot by William Finley," but the committee auditing the public accounts only "allowed £150—agreeable to the third Paragraph of the Negro Act past 17th May 1751."[109] Here, the committee was referring to the lower compensation cap for escapees killed by a White person who was not part of the patrols.[110] But departing from such a strict application of the law, the committee authorized compensation to be paid to Francis Rose "for a fugitive Slave Shot by a Negro the property of John Drayton Esquire": "this Charge the Committee are of opinion is not within the Law passed in May 1751. but as they are informed the Deceased was a Notorious Offender whose Conduct set very bad examples to the Negroes of this Province, the Committee therefore under an equitable Construction of the third Paragraph of said Law, recommend that the sum of £150 be allowed to M^r. Rose."[111]

The 1769 Tax-Act, which was the final property tax legislation enacted during the colonial period, included compensation for the execution of seven enslaved persons.[112] Only one of those payments merited mention of the enslaved person's name, let alone the crime committed. According to the House journal, Isaac McPherson was paid £200 for his enslaved man Cain, who was executed.[113] The *South Carolina Gazette* reported, "We hear that that most desperate villain, the negro CAIN, who attacked and dangerously wounded his master, Mr. *Isaac Macpherson*, and several of his family, in the year 1764, and made his escape, has lately been taken in the woods, by the *Cherokee Indians*, and by them delivered up to *Matthew Keough*, Esq; commandant at Fort *Prince George, Keebowie,* so that, after escaping almost innumerable pursuits and stratagems to take him, he is at last likely to be brought to justice."[114] Cain was brought to Charles Town under guard a few weeks later.[115] A month afterward, the *South Carolina and American General Gazette* reported that "Mr. Isaac Macpherson's Negro Man, named CAIN, was sent from hence to St. Paul's Parish, where the Crimes, he was charged with, were committed, and there was tried by a Jury of Magistrates and Freeholders, agreeable to the Negro-Act, and being found Guilty, was condemned and executed."[116]

Tax-Act Payments, 1770–75

South Carolina enacted no tax legislation from 1770 through the end of the colonial period due to a controversy between the House and imperial authorities over the scope of the House's spending powers, revealing tensions between the colonists and England over legislative power that, as described in later chapters, also surfaced in other American colonies in other guises.[117] Despite the controversy, the House continued to prepare tax bills—which the Council refused to approve[118]—and, in doing so, audited expenses to be included in the Tax-Act schedule. Despite the controversy, the House eventually created a mechanism to pay all the colony's public creditors, including slaveholders seeking compensation for enslaved persons killed or executed, while the impasse continued.

The accounts compiled in preparation of the 1770 and 1771 Tax-Acts included compensation for the execution of ten enslaved persons; however, the House journals provide no details regarding the circumstances surrounding these payments.[119] Nevertheless, the *South Carolina Gazette* indicates that £200 payments authorized to James Sands's estate and to Price, Hest & Head stemmed from a poisoning:

> On Friday last two Negroes, viz. Dolly belonging to Mr. James Sands, and Liverpoole, belonging to Mr. William Price, were burnt on the Workhouse Green, pusuant [sic] to the sentence that had been passed on them a fortnight before; the former for poisoning an infant of Mr. Sands's, which died some time since, and attempting to put her master out of the world the same way; and the latter (a Negro Doctor) for furnishing the means. The wench made a free confession, acknowledged the justice of her punishment, and died a penitent; but the fellow did neither. A mulatto named Dick, formerly a slave to Mr. d'Harriette, but afterwards manumised, who stands accused as instigator of these horrid crimes, has disappeared.[120]

Completing the story, the *Gazette* reported a few weeks later, "The Mulatto Fellow Dick . . . accused of being the Instigator to the poisoning of the late Mr. Sands and his Family, was on Friday last tried, upon the Negro Act, and adjudged to receive twenty-five Lashes on Saturday Morning at four different Corners, and the same Number last Tuesday, in all 100 each Day, and to lose his Right Ear; which Sentence has been executed. A Bill of Sale of him, from Colonel Laurens, to John Mitchell, a free Negro, being produced at his Trial, the Sentence could not be extended to Transportation."[121]

In 1774, the House compiled additional accounts from 1771, 1772, and 1773 that included compensation for the execution of twenty-one enslaved persons;[122] however, no Tax-Act was prepared because the House deemed it futile.[123] Although the House journal includes no details regarding these payments, a series of news items spell out the circumstances surrounding £200 paid to Lazarus Brown's estate. It was first speculated that a known criminal had killed Brown:

> On Tuesday the 23d past was shot, in the Woods, about Half a Mile from his own House, at the Three Runs, and expired in two Hours after, Captain Lazarus Brown, formerly a Captain of Rangers in the Service of this Government, and reckoned the tallest Man in this Province, being near Seven Feet high.—The Ball which killed him entered on the Left Side of his Back-Bone, and lodged in his Wrist. A Jury of Inquest brought in the Verdict *Wilful Murder*, by Persons unknown.—This Murder is supposed to have been committed by one Payne, belonging to a desperate Gang of Villains which urged the Settlers on the Western Frontiers, some Years ago, to the violent Measure of driving them out of the Province, in a Manner which our Laws did not justify, and who, of late, we are informed, are returned seven Times worse than they were.[124]

A week later, a follow-up report stated, "The Name of the Man who is suspected of having killed Captain Lazarus Brown, is not Payne, but Prine; a notorious Offender, who some Time ago escaped out of Savannah Jail, under Sentence of Death, and for apprehending whom the Government of Georgia hath offered a Reward of Fifty Pounds Sterling."[125] By the end of the month, however, the news reports completed their descent from the lurid to the perfunctory when it was reported, "It was not the notorious Felon Robert Prine, that lately killed Capt. Lazarus Brown. He was shot by one of his own Slaves, who has since been convicted and burnt alive."[126]

Demonstrating continued fealty to the letter of the law, the House journal includes the following notation in approving a £400 payment to Isaac Dutart: "a Certificate in his favor for a Negro Man and a Negro Woman executed: Your Committee observe that the Justices and Free-holders who sat on the trial of these Negroes, altho' they could not agreeable to the Act of Assembly Appraise them for more than £200 each; Yet they Certifie that the said Slaves were really worth £750. But as the Law will not allow more than the sum of £200. to be paid by the Public for each Negro that is executed, Your Committee have allowed £400. for the said Negroes who were executed."[127] The House agreed with the committee's judgment.[128]

That same day, however, the House decided to consider "what steps may be necessary to be taken to make the Owners of all Slaves who shall be hereafter Executed, full Compensation for the value of the said Negroes."[129] After debate the next day, the House resolved to "Provide such Sum or Sums, as a Compensation, to the Owner or Owners of such Slave or Slaves, as shall appear to this House reasonable Additional to the sum of Two hundred Pounds provided by Law."[130] The House then ordered its change in policy to be publicly announced and further indicated that "it is expected that all Magistrates and other Persons who shall be Concerned in the Valuation of any Slave or Slaves so Condemned and Executed, do have particular regard to the nature of the Offence which such Slave or Slaves are Convicted of and how much the value of the said Slave or Slaves are lessened thereby."[131]

A few days later, frustrated with the persistent impasse that prevented tax legislation from being enacted and the public creditors from being paid, the House took action: "RESOLVED, That this House being prevented by His Majesty's Council from providing for the Charges of this Government for several Years past, in the usual Method by a general Tax. It becomes the Duty of the House to take every step in their Power to alleviate the Distresses of their unfortunate fellow Subjects, the Creditors of the Public."[132] The House ordered its clerk to issue tax certificates to "any persons whose Accounts have been audited and Allowed by the House, and who shall require such Certificates for any Sum or

Sums not exceeding the Amount of their said Demands and Interest thereon . . . and that the same will be provided for in the next Tax Bill."[133] The House's message to the governor informing him of its actions (and his response) were published in the *South Carolina Gazette*.[134] The tax certificates issued by the House came to be used as a form of currency.[135]

The House accounts compiled in preparation of the 1775 Tax-Act included compensation for the execution of nineteen enslaved persons and the killing of another.[136] The House journal provides no details regarding most of these payments.[137] In one case, however, the journal describes a belated request for £50 made by Thomas Lynch, who in 1774 had "informed the House, that during the Time he was off the Province, a Negro of his was tried and Executed, for a Felony Committed by the said Negro, and agreeable to the direction of the Negro Act, the Justices and Freeholders, before whom the Negro was tried, did Appraise the said Negro to be valued at £50. and did give a Certificate thereof, which Certificate was mislaid."[138] The House referred Lynch's request to the committee auditing the public accounts and eventually authorized payment the following year.[139]

The House journal provides more detail regarding the circumstances surrounding the single extrajudicial killing. Sarah Edwards petitioned for compensation "for a Negroe . . . run away from her Plantation, and shot by a Party from the Patrol."[140] Edwards explained,

That Your Petitioner having had a Negro Man Slave run away and carried with him a Gun Ammunition &ca by which he did a good deal of Mischief and was so daring & desperate as to threaten to shoot any Person that attempted to take him That some time in August 1773 a Party from the Patrol with two Negroe Men was sent in pursuit of the said run away Negroe they came up with and he standing upon the defence and refusing to be taken a Negro Man belonging to Thomas Ferguson Esqr who went with the Party to assist to take the said Runaway Negroe shot him by which he died Your Petitioner therefore most humbly prays this Honorable House to take the case into Consideration and to make her such a Compensation for the loss of the said Negro as to this House shall seem meet.[141]

The committee auditing the public accounts "recommend[ed] that £200 may be allowed her for the loss of the said Negroe, as they find such Allowance has been made to other Persons for Negroes that were shot."[142] The House agreed and authorized £200 compensation for Edwards.[143]

Following the 1774 change to the compensation scheme, several accounts were grouped together as "Certificates in favor of the several Persons for Negroes executed, which have been valued and appraised by the respective Magistrates and Freeholders who tried the said Negroes, and who have valued the said Negroes in conformity of a Resolution of this House on the 23.ᵈ of March 1774."[144] The accounts included claims from

- Samuel Benoist, who submitted "two Certificates in his favor for two Negroes executed, one valued at £700 and the other at £450, making together £1150";
- John Syme, who submitted a claim "for a Negro executed valued at £600";
- Francis Gillispee, who submitted a claim "for a Negro executed £350";
- Daniel Droze, who submitted a claim "for a Negro executed valued at £250"; and
- John Mackintosh, who submitted a claim "for a Negro executed valued at £450."[145]

The committee auditing the public accounts referred all these claims to the House for its consideration.[146]

The House ordered its clerk to write to each slaveholder to request that they "get the respective Magistrates and Freeholders who tried and condemned the said Negroes, to render a particular description (on Oath) of the said Negroes, and whether any of them were Tradesmen and of the appraised value of them on Oath."[147] The first claims to be considered after receiving this additional information were those of John Syme and Daniel Droze. In Syme's case, the committee auditing the public accounts considered the court's valuation "and made all the enquiry relative thereto they possibly could, and having reason to believe it was not the first Crime that the said Negro had committed they think £400 will be full sufficient to be made to Doctʳ. Syme for the loss of his said Negroe."[148] The House agreed.[149]

Droze's claim for additional compensation was denied because the committee found that "the Negro belonging to Daniel Droze who was executed had committed the Offence for which he suffered Death before the Resolution of this House to provide the full value of such Negroes as should be executed after that Resolution."[150] As the court had then "altered the Certificate and made it agreeable to Law," the committee recommended payment of the legal maximum of £200.[151] The circumstances surrounding the payment to Droze, including the outcome of his compensation claim, garnered extended attention in the newspaper:

ON Tuesday last Week was tried, convicted and executed at Ashley Ferry, that notorious Offender Caesar, a Negro Man Slave, the Property of Mr. Daniel Drose of Dorchester, who, with sundry other Negroes, as their Captain or Chief, went from a Camp of Runaway Slaves at Beach-hill on or about the end of June last Year, with Horses, Fire-Arms, Cutlasses and other dangerous Weapons with Intent to, and in the Night did, break open the Dwelling and Stores of the Honourable John Drayton, Esq; at Drayton-Hall, and stole and carried away from thence Candles, Sugar, Rum, Bacon, Soap, Wine, a Bale of Cloth, and sundry other Articles to a very great Amount, his Property; which Goods Caesar and they carried to the Camp at Beach Hill, and there divided the Spoil. This Fellow, while the others were taking the Goods, stood Centry with a Gun loaded with small Shot, at the Dwelling House; and in that Case it appeared that if Mr. Drayton, or any other Person, had appeared or offered to molest the Thieves, they were to have been shot; providentially, this horrid Intention was not perpetrated.

There were seven Negroes in and belonging to this Camp, four of whom have been executed at different Times. . . .

Caesar had a Ticket to pass any where unmolested, with Mr. Drose's Name forged to it, and now in his Custody; Caesar said it was written by one of the half-breed People named Josiah Reed, alias, Scott. He also said that he himself had stolen many Horses and that the noted Tilly, a Horse Thief, harboured about the same Camp to the southward. He confessed the Fact for which he suffered, and he likewise confessed being one of those who robbed and shared the Plunder when Mrs. Pender was so cruelly beat, abused and robbed in April last. He accused two other Negroes of being concerned in robbing Mrs. Pender, as well as Andrew now out in the Woods: All possible Means will be taken to investigate the Truth of his Discovery.

This was one of the most daring Gangs of Fellows that ever infested the Province, and by the spirited Behaviour of the Prosecutor and some other Country Gentlemen, offering a handsome Reward withal for the apprehending the said Caesar, he was brought to Justice, being taken up near Silver-Bluff and brought from thence to Ashley Ferry. Caesar cost Mr. Drose full 520l. [i.e., £520] but had he not been so notorious a Rogue, yet as the Resolution made in the Commons House of Assembly of this Province, dated 23d March, 1774 expressly mentions these Words "for Felony, Murder or any other Crime to be *hereafter* committed," the Magistrates and Freeholders had it not in their Power to do more than give a Certificate for Fifty Pounds Proclamation Money.[152]

When the committee later reviewed the remaining claims, it summarily recommended that Gillispee's claim be approved in full.[153] However, Benoist's claim, which related to the execution of an enslaved man and an enslaved woman, was not allowed in full because, "by the best Information which your Committee could obtain of the true value of the said Negroes, they recommend that the Sum of Eight hundred and fifty Pounds be provided for the said Samuel Benoist as a full Compensation for the loss of those Negroes."[154] Similarly, the committee refused to allow Mackintosh's claim in full because the "Committee upon considering the same, think that the Sum of £300 will be a full Compensation for the loss of this Negro."[155]

Separately, Edward Blake and William Godfrey's estate submitted requests for compensation in excess of the £200 cap. Blake submitted a certificate "for a Negro executed and appraised at £700 which the Justices and Freeholders Certify that they think the said Negro was worth that Sum before he had committed the Crime for which he was put to Death."[156] The committee auditing the public accounts took a different view—and the House agreed: because "the value of the said Negroe was much reduced by his committing that Crime, they recommend that £400 be allowed to Mr. Edward Blake for the loss of the said Negroe."[157] The £350 claim made by Godfrey's estate was approved without comment.[158]

Once work on the schedule concluded, the House again ordered the clerk to issue tax certificates to the public creditors.[159] Additionally, the House ordered "that the several Demands of Persons for the Years 1769 1770 1771 1772 & 1773 who did not receive Certificates for the same be provided for in the present Schedule," ensuring that they, too, would be paid.[160]

Manipulating the Racial Balance

In addition to continuing to embrace targeted tax exemptions for White immigrants,[161] the legislature reenacted the prevailing import taxes on enslaved persons and then repeatedly extended them throughout the remainder of the colonial period.[162] In doing so, the legislature continued to set its sights on "raising and appropriating a fund sufficient for the better settling of this Province with white inhabitants" while imposing a prohibitive additional tax on the importation of potential troublemakers from other colonies to ensure the tractability of the enslaved population in place.[163] As illustrated in figure 3.2, between 1752 and 1765, the revenue raised from these taxes was greater than £10,000 in all but one year, and a significant spike occurred at the end of the period, when more than £60,000 was raised in 1765 alone.[164]

Three-fifths of the revenue from these import taxes was dedicated to paying bounties "to every poor foreign protestant whatever from Europe" as well as to poor Protestants from Great Britain and Ireland whose good character was appropriately attested, who were between two and fifty years of age, and who came to South Carolina to settle in

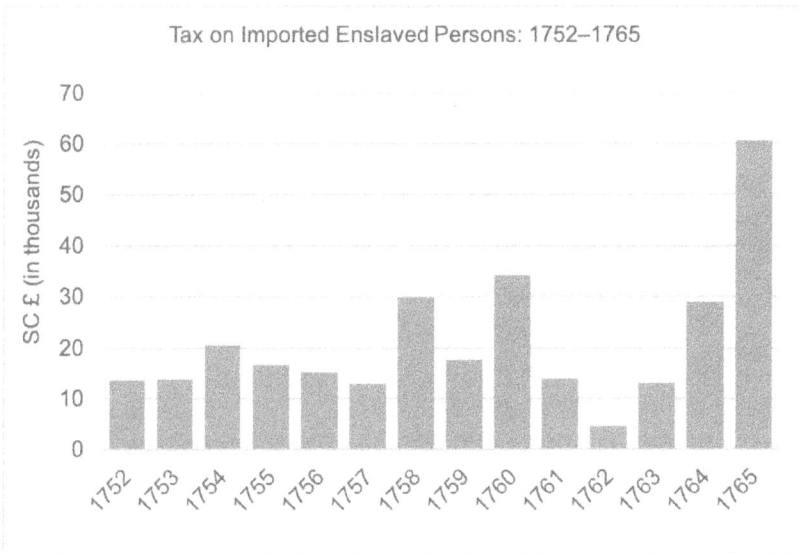

Figure 3.2. Tax on imported enslaved persons, 1752–65

designated areas in the central and southern portions of the colony.[165] The bounties were largest during the first three years and then reduced by one-third for the following two years.[166] After the expiration of this five-year period, it was anticipated that "there will be as many poor protestants settled on the southern frontier and central parts of this Province as there will be on the northern frontier."[167] Accordingly, the bounty was to be lowered further at that time but extended to "poor protestants" no matter where they settled in South Carolina.[168] An additional one-fifth of the revenue from these taxes was dedicated to "defraying the expense of surveying and running out lands, and passing grants to such poor protestants."[169]

It quickly became clear, however, that there was insufficient vacant land in the designated areas to accommodate the new arrivals.[170] Accordingly, in 1752, the import tax revenue was instead dedicated to providing in-kind assistance to new arrivals as well as "every free poor foreign Protestant from Europe" already in the colony who had not yet received the cash bounty—with that assistance taking the form of tools, "corn or other provisions," and "a cow and calf for every five such poor Protestants as shall be settled together."[171] Those who arrived more than four months after the act's passage received half the assistance.[172] In 1754, additional import tax revenue was redirected to "the passing of grants to such poor Protestants as have settled in this Province since the time of passing the above recited Act."[173]

In 1761, the legislature bemoaned the inefficacy of these efforts, noting that more than £57,575 of the appropriated funds still sat in the public treasury.[174] Given the surplus, the legislature decided "to increase the bounty to such settlers which may best answer the said good intentions."[175] The increased bounty provided funding to cover settlers' cost of passage from Europe and "to enable them to purchase tools and provisions."[176] The bounties were to be paid during the following three years but, like the import taxes, were repeatedly extended.[177]

In 1764, the legislature again professed concern that "an importation of negroes, equal in number to what have been imported of late years, may prove of the most dangerous consequence in many respects to this Province."[178] In order "to obviate such danger," the legislature imposed an additional £100 tax on "every inhabitant of this Province and other person first purchasing, or if not sold, every person importing for his,

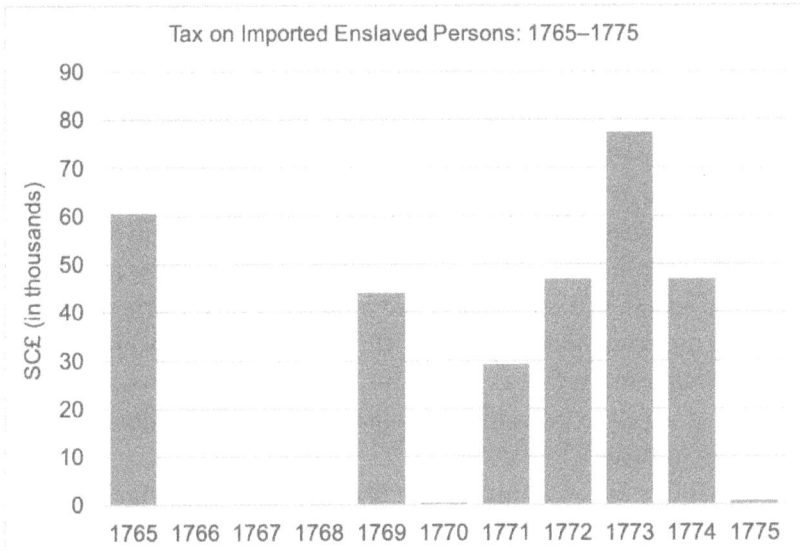

Figure 3.3. Tax on imported enslaved persons, 1765–75

her or their own use, any negro or other slave hereafter to be imported or brought into this Province, either by land or water."[179] This "prohibitory duty" mimicked the tenfold increase built into the 1740 General Duty Act after the Stono Rebellion, but it stiffened the disincentive by multiplying the highest rate of tax by ten and applying that additional tax to all imported enslaved persons on top of the base tax rate.[180] The additional tax was in effect for three years beginning January 1, 1766.[181] As indicated in figure 3.3, the additional tax—abetted by the Stamp Act controversy[182]—led to a steep drop in import tax collections, evidencing a correspondingly steep drop in the importation of enslaved persons while the tax was in force.[183] Nonetheless, import tax revenues—and imports—quickly bounced back in the early 1770s when a credit crisis led to a decline in demand in the eastern Caribbean that "caused captains . . . to seek more lucrative markets" in the leeward islands and South Carolina.[184]

Reflection

South Carolina's legislature spent the final decades of the colonial period fine-tuning the legal regime through which it deployed the power to tax in service of the evils of slavery, racism, and White supremacy. Having settled on its preferred mix of tax and nontax measures, the legislature eschewed its earlier practice of periodically rewriting the entire slave code in favor of renewing the 1740 Slave Code with selected additions and refinements (e.g., expanding slaveholder compensation to enslaved persons killed or injured under color of law and later relaxing the compensation cap). Similarly, the general rates of taxation on the importation of enslaved persons remained the same as under the 1740 General Duty Act—again with a brief resort to prohibitive taxes in the late 1760s that were aimed at inhibiting the growth of South Carolina's Black population. What is more, the revenue from these import taxes continued to be devoted largely to providing financial incentives for White migration to South Carolina.

The stability and routinization of these closely intertwined tax and nontax measures are evidenced by the legislature's repeated extension of both the basic import tax rates and the bounties for Whites migrating to the colony that were funded by those taxes as well as in the House's increasingly mechanistic treatment of slaveholder compensation claims as part of the annual tax legislative drafting process. Regarding the slaveholder compensation payments, which again open a revealing tax window onto South Carolina's slave society, it is worth recalling from chapter 2 that a separate section in the schedule was set aside specifically for payments related to "Criminal Slaves" beginning in 1750. This change permitted the drafters of the Tax-Act schedules to dispense with repeating the reason for payment, whether by grouping compensation payments together or by resorting to shorthand (e.g., "ditto" or, even more economically, "do."). Concomitantly, the drafters abandoned a short-lived practice of providing greater detail in the schedule regarding the crimes committed by the enslaved, preferring instead boilerplate references to "a Negro executed."

Further evidence that the machinery of the law had grown more efficient can be found in the contrast between how the House journals treated the payments cataloged in chapters 1 and 2 and how they treated those cataloged in this chapter. Invariably, the names of Whites were mentioned because, as slaveholders, they were the recipients of compensation payments. In chapters 1 and 2, the House journals were often the source of other details regarding the payments, sometimes including the names of the enslaved and more often the circumstances surrounding an execution or killing. By the mid-1760s, however, the House journals were nearly devoid of factual detail regarding executions. The mechanistic processing of slaveholder compensation claims was interrupted only to provide details regarding the occasional payment for an extrajudicial killing, an execution or killing that did not fit squarely within the parameters of the law, or quirky administrative situations (e.g., the need to pay interest on delayed compensation payments or the reimbursement of the public treasurer for monies advanced to cover compensation that had mistakenly been omitted from a prior schedule). Slaveholder compensation provided through the annual tax legislative drafting process had obviously become commonplace in the minds of legislators—a generally unremarkable part of the legal background that allowed White society to prosper through the exploitation of enslaved Black labor.

Indeed, during the period covered by this chapter, a smoothly operating tax legislative drafting process churned out significant amounts of slaveholder compensation that kept the slave codes' legal machinery humming as it churned out death and destruction among South Carolina's enslaved Black majority. Notwithstanding professions in the 1751 revision of the slave code that slave courts yearned to mitigate death sentences, the average number of compensated executions outpaced growth in the enslaved population by more than doubling in the late colonial period, rising from approximately three per year in the period covered in chapter 2 to approximately seven per year in the period covered here. Furthermore, every Tax-Act enacted in the late colonial period—as well as each Tax-Act prepared by the House but stymied by the Council in the years leading up to the Revolution—included slaveholder compensation payments. As indicated in figure 3.4, between 1752 and 1769, slaveholder compensation ranged from a low of 0.2 percent to a high of 2.85 percent of property tax revenue spent. Over the entire period covered by this chapter, the annual slaveholder compensation payments averaged £1,525—more than two and a half times the average in chapter 2—with the largest total occurring in 1775, when the legislature authorized nearly £5,000 in compensation after the House relaxed the £200 compensation cap.

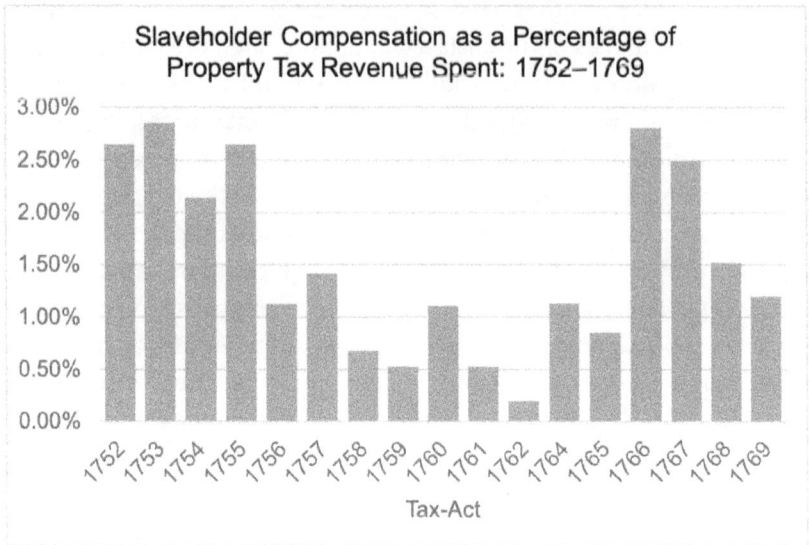

Figure 3.4. Slaveholder compensation as a percentage of property tax revenue spent, 1752–69

The Power to Destroy

Taken together, chapters 1 through 3 document the important role that taxation played in supporting and reinforcing the institution of slavery and the evils of racism and White supremacy in colonial South Carolina. Much like today's Internal Revenue Code, South Carolina's annual Tax-Acts in their time read like facially neutral statutes that aimed to distribute the burden of funding the shared expenses of government as fairly and efficiently as possible on the basis of taxpayers' ability to pay. Indeed, the Tax-Acts became so unremarkably boring and repetitive to the nineteenth-century editor of the *Statutes at Large of South Carolina* that, beginning with the 1740 Tax-Act, he chose to "hereafter insert no more than the titles; unless, in the course of perusing them, [he] should find new matter proper to be inserted."[185] Yet, in both cases, beneath the veneer of neutrality and objectivity lies a statute that is intimately connected with social forces and conveys messages both about those whom society values and supports and about those whom society has chosen to marginalize and oppress.

Through taxation, South Carolina repeatedly reinforced the message sent by the slave codes (but not only by the slave codes)[186] that enslaved persons were a dehumanized form of "property." When enslaved persons were "imported" into South Carolina—a term reserved for goods brought into the colony as opposed to the (White) people who were said to "settle" there[187]—the General Duty Act taxed them just as it taxed imported commodities like alcohol, tobacco, and sugar. Once imported, the enslaved became the object of annual property taxes under the Tax-Acts alongside land, storekeepers' stock-in-trade, and money lent for profit. Through these import and property taxes, the colonial government directly shared in the profits from slavery at all stages, beginning with the trafficking of human beings to and through South Carolina, continuing throughout the lifetimes of forced labor suffered by those who were brought to South Carolina in bondage, and extending to the forced labor of generations of their descendants. The story of taxation and slavery in colonial South Carolina thus demonstrates the expressive function of taxation—not to mention that one need not be a taxpayer at all to fall victim to those who would use the power to tax for evil ends.

But enslaved persons were not just "property" to be accounted for when determining the appropriate distribution of the colonial tax burden; they were also a large group of people to be subjugated and controlled, and for that reason, they found themselves at the source of determining both the amount of that tax burden and how the revenue raised would be spent. In the early tax experiments examined in chapter 1, enslaved persons who were killed or executed under color of law were valued, and that value was directly converted into taxes to be imposed—first, on local slaveholders and, later, on the region's slave- and land-holders. These tax experiments mixed efforts to deploy the redistributive power of taxation to the advantage of slaveholders with efforts to influence slaveholder behavior by providing financial incentives to reduce transgressions of the slave codes and, in turn, the harms and costs that exploitation of enslaved labor imposed on White society.

Beginning in this era of early tax experimentation and then more earnestly after enactment of the 1740 Slave Code, the legislature embraced a centralized, colonial-level process for vetting and funding slaveholder compensation claims on the theory that this compensation broadly benefited the public by ensuring that those who violated the slave code would be brought to "justice." Under this centralized process, the Commons House of Assembly vetted and approved slaveholder compensation claims as part of drafting the annual Tax-Act. Approved slaveholder compensation payments (together with other approved public expenses) then determined the precise amount of tax imposed under the Tax-Act. Completing the interconnected loop between taxing and spending, the Tax-Act specified each year that the revenue raised by the act could be spent only on the approved expenses included in the Tax-Act schedule and nothing else. It bears observing that South Carolina tax legislation enacted during and immediately after the Revolutionary War was not characterized by a similarly tight interdependence between taxing and spending. Schedules, if included at all, often contained only partial lists of expenses, and appropriation clauses became more general and did not limit the expenditure of tax revenue to enumerated expenses.[188]

In tandem with the intertwined tax and nontax efforts to control the enslaved population in place, the colonial legislature calibrated the level of taxation on the trafficking in enslaved persons to influence the number of Blacks brought into the colony. Giving a tax voice to White fears, these taxes were set so prohibitively high during the 1710s, 1740s, and 1760s that they significantly depressed the importation of enslaved persons.[189] But manipulating the racial balance of the colony was not only a matter of using tax sticks. The legislature also saw the revenue raised by these import taxes as a carrot—a steady but, due to historical circumstances, sometimes erratic stream of revenue[190] that could be used to lure White immigrants to South Carolina by funding in-kind or cash bounties, especially when legally mandated minimum ratios of Whites to Blacks in work areas simultaneously dangled the prospect of ready employment before them.

More than just a means of raising revenue and influencing behavior, taxation opened a window onto life in South Carolina's slave society. As described in chapter 1 and illustrated in chapters 2 and 3, this tax window opened fully once the legislature centralized the vetting of slaveholder compensation claims as part of the annual tax legislative drafting process. When possible, the contextual detail gleaned from tax legislative history was supplemented by records from the executive petition and pardon process as well as accounts in South Carolina newspapers. While the petition and pardon process belied the notion that the enslaved were fungible commodities for whom monetary compensation would easily suffice, the search for news reports revealed the same White fear of the colony's enslaved Black majority that was articulated more forthrightly in the text of South Carolina's tax legislation. In the space devoted to local news,[191] South Carolina's newspapers included few reports of the crimes or executions of enslaved persons as compared to the number of compensation payments documented here.[192] In fact, a study of newspapers throughout the American colonies noted how "only in South Carolina—where news of slave activity should have been most prevalent based on the black-to-white ratio of inhabitants—was there a noticeable lack of news of slaves. . . . The omission . . . speaks to the fear whites felt concerning blacks."[193]

Like the dearth of news reports, both the import taxes used to manipulate the colony's racial balance and the property taxes that purchased slaveholder cooperation in enforcement of the slave codes revealed Whites' persistent fears of enslaved Blacks' resistance to bondage. As South Carolina's ruling White minority wrestled with their fears of Black resistance, they dissonantly alternated between treating enslaved persons as human beings and treating them as a form of property.[194] Broadly speaking, the enslaved were viewed under the slave codes as human beings fully able to make—and be held criminally accountable for—choices that endangered the White minority; however, when time came to pay compensation for their execution or killing under color of law and to calculate the taxes that funded those compensation payments, the enslaved were treated as nothing more than property. This dissonance was on full display in Michael Jeans's 1742/3 request for clemency for Sampson. In his petition, Jeans acknowledged that Sampson's attempts at escape represented no more than the human desire for freedom, but when pleading for mercy, Jeans did so not on the grounds of Sampson's shared humanity but because Jeans's family would be rendered indigent without the income generated by its most valuable asset—that is to say, without the fruit of Sampson's forced labor as a skilled painter and glazier.

Moreover, when compensation for an execution or killing such as Sampson's was authorized, it was paid not to the family of the deceased but to the deceased's putative "owner," on the theory that they had been damaged in much the same way as if their crops or buildings had been destroyed. As reflected in the Tax-Acts and tax legislative history, these "owners" represented a broad swath of South Carolina's White population, including men and women; individuals and businesses; leaders of government; planters, butchers, and constables; and even churches. Representing a similarly broad swath of the enslaved population, the enslaved persons who were executed or killed included both men and women, the young and the old. Reinforcing their treatment as fungible "property," the enslaved mostly went unnamed, even though compensation was being paid for *their* deaths. What is more, compensation was not just paid to slaveholders themselves. Payments were also made to slaveholders' estates or heirs as the legal successors to the decedents' property rights in enslaved persons. Compensation was likewise paid to slaveholders' creditors—either when slaveholders assigned compensation claims to others or when payments on their claims satisfied outstanding mortgages secured by the value of the deceased enslaved person.

Slaveholders, feeling attached and entitled to their property rights, were persistent—but not always successful—in pressing claims for compensation from the public treasury. Chapter 2 included discussion of significant examples of slaveholder persistence involving Burrell Massingberd Hyrne and Deborah McCree, both of whom attempted to escape the prohibition against compensation for enslaved persons executed for murder or rebellion. Chapter 1 provided an earlier example in William Miles's unsuccessful claim for compensation from the public treasury at a time when the law dictated that slaveholders' economic losses were to be redistributed at the regional (rather than colonial) level, but officials had failed to follow through on that promise. Similarly, this chapter described how Daniel Droze submitted a claim for the full £250 value of his enslaved man Caesar following the House's relaxation of the £200 compensation cap. After investigating the claim, the House concluded that no more than £200 could be paid to Droze because Caesar had committed the offense for which he was executed *before* the 1774 change was made to the slaveholder compensation scheme. And when one of John Fryerson's enslaved men killed another, he requested compensation for the executed killer and for the victim, even though the law would at most have split the value of the killer between the two. Hewing to the letter of the law, the House responded by authorizing compensation only for the killer. Additionally, several claims vetted in the process of drafting the 1758 Tax-Act were unaccompanied by proof that the death sentence had been carried out, leading the House to condition payment on furnishing proof of execution. The thread running through all these examples is the importance that slaveholders placed on access to the tax system to broadly redistribute their losses as the price of securing their cooperation with enforcement of the slave codes when their capital investment in enslaved labor was threatened.

When not bound by the letter of the law, the House sometimes acted equitably in response to these claims, doing what it deemed "right" or to be within the spirit of the law. For instance, in chapter 1, the House authorized compensation to Thomas Hendley for the accidental killing of an enslaved person. In chapter 2, it authorized compensation to John McLeod and William Kelvert for the extrajudicial killing of enslaved persons before the slave code was amended to once again afford such compensation. In this chapter, the House authorized compensation to Francis Rose for one enslaved person who was shot by another, even though the law seemed to contemplate compensation in such situations only when a White person perpetrated the killing. This chapter likewise recounted how the House dealt with a claim from Thomas Shoemaker, who had not been satisfied with receiving £100—the maximum allowed to him by law—when Thomas Bradwell's enslaved man Sandy was executed for murdering his enslaved man Scipio. Shoemaker petitioned the House for additional compensation because Scipio was valued at £400 and had been murdered while attempting to apprehend Sandy, who had escaped Bradwell. The House was sympathetic to Shoemaker's plea and awarded him an additional £200—despite there being no legal basis for doing so—because "a very valuable Slave, lost his Life, not only in a lawful but commendable Action."[195]

Beyond providing insight into the White slaveholding mindset, taxation opens a window onto the world of the enslaved. Chapters 1 through 3 revealed the struggles of those who undertook the risks associated with attempted escape from slavery and who were killed before attaining freedom—a group that included two enslaved persons held by Speaker of the House Paul Jenys, Joseph Elliott Jr.'s enslaved man Daniel, and James McGirt's enslaved man Joe. These killings often occurred at the hands of organized patrols but could also occur when individual Whites attempted to apprehend escapees. For instance, James White was apparently acting alone when he killed John Edwards's escaped man Tony. In a case with an unrevealed backstory, Silas Miles's enslaved man Primus attempted escape after he shot not the overseer but the overseer's wife, which created panic in the surrounding area and resulted in two parties of the militia being sent in pursuit. After Primus crossed a river, he defiantly told his pursuers that he would shoot anyone who tried to take him rather than accede to their demands to surrender. Sending mixed messages about why Primus was then shot through the head, the House journal raises the possibility of self-defense, by asserting that Primus had been reaching for his gun at the time, but likewise pointed to more callous and self-interested motives for his killing when it observed that the patrol could not pursue Primus further without the men having to swim across the river.

Other enslaved persons chose to rise up and resist their bondage. Some did so en masse, as happened in the Stono Rebellion. Others did so individually or on a smaller scale, as when Hyrne's two enslaved men tied up the overseer and whipped him to death; when John Norman was maimed by an enslaved person; when two of John Miles's enslaved persons poisoned his infant son; and when Joseph Blake was poisoned—not once but twice—with the second, successful attempt on his life involving a quartet of enslaved persons that included two of his own and two held by others.

In contrast, some enslaved persons chose to enforce the slave codes against others—as July and Harry did in chapter 2 and as John Drayton's enslaved man did in this chapter when he shot an escapee previously held by Francis Rose. Other enslaved persons succumbed to pressure to aid in prosecutions under the slave code. For instance, pardons were dangled before enslaved persons in exchange for testimony—as happened when Kate testified against Boatswain in chapter 2. And family members were sometimes induced to testify against each other—as happened in chapter 2 to Kit (executed on the testimony of his wife, Venus) and in this chapter to Jinny (executed on the testimony of her daughter) and Jemmy and Robin (executed on the testimony of their sister). Faced individually with impossible circumstances, as also happened to Hagar in chapter 2, Robin ultimately confessed to his crime just before his death—but only after being tortured by hanging on a gibbet for a week.

The complexities of personal relationships among the enslaved surfaced in a different way in this chapter when Hannah recanted her testimony against her husband, Will, shortly before her death, possibly leading to his life being spared. As all personal relationships do, the relationships among the enslaved sometimes led to disagreements. Occasionally, these conflicts escalated to murder, as when Pompey poisoned Peter in this chapter and John murdered Duff in chapter 2. In all these ways, it becomes clear how closely taxation was (and is) bound up with everyday life and how it can open a window onto society.

These glimpses of life in colonial South Carolina have shown the destruction that taxation can wreak when its power is used in the service of societal oppression. Taxation was a key element in the multifaceted strategy that the ruling White minority employed to exert ever-tighter control over the colony's enslaved Black majority. Taxation was used to affect South Carolina's Black-White racial balance as well as the composition of its enslaved population. Prohibitive levels of taxation periodically deterred the importation of all enslaved Blacks but more routinely deterred the importation of troublemakers from other colonies. These prohibitive taxes acted as tax penalties aimed not at raising revenue but at shaping economic demand in South Carolina's market for enslaved labor. At the same time, the colonial government reaped significant profits from its revenue-raising taxes on the slave trade—more than £650,000 between 1735 and 1775[196]—profits that funded handouts to "poor protestants" to encourage the migration of select groups of Whites to the colony. Together, these tax carrots and sticks were employed to shape White society and enhance White control over an enslaved Black majority whose forced labor was vital to White prosperity.

Even more distressing, however, is the role that taxation played in facilitating the killing of enslaved persons, whether death came after summary trials by White slave courts or at the hands of individual Whites without even the semblance of judicial process. "Justice" was swift and punishment brutal, taking the form of public hangings, burnings at the stake, and public torture by being hung in chains. If the occasional news reports are any indication of general sentiment, these killings were met alternately with a disturbingly matter-of-fact acceptance or with self-righteous indignation at the impertinence of the enslaved. Throughout the colonial period, tax measures greased the palms of slaveholders to ensure the smooth operation of the colony's machinery of death. Naturally, the payments documented here cannot provide a full accounting of enslaved persons put to death in colonial South Carolina, whether because compensation was flatly denied (as happened following the 1739 Stono Rebellion), because the enslaved person's death was considered to be a domestic matter (as seemed to be the case with Alexander Fraser's withdrawn petition), because compensation was paid outside the Tax-Acts (e.g., when it was funded locally or regionally from the 1710s through the 1730s) or was the subject of a blanket authorization (as occurred in the early colonial period), because the killing legally occurred at the hands of a slaveholder inflicting punishment, or for some other reason (e.g., Thomas Lynch's "mislaid" certificate). Yet even this incomplete picture documents an anguishing death toll facilitated by the power of taxation. From the early 1720s through 1775, the Tax-Acts provide evidence of more than 250 enslaved persons who were executed or killed under color of law—executions and killings that not only punished the offender but also inflicted terror on all other enslaved persons for the express purpose of keeping them in subjugation.[197] Slaveholders were paid a total of nearly £47,000 in compensation for the loss of their "property" in the name of reinforcing and perpetuating the institution of slavery—blood money that was larger in amount than the total expenses reflected in the schedules of a number of South Carolina's annual Tax-Acts.

Given South Carolina's unique situation as both a slave society from its founding and the only American colony with an enslaved Black majority, it is no wonder that taxation reflected the centrality of slavery in South Carolina society. Having now explored at length the variety of tax tools that South Carolina used to oppress and kill human beings on the basis of their race, part 2 of this book turns to examining the connections that other American colonies forged between taxation and slavery. Before embarking on that examination, it bears noting that South Carolina was chosen for extended study here not because it was broadly representative of the experience elsewhere but because its unique situation illustrates how thoroughly taxation could be used in the service of evil ends by protecting and preserving the institution of slavery. Because of the close relationship between tax law and society, one can only expect to encounter differences in the nature and tenor of the relationship between taxation and slavery in other American colonies, especially given that some of those colonies never became slave societies like South Carolina and the pattern of life between slaveholders and the enslaved did not everywhere involve South Carolina's plantation life or the growing of staple crops like rice. Part 2 thus affords the opportunity to explore the deeper complexities of the relationship between tax law and society through the lens of colonial American slavery outside of South Carolina.

PART II

Taxation and Slavery in Other American Colonies

4

The Northern Colonies

This chapter begins exploring the relationship between taxation and slavery in other American colonies by moving north from South Carolina to New England. Slavery existed in New England decades before South Carolina's settlement and the establishment of its slave society; however, without an economy built around staple crops, New England's enslaved population never grew to the size of South Carolina's. Moreover, set in a different social, political, and geographic environment, the operation and legal regulation of slavery in New England differed markedly from the operation and legal regulation of slavery in South Carolina, producing quantitatively and qualitatively different connections between taxation and slavery. In addition to these regional-level contrasts, differences existed among the New England colonies regarding whether and how tax measures were employed to protect and promote slavery—and, utterly unlike South Carolina, eventually to put an end to the slave trade.

Through these points of contrast, this chapter's exploration of the relationship between taxation and slavery in the northern colonies deepens understanding of the connections between tax law and society. Building on the work in part 1, this chapter demonstrates how taxation is not a bland matter of economics—in other words, of merely identifying and then refining and perfecting a chosen tax base—but rather reflects and expresses societal values. Although New England's brand of racism and slavery led to the establishment of distinctive connections between taxation and these evils, that is not to say that tax law was in any way "special." To the contrary, tax law in New England was as intimately connected with slavery as were other areas of law.

Slaveholder Compensation

New England's Societies with Slaves

Slavery was present in New England by the 1630s.[1] The use of Native American and then Black enslaved labor grew and continued throughout the colonial period, powering the engine of colonization and an economy yoked to the slave trade.[2] Nevertheless, the number of enslaved persons in New England remained small in comparison to the size of South Carolina's enslaved population. On the eve of the Revolutionary War, when the Black population had grown to its largest size, Blacks in New England numbered approximately sixteen thousand and constituted about 2.4 percent of the population.[3] In contrast, South Carolina exceeded New England's high-water mark half a century earlier, and by that time, enslaved Blacks had been in the majority for two decades.[4]

In New England, significant differences in the size of the Black population existed from colony to colony. New Hampshire, with its lesser commercial importance, had the smallest Black population at the end of the colonial period (674 in 1773).[5] In contrast, as "the richest and most powerful New England province" and an active participant in the slave trade, Massachusetts had a Black population nearly eight times larger than New Hampshire's.[6] Connecticut's Black population was larger still, which, given an economy that lacked the concentrations of enslaved Blacks found on South Carolina plantations, has been attributed to the fact that wealth in Connecticut was more equally distributed and allowed "more persons to own slaves than in Massachusetts or Rhode Island, where wealth was concentrated to a greater degree among merchants and landed gentry."[7] Rhode Island had a smaller Black population than either Connecticut or Massachusetts; however, Blacks constituted a larger percentage of the population there than in any other New England colony. At the end of the colonial period, Blacks constituted 6.3 percent of Rhode Island's population—a significant dip from the peak of 11.5 percent in the 1750s but still nearly double the percentage in Connecticut and more than triple the percentage in Massachusetts.[8] The concentration of Blacks in South Kingstown, Rhode Island, was even greater—20 percent of the population, or more than triple the colony-wide average.[9] The concentration of Blacks in Rhode Island has been attributed to its leading role in the slave trade and the large-scale farming activity that occurred in the Narragansett Country (which included South Kingstown).[10]

Overall, these numbers indicate that New England was a "society with slaves"—one where "slavery was just one form of labor among many"—rather than a "slave society" like South Carolina, where "slavery stood at the center of economic production, and the master–slave relationship provided the model for all social relations."[11] Yet, slave societies did exist within New England. Rhode Island's Narragansett Country has been described as "a slave society within a society with slaves" because of the centrality of slavery to economic and social life there.[12] Nonetheless, without staple crops, enslaved labor became "highly diversified" to meet the demands of the New England economy, and "Negroes accordingly were taught and followed whatever calling their owners pursued, whether farming, lumbering, trading, fishing, whaling, manufacturing or privateering."[13] Rhode Island's leading role in the slave trade also required the enslaved to work "in the business of slavery" itself: "They assisted their enslavers in distilleries that manufactured rum and shops that manufactured barrels, and the barrels of rum were then packed onto slave ships and used to purchase slaves along the West African coast. Enslaved Rhode Islanders also cared for the livestock and cultivated the crops that eventually fed enslaved people in the West Indies. Their work, in other words, reflected the business of their enslavers."[14]

Slave Codes

By the turn of the eighteenth century, a growing population of enslaved Native Americans and, increasingly, enslaved Blacks led to the enactment of regulations aimed at controlling them.[15] Over time, all the New England colonies created slave codes through piecemeal legislation, and this colonial legislation was supplemented with more stringent local restrictions in cities with large concentrations of enslaved persons (e.g., South Kingstown).[16]

New England's piecemeal regulation of slavery fell far short of South Carolina's comprehensive slave codes but did starkly illustrate the tensions created when people were classified as property.[17] For instance, despite being treated as slaveholders' property, enslaved persons in New England were permitted to enter into contracts, hold property, testify in court against Whites, file lawsuits (including against their holders), enjoy the same legal process in criminal cases as Whites, and even legally marry.[18] New England's slave codes were also far less draconian than those of South Carolina. As harsh as the punishments prescribed specifically for the enslaved could be in New England, they generally involved only whippings, rarely entailed mutilation or sale outside the colony, and never extended to the death penalty, which was such a prevalent feature of South Carolina's slave codes.[19] New England's more "benign" legal treatment of enslaved persons has been attributed to, among other things, a New England economy that "could not absorb large numbers of slaves," which had given rise to fears of uprisings elsewhere; the fact that slaveholders and the enslaved often worked and lived together, permitting slaveholders more effectively to control and punish enslaved persons through near-constant surveillance; and religious influence that shaped "a patriarchal conception of slavery."[20]

Without the death penalty enshrined in slave codes to punish and instill terror in the enslaved population, the New England colonies apparently had no need to create slaveholder compensation schemes akin to South Carolina's.[21] Reflecting a less intense connection with slavery, the tax systems of Massachusetts, Rhode Island, Connecticut, and New Hampshire were spared the task of distributing the cost of slaveholder compensation among the White populace. Consequently, an important connection between taxation and slavery that existed in South Carolina's slave society was entirely absent from New England's societies with slaves.

Marking the Enslaved as Property

Though, at first blush, the New England colonies' treatment of the enslaved might seem comparatively benign, others have described it in more sinister terms: "In the North, the laws of slavery assigned the enslaved a status that simultaneously reduced them to chattel and made demands of them as legal persons—whichever suited their enslavers. This arbitrary treatment of slaves, as chattel in some instances and legal persons in other instances, made northern slavery particularly bewildering and appalling. The limited legal acknowledgment of personhood seemed technically mild but was in practice draconian."[22] For example, as mentioned earlier, enslaved Blacks could legally marry other Blacks in Massachusetts; however, being "property" of the slaveholder, those married couples and their children could be separated at any time through sale or bequest or even, as evidenced in newspaper advertisements, by giving away newborns because slaveholders saw them as a burden.[23] The tension created by alternately treating the enslaved as persons or property has, therefore, been described as "especially poignant in New England."[24]

New England tax laws add another dimension to the northern colonies' seemingly arbitrary alternation between treating the enslaved as people or property. Taxes on "polls and estates"—that is, a combination of head taxes and property taxes—were an important feature of colonial New England tax systems.[25] The poll tax applied to men, typically within a specified age range.[26] In Massachusetts and New Hampshire, it appears that enslaved men were initially treated as persons subject to poll tax, with slaveholders held responsible for payment.[27] Then, after some equivocation in the early 1690s and around the time that the colony began to legally regulate slavery, Massachusetts listed enslaved persons among the property assessed in determining the value of taxpayers' estates.[28] This change was not, however, without its opponents. In 1716, Samuel Sewall, then a member of the Massachusetts Governor's Council and later chief justice of the Superior Court of Judicature, recorded in his diary, "I essay'd June, 22, to prevent Indians and Negroes being Rated with Horses and Hogs; but could not prevail."[29] Similar to Massachusetts, when New Hampshire ordered a colony-wide inventory of polls and estates in 1727 to distribute the tax burden more fairly among its towns, it enumerated enslaved persons among the property to be inventoried, sandwiching them between livestock and real estate.[30]

Until the end of the seventeenth century, Rhode Island levied taxes "as lump sums, allocated to the towns in fixed amounts," leaving it to individual taxpayers to assess their own estates.[31] In 1695, even before the Rhode Island legislature began regulating slavery in earnest, it enacted the colony's first set of uniform rules regarding the property includible in taxpayers' estates, listing enslaved persons among taxable property and grouping them together with livestock.[32] Rhode Island continued this practice in later versions of that legislation.[33]

Departing from the path taken by other New England colonies, Connecticut provides an interesting contrast between the form and substance of the taxes on polls and estates.[34] Like Massachusetts and New Hampshire, Connecticut imposed poll taxes as early as 1650 on "all the male persons . . . from sixteene yeares old and vpwards"—making no distinctions based on race—and specified that "for such servants . . . as take not wages, theire . . . masters shall pay for them."[35] In 1678, the legislature clarified that "Indian male servants that live wth the English shall be put into the list and rated as other persons."[36] Then, in 1703, the legislature refined the scope of the tax on estates: "Whereas in the lawe . . . it is provided that all estate both reall and personall shall be entred in the lists of estates: It is now enacted by this Court that the intent of the said clause is that all male persons above sixteen years of age (except such as are exempted in said lawe) and all sorts of cattell, horses and swine, as are mentioned in said lawe, and no other shall be listed; and all personall estate not perticularly mentioned in the lawe is excepted."[37]

Over the ensuing decades, the Connecticut legislature made repeated adjustments to the tax base but never listed enslaved persons among the property included in taxpayers' estates.[38] Instead, the enslaved appear to have continuously been treated the same as indentured servants; in other words, males were nominally subject to poll tax, but payment was made by another (i.e., the slaveholder).[39] Thus, on the surface, Connecticut's treatment of the enslaved differed starkly—but for no readily apparent or articulated reason—from that of other New England colonies, with Massachusetts and Rhode Island, the two New England colonies that would later dominate the American slave trade, having led the way in deeming enslaved persons to be taxable property.[40]

Yet, despite formally treating the enslaved as people subject to tax, Connecticut always treated enslaved men as taxable property in substance. Because the poll tax was paid by the slaveholder, it effectively operated as a tax on the slaveholder's property—that is to say, the wealth-generating labor power under the slaveholder's control.[41] Unlike Connecticut, Massachusetts and New Hampshire eventually dispensed with the charade of formally treating the enslaved as people while in substance taxing them as property, opting instead more forthrightly to tax them as property in form *and* substance. Connecticut, however, never abandoned the subterfuge of exalting form over substance—

nominally treating enslaved men as taxable people but actually tax-ing them as property. This divergence of tax approaches mirrors the seemingly arbitrary legal treatment of the enslaved in New England described earlier—with the enslaved alternately treated as people or property depending on the whims of the Whites who exerted power and control over them.

Adding to the confusion, the choices made when taxing enslaved per-sons also sent mixed messages about whose labor was deemed valuable as a source of wealth.[42] In all New England colonies, the labor power of men was included in the tax base, sending the message that a man's work was valuable regardless of the color of his skin or whether he was free, indentured, or enslaved. But the labor power of women was not always seen as equally valuable. Massachusetts, New Hampshire, and Rhode Island eventually included the commodified labor power of enslaved women in the tax base but excluded the labor power of White women. In contrast, Connecticut systematically excluded the labor power of *all* women from the tax base. In doing so, Connecticut, whether wittingly or unwittingly, placed Native American, Black, and White women on the same plane but concomitantly sent the message that *all* their work lacked value—even if their labor was regularly sold in the market right beside men's.

Manipulating the Racial Balance

Rhode Island, Massachusetts, and New Hampshire all attempted to use the power of taxation to manipulate the racial balance of their popula-tions, whether by deploying the soft power of taxation to shape behavior with financial incentives or by deploying the hard power of punitive taxation to end deleterious behavior. But no matter whether the power of taxation was used to shape or stop behavior, the act of imposing taxes on the importation of enslaved persons marked the enslaved as prop-erty just as the taxes on polls and estates in those colonies did. Below these surface-level similarities, however, lie important differences in approach and motivation that further highlight both how taxation was just as intertwined with slavery as were other areas of colonial law and how the connections between taxation and slavery were influenced and shaped by the societies that forged them.

Shaping Behavior with Import Taxes

Among the New England colonies, only Massachusetts and Rhode Island, with their more active involvement in the slave trade, availed themselves of taxation as a tool to raise revenue while simultaneously creating financial incentives that encouraged the importation of White servants rather than enslaved Blacks and Native Americans. In contrast, having played "relatively minor roles" in the slave trade, Connecticut and New Hampshire never imposed revenue-raising taxes on the importation of enslaved persons.[43] Indeed, a telling incident occurred in 1732 when New Hampshire's governor relayed to its legislature the royal instructions restricting the enactment of taxes on the importation of enslaved persons—instructions that, as described earlier, South Carolina flouted for nearly a decade but that New Hampshire's governor was determined to heed.[44] The legislature responded by stating that it had "considered his Maj[ties] Instruction relating to an Impost on Negroes & Felons, to which this House answers, that there never was any Duties laid on either, by the Goverm[t], and so few bro't in that it would not be worth the Publick notice, so as to make an act concerning them."[45]

Massachusetts was the first to enact a tax on the importation of enslaved persons, doing so not as a stand-alone measure but as part of an act aimed at deterring interracial sex and procreation. As part of its 1705 "Act for the Better Preventing of a Spurious and Mixt Issue," Massachusetts enacted criminal punishments for "fornication" between Whites and Blacks and, beginning in 1706, imposed a £4 tax on "importing or bringing into this province any negro or negro's, male or female, of what age soever"—ostensibly to deter their importation in favor of "the bringing in of white servants."[46] Whereas South Carolina eventually allowed a portion of its import taxes to be drawn back on reexportation (thereby ensuring the collection of some revenue even on temporary importation), Massachusetts authorized a full refund upon reexportation within one year, upon proof of the enslaved person's sale "in any other plantation"—essentially creating "a free exchange-mart for slavers" as a sidelight to preventing miscegenation.[47] Furthermore, the high risk of mortality for new arrivals in the northern colonies was reflected in the legislature's decision to fully refund the tax "to the purchaser of any negro sold within this province, in case such negro happen to dye within the space of six weeks next after importation."[48] As part of a 1708/9 law authorizing the payment of a £2 bounty to those who imported "male servants, of the kingdom of Great Britain, being between the age of eight and twenty-five years," the import tax on enslaved Blacks was extended to "any Indian slaves, male or female, of what age soever," now making all enslaved labor more costly and discouraging the importation of enslaved Blacks and Native Americans in favor of the importation of White men, whose labor was temporarily subsidized.[49]

As happened elsewhere, the Massachusetts tax gave rise to smuggling aimed at avoiding payment.[50] To counter smuggling, the legislature first considered a bill for "An Act for the Encouraging the Importation of White Male Servants, and the preventing the Clandestine bringing in of Negroes, and Molatto's" in 1718; however, that bill died after a second reading.[51] Faced with a persistent problem, the legislature succeeded a decade later in creating steep fines for noncompliance.[52] After expiration in 1735, these enforcement provisions were revived in 1738/9 for an additional ten years, notwithstanding the royal instructions received in 1732 discountenancing import taxes like those imposed by Massachusetts.[53] Although the import tax was never formally repealed, subsequent events indicate that it came to be considered "expired or obsolete."[54]

Shortly after Massachusetts enacted its tax, Rhode Island enacted a £3 tax on the importation of enslaved Blacks in 1708.[55] The legislation aimed to prevent the "Dangers And Inconvenencies" that had been occasioned "by purchasing of Negros Lately Imported into this Collony being yᵉ worst Sort of Negros, Som Sent for murder Som for thifing Som Runaway & most Impodent Lame & Distempred which proves much to yᵉ Damage And Loss of Several Persons purchasing of Such Besides feares of putting in practis Inhuman And murderous Designes as they have bene Accustomed unto."[56] Like Massachusetts, Rhode Island initially authorized a full refund of the tax on reexportation; however, within months, the legislature reversed course and eliminated the drawback, obviously prizing revenue more than encouragement of through trafficking.[57] In 1711/2, Rhode Island instituted a £2 tax on the importation of enslaved Native Americans and, explaining that "the bringing of Negroes into this Colony, discourages the Importing of White Servants herein, and may in time prove Prejudicial to the Inhabitants, if not timely discouraged," strengthened the operation of the import tax to combat evasion through smuggling.[58] Yet, despite the professed desire to discourage the importation of enslaved labor and replace it with untaxed White labor, the legislature carved out an exemption for enslaved Blacks imported directly from Africa, perhaps to maintain a favorable balance of trade or to "mitigate England's opposition to slave tariffs."[59]

Three years later, the Rhode Island legislature again felt compelled to strengthen the operation of the import tax and now specified the use to which the revenue would be put.[60] All revenue already on hand from the tax as well as one-half of the revenue raised during the following seven years was given to the town of Newport for paving roads.[61] An additional £60 was dedicated to "erecting of a substantial bridge over Potowomut river."[62] In 1729, the Assembly once again specified the uses to which the import tax revenue would be dedicated, with one-half being given to Newport to pave and repair roads and the other half being used "towards the Support, Repairing and Amending the great Bridges on the Main, in the Country-Roads."[63] Taken together, these actions indicate how the import tax served as an important revenue-generating measure that benefited the public—not by attracting Whites to better control and subjugate an enslaved Black majority as occurred in South Carolina but by funding infrastructure projects: "The streets of Newport were paved and its bridges and country roads mended through the duties collected on slave imports. In many ways, the business of slavery literally built Rhode Island."[64] Nevertheless, in contrast to South Carolina and Massachusetts, Rhode Island repealed its import tax in 1732 after receiving the same royal instructions sent to other colonies restricting the imposition of import taxes on enslaved Blacks.[65]

Punitive Taxation to End the Trade in Enslaved Native Americans

In 1712, spurred by concerns associated with the importation of Native American war captives from the Carolinas (see chapter 1), Massachusetts banned the trade in enslaved Native Americans.[66] The legislation's preamble explained,

> WHEREAS divers conspiracies, outrages, barbarities, murders, burglaries, thefts, and other notorious crimes and enormities, at sundry times, and especially of late, have been perpetrated and committed by Indians and

other slaves within several of her majestie's plantations in America, being of a malicious, surley and revengeful spirit, rude and insolent in their behaviour, and very ungovernable, the over-great number and increase whereof within this province is likely to prove of pernicious and fatal consequence to her majestie's subjects and interest here, unless speedily remedied, and is a discouragement to the importation of white Christian servants, this province being differently circumstanced from the plantations in the islands, and having great numbers of the Indian natives of the country within and about them, and at this time under the sorrowful effects of their rebellion and hostilities,—*Be it therefore enacted . . .*[67]

Given the threat posed by continued importation of enslaved Native Americans, the act decreed that Native Americans imported after its publication would "be forfeited to her majesty for and towards the support of the government," unless a bond were posted to secure reexportation within one month.[68] In 1715, Connecticut and Rhode Island enacted like prohibitions.[69]

In 1714, New Hampshire passed an identically titled "Act Prohibiting the Importation or Bringing into This Province Any Indian Servant or Slaves," with a preamble taken nearly verbatim from the Massachusetts legislation. In its operation, however, this act differed markedly from Massachusetts's direct prohibition against the trade in enslaved Native Americans.[70] Notwithstanding its title, the legislation contained no actual prohibition at all, and unlike the bans enacted in the other New England colonies, it did not mandate the forfeiture of enslaved Native Americans on importation. Instead, the New Hampshire act required the importer of "All Indians, Male or ffemale or what age Soever" to "fforfeit to Her Majestie for the Support of the Government the sume of Tenn pounds per head."[71] In effect, New Hampshire chose a prohibitive tax on the importation of enslaved Native Americans as an alternative to direct prohibition of the trade.[72]

Punitive Taxation to Abolish the Slave Trade

Near the end of the colonial period, the New England colonies again illustrated the interchangeability of punitive taxation and direct prohibitions as deterrents to harmful behavior. Acting when the winds had shifted against the institution of slavery—but always with their own self-interest firmly in mind—Connecticut, Rhode Island, and Massachusetts all took steps toward abolishing the slave trade. As occurred earlier in the efforts to ban the trade in enslaved Native Americans, however, these colonies differed in their choices between direct prohibitions and punitive taxation as the means for abolishing the slave trade.

In 1774, amid growing antislavery activity among the colony's Quaker population and inspired by the dissonance between revolutionary rhetoric regarding the colonists' fight for freedom and liberty and the denial of that same freedom and liberty to the enslaved, Rhode Island prohibited the importation of enslaved Blacks—subject, however, to significant caveats.[73] Replicating (instead of eliminating) the dissonance that troubled the legislature, the act specifically exempted (1) those who were traveling through Rhode Island; (2) those who were coming from other British colonies "with an Intention to settle or reside, for a Number of Years"; (3) enslaved Blacks on Rhode Island ships who were taken from Africa to the West Indies but, unable to be sold there, were transported to Rhode Island (but only so long as they were reexported within one year); and (4) enslaved Blacks being transported on Rhode Island ships at the time of the ban's enactment.[74]

The latter two exemptions clearly reflect the importance of the slave trade to Rhode Island's economy.[75] As it has been observed, "The business of slavery, as distinct from the institution of slavery, allowed New England to become an economic powerhouse without ever producing a staple or cash crop."[76] Indeed, at the time the ban was passed, "nearly 66 percent of Newport slaveholders were . . . directly involved in the West Indian and Atlantic slave trades. They owned slaving vessels, imported molasses and rum, and supplied the West Indies with basic necessities such as candles, timber, and foodstuffs. Moreover, Rhode Island slave traders, who purchased African slaves with locally distilled rum, were responsible for more than 60 percent of all the North American traffic in slaves."[77] Rhode Islanders' economic self-interest obviously trumped their sense of justice.

Also in 1774, Connecticut banned the importation of enslaved persons—whether "Indian, Negro, or Molatto"—subject to a £100 penalty.[78] Unlike the Rhode Island legislation, the succinct preamble to Connecticut's ban made no mention of swirling antislavery sentiment, instead grounding its ban in the self-interested concern that "the Increase of Slaves in this Colony is injurious to the Poor, and inconvenient."[79] What the legislature left unsaid was that increasing Connecticut's enslaved population would be injurious to the *free White* poor and inconvenient for the *free White* majority—the impact of slavery on the enslaved did not even rise to the level of an afterthought.

Legislative moves to end the slave trade in Massachusetts began earlier but were less successful than in Connecticut or Rhode Island. Nevertheless, those moves demonstrate how heavy import taxes were seen as an effective substitute for direct prohibitions against the slave trade. Furthermore, the moves to end the slave trade in Massachusetts underscore how the New England colonies mixed moral objections with self-interested concern about the welfare of the White majority when curtailing the slave trade.[80]

In 1764, the Massachusetts House of Representatives created "a Committee to take under Consideration the Affair of Importation of Slaves, and to project some method to prevent the same for the future."[81] A bill titled "An Act to prevent the increase of Slaves within this Province" was drafted and read twice but died when it was denied a third reading.[82] Then in 1767, after first considering bills to "prevent[] the Importation of Slaves into this Province" and "to prevent the unwarrantable and unusual Practice or Custom of inslaving Mankind in this Province, and the importation of Slaves into the same," the House decided to let "the Matter subside" and instead form "a Committee to bring in a Bill for laying a Duty of Impost on Slaves imported into this Province."[83] A bill was drafted and passed by the House but died amid disagreement over changes proposed by the Council.[84] The surviving text of the bill reveals that its rationale was not grounded in a principled stand against slavery but rather in the notion that "the Importation of Slaves from Africa and Other Parts into this Province has Proved detrimental to the Publick, as it tends to Prevent & Discourage the Introduction of Useful Settlers & Inhabitants from Europe."[85] To deter the slave trade, the bill would have imposed a prohibitive tax—the rate was originally set at £100, but that number was struck through in the surviving draft and a still-hefty £40 inserted in its place.[86]

The effort to end the slave trade was renewed in 1771, when the Massachusetts legislature passed a bill to prevent the importation of enslaved persons from Africa.[87] The governor refused to approve the bill out of concern that it would contravene royal instructions and because he doubted "whether the chief motive to this Bill which, it is said, was a scruple upon the minds of the People in many parts of the province of the lawfulness, in a meerly moral respect, of so great a restraint of Liberty, was well founded."[88] In 1773, the House again considered bills to prevent the importation of enslaved persons at a time when Blacks were petitioning the government to end their enslavement and when sentiment was turning against the slave trade—with public support being voiced for the enactment of either direct prohibitions or heavy taxes to curtail the slave trade.[89] These matters were carried over to 1774, when the legislature twice passed bills that were broadly similar to the 1767 import tax legislation but styled as imposing fines (rather than taxes) on importers of enslaved persons, perhaps to convey a greater sense of moral condemnation; however, neither of those bills received the governor's assent.[90]

Reflection

Demonstrating how taxation is an expression of societal values rather than a cut-and-dried matter of economics, this chapter's exploration of the relationship between taxation and slavery in the New England colonies contains both echoes of and significant points of difference from part 1's exploration of the relationship between taxation and slavery in South Carolina. Most saliently, with much-smaller enslaved populations, the New England colonies cobbled together far less comprehensive and far less draconian slave codes than South Carolina did. Although these slave codes often prescribed severe corporal punishments, they never resorted to the death penalty as a means of terrorizing the enslaved population in the way that South Carolina did. Accordingly, none of the New England colonies created slaveholder compensation schemes akin to South Carolina's. Thus, a central and enduring link between taxation and slavery in South Carolina's slave society was absent from New England's societies with slaves.

But like South Carolina, the New England colonies had to confront the treatment of enslaved persons when crafting their taxes on polls and estates. South Carolina consistently treated the enslaved as a form of property for tax purposes, lumping them together with land to form the core of the property tax base each year. In contrast, after first treating the enslaved as people subject to poll tax and at a time when the two colonies were piecing their dehumanizing slave codes together, Massachusetts and New Hampshire decided to reserve the poll tax for White men and to lump the enslaved together with livestock under their property taxes. Rhode Island did not define its property tax base at the colonial level until the late seventeenth century; however, once it did, it likewise treated the enslaved as property. Connecticut, on the other hand, never ceased formally treating the enslaved as persons subject to poll tax. Yet, in substance, Connecticut always taxed the enslaved as property because payment of the tax never fell on the enslaved; rather, slaveholders were required to pay the tax as the persons who "owned" and legally controlled their wealth-generating labor power. Overall, the New England colonies evinced less conviction than South Carolina did in treating the enslaved as property for tax purposes, demonstrating how tax law was neither different nor detached from other areas of New England law in its alternation between treating enslaved persons as people or property.

Similarly, several of the New England colonies employed taxation as a lever for manipulating the racial balance of their populations— but again with important differences at both the regional and colonial levels. Import taxation, a commonly employed tool in South Carolina, was not used at all by Connecticut and not routinely used by New Hampshire to shape the racial balance of their populations due to their limited direct role in the slave trade. As a result, Connecticut was an outlier in both New England and the American colonies more generally because it did not formally mark the enslaved as property under either its taxes on polls and estates or its import tax legislation. It is not, however, possible to say whether this was a conscious choice or merely serendipity (e.g., a combination of inertia in the case of the poll tax and of Connecticut's generally sparing reliance on indirect taxation in the case of import taxes).[91]

With Massachusetts's and Rhode Island's more active roles in the slave trade, they both imposed taxes on the importation of enslaved persons. Their taxes, like South Carolina's, raised revenue while creating financial incentives to dampen the importation of enslaved Blacks and Native Americans and encourage the importation of White labor in their place—whether out of concern about miscegenation, the poor quality of imported enslaved labor, or the dangers posed by the enslaved population. Interestingly, Massachusetts and Rhode Island took different paths when addressing the reexportation of enslaved persons. Massachusetts chose to turn its harbors into a free-trade zone for slave traders by fully refunding its import tax upon reexportation. Rhode Island initially embraced Massachusetts's approach but quickly reversed course and eliminated its drawback, ensuring the collection of the full tax even upon prompt reexportation. Rhode Island then deployed the revenue raised from these import taxes to build and maintain the colony's infrastructure.

Whereas South Carolina occasionally employed prohibitive taxation to put a hard (but always temporary) brake on the slave trade, the New England colonies took things much further when they turned to taxation to end the slave trade, treating prohibitive taxation as just another tool in the legislative toolbox sitting right beside direct prohibitions against activity deemed harmful to society. Early in the eighteenth century, all four New England colonies ended the trade in enslaved Native Americans because imported Native American war captives from the Carolinas posed a threat to the White majority's personal safety while jeopardizing control of the enslaved population in place. Three of the colonies—Massachusetts, Connecticut, and Rhode Island—enacted prohibitions against the importation of enslaved Native Americans; however, New Hampshire opted instead for a prohibitive tax to stop that trade. Then near the end of the colonial period, Massachusetts, Connecticut, and Rhode Island took steps toward eliminating the slave trade altogether. But again, they diverged in their approaches: both Connecticut and Rhode Island enacted direct prohibitions against the slave trade, while Massachusetts unsuccessfully alternated between direct prohibitions and prohibitive taxation as a means of curtailing the slave trade. Notably, even though these steps were taken at a time when public sentiment in New England had shifted against the institution of slavery, both the tax and nontax moves to abolish the slave trade mixed growing moral objections to slavery with obvious self-interest—whether taking the form of explicit protections for the local economy (Rhode Island), expression of concern for the well-being of Whites (Connecticut), or the desire to influence the racial balance in favor of increasing the White majority (Massachusetts).

* * *

During the colonial period, racism and slavery were present in New England just as they were in South Carolina. Yet, in New England's different social, political, geographic, and economic environment, these evils took on a different shape than they did in South Carolina. Naturally, the different shape that slavery took in New England led to the creation of qualitatively and quantitatively different connections between taxation and slavery there. What is more, those regional differences were accompanied by differences even among the New England colonies with regard to how they used taxation in support of the evils of racism and White supremacy. To further deepen this understanding of the relationship between tax law and society, chapter 5 travels southward to examine the connections between taxation and slavery in the middle colonies.

5

The Middle Colonies

The middle colonies' positioning between North and South shaped the ties established there between taxation and slavery. With larger enslaved populations, the middle colonies forged stronger connections between taxation and slavery than existed in New England. These connections resembled South Carolina's through their deployment of tax law to (1) secure slaveholder cooperation in meting out capital punishment, (2) dehumanize the enslaved by marking them as "property," and (3) manipulate the racial composition of the population to better maintain the enslaved in subjugation. But these connections were not as sturdy as South Carolina's. For instance, as happened in New England, growing opposition to slavery eventually led the middle colonies to turn to taxation as a tool for curtailing the slave trade. In their use of taxation to support and promote slavery—and later to reduce or end the slave trade—the middle colonies invariably tailored their efforts to local conditions, even when the influence of slavery-related events, legislation, and organizing spilled across borders. Through the exploration of the multifaceted ties established between taxation and slavery in the middle colonies, this chapter further illustrates the close relationship between tax law and society, with taxation reflecting both the good and the evil in society.

Slaveholder Compensation

Having already been important to the development of Dutch and Swedish settlements in the area, slavery was present in the middle colonies long before the English takeover in the second half of the seventeenth century.[1] Under English rule, slavery continued to play an important role in the middle colonies' economies, as reflected in the growth of their enslaved populations during the eighteenth century.[2] With larger enslaved populations and greater fear of resistance to bondage, the middle colonies enacted more comprehensive and harsher slave codes than the New England colonies did. Enslaved persons in the middle colonies have therefore been described as "worse off than their brethren in New England" but, paralleling their location between North and South, "somewhat better off than their southern counterparts."[3] The middle colonies all established separate systems of justice for enslaved persons and included the death penalty as a form of punishment in their slave codes, causing them to share South Carolina's concern with securing slaveholder cooperation when the threat of capital punishment—and the destruction of slaveholders' financial investment in enslaved labor—loomed large. To address this concern, all the middle colonies created slaveholder compensation schemes, but each charted a different path when deciding how to use taxation to apply financial grease to the wheels of the legal machinery for killing enslaved persons.

New York

Early in the development of New York's slave code—and perhaps influenced by the experience of transplanted slaveholders from Barbados, who had similarly influenced the writing of South Carolina's slave codes[4]—the colony began a pattern of resorting to capital punishment in response to threats from resistance to bondage. In 1705, New Yorkers feared that enslaved persons from the frontier area of Albany were fleeing north to Canada, both "to the great loss & detriment of the Owner or Owners of Such Negro Slave or Slaves and also of very pernicious Consequence to the whole province" because escapees might provide valuable wartime intelligence to the French.[5] Reacting to these concerns, the legislature mandated the death penalty for escapees found above Saratoga and ordered that the full appraised value of executed escapees "be Rated Assessed and levyed on all and every person & persons having Slave or Slaves" in the city and county of Albany in the same manner as other taxes—which, as described later, meant by reference to the value of slaveholders' real and personal property.[6] To avoid valuation disputes when levying this tax, the legislature required the valuation of "Every Negro Slave male or Female from the Age of ffifteen Years and upwards being fitt for Service at Thirty pounds."[7] By confining the tax to county slaveholders, the 1705 compensation scheme forced slaveholders to internalize this cost of doing business with enslaved labor, much as South Carolina would do more than a decade later. But unlike South Carolina, New York fine-tuned the tax's progressivity by taking into account not only the number of enslaved persons but also the value of slaveholders' other property when levying the tax.

New York's second foray into enacting death penalty legislation was occasioned by "the Execrable and Barberous Murder comitted on the Person and family of William Hallet Junr late of New Town in Queens County."[8] The crime was committed "by an Indian Man Slave, and a Negro Woman, who have murder'd their Master, Mistress and five Children."[9] Both perpetrators were executed, along with two accomplices.[10] In 1708, reacting to these events, which "crossed the line between murder and rebellion,"[11] the legislature mandated the death penalty for "every Negro Indian or other Slave or Slaves . . . who . . . have has or shall Murder or otherwise Kill unles by Misadventure or in Execution of Justice or Conspire or attempt the Death of his her or their Master or Mistress or any other of her Majesties Leige People not being Negroes Mulattos or Slaves."[12] At the same time, the legislature expediently incorporated the 1705 compensation scheme and its tax mechanism by reference, altering it only by capping compensation at £25.[13]

In 1730, New York replaced its piecemeal slave code with comprehensive legislation that would endure for the remainder of the colonial period.[14] The 1730 slave code repeated the list of crimes punishable by death, which had been expanded in the wake of a 1712 insurrection in New York City (see box 5.1), and included a revised slaveholder compensation scheme.[15] Under that revised scheme, holders of executed enslaved persons were compensated a maximum of £25, funded through a tax on the property of taxpayers in the city or county where the enslaved person was convicted and executed.[16] Sending the message that slaveholder compensation provided some public benefit, the 1730 slave code embraced a limited form of redistribution because the tax was no longer imposed solely on slaveholders but on all property owners in the area. Despite two notable instances in which New York's localized slaveholder compensation scheme failed in its operation (see box 5.1), the legislature adhered to that scheme in 1745 when it reimposed the death penalty on escapees from the Albany area during the pendency of renewed hostilities with the French.[17]

Box 5.1. Pleas in New York for Compensation Funded at the Colonial Level

On two notable occasions, New York's localized slaveholder compensation scheme failed in its operation. Each time, those who were affected pleaded with the colonial legislature to provide the compensation authorized by law. While the South Carolina legislature rejected such entreaties, New Yorkers' pleas had some success.

1712 INSURRECTION

In April 1712, more than twenty enslaved persons armed with guns, swords, knives, and hatchets set fire to a building in New York City during the night. When Whites were drawn to the blaze, several of the enslaved fired on them. Although the Whites scattered on hearing the gunfire, the insurrectionists succeeded in killing nine Whites and wounding five or six others. The governor dispatched the militia after the rebels and apprehended all but six of them—those six having killed themselves. According to a June 1712 letter from the governor reporting on the events, the uprising had been occasioned by "some hard usage, they apprehended to have received from their masters."[a]

In all, nineteen enslaved persons were executed. As the governor's letter recounted, "one being a woman with child, her execution by that meanes suspended, some were burnt others hanged, one broke on the wheele, and one hung a live in chains in the town, so that there has been the most exemplary punishment inflicted that could be possibly thought of."[b] The affected slaveholders were entitled to compensation under the 1708 legislation authorizing compensation when executed enslaved persons were convicted of murdering a White person; however, local authorities failed to levy the tax on slaveholders to fund that compensation.[c] In 1712, the affected slaveholders petitioned the governor "to recommend it to the Generall Assembly of this Collony now Sitting to pass a Law to Enforce the payment of the Sumes of money intended to be paid to the Owner or Owners of Such Slaves as

a. Letter from Governor Hunter to the Lords of Trade (June 23, 1712), in 5 DOCUMENTS RELATIVE TO THE COLONIAL HISTORY OF THE STATE OF NEW-YORK 339, 341 (E.B. O'Callaghan ed., 1855).
b. *Id.*
c. Petition of the Owners of the Negro Slaves Executed for the Conspiracy (1712), 58 NEW YORK COLONIAL MANUSCRIPTS 22, *microformed on* New York (Colony) Council Papers, Ser. A1894, Roll 19, N.Y. State Archives.

Should be executed by virtue of An Act made for preventing the Conspiracy of Slaves."[d] The governor's Council recommended that the Assembly enact remedial legislation because "the Justices of the peace have neglected to raise the Sumes of money necessary for the payment of the Slaves so as aforesaid Executed notwithstanding the powers invested for soe doeing by virtue of the Aforesaid Act."[e]

In 1717, as part of a general appropriation bill addressing these and other arrears in payments, the New York legislature authorized the compensation payments set forth in the following table,[f] without naming the executed enslaved persons or providing other identifying details:

Slaveholder	Number executed	Compensation (in ounces of silver)
Rip Van Dam	2	100
John Barbarie	1	50
Walter Thong	1	50
Allanc Jarroet	1	50
Adrian Hoogland's estate	1	50
Peter Fauconier	1	50
Nicolas Rosevelt	1	50
Abraham Provoost	1	50
Isaac Governeur	1	50
Peter Moryne	1	50
John De. Honeur	1	50
Ruth Shepherd	1	50
Cornelia Norwood	1	50
John Cure	1	50
Richard Ray	1	50
David Lyell	1	50
Andrew Stuckey	1	50
Guysbert Van InBurg	1	50

With silver valued at eight shillings per ounce, each slaveholder was paid the equivalent of £20 per executed enslaved person.[g]

d. 1 JOURNAL OF THE LEGISLATIVE COUNCIL OF THE COLONY OF NEW-YORK 344 (1861) [hereinafter COUNCIL JOURNAL].
e. Id.
f. Act of Dec. 23, 1717, ch. 347, 1 COLONIAL LAWS OF NEW YORK FROM THE YEAR 1664 TO THE REVOLUTION 938, 983–84 (1896) [hereinafter N.Y. LAWS].
g. Act of Sept. 4, 1714, ch. 280, 1 N.Y. LAWS, supra note f, at 815, 819.

In the wake of this insurrection, the legislature expanded the slave code's list of crimes punishable by death.[h] Despite being debated when the slaveholders' petition for compensation was submitted to the governor and considered by the Council, that December 1712 legislation neglected to mention compensation for the holders of executed enslaved persons. When New York consolidated its slave code in 1730, the legislature corrected this omission.[i]

1741 CONSPIRACY

"The events of 1712 greatly increased suspicion and set the stage for a bloody panic a generation later, when the slaves were suspected of conspiring to burn New York City and massacre the white population."[j] This panic resulted in the execution of more than thirty enslaved persons and the deportation of seventy others to the even worse conditions of slavery in the Caribbean.[k] On this occasion, it was not slaveholders but the New York City government that petitioned for relief:

> That besides the great Loss and Damages, which the City and its Inhabitants have sustained, by the late wicked Conspiracy of the Negroes, a Demand is now made on the Corporation for the Money, allowed by a Law for Slaves executed in it, and for the Execution of them; which the said Corporation is in no Manner of Ways able to discharge, and that it would add a very great Hardship on the Inhabitants to lay it on them, as they have already so greatly suffered by the said Conspiracy; and therefore, pray the Premisses may be taken into Consideration, and order the Payment for the said Negroes, Trials and Executions, out of some of the publick Funds of the Province, or grant such other Relief, as shall seem just and reasonable.[l]

The Assembly ordered the petition to be considered at its next meeting; however, no record exists of any legislative action on the petition.

---

h. Act of Dec. 10, 1712, ch. 250, 1 N.Y. LAWS, *supra* note f, at 761, 765.

i. *See* N.Y.C. Chamberlain, Account Book: 1706–1736, BV New York City, Chamberlain's Office, N.Y. Hist. Soc'y (including no slaveholder compensation payments for the period when the 1712 legislation was in force but including an entry for 1733/4 after enactment of the 1730 Slave Code).

j. EDGAR J. MCMANUS, A HISTORY OF NEGRO SLAVERY IN NEW YORK 126 (1966).

k. *Id.* at 136.

l. 1 JOURNAL OF THE VOTES AND PROCEEDINGS OF THE GENERAL ASSEMBLY OF THE COLONY OF NEW-YORK 835 (1764) [hereinafter ASSEMBLY JOURNAL]; *see* 5 MINUTES OF THE COMMON COUNCIL OF THE CITY OF NEW YORK 67 (1905).

Nevertheless, just days after receiving the petition, the Assembly did give leave to draft a bill repealing the slaveholder compensation scheme altogether.[m] Although that legislation passed the Assembly, it was rejected by the Council.[n]

---

m. ASSEMBLY JOURNAL, *supra* note *l*, at 836.
n. *Id.* at 838; 1 COUNCIL JOURNAL, *supra* note d, at 810, 812.

New Jersey

In 1704, the newly reunified New Jersey legislature consolidated and expanded the colony's legislation regulating slavery.[18] Notwithstanding the governor's enthusiastic endorsement, the queen disallowed that legislation in 1709 on the basis of objections from the Board of Trade regarding the imposition of "inhumane penalties on negroes."[19] Before the act's disallowance, the governor had encouraged the legislature to supplement it with a slaveholder compensation scheme as a means of instilling terror: "I have Received Information from very good hands that the Negroes are grown very Insolent and Committ great Enormities, the best Expedient I can Recommend to you in that case is the passing a law to Settle a price upon the head of every Negroe who Shall be put to death in pursuance of the Law, to be paid to the owner of every such Negro, this I hope will be a means to frighten them from Committing any the like Enormities for the future."[20]

After a failed attempt in 1710/1, the legislature succeeded in enacting replacement legislation in 1713/4 when it reconvened after a two-year hiatus.[21] Drawing heavily from the legislation passed in New York in 1712, New Jersey established a separate criminal justice system for enslaved persons; mandated the death penalty for the same litany of crimes as in New York; and heeding the governor's advice, created a slaveholder compensation scheme patterned after New York's 1705 scheme.[22] The preamble to the compensation scheme echoes the concerns so often expressed by the South Carolina legislature:

And Whereas such Negro, Indian or Mullatto Slave so put to Death, will be a great Loss to the Owner of the same, who was no ways assisting, Countenancing or abetting his said Slave in the mischief done and perpetrated by the said Slave, and may induce the owner to transport the said slave out of the Province, by which means the said Slave will be secured from the Punishment to be inflicted on him for his said Crime, and other Negro, Indian or Mullatto Slaves encouraged to do the like Mischief, in hopes of the same security. For preventing of which for the future, and that the owner of any Indian or Mullatto Slave may not be under any temptation of with-drawing and securing said Slave from the prosecution of Justice, *Be it Enacted . . .*[23]

Under New Jersey's compensation scheme, slaveholders were paid £30 for every executed enslaved man and £20 for every executed enslaved woman.[24] To fund compensation, the justices of the peace in the county where the crime was committed imposed a tax on local slaveholders on the basis of a list of able-bodied enslaved persons in the area between the ages of fourteen and fifty, which the constable of each town was now annually required to file with the Court of General Quarter Sessions.[25] The New Jersey scheme, like the New York scheme it was patterned after, forced local slaveholders to internalize this cost of doing business with enslaved labor. But departing from New York's approach and embracing the approach that South Carolina would take a few years later, New Jersey levied its tax solely by reference to the number of enslaved persons held rather than more progressively distributing the tax burden on the basis of slaveholders' overall wealth. Evidence of the imposition of these taxes exists among surviving records; however, as described in box 5.2, the justices of the peace and freeholders in New Jersey were less than assiduous in recording the taxes levied to fund slaveholder compensation payments.

Box 5.2. Slaveholder Compensation Payments in Bergen County, New Jersey

Enslaved Blacks were a key source of labor in the primarily Dutch area of Bergen County, New Jersey.[a] Indeed, New Jersey's few colonial censuses reveal that Bergen County consistently had the highest concentration of Blacks in the colony.[b] During the period that New Jersey's slaveholder

a. GRAHAM RUSSELL HODGES, ROOT & BRANCH: AFRICAN AMERICANS IN NEW YORK & EAST JERSEY, 1613–1863, at 77, 107 (1999).
b. EVARTS B. GREENE & VIRGINIA D. HARRINGTON, AMERICAN POPULATION BEFORE THE FEDERAL CENSUS OF 1790, at 109–11 (1932).

compensation scheme was in force, the minutes of the Bergen County justices and freeholders record seven death sentences for enslaved persons; however, those minutes contain only a single order imposing the tax to fund slaveholder compensation.[c]

In that exceptional case, Harry was convicted in December 1731 of poisoning Colonel William Provoost's enslaved man Sepeo and of threatening to murder his own holder, Garret Hoppe.[d] "Justice" was swift: Harry allegedly poisoned Sepeo on November 25; Sepeo died on December 1; Harry was tried and convicted on December 13 (a seemingly perfunctory trial given that seventeen witnesses were summoned to testify but no testimony was recorded); and Harry was executed the following day. And that swift "justice" was far from impartially administered: Provoost, the victim's holder, served both as the justice of the peace who issued the arrest warrant and as a member of the panel that found Harry guilty.

Pursuant to the slaveholder compensation scheme (but showing far less haste than they did in putting Harry to death), the justices of the peace met at the aptly named New Barbadoes (present-day Hackensack, New Jersey) on April 26, 1732, to tally up the compensation that was due to Hoppe (£30) along with the costs of prosecution and execution (£15 10s). The justices ordered the county constables to collect a tax of "Six Shillings p^r head"—in other words, six shillings per enslaved person held by each of Bergen County's slaveholders—to defray the payment to Hoppe and the other costs associated with Harry's case. The constables were given one month to collect the taxes and pay them over to William Provoost—who, adding to his already deep involvement in the affair, had been appointed to make the payments to Hoppe and others.

c. Minutes of the Justices and Freeholders of Bergen County, 1715–1794, at 24–28, 36–39, 44–47, 53–59, 122–24, Board of Chosen Freeholders Records: Minutes: 1715–1795, Box 1, Bergen Cnty. Dep't of Parks, Div. of Cultural & Hist. Affs. Archives [hereinafter Minutes]. The Court of Quarter Sessions also appears to have tried criminal cases involving enslaved persons prior to repeal of the slaveholder compensation scheme. *See* HENRY SCOFIELD COOLEY, A STUDY OF SLAVERY IN NEW JERSEY 40 n.1 (1896). Nonetheless, on the basis of my discussions with the archivist, court personnel, and clerk's office personnel, the fragmentary records from that court no longer appear to be held by Bergen County. *Cf.* HIST. RECS. SURV., WORKS PROGRESS ADMIN., INVENTORY OF THE COUNTY ARCHIVES OF NEW JERSEY: BERGEN COUNTY 91–94 (1939); William Nelson, *Report on the Extent and Condition of the Records of Bergen County, in* 3 [2d Ser.] PROCEEDINGS OF THE NEW JERSEY HISTORICAL SOCIETY 174, 175 (1874).

d. Minutes, *supra* note c, at 24–28.

The only other mention of slaveholder compensation in the Bergen County records concerns problems with the administration of the "negro tax" that funded slaveholder compensation payments. In October 1752, the minutes of the justices and freeholders contain an oblique reference to the compensation paid some seven years earlier to the slaveholders Johonnes Van Houten and Eden Sipp following the execution in May 1744 of their enslaved men Ian and Tom for poisonings.[e] Noting (but not fully explaining) problems with the administration of the tax to fund these compensation payments, the justices and freeholders indicated that they "Do Agree that all those persons that have Over paid In the Negroes Tax In the Year 1744 May Come to the County Collector then In post and Receive all What they have Over paid And then the Charges that is Recrued by Executing the Said Negroes Shall be Levyed Upon the Whole County."[f]

---

e. *Id.* at 53–59.
f. *Id.* at 71.

In 1768, amid a climate of growing antislavery sentiment, New Jersey overhauled its system of criminal punishment for enslaved persons. The legislature eliminated the separate slave courts; expanded the list of crimes punishable by death; and apparently no longer convinced of slaveholders' lack of complicity or of the need for compensation to secure their cooperation in bringing the enslaved to justice, repealed the slaveholder compensation scheme that had been in operation for half a century.[26] Lending support to the notion that slaveholders were no longer seen as free of culpability when their enslaved persons committed crimes, New Jersey now required the individual slaveholder to fully absorb this cost of doing business with enslaved labor. After benefiting from the compensation scheme for more than fifty years, slaveholders surely felt a pronounced financial incentive to alter their behavior to avoid being saddled with a tax burden that had previously been distributed among all county slaveholders.

Pennsylvania

In 1700, the legislature that then governed both Pennsylvania and Delaware created a separate court system for trial and punishment of enslaved persons and mandated the imposition of the death penalty upon conviction for "rape or ravishment upon any white woman or maid, or . . . murder, buggery or burglary."[27] In January 1705/6, on the eve of this legislation's disallowance, Pennsylvania's now separate legislature enacted replacement legislation that governed the trial and punishment of enslaved persons for the remainder of the colonial period.[28]

But neither the original nor the replacement legislation included a mechanism for compensating the holders of executed enslaved persons. In 1707/8, the lack of compensation led to a complaint from the slaveholders William Righton and Robert Grace—who specifically noted its existence elsewhere—accompanied by a commutation request:

> That Tony a Negro the Slave to your Peticon[r]. William Righton, Quashy a Negro the Slave of yo[r] Pet[r]. Robert Grace were lately at a Special Court charged & convicted ffor the ffeloniously & Burglarly breaking and en-tring the Dwelling house of Ann Budd Widow & taking thence divers goods & are now under Sentence of Death for the Same. But forasmuch as it will be very great damage to yo[r] Pet[rs]. Should their said Slaves Suffer Death there being no provision made for a competent Restitution to the Owners of such Slaves being Offenders in such cases as is usual in other Governments Yo[r] Pet[rs]. humbly beg your Honour will be pleased to grant your pardon & mercy in the premises. And that they may be Suffer'd to transport the said Negroes out of this Governm[t] & inflict such Corporal punishm[t] as may be thought requisite for a Terror & Example to others of their Colour w[ch] yo[r] peticon[rs] will cause to be duly executed upon them.[29]

The governor referred this petition to the Provincial Council. The Council acceded to the commutation request and took up the invitation to detail the punishment the two men would suffer before being sold outside the colony; however, no steps were taken to provide compensation to slaveholders in future cases.[30]

The lack of compensation led not only to complaints but also to evasion of the law: "It too often happens that negroes commit felonies and other heinous crimes which by the laws of this province are punishable by death, but the loss in such case falling wholly on the owner is so great a hardship that sometimes may induce him to conceal such crimes or to convey his negro to some other place and so suffer him to escape justice, to the ill example of others to commit the like offenses."[31] In 1725/6, the legislature remedied this situation by requiring the slave court to value every executed enslaved person, "which value by them set shall be allowed and paid to the owner out of the duties, fines and penalties arising from this and one other act laying a duty on negroes imported into this province and no otherways, and the provincial treasurer is hereby empowered and required to pay the same by order under the said justices' hands, which said order they are hereby required to make, seal and deliver to the owner of any negro executed."[32]

The Pennsylvania slaveholder compensation scheme was thus funded through a combination of revenue raised from taxes on the importation of enslaved Blacks and fines and penalties imposed on free Blacks and Whites who transgressed the slave code. Having chosen to fund slaveholder compensation at the provincial rather than the local level (as New York and New Jersey did), it is unsurprising that Pennsylvania turned to import tax revenue as the primary source of funding. Before enacting its compensation scheme, Pennsylvania had ceased imposing a colonial-level property tax and instead turned to relying on "imposts, excises, and nontax revenues"—only reinstating the property tax decades later to meet wartime revenue demands.[33]

But the import tax did not prove to be a stable source of revenue. As described later, Pennsylvania acceded to the pressure that England soon placed on all American colonies and ceased collecting the import tax in the 1730s. Collection of the tax did not resume until the early 1760s, when it was reimposed to deter the importation of enslaved Blacks. Nevertheless, Pennsylvania had forged an inextricable link between the tax revenue raised from trafficking in enslaved Blacks and the monetary cost of ensuring the smooth operation of the colony's slave code—a connection that was reactivated as soon as collection of the import tax resumed. Pennsylvania thus took a different view from New York and New Jersey regarding who benefited from—and, in turn, should share in defraying the cost of—slaveholder compensation. Not confining ostensible beneficiaries to slaveholders, the Pennsylvania legislature also included the slave traders who made slaveholding possible. In effect, the legislature created a closed loop in which trafficking enslaved Blacks to Pennsylvania generated the revenue used to terrorize and control both the new arrivals and those who were already held in bondage.

Delaware

The three "lower counties" on the Delaware River were granted their own legislature in 1704.[34] Yet, Delaware did not enact its own slave code until 1726, responding to "the dramatic increase in the slave population after the end of Queen Anne's War in 1713."[35] Following Pennsylvania's lead, Delaware established separate courts for trying enslaved Blacks, authorized the death penalty for the same litany of crimes as Pennsylvania, and created a slaveholder compensation scheme.[36]

But when Delaware created its slaveholder compensation scheme, it took a different path than Pennsylvania did. Rather than fully indemnifying slaveholders, Delaware provided compensation equal to two-thirds of the value of an executed enslaved person.[37] Furthermore, Delaware could not replicate Pennsylvania's choice to fund slaveholder compensation primarily with import taxes because, as described later, Delaware never taxed the importation of enslaved persons. Instead, Delaware chose a hybrid approach that required the individual slaveholder to bear a portion of the loss but then spread the majority of the loss more broadly by having it paid "out of the public levy, to be raised in the same manner as the county levies."[38] Like South Carolina's Tax-Acts, these county-level property taxes— which, as described later, were the only direct taxes regularly imposed in Delaware during the colonial period—maintained a tight connection between taxing and spending. Each county set the annual property tax rate based on the local levy court's audit of existing public debts and estimated future expenditures.[39] As a result, the portion of slaveholders' economic losses that was borne by county taxpayers directly determined the size of their annual property tax burden. Concomitantly, the portion of the loss that was not redistributed among county taxpayers was borne by the affected slaveholder, imposing a sizeable additional tax that created an incentive to take steps to prevent the commission of capital crimes.

Unfortunately, neither Pennsylvania nor Delaware has tax records documenting slaveholder compensation payments as extensive as South Carolina's. Nonetheless, as described in box 5.3, the records that do exist provide a glimpse of life for the enslaved and those who held them in bondage.

Box 5.3. Slaveholder Compensation Payments in Pennsylvania
and Delaware

PENNSYLVANIA

In Pennsylvania, there are records of a handful of slaveholder compensation payments made in the late colonial period. Evidence of these payments can be found in the provincial treasurer's account books and in the legislature's regular audits of the colony's public accounts, where receipts from the import tax on enslaved Blacks were reported together with slaveholder compensation payments made from those funds. In contrast, audits from the 1720s and 1730s (i.e., before Pennsylvania temporarily ceased collecting its import tax) detail the revenue collected and even drawback payments made on reexportation but make no mention of slaveholder compensation payments.[a]

As detailed in the appendix (table A.2), the legislature's 1763–74 audits reveal only eight slaveholder compensation payments made in Pennsylvania.[b] The total compensation paid was £575, ranging from £55 to £120 per enslaved person executed. Although the audit reports are short on detail, it is sometimes possible to ascertain the circumstances surrounding a payment. For instance, the 1763 payments to Daniel Richards and John Philips's estate stemmed from the execution of their enslaved men Joe and Caspar for burglary. After conviction and before execution, "several petitions from the Inhabitants of Philadelphia" were submitted to the governor requesting a reprieve for Joe and Caspar; however, "the Council were unanimously of Opinion, that as there appeared no particular Circumstances in the case of either of the said two unhappy Criminals, which rendered them proper Objects of the Governor's mercy and favour, they could not advise him to interpose between the Laws and the

---

a. 3 VOTES AND PROCEEDINGS OF THE HOUSE OF REPRESENTATIVES OF THE PROVINCE OF PENNSYLVANIA 18, 29–30, 39, 57, 91, 104, 119, 160, 176, 193, 213 (1754) [hereinafter PA. HOUSE JOURNAL]; 5 *id.* at 278, 366, 430; 6 *id.* at 99, 284, 298, 438, 439, 536; Provincial Accounts of Pennsylvania (1758–1764), Smith Family Papers, Ser. I(b), Box 3, Folder 20, at 15, Hist. Soc'y of Pa.; Samuel Preston Moore Account Books (Oct. 17, 1764 & May 13, 1768), Collection LCP.in.HSP235, Hist. Soc'y of Pa.; Province of Pennsylvania Daybook (of Owen Jones, Sr.) (1768–1776), Jones Family Papers, vol. 19, Hist. Soc'y of Pa.
b. *See supra* note a.

Execution of them on this occasion, and the Governor was pleased to join with them in Opinion."[c]

Details regarding the 1768 compensation payment to James Burd stemming from the execution of Jem can be found in letters written by Burd's son-in-law, the attorney Jasper Yeates, which include a secondhand recounting of Jem's confrontation with his own mortality in the face of a justice system—and society—infected with racism. On March 7, 1768, Yeates wrote Edward Shippen, Burd's brother-in-law and himself a distinguished attorney (Yeates and Shippen served together on the Pennsylvania Supreme Court after the Revolutionary War),

> I have just returned from Middletown, whither I went on hearing the melancholy affair which lately happened there through the imprudence of some waggoners, & the villainy of Mr. Burd's Negroe, Jem. From the depositions forwarded you by the coroner, you will perceive the first origin of the quarrel which terminated in the death of Henry Corson, & the commitment of the perpetrator of the fact to this gaol. I would not attempt to excuse or palliate the offence of the negro, but am of opinion, if he had not been pushed to the last extremity he would not have committed the fatal deed. I was present at Mr Slough's holding his inquest, & was not a little surprized from the evidence adduced to the jury, that they found the facts stated in the inquisition. The first assault appeared from the testimony to have been made by the deceased, & tho' jem behaved rudely & saucily yet he was not proved to have formed any intention of doing mischief, until greatly provoked. The prejudices commonly entertained against slaves gave rise I fancy, to this verdict of the jury, added to the bad character the fellow generally bore.[d]

On March 23, Yeates wrote Burd with details regarding the upcoming trial: "I believe Jem expects to die. I saw him in Gaol, and he appears penitent, & heartily sorry for the Fact. The Dutch Calvinist Minister has paid him one or three Visits in his Confinement, & is endeavouring to prepare the poor unhappy Creature for another State of Existence."[e] The day after the trial, Yeates wrote Shippen to notify him that Jem had been

c. 9 Minutes of the Provincial Council of Pennsylvania 6 (1852).
d. Letter from J. Yeates to Edward Shippen (Mar. 7, 1768), *microformed on* Transcripts (2d roll), MG-30, Burd-Shippen Family Collection 1704–1900, Roll No. 7173, Pa. State Archives.
e. Letter from J. Yeates to J. Burd (Mar. 23, 1768), *microformed on* Transcripts, *supra* note d.

convicted and that Yeates had "got the justices' & freeholders' valuation of Jem, under their hands, being £90. & will procure an order on the provincial treasurer after his execution."[f] Yeates went on to explain, "From the evidence at the trial there appeared strong presumptive proof of malice against the unfortunate Corson previous to any stroke given on either side, or even assault:—the testimony of the waggoners who were present at the beginning of the quarrel, & who did not attend at the coroner's holding his inquisition sets the matter in a somewhat different light from what appeared before to be the case; and the general bad character of the negroe completed his unhappy fate." Yeates enclosed with his letter a letter from the court to the governor apprising the governor of Jem's conviction for the "felony & murder on Henry Corson in having given him two mortal wounds with a drawn knife, of which he shortly after died" and indicating that the execution had been set for April 18. The provincial treasurer registered the compensation payment to Burd on May 13.

In 1771, demonstrating slaveholders' persistence in gaining access to redistributive taxing mechanisms to spread their losses, Joseph Cook pressed a claim for compensation to the Pennsylvania legislature even though that claim did not fall within the parameters of the law:

> A Petition from *Joseph Cook*, of the County of *Cumberland*, was presented to the House and read, setting forth, that on the Twenty-fifth Day of *October* last the Petitioner's Barn, two Stables and a Sheep-House were destroyed by Fire;—that the Barn was full of Grain, and that four Barracks of Grain adjoining it were also consumed;—that the Petitioner's Loss on this Occasion amounted to at least *Two Hundred Pounds* lawful Money of this Province; that the Fire was willfully kindled by a certain Negroe (named *Candy*) belonging to the Petitioner, as appeared by the said Negroe's own voluntary Confession;—that immediately after committing the Crime, he fled into the Woods and concealed himself there two or three Weeks, during which Time his Feet and Ankles were so severely frostbitten, that had he continued but a very few Days longer so exposed to the Weather he must unavoidably have perished;—that after his Return, he was kept in the Petitioner's House, where, notwithstanding all proper Measures were taken for his Recovery, he died on the Eighth Day of *December* following, before

---

f. Letter from J. Yeates to E. Shippen (Apr. 5, 1768), *microformed on* Transcripts, *supra* note d.

a Commission could be obtained to try him for the Crime of which he had confessed himself guilty;—that the Petitioner cannot recover the Value of the said Negroe in the Mode directed by the Act of Assembly for the Trial of Negroes, and has no Prospect of ever receiving it, unless by an Application to the Honourable House, he therefore prays they would be pleased to take the Premises into Consideration, and give him such Compensation for the Loss of his said Negroe as they may think reasonable.[g]

One can only wonder whether the care taken to help Candy recover from hypothermia was motivated by human compassion or by a desire to seek criminal punishment followed by a payment of slaveholder compensation—not to mention whether the treatment Candy received prior to the arson was of a different character and had motivated his brazen act of resistance. The legislature debated Cook's petition on several occasions without ever reaching a recorded decision.[h]

DELAWARE

The surviving tax records in Delaware are fragmentary; however, there is evidence of slaveholder compensation payments in the minutes of the county levy courts. For instance, in 1742, the Sussex County Levy Court authorized a £14 payment to James Collet's estate "for 2/3 of the apprais'd Value of Negro Dick."[i] In 1770, the Kent County Levy Court authorized a £40 payment to Susannah Blundel, executrix for the estate of James Blundel, which represented "two thirds of the value of Negro Charles who was convicted & Executed for a Rape."[j] Charles had been valued at £60 by the court when it convicted him of "Committing a Rape on the Body of Mary Crippin a White Woman."[k] Then, in 1773, the Kent County Levy Court authorized a £46 13s 4d payment "to William Rhodes Esq[r]. in Satisfaction for Negro George his Slave, convicted & hanged, 2/3 of £70 the

g. 6 PA. HOUSE JOURNAL, *supra* note a, at 284.
h. *Id.* at 298, 438, 439.
i. Publick Charge 1742, *microformed on* Sussex County Appearance/Continuance Docket, 1741–1753, RG4815.017, Roll No. 2, Del. Pub. Archives.
j. Kent County Levy Court Minutes (1770), *microformed on* Minutes of the Kent County Levy Court, 1732–1817, RG3200.015, Roll No. 1, Del. Pub. Archives [hereinafter Minutes].
k. Docket, 1764–1773, Kent County Court for the Trial of Negro and Mulatto Slaves, RG3811, Del. Pub. Archives.

Value set on him by the Court for the Trial of Negroes."[l] George had been charged with the murder of Margaret Scanthin.[m]

In November 1768, the Kent County Levy Court authorized a £33 6s 8d payment to Vincent Loockerman, of the storied Dover family, which represented two-thirds of his enslaved man Darby's £50 "intrinsick value."[n] Darby had been convicted of burglary for breaking into the home of Mary Bloom at night and stealing coins and paper money, handkerchiefs, a woman's cap, a razor, shoe buckles, shoes, cloth, and thread—leaving only when he heard someone coming downstairs. Darby hid the stolen goods on Loockerman's property and the next day even "Cut himself a Waistcoat out of the blue Cloath" that "he had made up and now Wears."[o] Payment was conditioned on Darby's execution and was obviated when the king pardoned him on the court's recommendation.[p] Notwithstanding Darby's pardon, it appears that the payment was made—to the profit of the county—because the levy court noted the following year that the county treasurer (rather than Loockerman) had on hand £39 6s 2d cash from "the sale of Negro Darby."[q]

l. Kent County Levy Court Minutes (1773), *microformed on* Minutes, *supra* note j; *see* Docket, *supra* note k, at 17.

m. Dom. Rex v. Negro George (1773), Kent County Court for the Trial of Negro and Mulatto Slaves, RG3811, Del. Pub. Archives.

n. Kent County Levy Court Minutes 14 (1768), *microformed on* Minutes, *supra* note j. *See generally* Kathryn S. LaPrad, Thinking Locally, Acquiring Globally: The Loockerman Family of Delaware, 1630–1790 (2010) (M.A. thesis, University of Delaware), https://udspace.udel.edu.

o. Dom. Rex v. Negro Darby (1768), Kent County Court for the Trial of Negro and Mulatto Slaves, RG3811, Del. Pub. Archives; Docket, *supra* note k, at 7–8.

p. Pardon of Negro Darby (1768), 1 Deed Record S, at 232, *microformed on* RG3555.021, Kent County Deed Records, Roll No. 8, Del. Pub. Archives; *see* WILLIAM H. WILLIAMS, SLAVERY AND FREEDOM IN DELAWARE, 1639–1865, at 34 (1996).

q. Kent County Levy Court Minutes 14 (1769), *microformed on* Minutes, *supra* note j.

Marking the Enslaved as Property

The middle colonies relied less on direct taxes than the New England colonies did. Nonetheless, while creating slave codes and devising slaveholder compensation schemes, the middle colonies did take the opportunity to use direct taxation to reinforce the dehumanization of enslaved persons by classifying them as taxable property. Reminiscent

of Connecticut's divergence from the other New England colonies, however, New Jersey equivocated regarding the treatment of the enslaved as
property for tax purposes.

New York

In New York's early years under English rule, the Duke of York's Laws
drew directly from experience in New England and authorized the
imposition of taxes on polls and estates.[40] The poll tax applied to all
males sixteen years or older and, like contemporary New England laws,
specified that "for such . . . Servants as take not wages, their . . . Masters
shall pay for them."[41] After the establishment of New York's legislature,
the colony abandoned the poll tax in favor of taxing "reall and Personall Estates"—largely during times of extraordinary revenue need (e.g.,
wartime)—but without elaborating on what property was includible in
the tax base.[42]

Property taxation was not without its valuation problems, however,
and attempts to address those problems afford some insight into the
scope of the tax base. In 1693/4, after complaining to the governor about
the lack of a uniform method for property valuation, the Assembly developed its own set of valuation rules that mandated "all Negro and *Indian* Slaves, from twelve Years old to Sixty, be valued at *Twelve Pounds
per* Head," created similar valuation rules for livestock and land, and
closed with a request that the governor "appoint and commissionate fit
Persons upon Oath, in each respective City and County, throughout this
Province, for the making an Estimate" in accordance with these valuation rules.[43] When the Westchester Court of Sessions ordered an assessment of the county's "reall & personall Estates" in 1695, it required
assessors to use a valuation schedule patterned after the Assembly's—
including a £12 value for all "Negroe men 12 yeares to Sixty yeares"—
because that had been found to be "the Easiest & most Equall Meathod"
of assessment.[44]

Notwithstanding the Westchester Court of Sessions' confidence in
this approach, valuation proved to be a perennial issue. As mentioned
earlier, in the context of assessing tax on Albany's slaveholders to fund
compensation for executed escapees fleeing to Canada, the legislature
in 1705 provided specific rules for valuing enslaved persons. During the

remainder of the colonial period, the New York legislature periodically found it necessary to enact legislation aimed at promoting equal taxation in specific cities and counties.[45] For Orange County, these efforts culminated in the passage of a 1775 law detailing precisely how property would be assessed—with specific, age-based valuation rules provided for both enslaved men and women.[46]

New York also occasionally imposed special taxes to fund defense-related expenditures that marked the enslaved as property. In 1703, slaveholding was included along with wig wearing, being a lawyer or member of the legislature, and bachelorhood as a marker of status when tax was imposed on "Severall Ranks and Stations and Circumstances."[47] At other times, enslaved persons were taxed alongside chimneys, stoves, and fireplaces and imported cider, beef, and pork.[48] During the French and Indian War, New York's governor furnished some insight into the rationale behind such tax measures when he recommended that the legislature enact a head tax on enslaved persons because it "cannot be thought heavy, as none but Persons of some Substance possess Slaves, and the Tax will fall equally according to Mens Abilities."[49] When making a similar recommendation a few years later, the governor added that "a Poll Tax on Slaves . . . will naturally tend to Introduce white Servants, which will augment the Strength of the Country; besides, the Price of Labour is now become so high, and hence the Owners of Slaves reap such Advantage, that they cannot reasonably complain of a Tax on them."[50]

Pennsylvania

After first authorizing the imposition of a combination land/poll tax, the shared legislature governing Pennsylvania and Delaware shifted in 1693 to imposing tax largely on property, accompanied by a head tax on "all Freemen within this Province & Territoryes who have been out of their Servitudes by the Space of Six months, and Shall not be otherwise Rated by this Act nor worth One hundred pounds."[51] Beginning in 1710/1, the Pennsylvania legislature sandwiched "bound servants and negroes" between land and livestock when it embarked on a practice of mentioning specific types of property included in the tax base.[52] In contrast to the legislature's decision to impose a minimum tax on free men but not free women, the enslaved were included in the property tax base without distinction as to gender.

Delaware

After Delaware was granted its own legislature, direct taxation there occurred mostly at the county level.[53] Under colonial legislation that continued in force after statehood, Delaware's county-level taxes applied to "persons and estates" without elaboration regarding the composition of the tax base.[54] In 1796, the legislature amended the colonial-era tax laws "for the more equal and just assessment of the good people of the State."[55] That legislation both required detailed listings of assessable property (in place of the summary assessments issued under prior law) and specified the methods to be used for valuing property.[56] Tellingly, that legislation—without any recorded debate or controversy over the question of whether enslaved persons constituted property—included specific rules for valuing enslaved persons (both male and female) alongside those for silver plate and other personal property.[57] Immediately thereafter, the treatment of enslaved persons as property was reflected in the more detailed listings produced by county assessors.[58]

New Jersey

In the late seventeenth century, East New Jersey, perhaps reflecting the New England roots of its early settlers,[59] first included enslaved persons among the people subject to poll tax; however, it later moved them into the category of taxable property.[60] West New Jersey imposed taxes on property and business profits and even more quickly specified that enslaved persons were included in the tax base.[61] After reunification at the turn of the eighteenth century, however, New Jersey equivocated in its tax treatment of the enslaved.

Until turning to other sources of revenue in the early 1730s, the New Jersey legislature routinely included enslaved laborers in the category of "Lands and Chattels" when imposing taxes on property.[62] But on two occasions in the early 1710s, the legislature opted to impose a poll tax in addition to the tax on property and business profits, with deliberations that might shed light on this shift unfortunately left unrecorded due to the Assembly's decision to discuss the tax bill while sitting as a committee of the whole.[63] On those two occasions, echoing the dissonance between form and substance in Connecticut's tax laws, the New Jersey legislature nominally shifted the enslaved out of the category of property and into the category of people subject to poll tax. In substance, however, the legislature continued to treat enslaved persons as property—in other words, as valuable only for their wealth-generating labor power under slaveholder control—by exempting them from tax if they were "not able to work."[64] This shadowy dual status surfaced again when the legislature resumed taxing property in the early 1750s.[65] In these later tax acts, indentured servants and enslaved laborers seem to demarcate the transition from listings of profit-producing businesses operated by taxpayers (e.g., shops, mills, forges, brew houses, and freelance labor) to the enumeration of taxable property (i.e., bound laborers, livestock, and land).[66]

In a further echo of the New England colonies' tax treatment of the enslaved, the labor power of enslaved men was deemed valuable and subjected to tax in all the middle colonies. New York, Pennsylvania, and Delaware all deemed enslaved women's labor also to be valuable—and taxable. However, apart from several tax acts passed around the turn of the eighteenth century, New Jersey systematically excluded the labor power of enslaved women from the tax base.[67] Thus, like Connecticut's taxes on polls and estates, New Jersey's taxes on property and business profits conveyed the counterfactual message that enslaved women's work lacked value—even though their labor was commodified and sold in the market alongside enslaved men's.

Manipulating the Racial Balance

Before marking enslaved persons as taxable property in the hands of slaveholders, the middle colonies often treated them as valuable property upon their forced arrival—taxing them alongside imported cocoa, molasses, and liquor. The factors influencing whether and how the middle colonies taxed the importation of enslaved persons varied, just as they did elsewhere. Thus, despite the influence of slavery-related events and movements that spilled across borders, internal divisions and other factors caused the middle colonies to opt for distinct paths when using (or attempting to use) import taxation to shape the racial balance of their populations, demonstrating once again the close relationship between tax law and society.

Pennsylvania

In 1700, Pennsylvania began taxing the importation of enslaved Blacks to raise revenue, initially setting the rate at £1 on enslaved adults and six shillings on enslaved children but later increasing the rate to £2 on all enslaved Blacks.[68] In the wake of the 1712 insurrection in New York City, the legislature radically shifted course by enacting a tax aimed at restricting the slave trade.[69] Spurred by "a Petition signed by many of the Inhabitants of this Province, praying the Prohibition of *Negroes*," the legislature increased the tax tenfold to £20.[70] The legislature chose prohibitive taxation over the Quaker abolitionist William Southeby's contemporaneous suggestion to set the enslaved free—Southeby's petition having been described as "one of the most memorable incidents in the early struggle against slavery"—but freedom was an option that the legislature deemed "neither just nor convenient."[71] In 1713/4, the queen prospectively disallowed the 1712 tax, enjoining its future imposition based on concerns about the legislation's authorization of warrantless searches and, perhaps more importantly, its adverse impact on the British slave trade.[72]

Within days of discussing the disallowance of this tax, the Pennsylvania legislature opened debate on a revenue-raising package and quickly decided to include a £5 tax on the importation of enslaved Blacks.[73] By settling on a £5 tax, the legislature appears to have struck a balance between the need to raise revenue and a continued desire to discourage the slave trade—the new rate being one-fourth the prohibitive £20 tax but still more than double the earlier £2 tax.[74] Indeed, the same £5 tax rate was later imposed to deter the importation of servants who had been "convicted of heinous crimes, who, soon after their coming into this province, do often run away and leave their master's service and commit many heinous felonies, robberies, thefts and burglaries."[75] Lending support to the idea that the tax was likewise an important source of revenue, when the legislature created the colony's slaveholder compensation scheme a decade later, it dedicated the revenue raised by this tax to funding that compensation.[76]

The legislature repeatedly renewed the £5 import tax, dodging royal disallowance through short-term extensions that expired before royal review was completed or by refraining altogether from sending the legislation to England for approval.[77] On the same day in 1725/6 that the legislature renewed the £5 import tax for the last time, it enacted the 1725/6 Slave Code that introduced the colony's slaveholder compensation scheme.[78] The slave code also contributed to the project of controlling the colony's enslaved population by making a targeted adjustment to the import tax rate to influence the composition and tractability of Pennsylvania's enslaved population. To keep out known troublemakers, the import tax was doubled from £5 to £10 through the imposition of an additional tax "for every negro imported or brought into this province from the West Indies or any other place who shall or may have been transported or sent away for being principal or accessary to any felony or grand or petty larceny or other misdemeanors."[79]

In 1729, the Pennsylvania legislature again renewed the import tax but lowered the rate to £2.[80] According to scholarly speculation, the rate reduction might have been aimed both at dampening the incentive for smuggling to evade tax and at securing a more permanent source of revenue (in lieu of the short-term renewals employed after disallowance of the 1712 tax).[81] Whatever the reason for lowering the base tax, the legislature made no change to the additional tax on enslaved convicts enacted three years earlier. Though not formally repealed until 1761, the 1729 tax was enforced for only a few years and then went uncollected for three decades to comply with the royal instructions issued in the early 1730s restricting the imposition of taxes on the importation of enslaved persons.[82]

There has been some debate about what role (if any) burgeoning Quaker antislavery sentiment played in Pennsylvania's early taxation of imported enslaved persons.[83] Evidence of the influence of Quaker antislavery agitation does, however, surface later in the colonial period, when the tide turned in Pennsylvania toward restricting the slave trade.[84] In early 1761, following a spike in importation of enslaved Blacks due to the enlistment of White servants in the French and Indian War, "a Remonstrance from a great Number of Inhabitants of the City of *Philadelphia* was presented to the House and read, setting forth the mischievous Consequences attending the Practice of importing Slaves into this

Province, and praying a Law to prevent or discourage such Importation for the future."[85] Despite opposition from merchants, the legislature enacted a £10 tax on the importation of enslaved Blacks, replicating the rate of tax imposed earlier in the century to stem the importation of enslaved convicts.[86] In 1768, the £10 tax was extended for seven years because it had "been found by experience to be of public utility."[87]

In January 1773, with Quaker sponsorship, "a considerable Number of the Inhabitants of the City of *Philadelphia*" petitioned the legislature to have the colony's agent in London work to obtain a ban on "the future Importation of Negroes into this Province."[88] As happened in New England, the petition—which the Quaker abolitionist Anthony Benezet stated was signed by about two hundred people, but he claimed that "if time would have allowed we might have had several thousand hands to the Petition"—mixed moral and religious objections with appeals to self-interest, stating that the slave trade "has long been an occasion of deep concern to a great number of the Inhabitants of this Province, as well on account of its inconsistency with the whole tenor of the Christian Religion, as because of the evil Influence it has on the religious and moral conduct of the people and the dreadful consequence, which, it is to be feared, will one day attend, in those parts, where it prevails."[89] Citing the importance of the matter "to the welfare and safety of the British Colonies," the petitioners urged Pennsylvania's legislature to act in concert with other colonial legislatures to make "such representations to the King as to you [i.e., the legislature] may appear most effectual towards putting a stop to this mighty evil."[90]

Disappointing Benezet because, by that time, "the number imported in this province is so small," the legislature chose not to pursue an outright ban on the slave trade but instead to create "a Committee to prepare and bring in a Bill for laying an additional Duty upon the Importation of Negro and Mulatto Slaves into this Province."[91] The resulting act made the existing £10 tax "perpetual" and imposed an additional £10 tax because it would "be of still greater public advantage."[92] According to Benezet, the £20 tax constituted a "tacit prohibition of the Trade" aimed at eliciting a response from England (i.e., either approval or disallowance of the legislation) that would permit the legislature "to judge what farther Step to take, with respect to making head with the King and Parliament, that the Slave Trade may be put an end to."[93] But

Pennsylvania Import Taxes Collected: 1762–1775

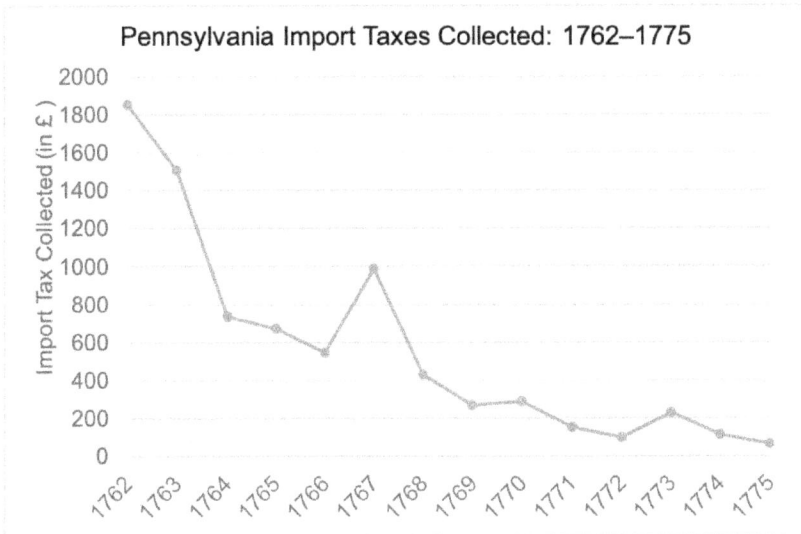

Figure 5.1. Pennsylvania import taxes collected, 1762–75

that signal never came because the act was allowed to become law by lapse of time.[94]

Evidence of the effect of these taxes on the importation of enslaved Blacks can be gleaned from figure 5.1, which is based on the legislature's annual audit of the provincial treasurer's accounts (see box 5.3). These data do not, however, provide a fully accurate accounting because (1) the audits occasionally included payments from prior periods or mentioned unpaid amounts from the current period; (2) the taxes did not apply to enslaved Blacks brought to Pennsylvania with Whites coming to settle there; (3) some officials failed to diligently collect the tax; and (4) smuggling and other subterfuges were used to evade tax.[95] Nonetheless, the available data point toward a steep decline in the importation of enslaved Blacks to Pennsylvania between 1762 and 1775.

Delaware

Despite Delaware having followed Pennsylvania's example when creating its slave code, the colony did not emulate Pennsylvania's decision to tax the importation of enslaved persons.[96] Delaware's different path may have been due to a combination of factors: On the one hand, taxation in Delaware occurred mostly at the county level during the colonial period.[97] On the other hand, even if taxation had occurred more frequently at the colonial level, taxing the importation of enslaved persons was not likely to generate significant revenue because Delaware, like New Hampshire and Connecticut, did not play an active role in the slave trade. Indeed, Delaware's inhabitants largely purchased enslaved persons at the neighboring ports of Annapolis and Philadelphia.[98]

Nonetheless, a notable attempt to tax the importation of enslaved persons did occur amid Pennsylvania's moves to curtail the slave trade through prohibitive taxation.[99] In 1767, the Delaware legislature appointed a committee to "bring in a Bill for the further and better Regulation of Slaves within this Government, and for imposing certain Duties on all Slaves brought into and sold in the same."[100] Five days later, the bill was brought before the legislature, and "many Debates arose for and against that Part of the Bill for imposing Duties on all Slaves brought into and sold in this Government."[101] When put to a vote, the taxing measure failed to pass.[102] A day later, the legislature "resumed the Consideration of the Bill for the further and better Regulation of Slaves, &c. and the several Clauses with Regard to imposing Duties being voted out, it was proposed, that a new Clause should be added, totally prohibiting the Importation of Slaves into this Government."[103] That proposal likewise failed; however, a motion to record the individual votes passed, with the legislative journal reflecting a total of seven votes in favor and nine against the proposal.[104]

William Williams has offered the following interpretation of these attempts to curtail the slave trade:

> On the surface, it looked like the first great clash in the legislature between supporters and opponents of slavery, but the reality was quite different.
>
> Because the leaders on both sides were slaveholders, the only important determinant in the debate seemed to be geography. The seven legislators who favored the slave-import ban included one from New Castle and Sussex and all five of the Kent delegation. Four of the nine opponents of the ban were from Sussex, with the other five from New Castle. A probable explanation is that the more established Kent planters

had a surplus of slaves by 1767 and were anxious to sell them to farmers in undeveloped sections of Sussex and southern New Castle County, where there was still a strong market for unfree blacks. An import ban would help keep prices high by eliminating the only competing source of supply. . . . Farmers and planters in the relatively undeveloped parts of Sussex and southern New Castle, however, were concerned about increasing their supply of slaves at bargain prices, and they considered the continued importation of even a small number of unfree blacks to be advantageous to their interests.[105]

Accordingly, Delaware's failed attempt to enact a prohibitive tax on the importation of enslaved persons or to impose an outright ban on the slave trade might have been motivated not by fear of uprisings or moral or religious opposition to slavery but rather by slaveholders' economic self-interest in manipulating the supply—and, in turn, the value—of human "chattel."

New Jersey

During much of the eighteenth century, New Jersey refrained from taxing the importation of enslaved persons—not because it lacked a direct connection with the slave trade but rather to promote the slave trade. At the turn of the eighteenth century, Queen Anne set the tone when she instructed the colony's first royal governor to encourage trade—particularly with the Royal African Company—and then continued, "whereas we are willing to recommend unto the said company, that the said Province may have a constant and sufficient supply of merchantable negroes, at moderate rates, in money or commodities, so you are to take especial care, that payment be duly made, and within a competent time according to their agreements."[106] Edgar McManus has observed that "these instructions became settled policy, and the slave traffic became one of the preferred branches of New Jersey's commerce."[107] In fact, New Jersey became a tax haven from which enslaved persons were smuggled into neighboring New York and Pennsylvania to evade their import taxes.[108]

Yet, beneath the surface of New Jersey's reputed status as a haven for slave traders lies significant tension within the legislature and between

the legislature and the governor over the use of import taxes to manipulate the racial balance of New Jersey's population. In 1713/4, inspired by
Pennsylvania's response to the 1712 insurrection in New York City, New
Jersey enacted a tax on the importation of enslaved persons simultaneously with the enactment of its slave code.[109] From 1714 to 1716, imported enslaved persons, except for those coming "directly from *Africa*,"
were subject to a £10 tax; from 1716 to 1721, the tax was extended to
all imported enslaved persons.[110] New Jersey's governor reported to the
Board of Trade that the tax was "Calculated to Encourage the Importation of white Servants for the better Peopeling that Country, a Law
something like that in Pensilvania haveing evidently had that effect."[111]

After this tax expired,[112] the legislature moved to enact fresh import
taxes. In 1738, demonstrating concern with controlling the enslaved
population, the Assembly simultaneously ordered the drafting of bills
"to lay Duty on Negroes imported into this province" and "for regulating Negro Slaves."[113] But only the import tax bill made it to the Council,
and when the Assembly refused to accept the Council's amendments,
the Council rejected the bill.[114] In 1744, the Assembly again presented
the Council with a bill to tax the importation of enslaved persons.[115] The
Council again rejected the bill, explaining to the governor, "This Bill the
Council considered abstractedly from any Instructions your Excellency
has in relation to the African Company, which many of the Gentlemen
of the Assembly we suppose are unacquainted with, and only weighed
the Advantages and Disadvantages that would arise to the People of this
Colony upon that Bill's passing into a Law. By that Bill was plainly intended an intire Prohibition of all Slaves being imported from foreign
Parts, no less than a Duty of Ten Pounds being imposed on all grown
Slaves imported from the West-Indies, and Five Pounds on all those
directly imported from Africa."[116] The Council then elaborated on the
causes of a recent shortage of labor that had resulted in rising wages,
leading the Council to conclude that "it would be more for the Interest
of the People of this Colony to encourage at this Time the Importation
of Slaves, than by a Law to prohibit them altogether."[117]

In 1761, the legislature moved to enact an import tax after receiving
two petitions "from a Number of the Inhabitants of this Colony . . . that
a Duty may be laid on all Negro Slaves imported into this Colony."[118]
Fragments of a surviving petition refer to the slave trade as "vile and

oppressive" but likewise express concern that Pennsylvania's prohibitive import tax would have spillover effects in New Jersey, where imported enslaved labor could be purchased more cheaply due to the absence of taxation.[119] When the governor learned of the proposed legislation, he sent the Assembly a message reminding them, "by the 26th Article of his Majesty's Instructions, I am forbid giving my Assent to any Act imposing Duties on Negroes imported into this Province, payable by the Importer; or upon any Slaves exported, that have not been sold in the Province, and continued there for the Space of twelve Months."[120] The Assembly dropped consideration of the bill but responded, "on Account of the Inconvenience the Province is exposed to, in lying open to the Importation of Negroes, at a Time when the Provinces on each Side have laid Duties on them; that we look upon it as a particular Hardship, to be denied the common Privilege of such a Prohibition; and therefore desire his Excellency would be pleased to represent the Inconveniences of the Instruction he has mentioned, and if possible, get it withdrawn."[121] The governor relayed the Assembly's concerns to the Board of Trade, noting that the absence of a tax in New Jersey had the effect that "great Numbers of Negros are landed in this Province every Year in order to be run into New York & Pensylvania besides overstocking this Country with Slaves of which in the general opinion there are already too many."[122]

In late 1762, New Jersey enacted an import tax that, at the governor's insistence, contained a suspending clause that prevented it from taking effect before receiving royal approbation.[123] The preamble to this legislation reiterated the "Inconveniences" associated with the importation of enslaved Blacks and particularly mentioned that it "prevents industrious People from our Mother Country, and Foreigners, to settle among us."[124] Belying this rationale, however, the legislation ensured the colony's competitive position vis-à-vis its neighbors: the legislation imposed a £2 tax in eastern New Jersey that, as described later, paralleled New York's tax on direct imports from Africa but was half the £4 tax on those coming from the Caribbean, and it imposed a £6 tax in western New Jersey that was significantly lower than Pennsylvania's £10 tax.[125] Additionally, the legislation allowed a drawback of three-fourths of the tax on reexportation within six months.[126] But these taxes never went into effect because the Board of Trade, despite having "no particular Objection to the Policy of imposing a reasonable duty upon the importation of Negroes," refused to submit the act to the king for approval on the ground that it violated royal instructions by both imposing the tax on the importer and not providing a full refund on reexportation.[127]

The New Jersey legislature finally succeeded in taxing imported enslaved persons in 1767. The preamble to this act reiterated the desire to use taxation as a means of discouraging the slave trade and of encouraging White immigration to New Jersey: "Whereas Duties on the Importation of Negroes, in several of the neighboring Colonies, hath, on Experience, been found beneficial in the Introduction of sober industrious Foreigners to settle under His Majesty's Allegiance, and the Promoting a Spirit of Industry among the Inhabitants in general: In order therefore to promote the same good Designs in this Government . . ."[128] Finally matching rate with rhetoric, the 1767 legislation imposed a £10 tax on the purchase of enslaved persons who had not been in the colony for one year (or previously been taxed)—including purchases "made upon the Water or Waters, along the Sea Coast of this Province, or those between this Province and the provinces of *New-York*, *Pennsylvania*, and the lower Counties of *Delaware*."[129] In 1769, the tax was renewed for ten years, but the rate was increased to £15.[130] In these later years, the persistence of the New Jersey legislature in seeking to tax the importation of enslaved persons has been attributed in part to the influence of the growing antislavery movement among Quakers in Pennsylvania and New Jersey.[131] In a seeming testament to the effectiveness of these taxes, the Assembly's regular audits of the provincial treasurer's accounts reveal only a single payment relating to this tax—of £9 10s from Daniel Ellis in 1768, which represented the prevailing £10 tax on a single imported enslaved person net of the tax collector's commission.[132]

In 1773, a series of petitions complaining of "the Mischiefs arising from personal Slavery" were presented to the Assembly, which was urged to end the slave trade and ease the manumission process.[133] In response, the legislature drafted two bills: one amending the import tax and another addressing manumissions.[134] Controversy over the manumission bill—which was the target of a number of petitions in support and in opposition[135]—quickly overshadowed the effort to amend the import tax and caused both bills to be carried over from one legislative session to the next, eventually to be buried by concerns related to the Revolutionary War.[136]

New York

With the largest enslaved population in the middle colonies, New York was the most consistent in taxing the importation of enslaved persons. After a failed attempt in 1702, the New York legislature succeeded in 1709 in imposing a £3 tax on enslaved Blacks not imported directly from Africa as well as other enslaved persons not imported directly from their native lands.[137] As indicated in table 5.1, over the following decade, the legislature repeatedly tinkered with tax rates that varied based on the origin of imported enslaved persons and the ownership of the vessel that transported them to New York.[138]

Notable for its absence from this table is any reaction to the 1712 insurrection in New York City. As described earlier, the legislatures of Pennsylvania and New Jersey were so alarmed by this insurrection that they both enacted prohibitive taxes to curtail the slave trade; however, New York took no such action.[139] In the wake of the insurrection, New Yorkers simply avoided purchasing enslaved persons from the areas in Africa that the insurrectionists hailed from.[140] At the same time, the colony's tax laws reaffirmed a steadfast commitment to enslaved labor, with the legislature exploiting the slave trade as a source of revenue while using the tax rate structure to shape slaveholder preferences and promote local participation in the slave trade.[141]

Beginning in 1720, the New York legislature simplified the rate structure by imposing a £2 tax on enslaved persons coming directly from Africa and a £4 tax on all others (subject to exceptions for small children and, later, those who were already sick and dying upon arrival).[142] Notwithstanding misgivings expressed by the Board of Trade and the royal instructions to the contrary issued in the early 1730s, this rate structure

TABLE 5.1. New York Taxes on Imported Enslaved Persons in the 1710s

Year	Imported directly from Africa in New York–owned vessels	Imported directly from Africa in British-owned vessels	Imported from West Indies	Others
1714	£3	—	—	£4
1715	£2	—	£5	£4
1716	£2	—	£4	£4
1718	£2	£2	£4	£4

continued in place for the remainder of the colonial period, with a higher £5 tax eventually imposed on enslaved persons coming over land to deter smuggling from neighboring colonies.[143]

Although part of general revenue-raising measures, these import taxes also aimed to shape the composition of New York's enslaved population by providing a financial incentive for slaveholders to prefer lightly taxed enslaved persons coming from Africa over more heavily taxed enslaved persons coming from the Caribbean.[144] New Yorkers initially preferred enslaved persons coming from the Caribbean because they were "seasoned"—in other words, they had already been subjected to harsh conditions of slavery there "to break them into the labor system"—in the hope "that slaves from the Caribbean would be easier to manage because of better slave conditions in New York than the Caribbean."[145] Notwithstanding this general preference, in a 1718 letter to the Board of Trade, New York's governor voiced a perennial complaint in the American colonies when he described the tax rate structure as designed to "discourage the importing their refuse & sickly Negroes here from other Colonies which they commonly do."[146] A few months later, the legislature sent a letter to the governor responding to a variety of complaints from the Board of Trade regarding the colony's import tax legislation. In that letter, the legislature echoed the governor's concerns and described them as so "obvious" that it felt no need to enter into a lengthy explanation, stating only that the tax rate structure aimed to "encourage a direct Importation from *Africa*, and discourage an Importation from the Plantations, by whom we [i.e., New Yorkers] are supplied with the Refuse of their *Negroes* and such Malefactors, as would have suffered Death in the Places from whence they came, had not the Avarice of their Owners, saved them from the publick justice by an early Transportation into these Parts, where they not often fail of repeating their Crimes."[147]

New Yorkers would not, however, alter their general preference for enslaved persons coming from the Caribbean until the 1741 conspiracy to burn New York City and murder its White inhabitants: "Before 1741, fewer than one third of the city's slave imports came from Africa, and almost three quarters from the Caribbean. After 1741, these numbers were exactly reversed. Evidently, New York merchants and slave owners hoped that African slaves would be more tractable, less able to communicate with one another and with city blacks, and less able to organize a revolt."[148] But this was the conspiracy's only repercussion on the slave trade because the New York legislature enacted no tax changes to more generally deter the importation of enslaved Blacks.[149] Following the 1739 Stono Rebellion, even South Carolina reacted by imposing a prohibitive tax on the importation of enslaved Blacks that, combined with other factors, curtailed the importation of enslaved persons for nearly a decade. In contrast, New York tax law continued to send the message that the colony was wedded to the slave trade, with New Yorkers finally bringing their behavior into line with the long-standing tax incentive to favor enslaved Blacks coming from Africa over those coming from the Caribbean.

Yet, as was the case in New Jersey, dissension existed beneath this surface of steadfast support for the slave trade. At times, it was suggested that the New York legislature should deter the importation of enslaved persons in favor of encouraging White immigration.[150] For instance, a 1737 editorial in the *New York Weekly Journal* published by John Peter Zenger contemplated the use of taxes to encourage White immigration. Reminiscent of South Carolina's use of import tax revenue to fund bounties to attract White settlers, the editorial asked "whether, if any such Taxes should be thought proper to be laid, for Discouraging the Use of Negroes, the Produce of it would not be most beneficial for the Country, to be disposed of in Bounties for encouraging the Importation of white Servants to supply their Places?"[151]

At the end of the colonial period, influenced by antislavery agitation emanating from Pennsylvania, the New York General Assembly passed bills to increase the import tax in 1773, 1774, and 1775.[152] According to Anthony Benezet, the 1773 bill would have raised the tax to match the £20 rate that prevailed in Pennsylvania.[153] That bill appears to have died without coming up for a final vote because, as Benezet reported, it "was not agreed to by the Governor and Council under pretence, as I hear that it would lay a difficulty on the West India people who come over for the recovery of their health with respect to their Servants, tho' there was a clause in the Bill I hear allowing Eighteen Months in that case."[154] The Council later rejected the 1774 and 1775 bills—an unsurprising turn of events given Benezet's observation that New Yorkers were "not in general so willing to hear of putting an end to Slavery as in [Pennsylvania] and the Jerseys."[155]

Reflection

The middle colonies, in keeping with their geographic position, proved to be more deeply wedded to slavery than New England's societies with slaves but less so than South Carolina's slave society. Reflecting their more fulsome embrace of slavery, the middle colonies forged connections between taxation and slavery that were both greater in number and stronger than those of the New England colonies. The middle colonies all entwined their tax systems in the multipronged efforts undertaken to control and subjugate their enslaved populations, demonstrating once again how tax law was no different from other areas of the law in being unable to escape the taint of slavery. Yet, even as the middle colonies' tax systems were deployed in service of the evils of racism and slavery, there were attempts—some more successful than others—to use taxation to curtail the slave trade, reflecting a growing discomfort with slavery in the middle colonies.

With larger enslaved populations, the middle colonies found it necessary to go to greater lengths to maintain control over their enslaved populations than the New England colonies did. The middle colonies all adopted slave codes that embraced the death penalty. Just as South Carolina did, the middle colonies endeavored to secure slaveholder cooperation in meting out capital punishment under their slave codes by compensating slaveholders for the economic loss incurred when their enslaved persons were executed. Nonetheless, the middle colonies acted at different times and used different tax mechanisms to fund these slaveholder compensation payments.

Taxation was fundamental to these compensation schemes because, without funding, slaveholder compensation would be a meaningless gesture. Faced with the need to choose a funding mechanism, each colonial legislature had to decide who benefited—and, therefore, who should share the burden—when slaveholders were paid to cooperate in the administration of the slave code's most draconian punishments. Among the middle colonies, New York was the first to grapple with this question, deciding that the cost of slaveholder compensation should be shared by all local slaveholders. In an instance of legislative borrowing and adaptation, New Jersey patterned its own slaveholder compensation scheme after New York's. But whereas New York took advantage of its administrative infrastructure to achieve a progressive distribution of the tax, New Jersey distributed the additional tax burden on slaveholders in an administratively simpler fashion—that is to say, through a head tax on enslaved persons.

Both New York and New Jersey later shifted their views regarding who benefited from compensation payments made to the holders of executed enslaved persons. On the one hand, New York saw a broader public benefit and transitioned to requiring all local property holders—and not just slaveholders—to bear the burden of compensation. On the other hand, New Jersey retrenched and chose to eliminate its slaveholder compensation scheme, perhaps motivated by a sense that slaveholders bore some culpability when their enslaved persons committed crimes and thus should themselves bear the costs imposed on society by those crimes.

Pennsylvania took longer to create its slaveholder compensation scheme but eventually acted in response to evasion of the law and complaints about the colony's lack of a compensation scheme. Answering the question of who benefits from smooth operation of the slave code differently, Pennsylvania funded its slaveholder compensation scheme primarily with revenue from taxes on the importation of enslaved persons. Pennsylvania thus required the cost of slaveholder compensation to be distributed among those who benefited from enslaved labor but on a broader scale than its neighbors—not only at the colonial rather than the local level but also including both slaveholders and slave traders.

Despite borrowing liberally from Pennsylvania's slave code, Delaware opted for a different funding mechanism—one that was tailored to its own tax system. Reflecting a sense that the smooth operation of the slave code broadly benefited society, Delaware spread the cost of slaveholder compensation through its county-level property tax system, just as it did other expenditures for the benefit of the public at large.

Through these varied choices, the middle colonies demonstrated both the influence that close neighbors with histories of shared governance could have on each other and the felt need to temper those influences to meet local conditions and concerns. Taken together, these choices evidence the important role that taxation played in all the middle colonies in ensuring the smooth operation of the legal machinery for

punishing—and killing—enslaved persons in the name of better maintaining control over them. The vignettes interspersed throughout this
chapter demonstrate how the middle colonies' tax records relating to the
operation of their slaveholder compensation schemes open a revealing
window onto their societies. Interestingly, these tax records evoke some
of the same themes encountered when earlier peering through the tax
window onto South Carolina's slave society—illustrating the persistence
of slaveholders in pursuing compensation, the haste with which "justice"
was meted out and enslaved persons were put to death, and the suffering
experienced by the condemned.

Also as in South Carolina, taxation's role in dehumanizing enslaved
persons was not limited to distributing the cost of compensating slaveholders for the economic loss they suffered from executions. Other
aspects of the middle colonies' tax systems reinforced this message by
treating the enslaved as a form of taxable property. New York, Pennsylvania, and Delaware all quickly moved to include enslaved persons in
the property tax base, while New Jersey equivocated in its treatment of
the enslaved, alternating between treating them as people or property
for tax purposes in ways that were redolent of the experience in New
England. Like New England, the taxing choices made by the middle colonies also sent mixed messages about whose labor was valued, with New
York, Pennsylvania, and Delaware all treating the labor of both enslaved
men and women as valuable while New Jersey generally treated only the
labor of enslaved men as valuable, even though the labor of enslaved
women was equally commodified.

Nevertheless, enslaved men and women were both treated as valuable
commodities for import tax purposes. Import taxation was not, however, only a means of dehumanizing the enslaved from the moment of
their arrival. Like South Carolina, the middle colonies also used import
taxation as a lever to manipulate the racial composition of their populations. New York employed its import taxes to shape slaveholder preferences to favor ostensibly more tractable enslaved persons imported from
Africa over troublemakers coming from the Caribbean. Pennsylvania
initially used import taxes to raise revenue but quickly shifted course
after the 1712 insurrection in New York City by enacting a prohibitive tax
to suppress the slave trade. After that tax was disallowed, Pennsylvania
struck a balance between raising revenue and putting a damper on the

slave trade, only to later lower the tax rate back to a purely revenue-raising level. New Jersey followed Pennsylvania's lead and succeeded in temporarily imposing a prohibitive tax on the importation of enslaved persons, with the aim of incentivizing the untaxed importation of White servants. For nearly five decades after that tax expired, however, New Jersey imposed no tax on the importation of enslaved persons and served as a haven for smugglers looking to evade New York's and Pennsylvania's import taxes.

As happened in New England, growing antislavery agitation in the middle colonies during the eighteenth century led to efforts to end the slave trade—but with the tool of choice in the middle colonies being prohibitive levels of taxation rather than outright bans on the slave trade. Pennsylvania succeeded first, imposing a heavy tax on the importation of enslaved persons in the early 1760s. Despite New Jersey's reputation as a tax haven, it repeatedly attempted to tax the importation of enslaved persons to reduce their numbers in the colony and incentivize White immigration. By the late 1760s, New Jersey succeeded in enacting a tax that was quickly increased to prohibitive levels. Both Delaware and New York attempted to impose prohibitive import taxes, but neither succeeded. Aside from demonstrating how taxation was used by the middle colonies to manipulate the racial composition of their populations, this chapter's examination of import taxation reflects growing tensions in the middle colonies between proponents and opponents of slavery as well as the tensions between the colonies and England as the royal government acted to advance the interests of British slave traders. What is more, this chapter illustrates the varied reasons behind colonists' embrace of import taxes as a tool for curtailing the slave trade—from the moral opposition and self-preservation witnessed both here and earlier in chapter 4 to the manipulation of the levers of supply and demand for personal gain witnessed in this chapter and that will again be on display in chapter 6.

The middle colonies, in keeping with their geographic position, produced a seeming admixture of the ties forged between taxation and slavery in New England's societies with slaves and South Carolina's slave society. Although the influence of legislation, events, and movements crossed borders within the middle colonies, the connections that these colonies established between taxation and slavery ultimately were shaped by local conditions, underscoring the close relationship between tax law and society. Next, chapter 6 travels farther southward to Maryland, Virginia, North Carolina, and Georgia to complete the work of documenting the ties between taxation and slavery in the American colonies.

6

The Southern Colonies

Unlike South Carolina, the other southern colonies did not begin as slave societies—they *became* slave societies. For instance, Maryland and Virginia only shifted to predominantly using enslaved labor to cultivate tobacco in the late seventeenth century.[1] And Georgia actually prohibited slavery shortly after its founding—not out of moral opposition but to avoid the "great inconveniences" slaveholding colonies encountered when defending themselves in times of war, insurrection, and rebellion due to dampened incentives for White immigration.[2] After much clamoring by its settlers, however, Georgia legalized slavery, and its Black population quickly grew to near parity with the White population.[3]

The southern colonies, like their counterparts to the north, were thus far from monolithic.[4] North Carolina exemplified this variety: its Cape Fear region had large plantations that produced rice and naval stores and resembled South Carolina's low country in terms of the concentration of enslaved persons; its northern region began as an extension of Virginia's economy, producing tobacco and other crops, and came to resemble the Chesapeake in the distribution of enslaved persons; by contrast, its western region had a "statistically insignificant" enslaved population, occasionally resulting in tensions with slaveholding regions.[5] As this chapter demonstrates, the patterns of similarity and difference that marked these southern societies that came to revolve around the evils of racism and slavery surfaced in stronger and more enduring connections between taxation and slavery than existed in the northern and middle colonies.

Slaveholder Compensation

The southern colonies all enacted harsh slave codes that established separate systems of justice for enslaved persons and authorized draconian punishments as part of "the apparatus of coercion" that slaveholders mobilized to sustain their burgeoning slave societies.[6] With harsher slave codes, the southern colonies more quickly adopted—and maintained a more steadfast commitment to—slaveholder compensation schemes than the middle colonies did. These schemes varied in their scope and generosity; however, through choices regarding tax funding mechanisms, the southern colonies sharply diverged from the middle colonies by rallying around the message that slaveholder compensation was of wide public benefit and, therefore, a burden to be shared by all.

Virginia

In 1672, having already absolved slaveholders and their agents from legal culpability for killing enslaved persons when "correcting" them (on the theory that no slaveholder would purposefully "destroy his owne estate"), Virginia temporarily authorized the killing of escaped enslaved persons who were "persued by warrant or hue and crye" and resisted apprehension.[7] Using the common medium of exchange at the time, the holders of those who were killed were to "receive satisfaction from the publique" in the amount of forty-five hundred pounds of tobacco for enslaved Blacks and three thousand pounds of tobacco for enslaved Native Americans (the holders of those who were injured were to receive "a reasonable satisfaction" for their damages).[8] In 1680, Virginia permanently authorized the killing of escapees who resisted capture but did not authorize slaveholder compensation.[9] In 1691, when the legislature enacted procedures for "suppressing outlying Slaves," it specified "that where any negroe or mulattoe slave or slaves shall be killed in pursuance of this act, the owner or owners of such negro or mulatto slave shall be paid for such negro or mulatto slave four thousand pounds of tobacco by the publique"—but notably omitted mention of compensation for enslaved Native Americans (who, in any event, "never became available in sufficient numbers to form a significant part of Virginia's labor force").[10]

Virginia steadily expanded the scope and generosity of its slaveholder compensation scheme. In 1705, compensation was extended to executed enslaved persons, with slave courts required to value them and "certify such valuation to the next assembly, that the said assembly may be enabled to make a suitable allowance thereupon, to the master or owner of such slave."[11] Additionally, Virginia formalized a procedure for slaveholders to "outlaw" escapees who "lie out, hid and lurking in swamps, woods, and other obscure places, killing hogs, and committing other injuries to the inhabitants of this her majesty's colony and dominion."[12] After two justices of the peace issued a proclamation against the escapee, the proclamation was to be published at the door of every church in the county. If the outlawed person "did not immediately return home," then the legislature legally authorized "any person or persons whatsoever, to kill and destroy such slaves by such ways and means as he, she, or they shall think fit."[13] The legislature permitted the holders of those who were killed to apply for judicial valuations that were to be submitted "to the assembly, with the rest of the public claims."[14] In 1723, following the discovery of two insurrectionary plots, the compensation scheme was further enlarged to cover enslaved persons killed "in the dispersing of any unlawful assemblies, pursuit of rebels or conspirators, or seizing the arms and ammunition of such as are prohibited . . . to keep the same."[15]

Uncapped and broadly applicable, Virginia's slaveholder compensation scheme was more generous than South Carolina's. For Virginia slaveholders, being granted access to the tax system to redistribute their losses secured more than their cooperation in enforcement of the slave code—it garnered their enthusiastic participation in the hunting and killing of their enslaved persons. Rather than dealing with troublemakers when taxpayer money was available to replace them, slaveholders like William Gregory publicly advertised their bloodthirstiness in the *Virginia Gazette*: "RUN away from the subscriber in *Charles City* county . . . a VIRGINIA born Negro fellow named PETER, about 44 years of age. . . . The said Negro is outlawed; and I will give 10l. [i.e., £10] to any person or persons that will kill him and bring me his head, separate from his body, or 40s. if delivered to the subscriber near the *Long Bridge*."[16]

Like South Carolina, Virginia centralized the vetting of slaveholder compensation claims as part of its tax legislative drafting process. That process began with the legislature's preparation of a book of approved public claims (many of which were first vetted by county courts of claims, just as slaveholder compensation claims were first vetted by the courts), followed by calculation of the tax rate by dividing the approved claims (less any funds on hand in the treasury) by the number of "tithables" (i.e., taxpayers), and finally passing an act levying the resulting poll tax.[17] Accordingly, the expenses in the book of claims—including slaveholder compensation payments—directly determined the poll tax rate in Virginia, much as the expenses in the Tax-Act schedules determined the amount of property taxes in South Carolina.

Despite these promising similarities, Virginia's tax legislative process does not afford the opportunity to document the legalized killings of enslaved persons in the same way that South Carolina's tax legislative process did. Most problematically, with a few exceptions, Virginia's books of public claims do not appear to have survived.[18] Among the remnants, an abstract of the 1702 book of claims includes two payments of four thousand pounds of tobacco—one to "William Brossio for his outlying Negro Slave Toby who was shott and killed" and another to "John Tullit for his Negro Slave Billy who was pursuant to Law shot & killed."[19] Unfortunately, the House of Burgesses journals are of limited assistance in reconstructing the missing claims. In the early years, the journals occasionally mentioned slaveholder compensation claims but only revealed their disposition when dealing with them summarily rather than referring them to the Committee for Public Claims.[20] By the 1730s, the journals included short descriptions of the claims and their disposition; however, with a handful of exceptions, these descriptions did not concern claims falling squarely within the compensation scheme.[21] As illustrated in box 6.1, however, what the claims described in the journals do shed light on is how the existence of a stable and generous compensation scheme whetted the appetite of Virginia slaveholders for redistributing their economic losses broadly among the colony's taxpaying populace.

Box 6.1. Virginia Slaveholders' Boundless Appetite for Redistribution

Virginia's stable and generous compensation scheme whetted the appetites of its slaveholders, enticing them to press the legislature to spread their losses widely among the colony's taxpayers in circumstances *not* squarely covered by the compensation scheme (e.g., for enslaved persons who were neither executed nor killed after being outlawed and refusing to return). In contrast to the occasional examples of persistent slaveholders in other colonies, between 1732 and 1775, Virginia slaveholders filed more than one hundred such claims that the House of Burgesses either approved (fifty-eight) or rejected (forty-nine) (see appendix tables A.3

and A.4, respectively).[a] A small number of additional claims were filed but have no recorded disposition.[b]

Evidence of slaveholder persistence is found not only in the number of claims submitted but also in their sometimes-questionable quality. For instance, in 1753, Francis Whiting requested compensation for Will, an escapee who he claimed had been "outlawed, after which some Persons being in pursuit of him, in Order to apprehend him, he ran into a Creek, and was drowned."[c] The House twice postponed consideration of Whiting's claim due to the failure of a witness to appear.[d] Eventually, the House rejected the claim, noting that Will had *not* been outlawed before his death. The House learned that one of Will's pursuers met "a Man with a Proclamation of Outlawry against him" several hours *after* Will's death and that the proclamation was not publicly posted until the next day.[e] Additionally, in 1766, the House summarily rejected a dilatory claim submitted by Charles Carter—a member of the House and of the prominent Carter family—seeking compensation for the loss of his enslaved man Harry, who tried to kill his overseer "about 14 or 15 Years ago" and was himself killed when escaping.[f]

Patterns among the adjudicated claims are equally revealing. Slaveholders initiated the outlawry process for nearly two-fifths of the enslaved persons covered by those claims and nearly always completed that process before their deaths. Through outlawry, slaveholders secured legal authorization to kill their enslaved persons in exchange for the promise—but, as Whiting discovered, not the guarantee—of

a. 6 JOURNALS OF THE HOUSE OF BURGESSES OF VIRGINIA 123, 254, 263, 325–27, 329, 335–36, 338, 341, 359, 369, 418, 420–21, 425 (H.R. McIlwaine ed., 1910); 7 *id.* at 8, 12, 14, 27–28, 35, 37, 43–45, 51, 84, 86, 94–95, 97, 99, 103–04, 109, 158, 162, 167, 176, 187–88, 194, 268, 273, 279–80, 297–98, 303, 308–09, 331; 8 *id.* at 9, 26–27, 31, 37, 39, 43–44, 55, 111–12, 115, 125, 138–39, 142–43, 145–46, 153–54, 158, 182, 236–37, 239–40, 242, 245, 248, 255–57, 259–62, 270–72, 434, 444; 9 *id.* at 19, 27, 64, 75–76, 79–80, 96, 107, 203, 210, 214–15, 218, 236, 239; 10 *id.* at 71, 97, 102, 119, 135–36, 141, 239, 258–59; 11 *id.* at 25, 36–37, 42, 83, 89, 91, 95, 107, 146, 193, 200, 207, 211–12, 234–35, 270, 274, 282, 289, 309, 330, 349, 354; 12 *id.* at 49, 75, 132, 158–60, 164–65, 167–70, 172, 174, 181, 189, 196, 208, 210–11, 259, 267; 13 *id.* at 92, 98, 104, 113–14, 181, 185–86, 189, 204, 222.
b. *E.g.*, 6 *id.* at 257, 262–63; 10 *id.* at 237; 12 *id.* at 38, 86, 166, 169, 270; 13 *id.* at 81–82, 184–86, 227.
c. 8 *id.* at 146.
d. *Id.* at 153–54, 242.
e. *Id.* at 256.
f. 11 *id.* at 3, 36–37.

compensation. The tantalizing possibility for Virginia slaveholders to spread their losses through redistributive tax mechanisms thus spurred them not simply to cooperate with but to actively engage the slave code's legal machinery of death.

The claims tell a different story from the perspective of the enslaved (as recounted by slaveholders in the context of an economically self-interested claims-filing process). Many claims document overt resistance to bondage, including escape to freedom and physical attacks against slaveholders and overseers and their families. In a final effort to seize control of their fates, more than one-fifth of these enslaved persons killed themselves rather than submit to Virginia's "justice" system. One early instance of suicide further hints at the bleakness of perpetual bondage. In 1736, William Cox was paid £60 because "his Negro Woman Slave had broke open his House, stolen several of his Goods, desperately wounded his Son, burnt his Tobacco-house, murdered Three other of his Slaves, her Children, and drowned herself; whereby, he is reduced to Poverty."[g] Absent from the description of Cox's dire financial straits, however, is any mention of why this woman might have chosen to kill herself *and* to kill her three children rather than leaving them at Cox's mercy in a state of bondage.

While enslaved persons clearly feared the draconian punishments that awaited them in Virginia, they also must have feared the mere prospect of incarceration. Even such minor transgressions as George Brett's enslaved man "having rambled a small Distance from his House," which resulted in his being "taken up" and placed in the Stafford County jail, resulted in his death when the jail "was soon after accidentally set on Fire, and the Slave burnt therein."[h] And he was not the only enslaved person among this group to die in a jail fire—eight others did too. Ten more died from exposure to the cold while jailed—some dying after acquittal or shortly following release. (Another four survived frostbite, with slaveholders compensated for the cost of medical care or loss of service.) Four more died in jail for no specified reason. In total, nearly one-fifth of these enslaved persons died while incarcerated.

---

g. 6 *id.* at 254.
h. 7 *id.* at 162.

Maryland

In 1712, even before enacting criminal laws specifically targeting enslaved persons, a committee of Maryland's Lower House suggested the creation of a slaveholder compensation scheme.[22] Five years later, to put an end to the practice of concealing the capital crimes of those who were held in bondage or of selling offenders outside the colony to mitigate losses, the legislature ordered that three-fourths of the value of those who were executed was "to be allowed in the Public Levy, to be paid to the Owner or Owners of such Negro, or Mulatto Slave, or Mulatto born of a White Woman."[23]

In 1729, when drafting gruesome legislation prescribing how enslaved persons would be put to death, the Upper House proposed removing the compensation cap.[24] The Lower House, however, disagreed: "We are apprehensive that paying the whole Value would make the Owners of Slaves less careful in keeping their Slaves within due Bounds, as they ought to be kept, & as they will probably be when the Interest of their Owners is joined with their Duty."[25] The Lower House thus eschewed full redistribution of slaveholders' economic losses in favor of maintaining a financial incentive for slaveholders to deter criminal behavior among their enslaved persons. Yet, "masters were loath to lose," and the legislature ultimately relented.[26] In 1737, the legislature removed the compensation cap and extended compensation to escapees killed when resisting apprehension and to those convicted of capital crimes who died while awaiting execution.[27]

Having gained significant ground, Maryland slaveholders sought to expand the redistributive compensation scheme through the petition process, albeit less frequently than Virginia slaveholders did. In 1739, William Ratcliffe narrowly lost his bid in the Lower House for "an Allowance for a Negro Slave who being apprehended and Committed for the Murther of another Slave died in Goal before Conviction."[28] In 1740, Ratcliffe resubmitted his request to the Upper House at the same time that John Blandford petitioned for compensation "for his Slave who dyed in Prison before Tryal, & who was there committed on Suspicion of conspiring the Death of sundry white persons."[29] Both petitions were granted, with the legislature ordering the payment of full compensation from the public treasury.[30] Three others later followed suit and received

compensation in similar circumstances.[31] The legislature was not, however, always so accommodating. In 1744, George Riddle unsuccessfully
sought compensation for his enslaved man James, who escaped jail after
conviction and was "not since retaken."[32]

Maryland's slaveholder compensation scheme was consolidated in
1751 and continued in force during the remainder of the colonial period.[33] Although the records of Maryland's colonial treasurers do not
appear to have survived,[34] the treasurers must have paid out significant
sums under the compensation scheme. Just between 1738 and 1770, the
governor, in consultation with the Council, issued death warrants for
the execution of nearly sixty enslaved persons,[35] with additional enslaved persons probably having been killed under other compensable
circumstances.

North Carolina

In 1715, North Carolina authorized compensation for enslaved persons
who "shall be killed in apprehending or that shall by Judgment . . . be
publickly executed to the Terror of other Slaves."[36] A judicial certificate of valuation entitled the slaveholder "to a Pole-Tax on all Slaves
in the Government to make up that sum to the Owner of such Slave
so publickly Executed or killed in Apprehending."[37] Despite ostensibly requiring the colony's slaveholders to internalize this cost of doing
business with enslaved labor, there is some evidence that the legislature instead paid compensation out of general poll tax revenues. For
instance, in January 1734/5, the House of Burgesses referred a petition
from Constance Williamson to the Committee of Claims because "some
years agoe She had two Negro Slaves condemned and executed . . . and
only valued at eighty five pounds and no part of the said sum paid."[38]
A month later, the House approved the list of public claims in preparation of general poll tax legislation and included an allowance of £250 for
Williamson (without specifying the payment's purpose) as well as £150
for "Allen Wells for a negro executed at Cape Fear."[39] Similarly, among
the claims approved in 1739/40, Rowland Williams's £200 compensation
payment "for a Negro named Will Executed according to Law" appears
to relate to a fragmentary court record in the General Assembly files
finding Will guilty of "ffeloniously bracking open [a] house and takeing

from thence Sundry Goods"—including the clothes Will was wearing at trial, though he denied this—and ordering him to "be carried to the next convenient Tree and there hanged up by the neck till he be dead."[40]

In 1741, taking inspiration from Virginia, North Carolina adopted an outlawry procedure, broadly authorized the killing of enslaved persons in enforcement of the slave code, and altered the slaveholder compensation scheme.[41] The 1741 Slave Code provided "that for every Slave killed in Pursuance of this Act, or put to Death by Law, the Master or Owner of such Slave shall be paid by the Public."[42] The court was required to certify an enslaved person's value upon conviction and transmit that valuation to the legislature to "make suitable Allowance . . . to the Master or Owner of such Slave."[43] In effect, North Carolina renounced its formal stance that slaveholders alone benefited from the compensation scheme (and should, therefore, bear the burden of funding it themselves) and instead announced that slaveholder compensation was of public benefit and that all taxpayers should bear a share of slaveholders' economic losses.[44] North Carolina slaveholders, like their counterparts in Virginia, took full advantage of this formal shift to a redistributive scheme by advertising "greater rewards for the return of their runaway slave's head than for the slave alive."[45]

As time passed, North Carolina trimmed the generosity of its slaveholder compensation scheme in recognition that a broadly redistributive scheme invited slaveholders to pursue profit regardless of societal impact. In 1753, North Carolina attempted to shape slaveholder behavior by denying access to compensation unless slaveholders demonstrated "that such Slave or Slaves, killed on outlawry, or capitally convicted, shall have been sufficiently cloathed, and shall likewise have constantly received, for the preceding Year, an Allowance not less than a Quart of Corn per Diem."[46] Five years later, when taxes were rising to cover the costs of the French and Indian War, the legislature complained that "many great Charges have arisen to the Province by Punishment of Slaves, who having Liberty from their Owners to hire themselves out, and having committed Robberies; by the Importation of Slaves from Foreign Parts for Crimes by them committed; by the condemnation of Slaves to Death for capital Crimes, for want of a punishment adequate to the Crimes they have been guilty of; and by the High Valuation of Slaves condemned to Death, or killed by Virtue of an Outlawry."[47] In response, the legislature denied compensation to those who allowed enslaved persons to hire themselves out or who knew of the criminal pasts of new arrivals at the time of purchase.[48] It changed the punishment for capital first offenses (other than rape or murder) for enslaved males to castration and provided compensation in the event of death following castration.[49] Finally, the legislature imposed a general £60 compensation cap.[50] In 1764, as war-related fiscal pressures eased, the legislature repealed the changes to the compensation scheme and to the punishment of capital offenses, replacing them with an increased £80 cap on compensation for executed enslaved persons.[51] Notably, the legislature set both the earlier and later caps sufficiently high that slaveholders "normally could purchase an acceptable replacement with the money paid . . . out of provincial revenues."[52]

In the early 1770s, the legislature twice considered authorizing counties to impose taxes to fund compensation for executed enslaved persons; however, the Council rejected the measure each time.[53] Having been "introduced by Thomas Polk, of Mecklenburg County, where there were very few slaves," the bill seems to have been motivated by a desire for "relief by counties that had few slaves."[54] By limiting redistribution to the county level, this change would have prevented eastern counties with large enslaved populations from forcing western counties with small enslaved populations to bear a portion of slaveholders' economic losses, effectively requiring slaveholding areas (rather than slaveholders individually) to internalize this cost of doing business with enslaved labor.

Consequently, whereas Maryland overcame reservations about increasing the generosity of its slaveholder compensation scheme, North Carolina expanded its scheme only to have second thoughts. North Carolina backtracked from Virginia's generous approach to slaveholder compensation with the aim of cutting costs while shaping slaveholder behavior. All or a portion of losses that had previously been redistributed broadly among North Carolina taxpayers were imposed on individual slaveholders, incentivizing them to take steps to avoid those losses. What is more, unsuccessful efforts at the end of the colonial period to cabin redistribution of losses at the county level suggest both internal tensions between slaveholding and nonslaveholding regions and further resistance to offering slaveholders a blank check to exploit the enslaved to maximize profits. As explored in box 6.2, additional insights into North Carolina's slave society can be gleaned from a review of surviving tax-related legislative records.

Box 6.2. The Tax Window onto North Carolina's Slave Society

In North Carolina, public claims were approved parallel to the process of enacting the poll tax that funded those claims.[a] As evidenced by appendix table A.5, the surviving lists of public claims document more than ninety slaveholder compensation payments, nearly all of which fell squarely within the parameters of the colony's compensation scheme.[b] These payments were made by North Carolina taxpayers over four decades between 1734/5 and 1774 with respect to more than one hundred enslaved persons killed or executed. Due to the number of missing lists—as well as surviving lists that include fees for executions without associated compensation payments[c]—these figures can represent only a partial accounting of the killings perpetrated under North Carolina's slave code.

Notably, among the surviving lists, there are only three recorded instances of the Committee of Claims recommending denial of a slaveholder compensation claim and only one instance of the legislature denying a claim recommended for approval:

- In 1758, the committee recommended denial of claims for two unnamed enslaved persons until the slave court certified "that they had provisions & cloaths agreeable to Law."[d] This procedural defect appears to have been corrected because there were two claims in the 1759 list for Isaac and Charles, whose place and timing of execution as well as valuations correspond to those in the denial.

a. *See* Coralie Parker, The History of Taxation in North Carolina During the Colonial Period, 1663–1776, at 97–124 (1928); *e.g.*, 1767 Report of the Committee of Claims, Treasurer's and Comptroller's Papers, Record ID SR.204.1.022, N.C. State Archives; 7 Colonial Records of North Carolina 627, 644, 667–68 (William L. Saunders ed., 1890) [hereinafter N.C. Records].

b. 4 N.C. Records, *supra* note a, at 123–24, 148–51, 529–31; 5 *id.* at 975–86; 6 *id.* at 209–15, 738–44; 8 *id.* at 141–43, 382, 475–76; 9 *id.* at 724, 771–72, 778, 953; 22 *id.* at 400–07, 815–66; Reports of the Committee of Claims: 1754–1760, Governor's Office Records, Record ID 67.1.134, N.C. State Archives; Reports of the Committee of Claims: 1760–1764, Governor's Office Records, Record ID 67.1.135, N.C. State Archives; Reports of the Committee of Claims: 1766–1773, Treasurer's and Comptroller's Papers, Record ID SR.204.1.022, N.C. State Archives; Treasurer's and Comptroller's Papers, Miscellaneous Group, Record ID SR.204.37, N.C. State Archives; General Assembly Session Records, N.C. Digital Collections, https://digital.ncdcr.gov.

c. *E.g.*, 1754 Report of the Committee of Claims, *supra* note b; 1768 Report of the Committee of Claims, *supra* note b.

d. 5 N.C. Records, *supra* note a, at 985.

- In 1764, Robert Howe, a sitting member of the Lower House, verbally applied for compensation on behalf of John Bell "for a Negroe Fellon who died in Wilmington Goal some Years Past."[e] The committee recommended denial because "such a Claim was formerly made more than once and Rejected," but it requested the Lower House to consider whether old claims submitted without supporting documentation should be approved.[f] Upon consideration, the Lower House authorized compensation. Indicating that Howe's advocacy was not disinterested, Bell promptly assigned his claim to Howe, who then sold it to another at face value.[g]
- In 1769, the Upper House requested the Lower House to reconsider James Walker and Thomas Craigg's claim "for a Negro Wench outlawed and afterwards drown'd" because the claim had been "disallowed by your Committee of Claims although claims of the same kind have heretofore been allowed."[h] The Lower House rejected the claim that same day.[i]
- In 1770, the committee approved Elizabeth Blaning's £80 claim "for a Negroe Man who being charged with an attempt to Poison M^{rs}. Hall and taken on Suspicion thereof poysoned himself on his Conveyance to Goal," but the Lower House denied the claim.[j]

Given the dearth of records of rejected claims (and of committee deliberations), it is impossible to determine how stringently the legislature scrutinized claims, though the committee's brief sittings point toward a perfunctory rather than punctilious process. Nevertheless, on the basis of extant records, there were comparatively few controverted claims in North Carolina.

Because payment of compensation was conditioned on a death sentence and seemingly not its execution, the legislature demonstrated its parsimoniousness when enslaved persons were granted reprieves. In

e. 1764 Report of the Committee of Claims, *supra* note b.

f. *Id.*

g. Assignment of Claim by John Bell to Robert Howe, 1760–1769 Payment to Master for Executed Slave, Treasurer's and Comptroller's Papers, Record ID SR.204.37, N.C. State Archives.

h. 8 N.C. RECORDS, *supra* note a, at 102.

i. *Id.* at 138.

j. 1770 Report of the Committee of Claims, *supra* note b.

1760, Joseph Watters was allowed £60 for his enslaved man Tom, who had been sentenced to death.[k] After the governor granted Tom a reprieve, the Committee of Claims recommended "that the House Order him to be Shiped of by the Treasurer to reimburse the Public."[l] Faced with a similar situation the following year, the Lower House requested the governor to order the enslaved person to be sold and transported out of North Carolina so "that the money arising by such sale may be paid into the hands of the Public Treasurer and applied to the Contingent fund."[m]

Given the summary nature of entries, it is remarkable that the Committee of Claims named 85 percent of the enslaved persons, either in the entry for slaveholder compensation or in a related entry. This acknowledgment of enslaved persons' humanity contrasts sharply with other southern colonies, where naming was a less frequent occurrence. The lists of claims also document enslaved persons' open resistance to bondage, as when they escaped and were later outlawed and killed. The lists also document more brazen acts of resistance, such as when a group of Henry Ormond's enslaved persons killed him in his bed in 1770—with, according to news reports, one telling him that "as he had no mercy on them, he could expect none himself."[n] And the lists hint at the complex personal relationships among the enslaved through their documentation of internecine acts of violence, as when Dick was executed for poisoning an enslaved man held by John Crawford and when Will was executed for murdering Caesar.[o]

For slaveholders, enslaved persons' trials could be family affairs—with no apparent concern for potential conflicts of interest. For example, Henry Ormond's brother Wyriot, as administrator of Henry's estate, received not only the compensation paid for the enslaved persons who murdered Henry but also £5 for his work on their trial—and on the separate trial of an enslaved person held by his brother Roger.[p] Beyond the evident disinterest in creating even the appearance of impartiality, the lists evidence White society's brutal determination to maintain control

k. 1760 Report of the Committee of Claims, *supra* note b.

l. *Id.*

m. 6 N.C. RECORDS, *supra* note a, at 680.

n. *New Bern*, VA. GAZETTE (Rind), Sept. 6, 1770, at 1.

o. 22 N.C. RECORDS, *supra* note a, at 839; 1754 Report of the Committee of Claims, *supra* note b.

p. 1771 Report of the Committee of Claims, *supra* note b.

of the enslaved through terroristic punishment. In matter-of-fact prose, the lists mention an enslaved person's punishment for murder by being burned to death and, even more cruelly, how Jemmy (on a second felony offense) and Isaac (for arson) were both castrated *and* executed.[q]

---

q. 6 N.C. RECORDS, *supra* note a, at 739, 742; 22 *id.* at 834; 1764 Report of the Committee of Claims, *supra* note b.

Georgia

In 1755, influenced by settlers from South Carolina and the Caribbean, Georgia enacted a slave code patterned after South Carolina's 1740 Slave Code.[55] This slave code authorized capital punishment in a wide variety of circumstances and created a slaveholder compensation scheme "to the End that Owners of Slaves may not be tempted to conceal the Crimes of their Slaves to the prejudice of the public."[56] Under the compensation scheme, the slave court valued enslaved persons sentenced to death "at any Sum not Exceeding Fifty pounds," with at least half of that amount awarded to the slaveholder and the remainder to the injured person.[57] But if an enslaved person was executed for "deserting out of this province," the compensation cap was lifted, and the slaveholder was paid full value.[58]

In 1765, the legislature revised the slave code by expanding the list of capital crimes, removing the cap on slaveholder compensation, shifting responsibility for appraisals to two freeholders, and omitting the provision regarding compensation to the injured party.[59] Yet within a year, the legislature sharply reversed course. To stem potential abuse, it reimposed a compensation cap (now £40) on the theory that a capital conviction should lower an enslaved person's value, and it recommitted responsibility for appraisals to the slave court.[60] Perhaps having escapees from South Carolina in mind, the legislature likewise expressed doubt about the public benefit of allowing slaveholders with no connection to the colony to redistribute their losses among Georgia taxpayers.[61] To close this loophole, the legislature denied compensation to nonresident slaveholders unless they had "a settled Plantation [in Georgia], whereon such Slave or Slaves, at the Time of the Crime committed, was or were employed."[62]

Much to the consternation of the legislature, the 1765 Slave Code met with royal disallowance in 1767 (not because of its harshness but out of concern for the inheritance consequences of classifying the enslaved as personal rather than real property).[63] The legislature quickly enacted a stopgap measure that included the revised version of the compensation scheme but with a lower £30 cap.[64] The governor assented to this legislation, notwithstanding that doing so contravened royal instructions.[65] In 1770, royal qualms having been assuaged, the legislature enacted a permanent replacement that was patterned after, but harsher than, the 1765 Slave Code.[66]

To fund the colony's compensation scheme, Georgia's slave codes consistently directed the colony's portion of fines and penalties as well as the proceeds from public sales of unclaimed escapees "to be appropriated towards paying for Negroes publickly Executed."[67] The legislature viewed this revenue stream as "in aid of the general tax"—that is to say, as a means of lessening the property tax burden, which was the primary mechanism for redistributing slaveholders' losses.[68] As described in box 6.3, the Georgia legislature adopted a practice of authorizing slaveholder compensation as part of the annual drafting of property tax legislation, much as South Carolina did.

Box 6.3. The Tax Window onto Georgia's Slave Society

Georgia followed South Carolina's example by factoring slaveholder compensation into the calculation of property taxes.[a] In many cases, however, Georgia prepared prospective estimates rather than vetting past claims, and it was not until 1757 that those estimates were incorporated into tax legislation.[b] Among the surviving tax acts,[c] several prospective estimates authorize £40 to be spent on "Negroes that may be apprehended &

---

a. JOURNAL OF THE COMMONS HOUSE OF ASSEMBLY [hereinafter COMMONS JOURNAL], reprinted in 13 COLONIAL RECORDS OF THE STATE OF GEORGIA 212, 341–42, 354–55, 487, 512–18, 603, 645 (Allen D. Candler ed., 1904) [hereinafter GA. RECORDS]; JACK P. GREENE, THE QUEST FOR POWER: THE LOWER HOUSES OF ASSEMBLY IN THE SOUTHERN ROYAL COLONIES, 1689-1776, at 68–70, 105–06 (1963).

b. E.g., COMMONS JOURNAL, 13 GA. RECORDS, supra note a, at 211–12, 342. Compare 18 GA. RECORDS, supra note a, at 72–73, 170, with id. at 246–47.

c. See Georgia, Laws: Tax Acts (LLMC Digital) [hereinafter LLMC]; 19 [pt. 1] GA. RECORDS, supra note a, at 481.

Executed," seemingly anticipating a single execution each year.[d] Eventually, past claims surfaced in the estimate, but slaveholder compensation claims did not first appear until 1766. These claims constitute "the main evidence concerning the incidence (but not always the type) of capital crimes committed by slaves" (for a listing, see appendix table A.6).[e]

Legislative and executive journals and surviving colonial newspapers reveal little about the circumstances surrounding these claims, but the few mentions attest to both the brutality of punishments and the reluctance to extend clemency to enslaved persons. In 1765, the *Georgia Gazette* reported, "Yesterday a negroe fellow, who belonged to Mr. Peter Nephew at Little Ogechee, and murdered another slave on the 23d May last, was hanged, and his head cut off in order to be fixed upon a post near the place where he committed the murder."[f] For this execution, Nephew received £49 compensation in the 1766 Tax Act. In 1767, William Mackenzie petitioned the governor for clemency for an enslaved person who was "under Sentence of Death for Robbery"; but the Council unanimously rejected the petition, and he was paid £40 compensation.[g] In 1771, the slave court submitted a report "Concerning the Trial of a Certain Negroe Man Slave Convicted of breaking a Shop and Stealing Sundry goods" in connection with the slaveholder John Glen's memorial to the governor "praying that the said Slave might be Transported and not executed."[h] Yet again, the Council rejected the petition, but it was not until the next tax act was passed in 1773 that Glen was paid £30 compensation (without interest, contrary to South Carolina's custom when tax legislation was delayed).[i]

Between 1766 and 1773, sixteen Georgia slaveholders were paid compensation for seventeen executed enslaved persons and another killed in a skirmish with escapees. Nearly two-thirds of these payments were authorized in a single year, 1768. Nearly one-third of compensated slaveholders

---

d. COMMONS JOURNAL, 13 GA. RECORDS, *supra* note a, at 645; 28 [pt. 1] GA. RECORDS, *supra* note a, at 342–45; 1763 Tax Act, para. XVI, LLMC, *supra* note c; 1764 Tax Act, para. XVII, LLMC, *supra* note c.

e. Betty Wood, *"Until He Shall Be Dead, Dead, Dead": The Judicial Treatment of Slaves in Eighteenth-Century Georgia*, 71 GA. HIST. Q. 377, 383 (1987).

f. *Savannah*, GA. GAZETTE, June 6, 1765.

g. PROCEEDINGS AND MINUTES OF THE GOVERNOR AND COUNCIL, *reprinted in* 10 GA. RECORDS, *supra* note a, at 246.

h. *Id.*, 11 GA. RECORDS, *supra* note a, at 305.

i. *Id.*

were (or soon became) politically prominent, including an attorney general (Charles Pryce), a member of the Commons House of Assembly (John Glen), a sitting House Speaker (Alexander Wylly), a future House Speaker and later Revolutionary War president and commander in chief of Georgia (Archibald Bulloch), and a Revolutionary War governor (John Houstoun).[j]

Unlike North Carolina, Georgia does not appear to have fixed its compensation caps with replacement cost in mind. The earliest recorded compensation payments, which appear to fall during the short period when no cap existed, are noticeably higher than later payments. After the cap's reinstatement, nearly all the April 1768 payments were at the £40 maximum, and both December 1768 payments were at the temporarily lowered £30 cap. The two 1773 payments relating to 1771 executions were at or near the £30 cap, probably because the 1770 Slave Code and its reinstatement of the £40 cap did not enter into force until royal approbation in mid-1771.[k] The final 1773 payment, for an execution that year, was at the reinstated £40 cap. With so many payments at the cap and the price of enslaved persons during this period generally ranging from £50 to £60, it appears that Georgia required slaveholders to internalize a significant portion of their losses.[l] By imposing what amounted to an additional tax on the affected slaveholders, Georgia created a financial incentive for them to shape their behavior in ways that reduced the risk of transgressions of the slave code.

---

j. *Id.*, 10 GA. RECORDS, *supra* note a, at 428; COMMONS JOURNAL, 14 GA. RECORDS, *supra* note a, at 140, 335, 365, 586; *id.*, 15 GA. RECORDS, *supra* note a, at 7, 305; KENNETH COLEMAN, THE AMERICAN REVOLUTION IN GEORGIA, 1763–1789, app. A at 283, 283–84 (1958).
k. Letter from the Earl of Hillsborough to Governor Wright (July 3, 1771), CO 5/661 (Adam Matthew, Colonial America).
l. BETTY WOOD, SLAVERY IN COLONIAL GEORGIA, 1730–1775, at 97 (1984).

Marking the Enslaved as Property

Southern slave societies were constructed around the notion that enslaved persons were not people but property, differing only regarding whether to classify them as real or personal property.[69] In combination with other areas of law, the southern colonies used their tax systems to consistently reinforce this message that the enslaved were held—and taxable—as property. Virginia and the colonies within its sphere of legal influence (i.e., Maryland and North Carolina) did so through poll taxes, while Georgia, influenced by South Carolina, did so through property taxes.

Virginia

Poll taxes were an important source of revenue in Virginia, alongside export taxes on tobacco and import taxes on enslaved persons that aimed to alleviate the constantly bemoaned poll tax burden.[70] Virginia's first poll tax was imposed in 1619 on "every man & manservant of above 16 yeares of age."[71] In 1644, the legislature made clear that "the masters of the severall familys within the collony shall be responsible for all the publique duties, tithes and charges, due from all persons in their familys."[72] Thus, "because some tithables owned other tithables in colonial Virginia, the tax functioned both as a poll tax on free men *and* as a property tax on the owners of slaves and servants."[73]

Virginia's legislature repeatedly tinkered with the list of "tithables" subject to poll tax, conveying messages about whose labor was valued and about the racial and social hierarchy of Virginia's burgeoning slave society. Most saliently, the labor of working-age men—of whatever color and whether free, indentured, or enslaved—was always treated as valuable and, therefore, taxable. By the early 1640s, racism was intertwined with this patriarchalism when the legislature classified Black women's labor as a valuable—and taxable—wealth-producing commodity in the hands of those who controlled that labor.[74] What is more, this treatment applied to free as well as enslaved Black women, as evidenced by a 1652/3 Northampton County order relieving a free Black family from this onerous tax burden. Anthony Johnson's wife, Mary, and his two daughters were relieved from paying taxes because of "ye great Losses they have sustayned (by an unfortunate fire)."[75] In fact, however, "the court's 'relief' amounted to no more than a concession to reduce the Johnsons' taxes to the level ordinarily assessed on a comparable white family."[76] In 1657/8, perhaps responding to confusion about the tax status of Black women, the legislature clarified that lists of tithables must include "all negroes imported whether male or female, and Indian servants male or female however procured, being sixteen years of age."[77]

In 1662, the legislature reinforced the racism and patriarchalism in the poll tax when it closed a loophole that encouraged Virginia planters to employ tax-free indentured White women in the fields in place of taxable male servants or enslaved persons. The move to tax "all women servants whose common imployment is working in the crop" appears to have been aimed at encouraging the return of White women to their "proper" place—that is, engaging primarily in domestic work that remained untaxed—because women of color were already taxed no matter what work they performed.[78] In 1668, the legislature further reinforced these messages when it reaffirmed that free Black women were taxable, explaining that "negro women, though permitted to enjoy their ffreedome yet ought not in all respects to be admitted to a full fruition of the exemptions and impunities of the English."[79] In 1680, the legislature further elaborated the racial hierarchy expressed through the poll tax when it required enslaved Blacks to be reported as tithables at an age two years younger than indentured Whites.[80] These moves made clear that, "when used to describe women, 'negro' connoted servile labor, a status that persisted even after one became free and regardless of the work one performed. In contrast, 'English' signified a set of privileges in which womanhood, dependence, and domesticity were intertwined."[81]

In 1705, the legislature reversed many of its earlier moves by revising the list of tithables to include "all male persons, of the age of sixteen years, and upwards, and all negro, mulatto, and Indian women, of the age of sixteen years, and upwards, not being free."[82] But in 1723, the legislature tacked back when it responded to complaints "of the great Numbers of free Negros of which the women pay no Taxes" by amending the list of tithables to include "all free negros, mullattos, or indians (except tributary indians to this government) male and female," as well as "all wives of such negros, mullattos, or indians."[83] That rule persisted until 1771, when a petition from "Mulattoes and free Negroes" spurred its repeal on the ground that it was "very burthensome . . . and is moreover derogatory of the rights of free-born subjects."[84]

Maryland

Maryland imposed poll taxes to defray public expenditures, and the poll tax became "the main source of revenue for the colony."[85] In contrast to Virginia, poll taxes were repeatedly described as the fairest means of levying taxes in Maryland "because as our [i.e., Marylanders'] Estates consist for the most part in Servants & Negroes those who have the most property pay the greatest Share of the Tax."[86] The poll tax was, therefore, viewed as an easily administrable surrogate for a property tax—which was possible only because bondspeople represented the bulk of colonists' wealth.

Like Virginia, Maryland tinkered with the poll tax base in telling ways. In 1662, Maryland marked the line between the free and unfree by specifying that males born in Maryland became subject to tax at age sixteen while imported male servants and male and female enslaved persons became taxable at age ten.[87] In 1676, the legislature erased this distinction when it set sixteen as the age when freemen, male servants, and enslaved persons all became taxable.[88] A few years later, the legislature debated adding White women servants "that work in the Ground" to the list of taxable persons; however, unlike Virginia, Maryland refrained from closing this tax loophole.[89] In 1712, enslaved persons who were "Adjudged by the County Courts to be past Labour" were declared exempt from taxation—in contrast, freemen were exempted only when they were so poor as to be living on "Almes from the County"—making it clear that enslaved persons were valuable only while laboring for slaveholders.[90] Finally, in 1725, the legislature underscored the centrality of race to Maryland's patriarchal poll tax structure when it continued to exempt White women from tax but added to the list of taxable persons "all Female Mulattoes born of White Women, and Free Negro Women, of the Age of Sixteen Years."[91]

North Carolina

In 1715, after encountering difficulty imposing a tax on polls and estates, North Carolina levied flat taxes on "every Tythable person or master of every Tythable person" and on "every Hundred acres of Land."[92] To resolve doubts about when individuals became tithable, the legislature provided that "all Males not being Slaves" became tithable at age sixteen while "All Slaves Male or Female" became tithable at age twelve.[93] In 1720, faced with rampant tax evasion, the legislature lowered the tax rates and strengthened information-reporting requirements.[94] Making clear that enslaved persons were a prized form of property, the legislature further decreed that, when collecting the fines imposed for concealing land or tithables, "no Negro shall be seized on or for any of the publick Taxes where there is any other personal Estate to be found to answer and pay the Fines."[95]

In 1722, the legislature abandoned taxing land in favor of levying only poll taxes.[96] The legislature then relied on poll taxes throughout the remainder of the colonial period, later declaring that "Taxation by the Poll, is found the most certain and easy Method of raising Money."[97] Nevertheless, the poll tax was perceived as burdensome to the poor and criticized for its inequitable operation as a surrogate property tax. For instance, in the late 1760s, during the Regulator Movement, petitioners from the western frontier urged the enactment of a property tax, arguing that the poll tax might adequately act as a surrogate property tax in eastern North Carolina, "where estates consist chiefly in Slaves; yet to us in the frontier, where very few are possessed of Slaves, tho' their Estates are in proportion (in many instances) as of one Thousand to one, for all to pay equal, is with Submission, very grievous and oppressive."[98] Treatment of the enslaved as property was thus at the heart of southern poll taxation.

Georgia

Georgia imposed property taxes patterned after South Carolina's annual Tax-Acts to defray expenses not covered through appropriations from the British Parliament.[99] Flat taxes on land and enslaved persons were at the core of Georgia's property tax, supplemented by taxes on town lots, cash lent out, and merchants' stock in trade.[100] As a result, Georgia marked enslaved persons as taxable property in much the same way that South Carolina did.

Although Georgia never experimented with poll taxes on Whites as South Carolina did, it did eventually impose a poll tax on free Blacks over the age of sixteen.[101] This tax was not, however, instituted with revenue raising as its primary goal, because it was estimated to apply to only twenty taxpayers and to raise no more than £15 in revenue.[102] Rather, this tax reinforced White supremacy in Georgia by depriving free Blacks of the tax privileges enjoyed by free Whites.

Manipulating the Racial Balance

Except for North Carolina, the southern colonies likewise marked enslaved persons as property immediately upon arrival by taxing them alongside other imported commodities. As happened elsewhere, import taxation also served as a tool for manipulating the racial composition of the colonies' populations—or, in Virginia, to purport to be doing so while pursuing other ends. Despite lacking an import tax, North Carolina was not left out of this story because it instead used poll taxes to manipulate the racial composition of its population.

Maryland

In 1695, Maryland began taxing the importation of enslaved Blacks to raise revenue.[103] The following year, the tax was raised to £1 sterling to alleviate the poll tax burden on "the Poorer sort."[104] The tax rate then continued at that level for two decades.[105] Revenue raising was not, however, the exclusive aim of this tax because Maryland soon carved out an exemption to encourage local participation in the slave trade. Beginning in 1704, enslaved Blacks imported on locally owned ships were exempted from tax "to encourage the Inhabitants of this Province to Adventure their Shipps and Vessells more freely abroad to import Rum Sugar Negroes and other Comoditys."[106]

In 1716, sensing an opportunity to raise additional revenue from the slave trade, the legislature imposed a tax of £4 local currency in addition to the £1 sterling tax.[107] This tax was disallowed because it also applied to imported Irish servants and would thus discourage the migration of Irish Protestants.[108] In response, the legislature enacted an additional tax of £1 local currency that applied to imported enslaved Blacks and Irish Roman Catholic servants, dedicating the revenue to funding the colony's schools so that its citizens would be well prepared "for the Discharge of their Duties in the several Stations and Employments they may be called to."[109] In 1728, the legislature clarified that the tax exemption for locally owned vessels did not apply to this additional tax.[110] The legislature then left these revenue-raising taxes—the basic tax of £1 sterling and the additional tax of £1 local currency—unaltered for decades.

It has been suggested that "by the middle of the century there was evidently some opposition rising to the further large importation" of enslaved Blacks.[111] Yet, the use of purely revenue-raising taxes on the importation of enslaved Blacks persisted. Amid controversy regarding the enlistment of White servants to fight in the French and Indian War,[112] Maryland included temporary additional taxes on the importation of enslaved Blacks among its wartime revenue measures in the mid-1750s; however, favoring White immigration does not seem to have been the goal given the simultaneous enactment of taxes on imported servants.[113] In 1763, after these temporary taxes expired, the legislature enacted an additional tax on the importation of enslaved Blacks, now to increase funding for the school system.[114] The Lower House proposed a rate of £10, but the Upper House reduced the rate to £2 local currency.[115] Though set to expire after three years, the £2 tax was twice extended and remained in force through the end of the colonial period.[116]

In late 1771, after rejecting a petition from Maryland Quakers to enact an outright ban on the slave trade, the legislature enacted an additional tax of £5 local currency and again dedicated the revenue to the school system.[117] The Quaker abolitionist Anthony Benezet later suggested that this tax "was too small to affect the Trade, fearing if larger to meet with opposition from the African Company."[118] But it is misleading to consider this tax in isolation—the import tax now totaled £1 sterling plus £8 local currency and has more recently been described as "prohibitive."[119]

Virginia

In 1699, Virginia enacted its first tax targeted at the importation of enslaved persons.[120] This measure was enacted in lieu of increasing the poll tax to fund the rebuilding of the colonial capitol after its destruction by fire.[121] The tax was renewed several times to continue funding public works.[122] Then, in 1710, the import tax was abruptly raised to £5 for enslaved Blacks but left at its historical rate of £1 for enslaved Native Americans.[123]

Amid fears of rebellion and calls for curbing the slave trade, the governor expressed concern that the sharp increase might be construed as a prohibition of the African slave trade and, therefore, violate royal instructions.[124] The House of Burgesses responded with the more benign explanation that import taxes on enslaved persons and liquor had long been accepted as the least burdensome means of raising revenue.[125] When submitting the legislation for royal approbation, the governor justified the tax as a revenue-raising measure and then explained how he had relented in his objections because, in the prevailing economic situation, the tax would not harm the slave trade:

> They [i.e., the Burgesses] urged what is really true, that the Country is already ruined by the great number of Negros imported of late years; that it will be impossible for them in many years to discharge the Debts already contracted for the purchase of those Negros if fresh Supplys be still poured in upon them while their tobacco continues so little valuable but that the People will run more and more in Debt, and must be forced to imploy their hands upon other manufactures. Whereupon finding them unanimously resolved rather to lose the Bill than to go contrary to the General inclinations of the Country I at last yeilded to pass the Act as they had prepared it, after having been assured by the most considerable Traders that this Duty will be no discouragment to the Negro trade if tobacco becomes valuable, and on the other hand, tho no Duty were laid on Negros, the Country is not in a Capacity to purchase any number while their tobacco is at so low a Rate, and that this Duty will only affect some few Merchants that perhaps may import Negros before they are acquainted with the Circumstances of the Country; but none that are thoroughly versed in this Trade.[126]

Based on a different economic calculus, the English slave trader Richard Harris later suggested to the Board of Trade that the import tax *was* intended to be prohibitive, having been "obtained by Overgrown Planters, who had Negroes In Abundance, In order To discourage & Disable Other Lesser Planters who had few or none from Increasing the Growth of Tobacco that theirs Might Sell the dearer In the Markets of Europe."[127]

After being renewed twice, the import tax was allowed to expire in 1718.[128] While in force, the tax might have restrained the slave trade, but it "did not end the traffic in slaves."[129] From late 1710 through 1718, more than forty-four hundred enslaved Blacks entered Virginia, as compared to the nearly seventy-three hundred imported during the prior decade.[130]

In the 1720s, Virginia twice attempted to reimpose a tax on the importation of enslaved persons. Early in the decade, Surry County suggested a £20 tax accompanied by legislation to better control the enslaved population in place, and other counties made similar suggestions.[131] Professing a fear of threats from the enslaved population and neighboring Native Americans but recalling that import taxes were a time-tested source of easy revenue, the legislature enacted a £2 tax on the importation of enslaved persons to defray defense-related expenditures without raising the poll tax.[132] Shortly after taking effect, this tax met with royal disallowance due to "the interferring interest of the *Affrican* Company"; however, repeal of the tax was not published in Virginia until some six months later.[133]

In 1727/8, the legislature reenacted the £2 tax—this time with a clause suspending its effect until royal approbation was announced.[134] When transmitting the law to England, the governor made the case for approbation by listing the expenses the tax would support, mentioning the need for alternative sources of revenue aside from the "grievous" poll tax, and citing the existence of "the like or a greater Duty on Negroes" in Maryland.[135] The governor even raised and dismissed the slave traders' argument that the tax was a burden on them: "The only objection I think that can be brought against this Law is, the private Interest of the Importer: but when it is considered that the price of Negroes will always be advanced in proportion to the Duty, they can't be sufferers by it. and the money will be taken out of their pockets, who are the advocates for it."[136] Despite the governor's arguments, the tax met with the same fate as the earlier measure.[137]

After issuance of the royal instructions in the early 1730s prohibiting the imposition of tax on the importer of enslaved Blacks,[138] the House of Burgesses resolved to draft a bill imposing a £1 tax that would comply with that instruction.[139] After the bill's second reading, the Burgesses shifted course and decided to impose a tax based on value instead of at a flat rate, still to be paid by the purchaser.[140] The enacted legislation, which was justified as a means of lessening the poll tax burden, imposed a 5 percent tax on the purchase price of all imported enslaved persons.[141] The governor successfully defended the tax on the ground

TABLE 6.1. Virginia Taxes on Imported Enslaved Persons, 1732–75

Years	Base tax	Additional taxes	Total tax
1732–40	5%	None enacted	5%
1740–44	5%	5%	10%
1744–51	5%	None enacted	5%
1751–52	Lapsed	None enacted	0%
1752–54	5%	None enacted	5%
1754–55	5%	5%	10%
1755–60	5%	5% + 10%	20%
1760–71	5%	5%	10%
1771–73	5%	Disallowed	5%
1773–75	Disallowed	Disallowed	0%

that it did not in "any way affect the British merchants trading in slaves, since they are not one farthing out of Pocket on Acc^t. of this Duty nor is their Price lessen'd by it, as may be clearly seen by comparing the Sales of Negros since the Comencement of this Duty with others when there was no Duty at all."[142] The tax was repeatedly extended over four decades, with a gap of only several months in 1751–52.[143] As set forth in table 6.1, beginning in 1740, the legislature imposed a series of temporary additional taxes to defray war-related expenses and, later, to lessen the poll tax burden.[144]

Virginia's import tax, at its peak, led to complaints to the legislature.[145] In 1760, the legislature reduced the tax by half on the ground that the "additional duty of ten per centum hath been found very burthensome to the fair purchaser, a great disadvantage to the settlement and improvement of the lands in this colony, introductive of many frauds, and not to answer the end thereby intended, inasmuch as the same prevents the importation of slaves, and thereby lessens the fund arising from the duties upon slaves."[146] The governor explained to the Board of Trade that the bill repealing the additional 10 percent tax passed by a single vote in the House because of "the contest . . . between the old Settlers who have bred great quantity of Slaves, and would make a Monopoly of them by a duty which they hoped would amount to a prohibition; and the rising Generation who want Slaves, and don't care to pay the Monopolists for them at the price they have lately bore, which was exceedingly high. These reasons your Lord[pps] may guess are not urged in the arguments on either side; but, I believe are the true foundation of the Squabble."[147]

In 1767, the legislature reinstated the additional 10 percent tax as a means of lessening the poll tax burden; however, that measure met with royal disallowance.[148] Another attempt at reinstating the additional 10 percent tax in 1769 likewise met with royal disallowance—and resulted in a sternly worded additional instruction from the Crown to the governor.[149] Up to this point, Virginia's import tax legislation depicted a firm commitment to profiting from the slave trade—even in the face of threats from a large enslaved population—because import taxation was a politically expedient means of raising revenue.[150] A tacit desire to suppress the slave trade surfaced only when wealthy planters could profit from manipulating the supply of enslaved labor to increase the prices of their own tobacco or enslaved persons.[151]

It was not until the end of the colonial period that Virginia's legislature expressed moral qualms about the slave trade. In 1772, while preparing import tax legislation, the House of Burgesses ordered an address to be drafted to the king requesting "his paternal Assistance in averting a Calamity of a most alarming Nature": "that the Importation of Negroes from *Africa* has long been considered as a Trade of great Inhumanity, and, under its present Encouragement, may endanger the Existence of his *American* Dominions; that Self-Preservation therefore urges us to implore him to remove all Restraints on his Governors from passing Acts of Assembly, which are intended to check this pernicious Commerce."[152] The final address further requested the king not to privilege the pecuniary interests of slave traders over those of the colonists, because the slave trade "greatly retards the Settlement of the Colonies, with more useful Inhabitants, and may, in Time, have the most destructive Influence."[153] The governor forwarded the address to England with his own endorsement, which focused squarely on the threats posed by the colony's large enslaved population.[154] These entreaties were to no avail because the 1772 legislation—which would have continued the base tax of 5 percent and revived the additional 5 percent tax that expired in 1771—also met with royal disallowance.[155]

Notably, moral opposition to slavery made no appearance in the text of the 1772 legislation. In keeping with the stated aim of continuing long-standing taxes, the 1772 legislation sought to maintain the status quo rather than return rates to their earlier, prohibitive peak. Interestingly, the House journal records no petitions urging the legislature to end the slave trade, which had been the spark for legislative action to end the slave trade in other colonies, even though Virginians had not hesitated to petition the legislature to *lower* the tax rate to mitigate the tax burden and encourage the slave trade when rates were at their peak. Rather than an expression of moral qualms about slavery, the 1772 legislation appears to have been an outgrowth of the routine work of the committee tasked with examining expiring legislation to determine which acts should be continued and which allowed to expire.[156] A final effort in 1775 to impose a 10 percent tax on the importation of enslaved persons—included as a revenue raiser in a bill relating to the militia—met with an unsurprising gubernatorial veto.[157]

What is more, the Virginia slave trade had peaked and tapered off long before the 1770s—not because of taxation but "because high rates of natural increase among native-born slaves reduced the need for new African imports."[158] Within the context of this overall decline, a variety of factors influenced short-term fluctuations in Virginia's slave trade.[159] Import taxes might have been one such factor, but as illustrated in figure 6.1,[160] there is no clear correlation between tax rates and the number of enslaved persons imported, except when the tax reached its peak of 20 percent. But even then, other factors probably contributed to the steep decline in imports, including depressed tobacco prices and the disruptions associated with the French and Indian War.[161] Nonetheless, had Virginians desired to end the slave trade, this correlation—which had figured prominently among the justifications for lowering the tax rate in 1760—militated in favor of a rate at least double that sought to be imposed by the legislature in 1772 and 1775. Yet, in apparent disregard of all facts to the contrary, when Virginians created their new government in 1776, they included among their grievances against King George III, "prompting our negroes to rise in arms among us, those very negroes whom, by an inhuman use of his negative, he hath refused us permission to exclude by law."[162]

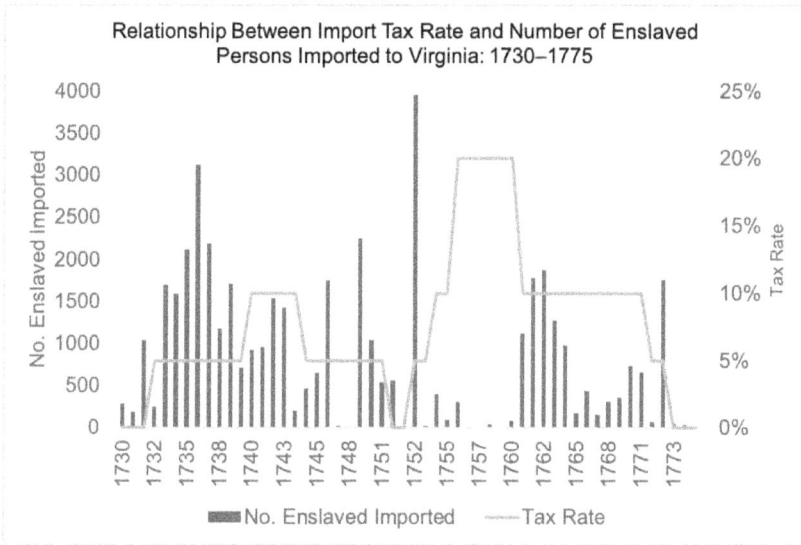

Figure 6.1. Relationship between import tax rate and number of enslaved persons imported to Virginia, 1730–75

Georgia

Simultaneous with the legalization of slavery, Georgia's Trustees enacted a revenue-raising duty of fifteen shillings for every imported enslaved Black twelve years or older.[163] After becoming a royal colony, Georgia took steps to establish a revenue-raising tax on the importation of commodities, including enslaved persons.[164] In 1761, these efforts first transformed into a "Bill to lay a Duty Equal to A prohibition to Prevent the Importation of seasoned Negroes into this Province" and later into a measure that combined that goal with meeting the need for revenue "to repair the Light House on Tybee Island."[165]

Echoing complaints voiced in other American colonies, the legislature explained that "it is greatly detrimental to the inhabitants of this province to purchase negroes imported from the *West-India* islands and colonies on the continent, who are in general transported thence by the courts of justice, or sent by private persons for their ill behaviour."[166] To deter this trade, the legislature imposed a £10 tax on all enslaved persons over age ten, unless they had "not been six months on shore in any part of *America*."[167] The first £36 of revenue was dedicated to lessening the property tax burden, and all additional revenue funded repairs to the lighthouse.[168] In 1767, the legislature reiterated the dangers posed by seasoned enslaved persons when it reenacted the tax and dedicated all the revenue to lighthouse repairs.[169] The tax was later extended until 1772 or until the additional funds authorized to be spent on the lighthouse had been fully expended.[170] Like South Carolina, Georgia thus strived to encourage the importation of enslaved Blacks from Africa with the hope of creating a more tractable enslaved population. At the same time, however, Georgia never aimed to end the intercolonial slave trade because it counted on import tax revenue to pay for public works.

In 1769, the legislature considered enacting a tax on the importation of enslaved Blacks and deploying the revenue to encourage the migration of Protestant settlers, as South Carolina had earlier done.[171] In 1773, after several failed attempts, the legislature instead enacted a tax on imported "Negroes or other Slaves, Goods, Wares, and Merchandize" to force nonresidents who traded in the colony to contribute to funding its government.[172] All imported commodities were taxed at 2.5 percent of their value.[173] Highlighting Georgia's unique position among the American colonies in relying heavily on grants from Parliament for its revenue, the report to the Board of Trade objected to the tax on the ground that it was both inequitable and impolitic "to call on such Persons to support the Government of a Country they trade to (unless under very Special Circumstances), and least of all to the Support of Government in Georgia, so great a part of which is defrayed out of the Revenue of Great Britain."[174] Based on this recommendation, the tax met with royal disallowance in late 1774, which the governor disseminated in a March 1775 proclamation.[175]

North Carolina

Unlike other southern colonies, North Carolina did not tax the importation of enslaved persons.[176] Like Delaware, Connecticut, and New Hampshire, North Carolina perhaps refrained from taxing imports because the slave trade to the colony was comparatively small, trade directly from Africa was rare, and significant trade from the West Indies did not begin until the mid-1760s.[177] Nevertheless, North Carolina did use taxation to manipulate the racial composition of its population, turning to poll taxes for this purpose.

In 1723, responding to complaints from "divers Freeholders and other Inhabitants of this Government, of great Numbers of Free Negroes, Mulattoes, and other Persons of mixt Blood, that have lately removed themselves into this Government, and that several of them have intermarried with the white Inhabitants of this Province; in Contempt of the Acts and Laws in those Cases made and provided," the legislature decreed that "all free Negroes, Mulattoes, and other Persons of that kind, being mixed Blood, including the Third Generation . . . both Male and Female, who are of the age of Twelve years and upwards"—along with their White spouses—would be tithable.[178] This change extended the rules for taxing enslaved persons to free persons of color and their spouses, leaving only White men (whether free or indentured) in the group that became taxable at age sixteen and only White women (whether free or indentured, unless married to a person of color) in the group that was exempt from poll tax.[179] The effect was to create a recurring, race-based tax penalty (or, as the 1723 legislation put it, "an additional Tax") on top of the existing £50 penalty paid by Whites who married "any Negro, Mulatto or Indyan."[180] In 1749, North Carolina reenacted this punitive additional tax and extended it to people of mixed race down to the fourth generation.[181] By relegating free people of color and their families to an inferior status, North Carolina not only deterred their migration to the colony but also worked to ensure that skin color would be synonymous with bondage—a fact that becomes abundantly clear when this additional tax is taken together with the simultaneous effort to shore up the mandate that all manumitted enslaved persons must permanently leave the colony within six months.[182]

The legislature received a series of petitions urging repeal of this tax, citing the financial burden that it created and, near the end of the colonial period, its inconsistency with "the Rights of Freeborn Subjects."[183] Not only did the legislature fail to act on these petitions, but it actually reaffirmed this punitive tax treatment in 1760.[184] North Carolina thus repeatedly chose to use taxation to advance White supremacy while deterring the migration of free people of color to the province.

Reflection

The southern colonies were "at once very alike, and yet significantly different. . . . They are not so dissimilar that comparison is fruitless. Rather, each society looks different in the light of the other; and our understanding of each is enlarged by knowledge of the other."[185] Unsurprisingly, given the close relationship between tax law and society, these patterns of similarity and difference likewise surface in the deep and enduring connections that the southern colonies forged between taxation and slavery as they became slave societies.

All the southern colonies enacted harsh slave codes to control their enslaved populations and included compensation schemes to secure slaveholder cooperation in their enforcement. Eschewing the more limited forms of redistribution adopted by the middle colonies, the southern colonies spoke with one voice when sending the message that slaveholder compensation provided a public benefit whose cost should be shared broadly by colonial taxpayers. But the southern colonies did not arrive at this consensus immediately, and they differed in the precise contours of its implementation.

For instance, Virginia and Maryland arrived at this destination earliest and consistently funded slaveholder compensation through provincial poll taxes. But whereas Virginia quickly moved to provide slaveholders full compensation, Maryland resisted doing so to incentivize slaveholders to reduce the incidence of transgressions of the slave code. Slaveholder persistence eventually succeeded, however, in eliminating this additional tax on individual slaveholders, shunting that burden instead onto the backs of all payers of Maryland's poll tax. Virginia slaveholders similarly demonstrated their persistence—and opened a tax window onto their slave society—through their unceasing efforts to expand the colony's generous compensation scheme through sometimes quite dubious petitions to the legislature.

North Carolina experimented with taxing slaveholders to fund compensation but soon gravitated away from this funding mechanism—first on an informal basis and later formally embracing Virginia's model of a generous slaveholder compensation scheme funded by colonial poll taxes. Yet, North Carolina's commitment to such a generous scheme proved to be tentative. When faced with financial headwinds, North

Carolina trimmed the generosity of its slaveholder compensation scheme to cut costs while providing slaveholders with a financial incentive to shape their behavior for the benefit of White society. Despite later easing some of these measures, North Carolina did not fully relinquish the use of financial incentives to shape slaveholder behavior as Maryland did, but it did resist a push from its frontier region to sharply limit the redistribution of slaveholders' economic losses. Surviving tax-related records provide a glimpse of the operation of this scheme and of North Carolina's slave society.

Georgia, too, felt the influence of a neighboring legal system: South Carolina's. Georgia borrowed heavily from South Carolina's slave code, including its slaveholder compensation scheme. Given its late legalization of slavery, Georgia leapfrogged South Carolina's early period of experimentation and always funded slaveholder compensation through colonial-level property taxes. Georgia did, however, depart from South Carolina's example by eventually removing the cap on slaveholder compensation, only to quickly reverse course and reinstate it due to concerns about abuse.

The southern colonies, with less hesitation or equivocation than their northerly neighbors, used their tax systems to mark the enslaved as property and to delineate racial and gender hierarchies. In the northern colonies, the combination of taxes on polls and estates necessitated the classification of enslaved persons either as people subject to poll tax or as property subject to the tax on estates. In Virginia, Maryland, and North Carolina, however, the poll tax alone served this combined function by subjecting free White men simultaneously to a poll tax on themselves and to the equivalent of a tax on their property. This was possible because enslaved persons served as a convenient proxy for wealth in southern slave societies, and the poll tax allowed that wealth to be taxed in a way that both was easily administered and avoided intrusive valuations of slaveholders' "property." Georgia, on the other hand, followed South Carolina's example by placing land and enslaved persons at the heart of its property tax.

The southern colonies' tax systems also reflected their societies' racial and gender hierarchies. As wealth-generating laborers, enslaved women were always taxed. In contrast, White women were consistently exempted from tax, except for a brief period when Virginia taxed White women servants to encourage their return to domestic work. To shrink the tax and social distance between free and enslaved Blacks (and correspondingly increase the distance between Whites and Blacks), Virginia and Maryland taxed free women of color, and Virginia taxed White women who married across racial lines to further reinforce that message. Ostensibly to the same end, Georgia eventually supplemented its property tax with poll taxes on free Blacks. Only Virginia repealed its discriminatory tax rules before the end of the colonial period.

North Carolina used its poll tax not only to delineate racial and gender hierarchies but also to manipulate the colony's racial composition. North Carolina's onerous tax penalties on free people of color and their families aimed to deter their migration to the colony and to ensure that skin color would be synonymous with bondage. Taxation was thus used to establish a rigid distinction between Whites and Blacks in North Carolina. Other southern colonies turned to import taxes to manipulate the racial composition of their populations; however, discouraging the importation of enslaved Blacks in favor of White migration was apparently a less pressing concern in the absence of an enslaved Black majority like that found in South Carolina. Most notably, Virginia paid lip service to using the power of taxation to depress the importation of enslaved Blacks in favor of encouraging White migration, but its actions spoke more loudly than its words. Virginia's import tax legislation evinced a deep commitment to the slave trade as a source of painless revenue that allowed the people in power to be seen as doing something about the onerous poll tax burden. When import tax rates did reach high levels, it was perceived not as a move to affect the colony's Black-White racial balance but as an attempt by wealthy and powerful Virginia slaveholders to manipulate the supply (and, in turn, the price) of enslaved labor to stymie competition in the tobacco trade or to exact higher prices on the sale of their own enslaved persons.

Georgia did use import taxes to curtail the slave trade but in a targeted fashion. Voicing widely held concerns regarding the hazards posed by enslaved persons from the Caribbean and other mainland American colonies, Georgia used taxation to encourage the importation of enslaved Blacks from Africa in the hope of creating a more tractable enslaved population. Nevertheless, Georgia sought only to softly shape behavior rather than to end the intercolonial slave trade because it relied on import tax revenue to fund public works. Maryland, on the other hand, did raise import taxes to seemingly prohibitive levels at the end of the colonial period, after long relying on those taxes both as a source of revenue and to encourage local participation in the slave trade—but after more recently rejecting an outright ban on the slave trade.

The southern colonies, like their northerly neighbors, forged common ties between taxation and slavery but diverged significantly in how they used taxation to advance the evils of racism and White supremacy to destroy the lives and liberty of their enslaved populations. Although the dominant slave societies in the region—Virginia and South Carolina—did exert influence over the legal development of their neighbors, that influence was tempered by local adaptations that illustrate the close relationship between tax law and society. From Maryland's late moves to curtail the slave trade after a long history of encouraging and profiting from it to Georgia's efforts to keep out troublemakers while still profiting from the intercolonial slave trade to North Carolina's sectional tensions related to slaveholder compensation to Virginia's greedy gentry feeding at the public trough, the southern colonies established deep and enduring connections between taxation and slavery that provide a unique vantage point from which to observe the development of their slave societies.

* * *

With this survey of the ties forged between taxation and slavery in the American colonies now complete, the concluding chapter will turn to considering the lessons that tax history might hold for those who are presently interested in obtaining reparations for the harms perpetrated in connection with, and in the long wake of, American slavery.

Conclusion

Due to the close relationship between tax law and society, the political choices made when constructing tax laws send messages about those whom society values and validates *and* about those whom society has chosen to marginalize and oppress.[1] Given that all of the American colonies exploited the labor of enslaved Blacks and Native Americans, it is no wonder that their tax systems reflected White fears of resistance to bondage and tell a story of power and profit that graphically demonstrates enslaved persons' degradation in the name of allowing White societies to flourish and prosper.[2]

Viewing Colonial Society Through a Tax Lens

The advice to "follow the money" applies equally to deeply politicized tax laws as it does to politics more generally.[3] After all, taxes cannot be raised from people without income or assets, and individual capacity to contribute increases as income and assets rise. In the American colonies, enslaved human beings constituted both a significant source of income and highly valuable capital assets; indeed, they were treated as property in law and in everyday life when they were bought and sold, bequeathed and gifted, mortgaged and rented out, or even reported missing in newspaper advertisements to elicit the aid of others in restoring this human "property" to its putative "owner." Unsurprisingly, then, tax law was no mere bystander to the legal project of dehumanizing enslaved persons; rather, it was an active participant through its marking of enslaved persons as taxable property in the hands of their holders.

Most American colonies marked enslaved persons as property immediately upon their forced arrival by taxing them alongside other imported commodities. Thereafter, the wealth-generating labor power of enslaved persons became the object of poll or property taxes that provided periodic, ritualistic reinforcement of enslaved persons' status as capital assets when taxpayers were required to account for their property—human and nonhuman—so that their individual contributions to the commonweal could be determined. Being associated with wealth, slaveholding was also a marker of power and privilege that was sometimes targeted for special exactions, as occurred from time to time in New York. In fact, a common refrain among colonial legislatures was that taxing slaveholding and slave trading was a painless means of raising revenue that often had the added benefit of enhancing the tax system's progressivity.

Profiting from enslaved labor required more, however, than merely classifying people as property along with land and livestock. To forcibly extract human labor through quiescent compliance that would safeguard White society, it proved necessary to establish systems of control over enslaved persons' lives and actions. As was the case with the legal project to dehumanize enslaved persons, this vast project of social engineering also had important tax components. At a general level, colonial legislatures became preoccupied with the racial mix of new arrivals out of concern about the ability to muster sufficient forces to defend against external enemies as well as against internal uprisings that might occur among the enslaved population. Import taxes proved to be a convenient mechanism to address these concerns. Whether by discouraging the importation of all enslaved persons or only those viewed as troublemakers, colonial legislatures used import taxes to cement White control by encouraging the importation of White servants, more tractable enslaved labor, or both. Even revenue-raising import taxes participated in this project, as when South Carolina dedicated the revenue from taxes on the importation of enslaved Blacks to subsidizing White migration and easing the acclimation of new White immigrants to life in the colony.

To exert control at the individual level, the American colonies adopted slave codes of varying severity and harshness. The middle and southern colonies, with their larger enslaved populations, authorized terroristic displays of force to maintain the enslaved population in subjugation. Their slave codes often resorted to capital punishment for criminalized forms of resistance and, in the southern colonies, absolved Whites from liability for the extrajudicial killing of enslaved persons. But if the threat of terroristic punishment was to have any effect, it was necessary to ensure slaveholders' cooperation in the administration of "justice" and the destruction of their valuable capital assets. To this end, the middle and southern colonies created slaveholder compensation schemes that varied in their scope and generosity as well as in how they distributed the burden of defraying the cost of slaveholder compensation.

Slaveholders, colonial legislators, and local officials all seem to have been keenly aware that the choice of tax mechanisms for funding slaveholder compensation conveyed a judgment about who benefited from these payments and, more importantly, determined how widely slaveholders' economic losses would be redistributed through the tax system. Reflecting the relative centrality of slavery to their societies, the middle and southern colonies made different choices regarding the tax mechanisms used to fund slaveholder compensation. As societies with slaves, the middle colonies sent the message that slaveholder compensation was of limited public benefit, with the cost of compensation defrayed through taxes on local slaveholders, local property holders, or people participating in the slave trade (i.e., slaveholders and slave traders). But New Jersey eventually repealed its compensation scheme—sending the signal that compensation provided no public benefit at all—and effectively taxed individual slaveholders alone. In contrast, as slave societies, the southern colonies coalesced around the use of broadly applicable poll or property taxes to fund slaveholder compensation, sending the message that slaveholder compensation broadly benefited the public and, therefore, that the burden of its payment should be shouldered by all colonial taxpayers. These varied choices for funding slaveholder compensation also open enlightening tax windows onto these societies, often adding new texture or depth to existing portraits of colonial American societies.

The American colonies used taxation in a coordinated, multipronged effort to protect and promote slavery and slaveholding in ways that reflected the prevalence and operation of the institution of slavery in their different societies, local attitudes and mores, and the tensions both within and among the colonies and between the colonies and England. But the story told by colonial tax laws is not just one of advancing slavery and racism so that Whites might profit from enslaved labor. As the end of the colonial period approached and public questioning of and opposition to slavery grew, some colonies used the power of taxation for more salutary ends—namely, as a more palatable means of ending the slave trade than an outright ban. Though often motivated by self-interest, these efforts show how taxation can be used not only in the service of evil but also to correct or mitigate societal injustices.

This examination of the role that taxation played in entrenching and perpetuating slavery in colonial America underscores how today's claims that taxation is a form of legalized theft or slavery are nothing more than overblown and bombastic rhetoric that inappropriately taps into the suffering of persons who experienced actual slavery and theft. This historical context also provides a firm anchor point for the efforts of critical tax scholars to shine a spotlight on the ways in which present-day tax laws continue to further racial and other forms of subordination. Furthermore, as discussed next, this historical context holds important lessons for people seeking reparations for the harms inflicted through slavery, the Jim Crow system of racial segregation that followed it, and the structural racism that persists in US society today.

Reparations

Recent rekindling of the "debate over reparations was fueled in part by the rise of the Black Lives Matter movement, as well as the writings of Ta-Nehisi Coates," whose essay "The Case for Reparations" appeared in *The Atlantic* in 2014.[4] The movement then garnered attention during the 2020 election campaign, with candidates for the US House and Senate as well as the presidency addressing the question of reparations.[5] Spurred by this renewed debate, legislative breakthroughs have occurred at the federal, state, and local levels.

After thirty years, a subcommittee of the US House of Representatives' Judiciary Committee finally held a hearing in 2019 on H.R. 40, a bill to create a commission to study reparations.[6] In 2021, the House Judiciary Committee approved the bill on a party-line vote, but the bill died on the House floor.[7] Additional breakthroughs have occurred at the state and local levels.[8] For instance, in 2019, Evanston, Illinois, approved a $10 million restorative housing program aimed at addressing its history of housing discrimination.[9] In 2020, Asheville, North Carolina, approved a reparations initiative to "provide funding to programs geared toward increasing homeownership and business and career opportuni-

ties for Black residents."[10] Also in 2020, the California legislature created a task force to study reparations, with that study culminating in a
comprehensive report issued in 2023 that recommended a combination
of apology, policy changes, and monetary compensation.[11] Acting in the
wake of that report, in 2024, the California legislature set aside $12 mil-
lion in the state budget to fund reparations-related initiatives that were
then making their way through the legislature.[12] Statewide task forces to
study reparations have also been established in Illinois and New York.[13]
And in 2022, Providence, Rhode Island, created a $10 million repara-
tions program that "will fund various social programs, including work-
force training, homeownership and financial literacy courses and small
business accelerators."[14]

Program Design

Equally important as acknowledging the need for reparations, however,
is the construction of meaningful programs.[15] For instance, ostensibly to
avoid the taxation of cash payments, Evanston chose to provide housing
vouchers for use toward the down payment on a house, paying down a
mortgage, or repairs to an existing home—with a third party interposed to
disburse funds to the bank or contractor.[16] But given the well-established
rule that income is taxable no matter its form and the "cornerstone" prin-
ciple that the substance of financial arrangements governs taxation, it is
unclear that local officials were correct in rejecting their Black constitu-
ents' pleas for unrestricted cash payments in favor of a more complicated
and restrictive voucher program aimed at circumventing taxation.[17]
Indeed, two recipients even found themselves in danger of losing their
reparations for failure to use vouchers before their expiration.[18]

As of early 2023, Evanston had authorized only $400,000 worth
of housing vouchers for sixteen Black residents—out of hundreds of
applicants—with some applicants having died while on the waiting list.[19]
This delay resulted from the city's choice to fund the program with revenue from the cannabis tax imposed when Illinois legalized the use of
marijuana in 2019, because city coffers received only "a trickle of the
tax money initially forecast."[20] Ultimately, Evanston corrected course
by authorizing an additional source of revenue in late 2022 and cash
payments in 2023, after which the pace of reparations payments picked

up—with $2.2 million distributed by October 2023 (split nearly evenly between cash and vouchers).[21]

Belying the notion that money is fungible, Providence's program was mired in controversy because the city's decision to fund the program with federal dollars provided under the American Rescue Plan Act (ARPA) for COVID-19 pandemic recovery efforts meant that the program had to be race-neutral.[22] To achieve race neutrality, "Black and Native American Providence residents qualify automatically, but the city has also established a separate, income criteria that could include about half its White residents."[23] But even when such constraints are avoided, choices among tax mechanisms for funding reparations programs convey important messages about how the cost of reparations should be distributed and who exactly should bear the burden of redressing a community's racist past. Unlike colonial slaveholders and legislators, present-day legislators seem to lack an appreciation of both taxation's importance and its expressive function. For instance, Providence's decision to use ARPA funding for its reparations programs effectively shifted the burden of confronting and redressing its deep involvement in and profiting from the slave trade—not to mention its more recent racist past—away from its own small number of residents and onto the more diffuse population of *all* American taxpayers. The decision of Providence, which occupies the lowest level on the ladder of US governmental entities, to shift the burden of reparations upward is akin to New York City's unsuccessful pleas for the entire colony of New York to absorb the cost of slaveholder compensation associated with the 1741 conspiracy to burn the city and murder its White inhabitants. New York City then explicitly sent the message that Providence is implicitly sending now: that it would simply be too much to ask city taxpayers to take on this burden themselves, so it should be shared at the broadest possible level of taxation.

Similarly, Evanston's initial choice to fund its reparations program with cannabis taxes rather than general city revenue was motivated by a desire to make amends for the city's history of disproportionately arresting African Americans on marijuana-related charges.[24] However laudable that motivation might be, Evanston's choice of tax-funding mechanism simultaneously bespeaks a decision to opt for an easy source of revenue—one that the city did not already count on for its operations and that avoided distributing the burden of reparations across the entire community that claimed responsibility for past discrimination.[25] This message that reparations were acceptable so long as payment did not create a burden for the community as a whole was only reinforced when the cannabis tax revenue fell short of expectations. At that time, the city council rejected a request to dedicate $5 million in ARPA funding to reparations, concerned that this would deplete the city's ARPA funding and potentially trigger lawsuits due to restrictions regarding the race-neutral use of those funds.[26] The city council did, however, accede to a request to tap into revenue from a real estate transfer tax on properties worth $1.5 million or more, which, like the cannabis tax, was a new source of revenue that had not yet been dedicated to specific programs and impacted only a segment of the local population.[27]

These examples highlight the need for those who are designing reparations schemes to consider the messages sent by the tax mechanisms chosen to fund reparations programs. As an ancillary matter, attention must also be paid to whether those who benefit from reparations programs will be taxed on the benefits received—a problem that could be solved in many cases through the enactment of a federal tax exemption for reparations that could then be incorporated by reference in the many state income taxes that adopt the federal income tax base as a starting point.[28] Furthermore, consideration should be given to addressing the presence of those who benefit from reparations programs in the group of taxpayers among whom the cost of reparations is being distributed.

Removing Artificial Constraints

Even when careful consideration is given to matching sources of revenue with the motivations behind reparations programs, governments are not free to adopt whatever reparations programs best achieve their goals from among the many different models that have been discussed and debated.[29] Rather, those who grapple with the design and implementation of reparations programs are constrained by the US Supreme Court's reactionary "colorblind" interpretations of the equal protection guarantee under the Fifth and Fourteenth Amendments to the US Constitution.[30] These interpretations limit the universe of workable reparations proposals by applying strict scrutiny to *all* racial classifications regardless of their aim, effectively requiring racial classifications in reparations programs to meet the high bar of being narrowly tailored to achieve compelling government interests.[31] Moreover, because the constitutional analysis of reparations programs relies heavily on the Supreme Court's affirmative action jurisprudence, the already constrained range of workable programs has probably been further narrowed following the 2023 decision in *Students for Fair Admissions, Inc. v. Harvard College*, in which the Supreme Court's conservative majority doubled down on its embrace of a "colorblind" Constitution.[32] In fact, in 2024, a legal challenge was filed against Evanston's reparations program on the basis of that Supreme Court decision, with the plaintiffs arguing that the program "discriminates against the suburb's non-Black residents."[33] Given already-tight constraints and the looming threat of litigation, the hazy contours of strict scrutiny analysis may lead designers of reparations programs to narrow the range of options even further by eschewing constitutionally questionable proposals to diminish the likelihood of successful legal challenges.[34]

These artificial constraints stand in stark contrast to the creativity that colonial legislators displayed when they constructed and reinforced the foundations of the institution of slavery so that Whites might profit from enslaved labor. Unlike present-day reparations advocates, colonial legislators were free to let loose their tax imaginations, which afforded them the legal space to, among other things, (1) experiment widely with tax mechanisms to fund slaveholder compensation schemes that were key to the smooth operation of draconian slave codes; (2) use taxation to shape slaveholder preferences and behavior to the benefit of White society, including by incentivizing local participation in the slave trade and encouraging the purchase of ostensibly more tractable enslaved persons; and (3) generate revenue from the slave trade dedicated to building the physical infrastructure (e.g., roads, bridges, and lighthouses) and human capital (i.e., educating future White leaders and workers) necessary for the colony's prosperity.[35] And when the Crown endeavored to constrain the actions of colonial legislators, some refused to accede to royal directives and instead created their own, more favorable legal terrains. To take but one example, South Carolina ignored royal instructions restricting the imposition of taxes on the importation of enslaved Blacks for nearly a decade to continue reaping profits from the slave trade that could be spent on attracting White settlers to the province. The legislature did eventually conform its import tax to those instructions—but only when the colony's interests aligned with royal dictates.

Faced with a more openly hostile legal terrain, reparations proponents might consider taking a page from the twentieth-century conservative movement, which worked for decades simultaneously to make the case against abortion and to seed the federal courts with judges who shared their views and would reshape the legal landscape in their favor—efforts that culminated in the 2022 US Supreme Court decision overturning *Roe v. Wade*.[36] Reparations proponents could similarly transform the federal courts by partnering with like-minded organizations dedicated to the appointment of judges with a commitment to civil and human rights.[37] Together, they could work to identify and advocate for the appointment of judges who, in the mold of Supreme Court Justice Ketanji Brown Jackson, are open to readings of the Equal Protection Clause that are in keeping with the roots of the Reconstruction Amendments in the abolition of slavery and protection of the rights of the formerly enslaved—protections whose scope, it has been said, "must be at least as great as the power to protect the rights of slaveholders before the Civil War."[38] Were these efforts to bear fruit, they might permit those who are fashioning reparations programs to unleash their legal imaginations in the way that colonial legislators did when laying the legal foundations for the institution of slavery that underpins reparations claims.[39]

That this suggestion comes in a book concerning the relationship between taxation and slavery might seem surprising, but it should not be. To many people, taxes are just something to gripe about—a dread-inducing annual chore that evokes fears of an Internal Revenue Service (IRS) audit. From a different vantage point, however, taxation gives way to flights of the imagination.[40] Taxpayers together with their tax advisers have devised an endless array of imaginative schemes for lowering their tax bills, and legislators are always finding new ways to use the tax system to shape behavior or deliver financial benefits. For instance, whether recipients realized it or not, the "stimulus checks" that the federal government distributed during the COVID-19 pandemic were not part of a direct spending program but rather advance payments of tax credits.[41] Indeed, the tax system's potential role in reparations programs has already begun to be explored, especially as it relates to taxing mechanisms for funding reparations, the qualification of community-building reparations funds for tax-exempt status, and the use of tax credits as a mechanism for delivering individual reparations payments.[42]

In fact, in a 1993 commentary in *Essence* magazine, it was suggested that Black taxpayers should claim a $43,209 rebate "for the 60 years of segregation and Jim Crow that followed slavery": "Although we were consigned by law to second-class citizenship then, we were still forced to pay first-class taxes."[43] The idea of a "Black tax" credit seemed so natural that the *New York Times* reported in 1994 that the IRS had already received more than twenty thousand claims for the credit.[44] Although the IRS warned of potential penalties, "some income tax return preparers and some con artists" who profited from fees charged to collect the credit urged taxpayers on, with more than ninety thousand claims filed in 2000–2001.[45]

Considering how many people readily believed in a nonexistent Black tax credit, it is quite plausible to expect that the tax system will play a role in reparations programs. The likelihood only increases after taking account of Congress's penchant for funneling spending programs through the tax system[46]—which just takes a page from the playbook of colonial legislators, who often preferred prohibitive taxes on the importation of enslaved Blacks over direct prohibitions against the slave trade. Given how intertwined colonial tax systems were with supporting and entrenching the institution of slavery and, later, with more salutary efforts to end the slave trade, it seems fitting both that lessons from tax history should aid in shaping a hospitable legal landscape for the construction of reparations programs and that the present-day tax system should participate in financial aspects of the resulting reparations programs.

As recounted in the introduction to this book, US Supreme Court Chief Justice John Marshall was correct when he observed that "the power to tax involves the power to destroy; . . . the power to destroy may defeat and render useless the power to create."[47] But as Justice Marshall intimated, simply because the power to tax has been used to destroy Black and Native American lives in the past does not necessarily and ineluctably render the current creative potential of the power to tax useless. To the contrary, by learning from the past, it might just be possible now to tap into the creative potential of the taxing power to work toward correcting those and other racial injustices, much as colonial legislators did long ago when they elected to use the power to tax to bring an end to the slave trade.

ACKNOWLEDGMENTS

This book began with a question from my colleague and former dean Chip Carter. Passing in the hall one day, Chip, who is a Thirteenth Amendment scholar, told me that he had encountered passing references in his research to how tax law had been used to pay compensation to slaveholders for enslaved persons who had been executed. Chip asked whether I had ever heard of this practice. I told him that I had not, but as someone who studies the impact of tax law on subordinated groups, I was intrigued by what he described. Because I was then writing *Tax and Time: On the Use and Misuse of Legal Imagination*, I asked Chip to send me copies of the references he had seen so that I could follow up on them later. After completing that book, I started to do some digging. What I found were deep connections between taxation and slavery in colonial America that both fascinated and horrified me—and led to the writing of this book. For setting me down what has proved to be a stimulating path of historical research, I owe Chip a deep debt of gratitude.

Naturally, however, there are many others to whom I owe thanks for their assistance in bringing this project to fruition. Thanks go to participants at the 2021 Annual Meeting of the Law & Society Association and to Roberta Mann and the students in her tax policy colloquium for their comments on early drafts of the first part of this book. Thanks go to participants at the American Tax Policy Institute's 2023 program "The Federal Income Tax: Racially Blind but Not Racially Neutral" for their comments and reactions to this project. For helpful comments on the final manuscript, thanks go to Chip Carter, Bridget Crawford, Diane Kemker, and Lu-in Wang. Thanks go to Jordan Fields, Ryan Jaffe, Danielle Pitrone, and Evan Sebio, as well as to the Pitt Law Library's staff of fellows and their supervisor, Linda Tashbook, for research assistance; to Helen Jarosz for handling endless interlibrary loan requests; and to the staffs at the archives and historical societies cited throughout this book for their help, with special thanks to Wayne Dorsey at the

South Carolina Department of Archives and History, Lisa Hayes at the Charleston Library Society, Margaret Dunham at the Delaware Public Archives, and Elizabeth Shepard at the Bergen County Archives. Thanks also go to my editor at NYU Press, Clara Platter, for her help in shaping this project as well as her unflagging support and hard work in shepherding it through the publication process. And above all, thanks go to my family for their patience and understanding during the time that I was working on this project.

APPENDIX

TABLE A.1. Slaveholder Compensation Paid through the South Carolina Tax-Acts

Tax-Act	Amount	Purpose
1721	£1,000	"to slaves condemned and shot"
1723/4	£500	"to arrears due for negroes killed"
1725	£100	"to Thomas Hendley for a negro killed"
	£100	"to Mr. William Cattell, for a negro killed"
1733	£80	"Benjamin Izard, for a negro killed"
	£80	"Ann Donovan, an Indian woman killed"
	£80	"James Rothford, for a negro killed"
	£80	"John Carmichael, ditto"
	£80	"Benjamin Child, ditto"
	£80	"William Ceely, ditto"
	£80	"The Hon. Arthur Middleton, Esq. allowed for a negro killed"
1734	£80	"To Peter Cowley, for a negro killed"
	£80	"To John Daniell, for a negro executed"
	£80	"To John Colleton, Esq. for a negro killed"
	£80	"To James Thomson, for a negro executed"
	£80	"To Isaac Mazyck, for a negro executed"
	£80	"To Andrew Broughton, for a negro executed"
	£160	"To Catharine Cattell"
1735	£80	"To Mr. William Elliott Senr."
	£80	"To Gerit Vanderheydon"
	£80	"To Isaac Cordes"
	£80	"To Major Tobias Fitch"
	£160	"To paul Jenys Esqr."
	£80	"To James Kerr"
	£80	"To Isaac Lessene Junr."
1741/2	£150	"To Mr. John Garnier for a Negro executed"
	£200	"To Mr. John Roberts for a Negro executed"
	£178	"To John Skene Esq"
	£22	"To Edward Perry"
1743	£100	"To Mrs. Elizabeth Cheeseman, for a negro executed"
	£200	"To Michael Jeans for a negro that was executed"
1745/6	£100	"To the Honorable Joseph Blake Esqr."
1746	£118 11s 5d	"To William Walker"
	£22 17s 1d	"To Christopher Smith"

(continued)

Tax-Act	Amount	Purpose
	£38 11s 6d	"To John Pollock"
	£200	"To Alexander Rantowl"
	£150	"To Mʳ. Francis Gracia"
	£50	"To Mʳ. William Roper"
1747	£400	"To Thomas Mellichamp for 2 Negroes which were executed"
	£155	"To Edward Bond for a Negro which was executed"
	£400	"To Burrell Massingberd Hyrne for two Negroes that were executed"
1748	£200	"To Abraham Mathison for a Negro executed"
	£180	"To William Waties Esqʳ. for a Negro executed"
1749	£150	"To Barnaby Raily for a Negro that was executed"
	£200	"To Frances Fitch Widow for a Negro executed"
1750	£200	"To William Cattell junior esqʳ. for a slave executed"
	£200	"To Josiah Parry for a slave executed"
	£200	"To Algernoon Wilson for a slave executed"
	£200	"To John Thompson for a slave executed"
	£164	"To the estate of a person in North Carolina dec̄ed owner of a slave executed in this province named Santee Jemmy to be paid when the proprietor's representative shall make a demand of the same"
	£36	"To the estate of Richard Fuller deceased for damages done by the said Santee Jemmy"
	£200	"To messʳˢ. Smith and Palmer on an order drawn by William Harvey for a slave executed belonging to him"
	£200	"To James Akin esqʳ. for a Negro executed"
	£100	"To Walter Holman for a negro executed"
	£100	"To William Walter esqʳ. for damages done by the said Holman's Negro to a negro mortgaged to him"
	£300	"To James Mᶜ.Cree for two slaves executed"
	£600	"To the estate of William Mᶜ.Cluer deceased for four slaves executed"
1751	£200	"To Thomas Miles for a slave executed"
	£150	"To John Brunson for a slave executed"
	£30	"To Jeremiah Cuttineau for damages sustained by the said Slave"
	£20	"To John Greene of Winyaw for damages sustained by the said Slave"
	£200	"To William Elliott for a slave executed"
	£192	"To John Ainger for a slave executed"
	£4	"To William Branford Junior for damages sustained by the said Slave"
	£4	"To Elizabeth Butler for damages sustained by the said Slave"
	£125	"To Mʳ. John Mᶜ.Leod for a Man Slave shot by the Patrol"
	£200	"To William Kelvert for a Man Slave shot by an Indian"
1752	£200	"To *Parmenas Way*, for a Slave executed for Poisoning"
	£80	"—*William Simmons*, for the use of the Estate of *John Sumner* deceased, for a Slave executed for Poisoning"
	£400	"—the Estate of the Honourable *Joseph Blake*, Esq; deceased, for *two* slaves executed for Poisoning him"
	£200	"—Mr. *Alexander Hext*, for a Slave executed for Murder"
	£200	"—*Samuel Wells*, for a Slave executed"
	£200	"—the Estate of Mr. *William Waties* deceased, for a Slave executed for Poisoning him"

Tax-Act	Amount	Purpose
	£175	"—the Estate of *William Brown* deceased, for a Slave executed"
	£25	"—*John Brunson*, for Damages which he sustained by the said Slave"
1753	£100	"To George Somers Esqr. for a Negro executed for Murder"
	£100	"To Benjamin Harvey of Stono Planter for damages sustained by the sd Negro"
	£50	"To Hugh Anderson for a Negro executed"
	£30	"To John Methringham for damages sustained by the said Negro"
	£200	"To M^r. John Cattell (son of William) for a Negro executed"
	£150	"To M^{rs}. Rachel Russ for a Negro executed"
	£200	"To M^r. John Cook for a fugitive slave killed by the Patrol"
	£200	"To M^r. Joseph Elliott Junior for a fugitive Slave killed in a like manner"
	£200	"To M^r. Silas Miles for a fugitive Negro killed by the Patrol"
1754	£100	"To Thomas Drayton Esqr. for a Slave executed"
	£200	"To William Main for the use of the estate of M^r. Richard Baker deceased for a Negro executed for Murder"
	£200	"To Captain Robert Sams for a Slave executed"
	£200	"To the Estate of Maurice Keating deceased for a fugitive Slave killed by a Party of the Militia"
	£200	"To Mary Hughes for a Slave executed"
1755	£150	"To James Anderson for a Slave executed"
	£50	"To the Estate of John Atcheson deceased for damages sustained by the said Slave"
	£200	"To William Chicken for a Slave executed"
	£200	"To Joseph Edward Flower for a Slave executed"
	£200	"To the Estate of David Godin deceased for a Slave executed"
	£175	"To John Joiner for a Slave executed"
	£200	"To Childermas Croft for a Slave executed"
	£200	"To Charles Pinckney junior Esqr. for a Slave executed"
	£150	"To Richard Field for a Slave executed"
	£200	"To James Michie Esqr. for a Slave killed by a Party of the Militia who were in pursuit of fugitive Slaves"
1756	£400	"To John Miles for two Slaves executed"
	£400	"To John Delagaye on two Orders of Sarah Purry for two Slaves executed belonging to the Estate of Charles Purry deceased"
	£200	"To the Estate of Charles Field deceased for a Slave executed"
	£50	"To John Edwards for a fugitive Slave killed on resisting the Person who attempted to apprehend him"
1757	£200	"To John McQueen . . .
	£200	"To Joseph Poole . . .
	£200	"To Joseph Brown & William Drakeford on an Order of William Flen . . .
	£200	"To Thomas Waties . . .
	£200	"To Joseph Seally . . .
	£200	"To Thomas Hale . . .
	£200	"To John Gordon of Beaufort . . .

for Slaves Executed"

(continued)

Tax-Act	Amount	Purpose
	£200	"To James McGirt for a fugitive Slave killed on resisting the Person who attempted to apprehend him"
1758	£200	"To John Geissendanner, for slaves executed"
	£400	"To William Dalton, do."
	£200	"To Hugh McCulchin's estate, do."
	£200	"To James Ladson, do."
	£90	"To James Ash's estate, do."
	£90	"To Joseph Ash, do."
1759	£150	"To William Glen . . .
	£50	"To John Sikes . . .
	£200	"To Thoˢ Wilson . . . For Slaves Executed"
	£100	"To Robert Weaver . . .
	£100	"To John Cleland Esqʳ. . . .
1760	£160	"To Martha Logan, for slaves executed"
	£40	"To Ann Clark, ditto"
	£200	"To Margaret Handlin, ditto"
	£600	"To William Raven, ditto"
	£100	"To John Pamor, ditto"
	£100	"To Padden Pond, ditto"
	£100	"To Thomas Bradwell, ditto"
	£100	"To Thomas Shoemaker, ditto"
	£100	"To Archibald Stanyarne, ditto"
	£100	"To Elizabeth Snipes, ditto"
	£200	"To John Hamilton, ditto"
	£200	"To Thomas Shoemaker, for a slave that was killed in apprehending a fugitive slave"
1761	£200	"Francis James
	£200	"John Remington
	£200	"Abel Johnson
	£200	"Charles Canty
	£200	"Morris Williams "For Slaves Executed"
	£200	"Susannah Bee
	£200	"Lemuel Nesmith
	£25	"Catherine Cattell
	£200	"John Fryerson
1762	£200	"To Alexander McGillivery for a Negro Executed"
	£200	"James Talbot for a Negro Executed"
1764	£205 4s	"To Thomas Elf, for a slave executed"
	£120	"Estate of William Coomer"
	£80	"Thomas Smith, Jr."
	£216	"Charles Bedingfield, on an order of John Bedingfield"

Tax-Act	Amount	Purpose
	£216	"The estate of Hugh Dowse"
	£216	"Fotheringham & McNeil"
	£216	"Henry Filder"
	£200	"William Fytte"
	£216	"The Churchwardens of St. George's Parish"
	£140 8s	"Jacob Motte, on an order of Joseph Shute and Benjamin Joy"
	£200	"Benjamin Smith, for Paul Jenys, deceased"
	£216	"Benjamin Smith, on an order of Antony White"
	£216	"Austin & Laurens"
	£216	"Micajah Williams"
	£216	"Joshua Screven"
1765	£200	"Cholmondely Deering, for a slave executed"
	£80	"Benjamin Jenkins, ditto"
	£200	"John Sims, ditto"
	£200	"William Hall, ditto"
	£100	"Isaac Rippon, ditto"
	£350	"Jacob Motte, Esq. Public Treasurer, advanced Gibbons & Tickling, for slaves executed"
1766	£200	"To Andrew Allison, for a negro executed"
	£400	"The Estate of William Anderson, deceased, for two negroes executed"
	£200	"Miles Brewton Esq. for a fugitive slave killed by a party in pursuit of runaway negroes"
	£200	"John Drayton, Esq. for a negro executed"
	£200	"Thomas Dixon, for a negro executed"
	£400	"Lewis Reeve and John Strickling, for two negroes executed, at £200 each"
	£200	"Aaron Fryerson, for a negro executed"
	£200	"To Francis Stuart, on a certificate of Richard Capers, for a negro executed"
1767	£180	"To John Becket, for his proportion of the valuation of a slave executed"
	£200	"Thomas Commander, for a slave executed"
	£200	"Daniel Desaussure, for a negro executed"
	£200	"William Miller, for a negro executed"
	£200	"John Myars, for a negro executed"
	£200	"Lewis Mourzon, for a negro executed"
	£150	"George Marshall, for a negro executed"
	£200	"Estate of Isaac Nichols, for a negro executed"
	£200	"Alexander Rantowle, for a negro executed"
	£200	"Philip Spooler's estate, for a negro executed"
	£200	"Samuel Sealy, for a negro executed"
	£200	"Estate of Champernoon Williamson, for a fugitive slave killed by the militia"
	£150	"Catharine Wigfall, for a negro executed"
1768	£150	"To John Ainslie Esquire for a Negro Shot"

(continued)

Tax-Act	Amount	Purpose
	£400	""Estate of William Brown deceased, for two Negroes executed"
	£100	""Shem Butler, for One half of the value of a Negro executed"
	£100	""Estate of Thomas Law Elliott deceased, for the other half of the value of the same Negro"
	£200	""Robert Duke, for a Negro executed"
	£200	""Samuel Green, for a Negro executed'
	£200	""Daniel Legare, for a Negro executed"
	£200	""Jane Pepper, for a Negro executed, belonging to the Estate of Gilbert Pepper deceased"
	£150	""Francis Rose, for a Negro shot"
	£200	""Peter Sinckler, for a Negro executed, belonging to the Estate of Philip Williams Deceased"
	£200	""William Withers, for a Negro executed"
	£180	""Elizabeth Young, for a Negro executed (payable to John Boone and Paul Townshend"
1769	£160	""To Simon Berwicke, for part of the valuation of a negro Executed"
	£40	""Elizabeth Payne for the other part of the valuation of the said Negro"
	£75	""The Honorable John Drayton Esquire for the valuation of a Negro Executed"
	£200	""John McElveen for a Negro executed"
	£100	""John Miles, for One Moiety of a Negro executed"
	£100	""William Pinckney, for the other Moiety of the said Negro"
	£200	""Isaac McPherson, for a Negro Executed"
	£200	""John McFaddian, for a Negro Executed"
	£200	""Miss Ann Wragg for a negro executed"
1770	£200	To James Akin "for a Negro Executed"
	£200	To William Campbell "for a Negro Executed"
	£200	To Thomas Ferguson "for a Negro Slave Executed"
	£200	To Price, Hest & Head "for a Negro Executed"
	£200	To James Sands's estate "for a Negro Executed"
	£100	To Benjamin Simons, Esquire "for a Negro Executed"
1771	£200	To Robert Allyne "for a Negro Executed"
	£200	To Isaac Dubose "for a Negro Executed"
	£200	To Christopher Rich and Thomas Wells "for a Negro Executed"
	£100	To Robert Croft "for a Negro Executed"
1774	£200	To Jonathan Wilkins "for a Negro Executed"
	£200	To John Baskerfield "for a Negro Executed"
	£200	To Lazarus Brown's estate "for a Negro Executed"
	£200	To Robert Cahusac "for a Negro Executed"
	£200	To Edward Davies "for a Negro Executed"
	£200	To Daniel Ravenel Jr. "for a Negro Executed"
	£200	To Thomas Williams's estate "for a Negro Executed"
	£200	To the Honorable John Drayton, Esquire "for a Negro Executed"
	£200	To Benjamin Fuller "for a Negro executed"
	£200	To John Harleston (in trust for Ashby Harleston) "for a Negro executed"

Tax-Act	Amount	Purpose
	£200	To Andrew Lord "for a Negro Executed"
	£200	To John Seabrook "for a Negro Executed"
	£200	To Daniel Stuart "for a Negro Executed"
	£200	To Humphry Sommers "for a Negro Executed"
	£200	To John Tygirt "for a Negro Executed"
	£200	To Benjamin Young "for a Negro Executed"
	£135 10s	To Robert Goodwin "for a Negro Executed"
	£128	To Gasper Fogely "for a Negro Executed"
	£100	To Samuel Dunlap "for a Negro Executed"
	£400	To Isaac Dutart "for a Negro Man and a Negro Woman executed"
1775	£400	To Thomas Elfe "for two Negroes executed"
	£200	To John Champneys "for a Negro executed"
	£200	To Joseph Dobbins "for a Negro executed"
	£200	To Henry Saltus "for a Negro executed"
	£200	To Samuel Thomas "for a Negro executed"
	£200	To Job Rothmahler "for a Negroe executed"
	£200	To Hugh Ferguson's estate "for a Negroe executed"
	£150	To William Young "for a Negro executed"
	£135 10s	To George Eigner "for a Negro executed"
	£50	To Thomas Lynch "for a Negro executed"
	£200	To Sarah Edwards "for a Negroe who had run away from her Plantation, and shot by a Party from the Patrol"
	£350	To Francis Gillispee "for a Negro executed"
	£850	To Samuel Benoist "for two Negroes executed"
	£300	To John Mackintosh's estate "for a Negro executed"
	£400	To John Syme "for a Negro executed"
	£200	To Daniel Droze "for a Negro executed"
	£400	To Edward Blake "for a Negro executed"
	£350	To William Godfrey's heirs "for a Negroe executed"

TABLE A.2. Pennsylvania Slaveholder Compensation Payments

Audit (import taxes/ fines collected)	Slaveholder	Enslaved person	Compensation	Purpose
1763 (£1,509 18s 6d)	Daniel Richards	Joe	£60	"for a Negroe (Joe) executed for Burglary"
	Executors of John Philips	Caspar	£60	"for a Negroe, Ditto"
1764 (£737 18s 6d)	Redmond Conyngham, attorney for Edward Stiles	Unnamed	£60	"for a Negroe executed for Murder"
	William Smith, agent for William Morrison	Unnamed	£60	"for a Negroe executed"
1765 (£670 10s 6d)	Joseph Richardson	Unnamed	£55	"for a Negroe Woman executed"
	Jac. Grojean	Unnamed	£120	"for a Negroe Man executed in Lancaster County"
1768 (£427 15s 9d/£2 10s)	James Burd	Jem	£90	"for a Negro executed"
1774 (£112)	Robert McKees	Unnamed	£70	"Cash paid for Robert McKees, Negro Slave, per Order certified by Emanuel Carpenter and Isaac Saunders, Esquires"

TABLE A.3. Claims outside the Slaveholder Compensation Scheme Approved by the Virginia House of Burgesses

Session	Slaveholder	Enslaved person	Amount	Accused criminal (alleged crimes)	Outlawed	Escapee	Details
						Basis of claim	
1732	Moss Armistead	Unnamed man	£40			N	Drowned while being pursued
1736	William Cox	Unnamed woman	£60	Suicide (arson, theft, wounding of slaveholder's son, murder of her three children)		N	
1738	Rebecca Collier (holder for life) and Thomas Lankford's wife (holder after Collier's death)	Unnamed man	£30			Y	Suicide	After being discovered onboard a ship, leaped into the river rather than be taken
	Peter Hay on behalf of himself, Philip Johnson, and Oriana Littlepage for an enslaved person held by William Johnson's estate	Unnamed man	£30	Died of jail frostbite after acquittal (felony)		N	
	Richard Randolph	Unnamed	£40	Died in jail fire he set (felony)		N	
	William Norvell	Unnamed	£20	"died during his Confinement" ("stabbing one *William Compton*")		N	
May 1740	Elizabeth Monday	Sharper	£25			Y	Suicide	"hanged himself"
1742	John Shelton	Unnamed woman	£35			Y	"murdered by another Negro"
	Zachary Lewis	Sacco	£40	Suicide (murdered overseer)		N	"hanged himself"
	Lewis Delony	Two unnamed	£52 12s 6d			Y	Found dead
	Charles Brown (on behalf of his children John and Mary)	Unnamed man	£30	Suicide (arson)		Y	"hanged himself"; Burgesses directed "that the Money be applied towards the Purchasing of another Slave, for the same Uses"

(*continued*)

Table A.3. (continued)

Session	Slaveholder	Enslaved person	Amount	Accused criminal (alleged crimes)	Outlawed	Escapee	Details
						Basis of claim	
1744	John Lewis	Unnamed man	£35	Escaped jail (robbery)	N		
	Joseph Molton Jr.	Unnamed man	£30	Found dead (murdered overseer's wife)	In process		
	Robert Powell	Unnamed man	£31		Y	Found dead with stolen goods	
	Henry Wythe	Unnamed man	£30	Suicide (poisoning)	Y		Ran away after being suspected of poisoning overseer and drowned himself before apprehension
	William Hodges	Unnamed man	Unspecified	Died in jail before trial (felony)	N		
	Charles Ewell and Rappahannock Iron-Mine Company	Will	£34		In process	"surrounded by the Neighbours, and refusing to surrender, was by them shot dead"	
	Moor Fantleroy	Harry	£25	Suicide (murder)	Y		Drowned himself after murdering his own wife
1745	Mary Griffin	Two unnamed	£60	Suicide (robbery)	Y		"in order to clear them, [Griffin] searched their Cabbins and found some Linen and other Goods which were stole, on which they ran away" and were found drowned
	William Beverley	Guy Maria	£94	Died of jail frostbite after acquittal (murder of overseer; two others were convicted and executed)	N		Later awarded additional £36 3s 6d for damages related to others who were acquitted and survived frostbite
	Thomas Lorton	Unnamed man	£5		Y	Shot and "so disabled, that he is of no Service"	Compensated only for medical care

Date	Petitioner	Enslaved Name	Amount	Circumstance	Y/N	Notes
1748	Joel Walker	Unnamed man	£45	Found dead (murder of Walker's son)	Y	
	Joseph Strother Jr.	Unnamed	£40	Died in jail fire (felony)	N	
	Jacob Sellers	Unnamed	£35	Died of jail frostbite after acquittal (felony)	N	
1752	William Broadnax	Unnamed man	£50	Suicide	Y	"to prevent being taken, threw himself into a Mill-Pond and was drowned"
	Francis Willis, guardian for infant Lewis Willis	Unnamed man	£50	Escaped jail before execution, later shot and killed (felony and burglary)	N	
	Executors of Rev. John Reade	Unnamed man	£30	Stabbed person attempting to apprehend him and while in jail "was Frost-bitten, and lost his Feet"	N	Payment for loss in value and cost of care
May 1755	George Purcelley	Guy	£45	Escaped jail before execution (unspecified crime)	N	
	James Graham and John Thompson	Will	£40	Died in jail of gunshot wounds received during apprehension (stealing)	N	
	Stephen Watkins	Unnamed man	£40	Suicide (murder of enslaved person and one of Watkins's children)	N	"hanged himself, to avoid as the Petitioner supposes, the Punishment of the Law"
Feb. 1759	George Brassfield	Sampson	£90	Died in jail before trial (murder)	N	
	John Baskerville	Unnamed man	£85	Died of the cold in jail before trial ("poisoning some of his Neighbours Negroes")	N	
Oct. 1760	Elizabeth King	Unnamed man	£70	Suicide (murder of King's husband)	N	"destroyed himself"
	Elizabeth Buchanan	Unnamed man	£80	Died in jail fire before trial (burglary)	N	

(continued)

TABLE A.3. (*continued*)

Session	Slaveholder	Enslaved person	Amount	Accused criminal (alleged crimes)	Basis of claim		
					Outlawed	Escapee	Details
	William Harris	Unnamed	£100		Y		"shot in attempting to break open a House"
	Francis Conway	Unnamed man	£30	Died in jail before trial (murder)	N		
Nov. 1762	Heirs of John Gatewood	Tom	£80 plus £11 16s for medical care	Died of jail frostbite after acquittal and shortly following amputation of his legs (burglary)	N		
	Richard Doggett	Nelson	£80	Escaped jail (felony)	N		
	James Patty	Unnamed	£3 15s (30 days lost time)	Acquitted (felony)	N		"whilst imprisoned was frostbitten and rendered incapable of Service"
Oct. 1764	James Boyd	Bob	£65		N		"apprehended . . . for a Runaway" then "made a desperate Attempt on the Life" of the constable, who killed him "in his own Defence"
1767	Junior Turner	Lucy	£60	Died after acquittal (murder of her newborn)	N		"while in Gaol she was taken sick of a Fever, and though the Weather was very cold, she . . . was removed Home the same Evening; That she languished under the Fever about three Months, and died"
	Henry Mitchell	Unnamed man	£35 7s 9d for medical care	"sentenced to be hanged" (burglary)	N		Pardoned but "was frost-bitten while in Gaol; in Consequence whereof he lost his right leg, and Half his left Foot"
	Benedict Rust	Morris	£20	Died of the cold in jail before trial (poisoning)	N		

Date	Owner	Slave	Value	Disposition	Outlawed	Fate	Notes
	Thomas Bullett	Ben	Unspecified	Escaped jail (felony)	N		
	Fortunatus Crutchfield	Unnamed man	£40		N	"happened, by Mistake, not to be outlawed, but was shot with other Slaves who were outlawed"	
1768	David Chivis	Unnamed man	£90	Escaped jail before execution (felony)	N		
Nov. 1769	Robert Higginson	Unnamed man	£60		Y	Suicide	"was surprised sleeping in a Canoe in Mr Holt's Mill-Pond, by one *Thomas Fear*, and being unable to rescue himself from the said *Fear* . . . jumped over board into the Water, and was drowned"
	Henry Kidd	Fortune	£60	Died of jail frostbite after trial (felony and burglary)	N		
	Thomas Field	Shropshire	£60		In process	"attempting to murder one *Shurles*, was killed by the said *Shurles*, in his own Defence"	Outlawry published at two churches in Bristol parish but not at other churches in the county
	Charles Tomkies	Sey	£30	Jail frostbite rendered him "unprofitable" (felony)	N		
1770	John Tayloe	Toby	£70	Died of jail frostbite after conviction (hog stealing)	N		
1772	Brett Randolph's estate	Charles	£80		Y	"died of Wounds he received when he was apprehended"	
	William Hoye	Limbo	£85		Y	Apprehended as an outlaw and put in jail; broke out while setting the jail on fire; died "of a Wound received" when being apprehended for the second time	Hoye purchased Limbo from John Glover *after outlawry*

(continued)

TABLE A.3. (continued)

Session	Slaveholder	Enslaved person	Amount	Accused criminal (alleged crimes)	Outlawed	Basis of claim Escapee	Details
	Elizabeth Derrick, on behalf of herself and her infant son Benjamin Goff	Jack	£75	Died of jail frostbite after trial (hog stealing)	N		
	John Young	Moses	£80		Y	Died "as was supposed, by the great Fatigue he underwent in endeavouring to escape his Pursuers"	
1774	Thomas Patterson	Tom	£85	"found dead" (murder)	Y		"having shot himself as it is supposed with a Gun he had stolen [from Patterson], to prevent his being apprehended and tried"
	John Durett	Jacob	£75	Died in jail fire he allegedly set to escape (felony)	N		
1775	Stephen Ham	Juda	£50	Suicide (murder of her son, arson)	N		"to escape punishment, she rushed into the dwelling House, where it was on fire, and was much burnt before she could be taken out; and that she was apprehended and committed in order to be tried for the said Crime, but died before the time of trial"

TABLE A.4. Claims outside the Slaveholder Compensation Scheme Disallowed by the Virginia House of Burgesses

Session	Slaveholder	Enslaved person	Accused criminal (alleged crimes)	Basis of claim			Details
				Outlawed	Escapee		
1736	Benjamin Morris	Unnamed man			N		"hang'd himself"
1738	John Carter	Unnamed woman			N	Suicide	"was endeavouring to make her Escape by Water, in a Canoe; and being closely pursued, threw herself into the Water, to avoid being taken, and was drowned"
	John Carter	Unnamed man			N		"killed by another Slave belonging to *John Steptoe*; for which Fact, the said *Steptoe's* Slave was condemn'd and executed"
	Robert Cobbs	Unnamed man			N		"hanged himself"
	Benjamin Needler	Unnamed			N		"ran away with an Outlaw'd Slave of the Petitioner's to *North-Carolina*; and having there committed a Robbery, and being pursued and over-taken, presented a Gun against his Pursuers, and was by one of them shot dead on the Spot"
May 1740	Peter Richeson	Seven unnamed			N		"ran away . . . shortly afterwards found dead in *Mattapony River*"
1742	Joseph Anthony	Two unnamed women			N		"a Negro Man Slave belonging to the Petitioner, and convicted . . . of the Murder of a Negro Woman belonging to the Petitioner, had also been the Occasion of the Death of another Negro Woman of the Petitioner's"
	Nathaniel Harrison	Unnamed			N		"killed by a White Man, in his own Defence"

(continued)

Table A.4. (continued)

Session	Slaveholder	Enslaved person	Basis of claim			
			Outlawed	Escapee	Accused criminal (alleged crimes)	Details
	Anthony Walke	Amos	N		Suicide (theft)	"it does not appear . . . that . . . Amos . . . was confederate with the other Negro *Devonshire* . . . in the Felony for which the said *Devonshire* was convicted, and executed: And that the Petitioner only endeavoured to apprehend, whip, and examine him, about Two Pair of *Virginia* Shoes; telling the said *Amos*, if he could prove he had been Confederate with the said *Devonshire*, he would prosecute him for it: Upon which the said *Amos* broke away from his Overseer, and drowned himself"
1744	John Chew	Unnamed woman	Y	"found dead"		
	Robert Farish	Unnamed	Y		"found dead in the Woods" (attempted murder of enslaved woman)	
1745	George Brett	Unnamed man	N	Died in jail fire		
1748	John Evans	Unnamed woman	Y	Suicide		"being apprehended and tied to be brought home . . . she made her Escape and drowned herself"
	Robert Daniel	Unnamed man	Y	Suicide		"that a Negro of his attacked him and his Brother, and having much wounded his Brother, to avoid Punishment he absconded: That he procured him to be out-lawed, some time after which, he hanged himself"
	John Hudgin	Unnamed	N			"murdered by another Negro"

1752	Abraham Estes	Unnamed		N	"found dead in the Woods"
	Robert Adams	Unnamed		Y	Suicide "hanged himself"
	Gideon Marr	Unnamed		Y	"found dead"
	Benjamin Branch	Unnamed man	"from a Sense of his Crimes, as the Petitioner conceives, and fearing to be brought to Justice, shot himself" ("many Robberies and Misdemeanors")	In process	
1753	Miles Cary	Unnamed man	Suicide (theft)	Y	"Petitioner employed some *Indians* to go in search of the said Slave, who afterwards drowned himself"
	Joseph Haile	Unnamed man	Suicide (murder)	N	"hanged himself, having first committed Murder on another Negroe"
	Nathaniel Harrison	Unnamed man	Escaped from jail before execution (felony)	N	
	William Byrd	Unnamed	"burnt in the Goal"	N	
Feb. 1754	Mary Jones	Harry	Died after being whipped and having both his ears cut off "on a very cold Day" (stabbing and wounding slaveholder)	N	
May 1755	Francis Whiting (guardian of orphans John and Mary Whiting)	Will		In process	"some Persons being in pursuit of him, in Order to apprehend him, he ran into a Creek, and was drowned"
	John Brummel	Unnamed man	Escaped from jail before execution (rape)	N	Pardoned

(continued)

TABLE A.4. (continued)

Session	Slaveholder	Enslaved person	Accused criminal (alleged crimes)	Outlawed	Escapee	Details
	Alice Catlett	Ned	Died in jail after being held postconviction until "Security for the Peace" was posted because of persons who "apprehended some Mischief . . . in Case he was discharged"	N		
	James MacDewell	Matt	Apparent death (felony and burglary)	Y		"ran away and committed a Felony and Burglary, by breaking open a House, and stealing an Ax and Case Knife, which were found on him when he was taken and carried before a Justice of the Peace, who ordered him to be whipped and conveyed to his Master; that he ran away soon afterwards, and was outlawed, and about 10 Months after his Outlawry, a Person's Bones were found in the Woods, and the Cloaths found with them, appeared to be the same the said Negroe had on when he ran away"
	George Mason	Dick		Y	Either died of wounds from apprehension or suicide by poisoning after apprehension	
	William Southall	Unnamed man	Suicide (arson)	N		Set fire to Southall's barn, destroying "all his Tobacco, Corn, Wheat, and Oats, and other Goods, and then hanged himself"
	William Lightfoot	Jasper		Y	Suicide	After apprehension in North Carolina, "on his Return, in order to avoid Hanging, which he often said he expected if he was brought back into this Colony, he dashed his Brains out against a Rock"

Basis of claim

Date	Owner	Slave	Suicide (attempted murder)	In process	Outcome	Notes
	Kenneth MacKenzie	Harry	Suicide (attempted murder)			"having quarreled with his Wife, stabbed her in several Places, and imagining that she would die thereof, ran away," but before the outlawry could be published, "the said Slave hanged himself"
1757	John Peyton Jr.	Unnamed man		N		"Allowance for the Loss of his Negroe Man's Service, during his Confinement . . . for Felony, he never receiving any Trial on the Commission of Oyer and Terminer obtained for that Purpose"
Sept. 1758	Jacob Valentine	Unnamed man		Y	Not found or recaptured	
	William Dobson	Unnamed woman		Y	"found dead in the Woods"	
Feb. 1759	Edward Carter, guardian to the orphans of James Carter	Unnamed		Y	"found dead in the Woods"	
	Hugh Moore	Tom		Y	"found dead in the Woods"	
Nov. 1762	Rev. Archibald Dick	Bob	Escaped jail before execution (felony)	N	Pardoned	
1766	William Pemberton	Bob		Y	"found dead in the Woods"	
	Charles Carter	Harry	Killed in apprehension (attempted murder of overseer "14 or 15 Years ago")	N		
Nov. 1769	John Beasley	Unnamed woman		Y	"was disabled by a Tree which fell upon her as she lay hid, and afterwards was burned to Death"	
	John Burke	Sam		Y	Suicide	In 1764, "to avoid Punishment, hanged himself"

(continued)

TABLE A.4. (*continued*)

Session	Slaveholder	Enslaved person	Accused criminal (alleged crimes)	Outlawed	Escapee	Details
						Basis of claim
	Elizabeth Emerson	Unnamed		Y	"found dead"	
1772	Wills Cowper	Frank		In process	Killed	"being discovered by one *James Bates*, and not only refusing to surrender, but attacking the said *James Bates*, he the said *James Bates*, in Defence of himself, discharged a loaded Gun at the said Slave, by which he was irrecoverably wounded in one of his Legs, and soon after died"
	Daniel Hamlin	Parriot	Alleged suicide by hanging (attempted murder of slaveholder's wife)	Y		Detailed fact finding revealed that only some bones and clothing were found
	William Robinson	Edinburg		In process	"having been apprehended and confined, was let loose by another Slave, and running into the River was drowned"	
1775	John Martin	Lemon		N	Died in jail fire that he allegedly set to escape	
	David Donnan	York Abram		N	Died in jail fire (with Lemon)	
	John Robinson, Peter Robinson's executor	Will		N	Died in jail fire	

TABLE A.5. North Carolina Slaveholder Compensation Payments

Session	Slaveholder	Enslaved person	Amount	Executed (alleged crime)	Killed	Outlawed
1734/5	Constance Williamson	Two unnamed	£250	✓		
	Allen Wells	Unnamed	£150	✓		
1738/9	Joseph Buncomb	James	£250	✓		
1739/40	William Bartram	Unnamed	£200	✓		
	Daniel Pugh	Unnamed	£180	✓		
	Rowland Williams	Will	£200	✓		
1740/1	Thomas Barker	Essex	£200	✓		
	Isaac Nichols (South Carolina)	Davie	£175	✓		
1743	William Hoskins	Nedd	£33 6s 8d	✓ (burglary and felony)		
	Bartholomew Evans	Sipio	£29 7s	✓ (burglary and felony)		
1751	[Illegible] Freeman	Quash	£36 13s 4d	✓		
	John Macon	Georg	£42 10s	✓		
1754	Thomas Barret	Will	£60	✓ ("Murder of a Negroe Man named Caesar")		
	Charles Chapman	Bob	£35	✓ ("ravishing a white Woman named Phebe Hawkins")		
	David Meade	Hampshire Adam	£50	✓ (murder of Edward Ball)		
	Newman Dun	Jack	£20	✓		
	Elizabeth Lee	Ben	£35	✓ (poisoning of Thomas Lee)		
1755	Capt. John DuBois	Tom	£70	✓		
1756	George Moore	Toney	£70		✓	
1757	Ann Walker	Cooper	£80		✓	✓
	Ralph Taylor	Mary	£80	✓		
	John McKinzie	Peter	£80	✓		
	John Campbell	Moses	£60	✓		
1758	Lewis De Rossett	Unnamed ("Carpenter by trade")	£75		✓ (jail fire)	✓
	Thomas Uzzell	Peter	£55	✓ (rape)		
	William Mace Sr.	Unnamed	£50		✓	

(continued)

Session	Slaveholder	Enslaved person	Amount	Executed (alleged crime)	Killed	Outlawed
1759	William Teague	Isaac	£80	✓		
	William Pratt	Charles	£75	✓		
1760	John Dalrymple	Jack	£60		✓	
	Joseph Watters	Tom	£60	Reprieved		
1762	John Oliver	Tom	£30	✓ (died of castration)		
	John Roberts	Jack	£60	✓		
	Richard Spaight	Cato	£60		✓	✓
	William Peacock	Morrise	£50	✓ (murder)		
	Thomas Jones	Jemmy	£60	✓		
	James Parker's estate	Caesar	£20	✓ ("Murder of his Master")		
	Thomas Corprew's estate	Dublin	£45	✓ (1754 murder)		
1764	John Daniel's executors	Titus	£60		✓	✓
	Hezekiah Russ	Dick	£60	✓ ("poisoning a Negroe Fellow belonging to John Crawford")		
	Peter Clear, guardian for Cornelius, William, and Demcy Leary	Isaac	£60	✓ (arson)		
	Mary Collins	Lettiss	£60	✓ (murder)		
	John Bell	Tom	£45		✓ (died in jail "some Years Past")	
1766	Matthew Rabourn	Rose	£50	✓ (arson)		
	Richard Yates	Pompey	£60	✓		
	John Cherry	Luke	£80	✓		
	Lewis Henry DeRosset	London	£75		✓ (drowned)	✓
	Cullen Pollock	Toddy Moses	£120	✓		
	Alexander Grant	Simon	£80	✓		
	Thomas Cook	Ben	£60	✓		
	Elizabeth Bonner, Henry Bonner's administratrix	Cato Peter	£160	✓		
1767	William Cannon	Simon	£60	✓ ("Murder of Lewis Bell")		

Session	Slaveholder	Enslaved person	Amount	Executed (alleged crime)	Killed	Outlawed
	Richard Ward	Boston	£80	✓		
	Thomas Edwards	Dick	£60	✓ (murder)		
	Evan Jones	Unnamed	£80	✓		
	John Bravard	Dick	£35	✓		
	Martha Hill	Bacchus	£50	✓ (rape)		
	Francis Corbin's administratrix	Cudgo	£80	✓		
	George Campbell	Quash	£70	✓ (murder)		
1768	Ezekiel Moore	Jack	£80	✓		
	Sam Thomas's executors	Robin Jack Jemmy	£160	✓ (murder)		
	James Hasell	Phillis	£80		✓	✓
	John Dubois's executors	Quamino	£80	✓		
	William Salter	Unnamed	£75	✓		
	Thomas DeVaughan, Bryan Lee's administrator	Will	£80	✓ (murder)		
	James Hasell Jr.	Johnny	£80	✓		
	William Campbell	Cudgoe	£80		✓ (drowned) ✓	
	Col. Wilson Cary	Harry	£80	✓		
	Charles Jordan	Unnamed	£80	✓		
1769	John Rowan	Gwyn	£80	✓		
	Christopher Robinson	Batt	£80	✓		
	Francis Clayton	Jack Toney	£160	✓		
1770	James Moore	George	£80	✓		
	Mary Ward, Benjamin Ward's administratrix	Cuff	£60	✓ ("Poisoning his late Master")		
	John Thornton and Martha Williamson, William Williamson's executrix	Two unnamed	£155	✓		
	Wyriot Ormond	Cuff Annis Phillis Lucy	£80 £70 £20 £65	✓ ("Murder of Henry Ormond")		

(*continued*)

Session	Slaveholder	Enslaved person	Amount	Executed (alleged crime)	Killed	Outlawed
	Dr. John Corbyn	Jack	£60	✓		
	Mills Reddick (Virginia)	Caesar	£80	✓		
	Richard Brownrigg	Three unnamed	£216	✓		
	John Stevens	Dick	£80	✓		
	Frederick Gregg	Quammee	£80		✓ (drowned himself)	✓
1771	John Ramsey	Phebe	£80	✓ (murder)		
	James Coar	Scip	£80	✓		
	John Simpson	Jack	£80	✓		
	Roger Ormond	Jem	£70	✓		
	James Harris	Mark	£80	✓		
	Robert Howe	Unnamed	£80	✓ (murder)		
1773	Catherine Henry, John Henry's administratrix	Toney	£80	✓		
	Richard Quince	Peach	£80	✓ (murder)		
	Frances Daniel	Scipio	£80	✓ (rape)		
	Ralph McNair	Jem	£80	✓		
	Rothias Latham	Oxford	£70	✓		
	Peter Mallet	Biscuit	£75		✓	✓
1774	Joseph McDonald	Sanders	£80	✓		
	Jacob Ryley	Bob	£80	✓		

TABLE A.6. Georgia Slaveholder Compensation Payments

Tax act	Slaveholder	Enslaved person	Amount	Executed (alleged crime)	Killed
1766	Peter Nephew	Unnamed	£49	✓	
	Alexander Wylly	Unnamed woman	£49 10s	✓	
	Archibald Bulloch	Colley	£50		✓
1767	Mary Douglass	Ben	£70	✓	
April 1768	John Rivers	Two unnamed	£80	✓	
	John Goulding	Unnamed	£37	✓	
	Samuel Salters	Unnamed	£40	✓	
	Samuel Stevens	Two unnamed	£80	✓	
	William Mackenzie	Unnamed	£40	✓	
	Peter Tondee	Unnamed	£40	✓	
	Roger Kelsall	Unnamed	£40	✓	
December 1768	Charles Pryce	Unnamed	£30	✓	
	William Gibbons	Unnamed	£30	✓	
1773	John Glen	Unnamed	£30	✓ (robbery)	
	Mary Maxwell	Crop ear'd Tom	£25	✓	
	John Houstoun	George	£40	✓ (robbery)	

NOTES

INTRODUCTION

1 Fernando Purcell, *"Too Many Foreigners for My Taste": Law, Race and Ethnicity in California, 1848–1852, in* EVIL, LAW AND THE STATE: PERSPECTIVES ON STATE POWER AND VIOLENCE 17, 24–26 (John T. Parry ed., 2006). *See generally* EVIL, LAW AND THE STATE, *supra*; RIGHTS, CITIZENSHIP, AND TORTURE: PERSPECTIVES ON EVIL, LAW AND THE STATE (John Parry & Welat Zeydanlıoğlu eds., 2009).

2 *E.g.*, Ruud De Mooij & Michael Keen, *Taxing Principles: Making the Best of a Necessary Evil*, FIN. & DEV., Dec. 2014, at 50; Alisha Hill, Opinion, *Is Taxation a Necessary Evil?*, CLEAR CREEK COURANT (Idaho Springs, Colo.), Aug. 31, 2017; Edward Lotterman, Opinion, *Taxes Are a Necessary Evil; Tax Evaders Really Are Evil*, PIONEER PRESS (St. Paul, Minn.), Oct. 27, 2002, at 2D; Robert Minsky, Opinion, *Paying Taxes Is Necessary Evil*, ST. LUCIE NEWS TRIBUNE (Fort Pierce, Fla.), Apr. 25, 2009, at A7; Gary Richards, *Roadshow: Most Readers Agree Taxes Are a Necessary Evil*, CONTRA COSTA TIMES (Walnut Creek, Cal.), May 24, 2009.

3 A.H. Carter, *The Lesser Evil: Some Aspects of Income Tax Administration in the U.S.A. and the U.K.*, 40 PUB. ADMIN. 69 (1962).

4 FRANK CHODOROV, THE INCOME TAX: ROOT OF ALL EVIL 14 (Ludwig von Mises Inst. online ed. 2002) (1954).

5 *Id.* at 1, 13, 23, 37.

6 ROBERT NOZICK, ANARCHY, STATE, AND UTOPIA 169–72 (1974); MURRAY N. ROTHBARD, THE ETHICS OF LIBERTY 162–68 (N.Y. Univ. Press 1998) (1982); CHARLES ADAMS, FOR GOOD AND EVIL: THE IMPACT OF TAXES ON THE COURSE OF CIVILIZATION, at xviii, xxii, 1, 282, 364, 475–80 (2d ed. 1999); Andrew Kaczynski, *Rand Paul Philosophizes on Tax Rates: "If We Tax You at 50%, You Are Half Slave, Half Free,"* BUZZFEED NEWS (July 6, 2015), www.buzzfeednews.com; Grover Norquist (@GroverNorquist), TWITTER (Jan. 5, 2019), https://twitter.com.

7 ROMAIN D. HURET, AMERICAN TAX RESISTERS 22, 30, 47–48, 53–54, 81, 91, 126–27, 185, 187, 190, 213, 231 (2014); INTERNAL REVENUE SERV., THE TRUTH ABOUT FRIVOLOUS TAX ARGUMENTS 32 (2022); *e.g.*, Denison v. Comm'r, 47 T.C.M. (CCH) 1496 (1984); McCoy v. Comm'r, 76 T.C. 1027 (1981).

8 ADAMS, *supra* note 6, at 476. This rhetorical move also has deep roots. On the eve of the Revolutionary War, the case for liberty was often made by comparing

British treatment of (White) Americans to slavery, even as (White) Americans themselves reaped the benefits of enslaving others. *E.g.*, *To the Inhabitants of the Province of South Carolina*, N.Y. Journal, No. 1647, July 28, 1774; *To the People of Great-Britain*, Pa. Gazette, No. 2393, Nov. 2, 1774, postscript.

9 Joseph Conrad, Heart of Darkness 113 (D.C.R.A. Goonetilleke ed., Broadview Literary Texts 1995) (1899). Conrad's novella is an apt source for this quotation because it partakes of a duality like that inherent in the power to tax. Taxation is simultaneously seen as a power that can create and uplift societies and as a destructive force that, as described throughout this book, can be—and has been—used to crush human lives as part of projects to entrench and perpetuate racism. Similarly, some people see *Heart of Darkness* as a trenchant critique of nineteenth-century colonialism and racism that points toward the path away from those evils, while others see it as a profoundly racist and dehumanizing text that should cease to be classed among the great works of literature. *Compare* D.C.R.A. Goonetilleke, *Introduction* to Heart of Darkness, *supra*, at 9, *with* Chinua Achebe, *An Image of Africa*, 18 Mass. Rev. 782 (1977).

10 17 U.S. 316, 431 (1819).

11 Anthony C. Infanti, Our Selfish Tax Laws: Toward Tax Reform That Mirrors Our Better Selves 10–11, 35–43, 135–59 (2018); *cf.* Sanford Levinson, McCulloch *II: The Oft-Ignored Twin and Inherent Limits on "Sovereign" Power*, 19 Geo. J.L. & Pub. Pol'y 1, 12 (2021).

12 *See, e.g.*, Cottage Sav. Ass'n v. Comm'r, 499 U.S. 554, 559 (1991).

13 Anthony C. Infanti, *LGBT Taxpayers: A Collision of "Others*,*"* 13 Geo. J. Gender & L. 1, 8 (2012).

14 *See id.* at 15–17; Infanti, *supra* note 11, at 10–11, 39, 141.

15 *See generally* Infanti, *supra* note 11; Dorothy A. Brown, The Whiteness of Wealth: How the Tax System Impoverishes Black Americans—and How We Can Fix It (2021); Critical Tax Theory: An Introduction (Anthony C. Infanti & Bridget J. Crawford eds., 2009).

16 For a reckoning of the relationship between slavery and accounting—which, like tax law, has been portrayed as a values-free zone—see, for example, Richard K. Fleischman & Thomas N. Tyson, *Accounting in Service of Racism: Monetizing Slave Property in the Antebellum South*, 15 Critical Persps. on Acct. 376 (2004); David Oldroyd et al., *The Culpability of Accounting Practice in Promoting Slavery in the British Empire and Antebellum United States*, 19 Critical Persps. on Acct. 764 (2008); Lúcia Lima Rodrigues & Russell Craig, *The Role of Government Accounting and Taxation in the Institutionalization of Slavery in Brazil*, 57 Critical Persps. on Acct. 21 (2018).

17 *See generally* Thomas D. Morris, Southern Slavery and the Law, 1619–1860 (1996).

18 *E.g.*, A. Leon Higginbotham, Jr., In the Matter of Color: Race and the American Legal Process: The Colonial Period (1978); Morris, *supra* note 17.

19 Brian Sawers, *The Poll Tax Before Jim Crow*, 57 AM. J. LEGAL HIST. 166, 166–67 (2017); *e.g.*, MORRIS, *supra* note 17, at 255. The few instances of scholars focusing sustained attention on taxation and slavery—mostly in the form of unpublished theses and dissertations—are cited in later chapters of this book.

20 William Michael Treanor, *The Original Understanding of the Takings Clause and the Political Process*, 95 COLUM. L. REV. 782, 785–91 (1995).

21 Ann Thúy Nguyễn & Maya Pendleton, *Recognizing Race in Language: Why We Capitalize "Black" and "White,"* CTR. FOR STUDY OF SOC. POL'Y (Mar. 23, 2020), https://cssp.org; *see, e.g.*, Kwame Anthony Appiah, *The Case for Capitalizing the B in Black*, ATL. (June 18, 2020), www.theatlantic.com.

1. EARLY EXPERIMENTATION

1 On how slavery shaped taxation in colonial America, see ROBIN L. EINHORN, AMERICAN TAXATION, AMERICAN SLAVERY (2006).

2 Given space constraints and the focus here on bringing taxation to the fore, a full description of economic, political, and social life in South Carolina (or, for that matter, any of the other American colonies) is beyond the scope of this book. Entire volumes have been written on these subjects, and many of them are cited in the notes to this book, making those notes a good source for identifying further reading about colonial American society.

3 PETER H. WOOD, BLACK MAJORITY: NEGROES IN COLONIAL SOUTH CAROLINA FROM 1670 TO THE STONO REBELLION 6 (1974); *see* ROBERT M. WEIR, COLONIAL SOUTH CAROLINA: A HISTORY 3–9 (1983).

4 WOOD, *supra* note 3, at 13–34; *see* PETER A. COCLANIS, THE SHADOW OF A DREAM: ECONOMIC LIFE AND DEATH IN THE SOUTH CAROLINA LOW COUNTRY, 1670–1920, at 22, 61 (1991); Thomas J. Little, *The South Carolina Slave Laws Reconsidered: 1670–1700*, 94 S.C. HIST. MAG. 86, 88–90 (1993).

5 WOOD, *supra* note 3, at 8; *see id.* at 6–8.

6 ROBERT OLWELL, MASTERS, SLAVES, & SUBJECTS: THE CULTURE OF POWER IN THE SOUTH CAROLINA LOW COUNTRY, 1740–1790, at 5 (1998); *see* IRA BERLIN, MANY THOUSANDS GONE: THE FIRST TWO CENTURIES OF SLAVERY IN NORTH AMERICA 7–8 (1998).

7 OLWELL, *supra* note 6, at 5; *see* Daragh Grant, *"Civilizing" the Colonial Subject: The Co-evolution of State and Slavery in South Carolina, 1670–1739*, 57 COMPAR. STUD. IN SOC'Y & HIST. 606, 611–14 (2015).

8 WOOD, *supra* note 3, at 20–21; A. LEON HIGGINBOTHAM, JR., IN THE MATTER OF COLOR: RACE AND THE AMERICAN LEGAL PROCESS: THE COLONIAL PERIOD 151 (1978).

9 WOOD, *supra* note 3, at 25; *see id.* at 131; OLWELL, *supra* note 6, at 11.

10 HIGGINBOTHAM, *supra* note 8, at 165; *see* Meghan N. Duff, *Creating a Plantation Province: Proprietary Land Policies and Early Settlement Patterns*, *in* MONEY, TRADE, AND POWER: THE EVOLUTION OF COLONIAL SOUTH CARO-

LINA'S PLANTATION SOCIETY 1, 7–8 & tbl.1.2, 16–17 (Jack P. Greene et al. eds., 2001) [hereinafter MTP]; Jennifer Lyle Morgan, *This Is "Mines": Slavery and Reproduction in Colonial Barbados and South Carolina*, in MTP, *supra*, at 187, 197–98.

11 WOOD, *supra* note 3, at 37; *see* HIGGINBOTHAM, *supra* note 8, at 164–66.

12 BASES OF THE PLANTATION SOCIETY 63 (Aubrey C. Land ed., 1969) [hereinafter LAND]; *see* WEIR, *supra* note 3, at 170; *see also* WOOD, *supra* note 3, at 35–91; DANIEL C. LITTLEFIELD, RICE AND SLAVES: ETHNICITY AND THE SLAVE TRADE IN COLONIAL SOUTH CAROLINA 74–114 (1981).

13 HIGGINBOTHAM, *supra* note 8, at 164; *see* WOOD, *supra* note 3, at 26 n.36.

14 WOOD, *supra* note 3, at 36.

15 *Id.* at 36, 143–44; EVARTS B. GREENE & VIRGINIA D. HARRINGTON, AMERICAN POPULATION BEFORE THE FEDERAL CENSUS OF 1790, at 173 (1932); Gary L. Hewitt, *The State in the Planters' Service: Politics and the Emergence of a Plantation Economy in South Carolina*, in MTP, *supra* note 10, at 49, 51.

16 WOOD, *supra* note 3, at 143; *see* CONVERSE D. CLOWSE, ECONOMIC BEGINNINGS IN COLONIAL SOUTH CAROLINA: 1670–1730, at 108–09 (1971); HIGGINBOTHAM, *supra* note 8, at 151–52, 160–62; Hewitt, *supra* note 15, at 57–58; William L. Ramsey, *"All & the Singular the Slaves": A Demographic Profile of Indian Slavery in Colonial South Carolina*, in MTP, *supra* note 10, at 166, 168, 173–74. *See generally* Denise I. Bossy, *The South's Other Slavery: Recent Research on Indian Slavery*, 9 NATIVE S. 27 (2016).

17 *See* Act of Apr. 24, 1708, No. 277, paras. V–VI, 2 STATUTES AT LARGE OF SOUTH CAROLINA 324, 325 (Thomas Cooper ed., 1837) [hereinafter STATUTES]; HIGGINBOTHAM, *supra* note 8, at 160–62; WOOD, *supra* note 3, at 37–40; *see also* CLOWSE, *supra* note 16, at 65–66, 84–85, 87, 109. Dates given for legislation refer to the date of enactment and include the use of hybrid old-style/new-style dating for acts passed between January 1 and March 24 in years before 1752.

18 D. Andrew Johnson, *Displacing Captives in Colonial South Carolina: Native American Enslavement and the Rise of the Colonial State After the Yamasee War*, 7 J. EARLY AM. HIST. 115 (2017).

19 Ramsey, *supra* note 16, at 179; *see id.* at 178–79; *see* PHILIP D. MORGAN, SLAVE COUNTERPOINT: BLACK CULTURE IN THE EIGHTEENTH-CENTURY CHESAPEAKE AND LOWCOUNTRY 481 (1998).

20 WOOD, *supra* note 3, at 43.

21 *Id.* at 145; *see* Hewitt, *supra* note 15, at 63–64; Ramsey, *supra* note 16, at 179.

22 WOOD, *supra* note 3, at 146–47 tbl.II.

23 *Id.* at 150.

24 *Id.* at 166; *see* COCLANIS, *supra* note 4, at 64 tbl.3-1.

25 R.W. Kelsey, *Swiss Settlers in South Carolina*, 23 S.C. HIST. & GENEALOGICAL MAG. 85, 90 (1922) (translating and reproducing Letter from Samuel Dyssli to His Mother, Brother, and Friends in Switzerland (Dec. 3, 1737)).

26 OLWELL, *supra* note 6, at 30; *see* COCLANIS, *supra* note 4, at 64 tbl.3-1, 68 tbl.3-4; *see also* MORGAN, *supra* note 19, at 95, 96–97 map 2.

27 RACHEL N. KLEIN, UNIFICATION OF A SLAVE STATE: THE RISE OF THE PLANTER CLASS IN THE SOUTH CAROLINA BACKCOUNTRY, 1760–1808, at 19 (1990); *see id.* at 19–20.

28 HIGGINBOTHAM, *supra* note 8, at 152.

29 1690/1 Slave Code, No. 57, 7 STATUTES, *supra* note 17, at 343 (disallowed); 1693 Slave Code, No. 101, 2 STATUTES, *supra* note 17, at 78 (title only); 1695/6 Slave Code, No. 141, GOVERNOR ARCHDALE'S LAWS [1696], at 60, S.C. Dep't of Archives & Hist.; *see* COMMISSIONS AND INSTRUCTIONS FROM THE LORDS PROPRIETORS OF CAROLINA TO PUBLIC OFFICIALS OF SOUTH CAROLINA: 1685–1715, at 23 (A.S. Salley, Jr. ed., 1916); JOURNALS OF THE COMMONS HOUSE OF ASSEMBLY OF SOUTH CAROLINA: FOR THE FOUR SESSIONS OF 1693, at 34–35 (A.S. Salley, Jr. ed., 1907); CHARLES H. LESSER, SOUTH CAROLINA BEGINS: THE RECORDS OF A PROPRIETARY COLONY, 1663–1721, at 258 (1995); Little, *supra* note 4, at 96–101.

The separate legislature that governed the southern portion of the colony of Carolina (for convenience, here referred to as "South Carolina" before and after the formal split) quickly evolved into a bicameral body, with an elected "Commons House of Assembly" and an appointed "Council." EDSON L. WHITNEY, GOVERNMENT OF THE COLONY OF SOUTH CAROLINA 31, 42–44, 47–50 (1895). Both voters and members of the House were limited to White male property owners. *E.g.*, Act of Dec. 15, 1716, No. 365, para. XX, 2 STATUTES, *supra* note 17, at 683, 688–89. During both the proprietary and royal colony periods, the governor possessed the power to veto legislation, and all enacted legislation was to be submitted for ultimate approval either to the colony's proprietors or to the Crown, as appropriate. WHITNEY, *supra*, at 52–54. For an overview of the development, structure, and operation of other colonial legislatures, see PEVERILL SQUIRE, THE EVOLUTION OF AMERICAN LEGISLATURES: COLONIES, TERRITORIES, AND STATES, 1619–2009, at 11–71 (2012).

30 Little, *supra* note 4, at 97, 100; M. Eugene Sirmans, *The Legal Status of the Slave in South Carolina, 1670–1740*, 28 J.S. HIST. 462, 464–66 (1962).

31 WINTHROP D. JORDAN, WHITE OVER BLACK: AMERICAN ATTITUDES TOWARD THE NEGRO, 1550–1812, at 85 (2d ed. 2012); *see* Little, *supra* note 4, at 100–01.

32 HIGGINBOTHAM, *supra* note 8, at 169–90.

33 *Id.* at 170; *see* Grant, *supra* note 7, at 615–17.

34 1712 Slave Code, No. 314, pmbl., 7 STATUTES, *supra* note 17, at 352, 352; *see* 1722/3 Slave Code, No. 476, pmbl., 7 STATUTES, *supra* note 17, at 371, 371; 1735 Slave Code, No. 586, pmbl., 7 STATUTES, *supra* note 17, at 385, 385; John Samuel Harpham, *Two Concepts of a Slave in the South Carolina Law of Slavery*, 39 SLAVERY & ABOLITION 101, 116–17 (2018).

35 Little, *supra* note 4, at 101.

36 1722/3 Slave Code, *supra* note 34, paras. VIII, X; *see* 1735 Slave Code, *supra* note 34, paras. VIII, X.

37 1722/3 Slave Code, *supra* note 34, para. XII; *see* 1735 Slave Code, *supra* note 34, para. XI; HIGGINBOTHAM, *supra* note 8, at 182–83.

38 1712 Slave Code, *supra* note 34, para. XII; 1722/3 Slave Code, *supra* note 34, para. XIV; 1735 Slave Code, *supra* note 34, para. XIII.

39 1712 Slave Code, *supra* note 34, paras. XV, XIX.

40 1722/3 Slave Code, *supra* note 34, para. XVII.

41 MORGAN, *supra* note 19, at 446–47.

42 1722/3 Slave Code, *supra* note 34, para. XVII.

43 1735 Slave Code, *supra* note 34, para. XVI.

44 1695/6 Slave Code, *supra* note 29, para. 10; 1698 Slave Code, *microformed on* Acts, Bills, and Joint Resolutions: 1691–1716, ST731, at 8, S.C. Dep't of Archives & Hist.; 1701 Slave Code, *reprinted in* L.H. Roper, *The 1701 "Act for the Better Ordering of Slaves": Reconsidering the History of Slavery in Proprietary South Carolina*, 64 WM. & MARY Q. 395, 413 (2007); 1712 Slave Code, *supra* note 34, para. XVII.

45 *See supra* note 44.

46 Act of Dec. 18, 1714, No. 344, para. VI, 7 STATUTES, *supra* note 17, at 365, 366–67; HIGGINBOTHAM, *supra* note 8, at 187.

47 1722/3 Slave Code, *supra* note 34, para. XIX; 1735 Slave Code, *supra* note 34, para. XVII.

48 *E.g.*, 1712 Slave Code, *supra* note 34, paras. IX–X, XII, XV, XVII, XIX; *see* Robert Olwell, *"Practical Justice": The Justice of the Peace, the Slave Court, and Local Authority in Mid-Eighteenth-Century South Carolina, in* MTP, *supra* note 10, at 256; HIGGINBOTHAM, *supra* note 8, at 179–81; OLWELL, *supra* note 6, at 71–101; MORGAN, *supra* note 19, at 263–64.

49 Act Inhibiting the Trading with Servants or Slaves, No. 34 (1686/7), 2 STATUTES, *supra* note 17, at 22, 23; Little, *supra* note 4, at 94–95.

50 *E.g.*, 1695/6 Slave Code, *supra* note 29, para. 2.

51 1698 Slave Code, *supra* note 44, at 2; *see* 1701 Slave Code, *supra* note 44, at 408; 1712 Slave Code, *supra* note 34, para. II; 1722/3 Slave Code, *supra* note 34, para. II; 1735 Slave Code, *supra* note 34, para. III.

52 *E.g.*, 1701 Slave Code, *supra* note 44, at 414; 1712 Slave Code, *supra* note 34, para. XXX; 1722/3 Slave Code, *supra* note 34, para. XXXI; 1735 Slave Code, *supra* note 34, para. XXVIII.

53 1712 Slave Code, *supra* note 34, para. XXX; *see* 1722/3 Slave Code, *supra* note 34, para. XXXI; 1735 Slave Code, *supra* note 34, para. XXVIII.

54 1712 Slave Code, *supra* note 34, para. XXX.

55 WOOD, *supra* note 3, at 279.

56 HIGGINBOTHAM, *supra* note 8, at 184.

57 *E.g.*, 1695/6 Slave Code, *supra* note 29, para. 4; 1698 Slave Code, *supra* note 44, at 10; 1701 Slave Code, *supra* note 44, at 409, 414; 1712 Slave Code, *supra* note 34, paras. XI–XII, XVI; 1722/3 Slave Code, *supra* note 34, paras. XIII–XIV, XVIII; 1735 Slave Code, *supra* note 34, paras. XII–XIII.

58 1695/6 Slave Code, *supra* note 29, para. 18.

59 1712 Slave Code, *supra* note 34, para. XVI.

60 *Id.*

61 *Id.*

62 *Id.* para. XIX.

63 *Id.* para. XII.

64 Act of Dec. 18, 1714, *supra* note 46, para. IV.

65 *Id.*

66 *Id.* para. V; WOOD, *supra* note 3, at 280.

67 Act of Dec. 11, 1717, No. 388, pmbl., 7 STATUTES, *supra* note 17, at 368, 368–69. For readers familiar with the tax academic literature, the changes made by this statute (as well as some later experimentation with the tax mechanisms for funding slaveholder compensation) may call to mind Pigouvian taxation; however, an examination of these changes (and that later experimentation) through the lens of Pigouvian taxation is beyond the scope of this book. *See* A.C. PIGOU, THE ECONOMICS OF WELFARE 159–63, 168–71 (1920); Agnar Sandmo, *Pigouvian Taxes, in* THE NEW PALGRAVE DICTIONARY OF ECONOMICS 10312, 10312 (2018).

68 Act of Dec. 11, 1717, *supra* note 67, para. II.

69 *Id.*

70 *Id.*

71 *Id.* pmbl., para. I.

72 *Id.* para. I.

73 WOOD, *supra* note 3, at 285–307.

74 2 WALTER B. EDGAR & N. LOUISE BAILEY, BIOGRAPHICAL DIRECTORY OF THE SOUTH CAROLINA HOUSE OF REPRESENTATIVES 120, 146, 153, 159, 198, 234, 246, 282, 320, 337, 359, 362, 409, 419, 454, 472, 475, 505, 550, 571, 653, 677, 700, 717, 724, 729 (1977).

75 1722/3 Slave Code, *supra* note 34, para. XVIII.

76 *Id.* paras. XIV, XVII–XVIII.

77 *Id.* para. XXII.

78 *Id.*

79 HIGGINBOTHAM, *supra* note 8, at 190.

80 1722/3 Slave Code, *supra* note 34, para. XVIII.

81 *Id.*

82 *Id.*

83 *See generally* Act for Establishing County and Precinct Courts, No. 16 (1721), 1721 S.C. Sess. Laws (LLMC Digital); John E. Douglass, *Judiciary Without Jurisdiction:*

South Carolina's Experiment with a County and Precinct Court System, 1720–1730, 90 S.C. HIST. MAG. 237 (1989).

84 *See* WEIR, *supra* note 3, at 214.

85 1722/3 Slave Code, *supra* note 34, para. XXXVII.

86 *Id.*

87 W. ROY SMITH, SOUTH CAROLINA AS A ROYAL PROVINCE, 1719–1776, at 280–82 (1903).

88 OLWELL, *supra* note 6, at 78–79; Edson L. Whitney, History of the Colony of South Carolina 675–80 (1890) (Ph.D. dissertation, Harvard University) (on file with Harvard University Archives); *cf.* John Donald Duncan, Servitude and Slavery in Colonial South Carolina, 1670–1776, at 708 tbl.XXXVI (1971) (Ph.D. dissertation, Emory University) (ProQuest).

89 MAURICE A. CROUSE, THE PUBLIC TREASURY OF SOUTH CAROLINA 109–14 (1977); SMITH, *supra* note 87, at 289–329; WHITNEY, *supra* note 29, at 47–48; WEIR, *supra* note 3, at 125–31.

90 This view cannot, of course, be fully contextualized because of the inability to account for the perspective of the enslaved persons who were killed, executed, or threatened with death. Even when an enslaved person's perspective is recounted here, one must bear in mind that it is filtered through the eyes of slaveholders or other Whites, whether recounted in a slaveholder's petition for compensation or clemency, by the legislature or executive investigating and considering those claims, or by the publishers of South Carolina's newspapers.

91 OLWELL, *supra* note 6, at 82; *see* Email from Wade H. Dorsey, Supervisor, Reference Servs., S.C. Dep't of Archives & Hist., to author (Dec. 14, 2021) (on file with author).

92 1721 Tax-Act, No. 451, para. XXVIII, 3 STATUTES, *supra* note 17, at 149, 155. The 1721 Tax-Act also included a £200 payment "to the Rev. Mr. Guy, for the loss of a negro," but the circumstances of the "loss" are nowhere spelled out. *Id.* para XXXI.

93 *Id.* para. XXVIII.

94 *See supra* notes 81–82 and accompanying text.

95 1723/4 Tax-Act, No. 479, para. XXVII, 3 STATUTES, *supra* note 17, at 206, 213.

96 JOURNAL OF THE COMMONS HOUSE OF ASSEMBLY OF SOUTH CAROLINA: FEBRUARY 23, 1724/5–JUNE 1, 1725, at 76 (A.S. Salley ed., 1945) [hereinafter 1725 JOURNAL].

97 JOURNAL OF THE COMMONS HOUSE OF ASSEMBLY OF SOUTH CAROLINA: JUNE 2, 1724–JUNE 16, 1724, at 14 (A.S. Salley ed., 1944).

98 JOURNAL OF THE COMMONS HOUSE OF ASSEMBLY OF SOUTH CAROLINA: NOVEMBER 1, 1725–APRIL 30, 1726, at 22 (A.S. Salley ed., 1945) [hereinafter 1725–1726 JOURNAL].

99 1724/5 Tax-Act, No. 493, para. XXV, 3 STATUTES, *supra* note 17, at 238, 245.

100 1725 JOURNAL, *supra* note 96, at 45; *see id.* at 25, 34, 109–12.

101 *Id.* at 49.

102 1725–1726 JOURNAL, *supra* note 98, at 22.

103 *Id.* at 22–23.

104 *Id.* at 38; *see* Richard Waterhouse, South Carolina's Colonial Elite: A Study in the Social Structure and Political Culture of a Southern Colony, 1670–1760, at 165, 198, 293 (1973) (Ph.D. dissertation, Johns Hopkins University) (ProQuest).

105 1725 Tax-Act, No. 509, para. XXIV, 3 STATUTES, *supra* note 17, at 257, 264.

106 1722/3 Slave Code, *supra* note 34, para. XLI; *see* CLOWSE, *supra* note 16, at 239; SMITH, *supra* note 87, at 269; WEIR, *supra* note 3, at 110.

107 Act of Aug. 20, 1731, No. 540, 3 STATUTES, *supra* note 17, at 326; Act of Sept. 22, 1733, No. 566, 3 STATUTES, *supra* note 17, at 373.

108 1733 Tax-Act, No. 551, sched., 3 STATUTES, *supra* note 17, at 352, 361.

109 JOURNALS OF THE COMMONS HOUSE OF ASSEMBLY: JANUARY 9, 1732/3–MARCH 17, 1732/3, at 896, 945, 950 (LLMC Digital) [hereinafter 1732/3 JOURNAL].

110 *Id.* at 902, 934–35.

111 *Charles-Town*, S.C. GAZETTE, Jan. 27–Feb. 3, 1732.

112 1732/3 JOURNAL, *supra* note 109, at 927.

113 1734 Tax-Act, No. 572, sched., 3 STATUTES, *supra* note 17, at 384, 391–93.

114 JOURNALS OF THE COMMONS HOUSE OF ASSEMBLY: JANUARY 8, 1733/4–FEBRUARY 9, 1733/4, at 93–94, 106 (LLMC Digital) [hereinafter 1733/4 JOURNAL]; *see id.* at 76.

115 *Charles-Town*, S.C. GAZETTE, Jan. 20–27, 1732.

116 1733/4 JOURNAL, *supra* note 114, at 94; *see id.* at 73.

117 *Id.* at 72.

118 *Id.* at 74.

119 *Charles-Town*, S.C. GAZETTE, Aug. 18–25, 1733.

120 1735 Tax-Act, sched., *microformed on* South Carolina Manuscript Acts (Certified Copies) Sent to England (CO5/413-416): 1731–1738, GR41 (BMP D475-78), S.C. Dep't of Archives & Hist.

121 JOURNAL OF THE COMMONS HOUSE OF ASSEMBLY OF SOUTH CARO-LINA: NOVEMBER 8, 1734–JUNE 7, 1735, at 68 (A.S. Salley ed., 1947); *see id.* at 67, 69, 119, 170, 172, 174.

122 *Id.* at 70; *see id.* at 119, 170.

123 *Id.* at 76; *see id.* at 82, 83, 120, 170.

124 *Id.* at 82; *see id.* at 83.

125 *Id.* at 94, 107; *see id.* at 96, 120–21, 171.

126 1735 Slave Code, *supra* note 34, para. XXX.

127 *Id.* paras. XIII, XVI.

128 *See* LAND, *supra* note 12, at 206; MORGAN, *supra* note 19, at 298.

129 Act for the Encouragement of the Importation of White Servants, No. 167, pmbl., para. III (1698), 2 STATUTES, *supra* note 17, at 153, 153; *see id.* paras. I, III.

130 LAND, *supra* note 12, at 206; Repealing Act, No. 179 (1700/1), 2 STATUTES, *supra* note 17, at 165.

131 Act to Encourage the Importation of White Servants into This Province, No. 358 (1716), para. II, 2 STATUTES, *supra* note 17, at 646, 646–47; *see id.* para. I.

132 *Id.* para. VIII.

133 Act of June 29, 1717, No. 374, para. VI, 3 STATUTES, *supra* note 17, at 5, 6.

134 1701 Slave Code, *supra* note 44, at 416; *see* 1695/6 Slave Code, *supra* note 29, para. 22; 1698 Slave Code, *supra* note 44, at 12.

135 1712 Slave Code, *supra* note 34, para. XXIX.

136 1722/3 Slave Code, *supra* note 34, para. XXX.

137 Act of Mar. 11, 1726/7, No. 523, tit., pmbl., 3 STATUTES, *supra* note 17, at 272, 272.

138 *Id.* para. I.

139 *Id.*

140 1735 Slave Code, *supra* note 34, para. XXVII.

141 *See* WEIR, *supra* note 3, at 180–81, 188.

142 1703 General Duty Act, No. 204, para. IV, 2 STATUTES, *supra* note 17, at 200, 201; *see* 1716 General Duty Act, No. 359, 2 STATUTES, *supra* note 17, at 649; 1721 General Duty Act, No. 455, 3 STATUTES, *supra* note 17, at 159; 1722/3 General Duty Act, No. 477, 3 STATUTES, *supra* note 17, at 193; Act of Apr. 30, 1726, No. 520, 3 STATUTES, *supra* note 17, at 270; Act of Aug. 20, 1731, No. 543, para. VII, 3 STATUTES, *supra* note 17, at 334, 340–41; SMITH, *supra* note 87, at 286; W. Robert Higgins, The South Carolina Negro Duty Law 15–16, 20–22, 42–59, 127–34 (1967) (M.A. thesis, University of South Carolina) (on file with Milner Library, Illinois State University).

143 CROUSE, *supra* note 89, at 56.

144 Act of Dec. 18, 1714, *supra* note 46, para. IX.

145 *Id.*

146 Act of Dec. 11, 1717, *supra* note 67, para. III; 1716 General Duty Act, *supra* note 142, paras. III–IV.

147 Act of Dec. 11, 1717, *supra* note 67, para. IV; Higgins, *supra* note 142, at 19 n.21.

148 Higgins, *supra* note 142, at 19; *see* REPORT OF THE COMMITTEE OF THE COMMONS HOUSE OF ASSEMBLY OF THE PROVINCE OF SOUTH-CAROLINA ON THE STATE OF THE PAPER-CURRENCY OF THE SAID PROVINCE app. at 8 (1737) (LLMC Digital); Hewitt, *supra* note 15, at 51, 65.

149 1719 General Duty Act, No. 395, paras. I, III, XXX, 3 STATUTES, *supra* note 17, at 56, 56, 57–58, 65–67; *see* 3 STATUTES, *supra* note 17, at 68–69; WEIR, *supra* note 3, at 98–99.

150 1722/3 General Duty Act, *supra* note 142, para. III; *see* Act of Feb. 18, 1714/5, *No. 349, 2 STATUTES, *supra* note 17, at 622; 1716 General Duty Act, *supra* note 142, para. IV; 1721 General Duty Act, *supra* note 142, para. IV; CROUSE, *supra* note 89, at 55–56.

151 1722/3 General Duty Act, *supra* note 142, para. IV; *see id.* para. I; 1721 General Duty Act, *supra* note 142, para. I; *see* Higgins, *supra* note 142, at 20.

152 1721 General Duty Act, *supra* note 142; 1722/3 General Duty Act, *supra* note 142; Act of Apr. 30, 1726, *supra* note 142; Act of Aug. 20, 1731, *supra* note 142; *see infra* fig. 2.1.

153 2 ROYAL INSTRUCTIONS TO BRITISH COLONIAL GOVERNORS, 1670–1776, at 673–74 (1967).

154 *See* James A. Rawley, *Richard Harris, Slave Trader Spokesman*, 23 ALBION 439, 449–51 (1991).

155 Act to Encourage Persons to Become Settlers in the Province of South Carolina (1725), 1725 S.C. Sess. Laws (LLMC Digital).

156 1735 Tax-Act, *supra* note 120, at 1; 1736 Tax-Act, No. 608, para. II, 3 STATUTES, *supra* note 17, at 438, 438–39; 1736/7 Tax-Act, No. 628, para. II, 3 STATUTES, *supra* note 17, at 472, 473; 1738 Tax-Act, No. 650, para. II, 3 STATUTES, *supra* note 17, at 502, 502; 1739 Tax-Act, No. 663, para. II, 3 STATUTES, *supra* note 17, at 527, 527–28.

157 Act of June 7, 1735, No. 593, para. I, 3 STATUTES, *supra* note 17, at 409, 409.

158 *Id.* pmbl.; *see* Higgins, *supra* note 142, at 259.

159 WOOD, *supra* note 3, at 227.

160 Payments from 1740 to 1751 are omitted because compensation for extrajudicial killings was legally unavailable during that period, and the earliest payments are likewise omitted because they stemmed from undifferentiated, blanket authorizations.

161 *See* HERBERT APTHEKER, AMERICAN NEGRO SLAVE REVOLTS 182–87 (1943); MARVIN L. MICHAEL KAY & LORIN LEE CARY, SLAVERY IN NORTH CAROLINA, 1748–1775, at 98 (1995).

2. THE STONO REBELLION AND ITS AFTERMATH

1 PETER H. WOOD, BLACK MAJORITY: NEGROES IN COLONIAL SOUTH CAROLINA FROM 1670 TO THE STONO REBELLION 308 (1974); *see* HERBERT APTHEKER, AMERICAN NEGRO SLAVE REVOLTS 187–89 (1943); ROBERT OLWELL, MASTERS, SLAVES, & SUBJECTS: THE CULTURE OF POWER IN THE SOUTH CAROLINA LOW COUNTRY, 1740–1790, at 21–25 (1998).

2 WOOD, *supra* note 1, at 319 (quoting BOS. WKLY. NEWSL., Nov. 30, 1739).

3 *Id.* at 319–20 (footnote omitted).

4 *Id.* at 322 (quoting BENJAMIN MARTYN, AN IMPARTIAL INQUIRY INTO THE STATE AND UTILITY OF THE COLONY OF GEORGIA 173 (1741)).

5 *Id.* at 323.

6 *Id.*

7 *Id.* at 324; *see* 1740 Slave Code, No. 670, 7 STATUTES AT LARGE OF SOUTH CAROLINA 397 (David J. McCord ed., 1840) [hereinafter STATUTES] (renewed by Act of May 7, 1743, No. 702, para. V, 7 STATUTES, *supra*, at 417, 418, and renewed and amended by Act of Mar. 22, 1745/6, No. 725, paras. IX–X, 3 STATUTES, *supra*, at 647, 649–50); OLWELL, *supra* note 1, at 62–63; John Samuel Harpham, *Two Concepts of a Slave in the South Carolina Law of Slavery*, 39 SLAVERY & ABOLITION 101, 117 (2018).

8 1740 Slave Code, *supra* note 7, pmbl.

9 *Id.* paras. XVI–XVII.

10 *Id.* para. XVII.

11 Act of Mar. 22, 1745/6, *supra* note 7, para. IV.

12 *Id.* para. V.

13 1740 Slave Code, *supra* note 7, para. IX; *see id.* para. XV.

14 PHILIP D. MORGAN, SLAVE COUNTERPOINT: BLACK CULTURE IN THE EIGHTEENTH-CENTURY CHESAPEAKE AND LOWCOUNTRY 613 (1998).

15 1740 Slave Code, *supra* note 7, para. XXIV.

16 *Id.* paras. III–V.

17 *Id.* para. XLVII; *see* WOOD, *supra* note 1, at 306–07.

18 1740 Slave Code, *supra* note 7, para. XLVII.

19 *Id.*

20 *Id.* para. LVI.

21 *Id.*

22 *Id.* para. XVIII.

23 MORGAN, *supra* note 14, at 265; *see id.* at 264–65; ROBERT M. WEIR, COLONIAL SOUTH CAROLINA: A HISTORY 177 (1983).

24 1740 Slave Code, *supra* note 7, para. XVIII.

25 JOURNAL OF THE COMMONS HOUSE OF ASSEMBLY: SEPTEMBER 12, 1739–MARCH 26, 1741, at 117 (J.H. Easterby ed., 1952) [hereinafter 1739–1741 JOURNAL].

26 *Id.*

27 OLWELL, *supra* note 1, at 64.

28 1740 Slave Code, *supra* note 7, para. XLIX.

29 MAURICE A. CROUSE, THE PUBLIC TREASURY OF SOUTH CAROLINA 111–14 (1977); JACK P. GREENE, THE QUEST FOR POWER: THE LOWER HOUSES OF ASSEMBLY IN THE SOUTHERN ROYAL COLONIES, 1689–1776, at 53–65, 88–96 (1963).

30 1740 Tax-Act, No. 673, sched., S165001, Box 20, S.C. Dep't of Archives & Hist.; 1741 Tax-Act, No. 689, sched., S165001, Box 21, S.C. Dep't of Archives & Hist.

31 1739–1741 JOURNAL, *supra* note 25, at 166.

32 *Id.*

33 *Id.*

34 *Id.* at 172; *see id.* at 165–66, 171–72.

35 1740 Tax-Act, *supra* note 30, sched.

36 1739–1741 JOURNAL, *supra* note 25, at 63–64.

37 *Id.* at 64; *see id.* at 65–66, 220–21; JOURNALS OF THE SOUTH CAROLINA COUNCIL AND SENATE: NOVEMBER 10–DECEMBER 18, 1739, at 265–67, 270–71 (LLMC Digital); JOURNALS OF THE SOUTH CAROLINA COUNCIL AND SENATE: FEBRUARY 26–MARCH 8, 1740, at 300 (LLMC Digital).

38 1739–1741 JOURNAL, *supra* note 25, at 64.

39 *See id.* at 63–66, 76–77, 82–83, 528–29.

40 *Id.* at 83, 220–21, 322.

41 1741/2 Tax-Act, No. 688, sched., S165001, Box 21, S.C. Dep't of Archives & Hist; *see* JOURNAL OF THE COMMONS HOUSE OF ASSEMBLY: MAY 18, 1741–JULY 10, 1742, at 343–44 (J.H. Easterby ed., 1953) [hereinafter 1741-1742 JOURNAL].

42 1741/2 Tax-Act, *supra* note 41; 1741–1742 JOURNAL, *supra* note 41, at 364, 416, 422, 442.

43 *Charles-Town*, S.C. GAZETTE, Aug. 6–15, 1741.

44 1743 Tax-Act, No. 696, sched., S165001, Box 21, S.C. Dep't of Archives & Hist.; JOURNAL OF THE COMMONS HOUSE OF ASSEMBLY: SEPTEMBER 14, 1742–JANUARY 27, 1744, at 109–10, 199–200, 250, 256–57, 396–97 (J.H. Easterby ed., 1954) [hereinafter 1742-1744 JOURNAL].

45 OLWELL, *supra* note 1, at 73–74; *Charles-Town*, S.C. GAZETTE, June 21–28, 1742.

46 *Charles-Town*, S.C. GAZETTE, Jan. 10, 1743.

47 *Charles-Town*, S.C. GAZETTE, Jan. 17, 1743.

48 JOURNAL OF HIS MAJESTY'S HONORABLE COUNCIL: MARCH 15, 1742–FEBRUARY 19, 1743, at 397–98 (LLMC Digital).

49 *Id.* at 398.

50 *Id.* at 409.

51 *Id.* at 412–13.

52 *Id.* at 413.

53 *Charles-Town*, S.C. GAZETTE, Jan. 24, 1743.

54 1743 Tax-Act, *supra* note 44.

55 1742–1744 JOURNAL, *supra* note 44, at 387.

56 *Id.*; *see* 1740 Slave Code, *supra* note 7, para. VIII; *cf. id.* para. XLVII.

57 1742–1744 JOURNAL, *supra* note 44, at 388.

58 JOURNAL OF THE COMMONS HOUSE OF ASSEMBLY: FEBRUARY 20, 1744–MAY 25, 1745, at 278 (J.H. Easterby ed., 1955) [hereinafter 1744-1745 JOURNAL]; 1745/6 Tax-Act, No. 724, sched., S165001, Box 22, S.C. Dep't of Archives & Hist. The 1744 Tax-Act, No. 712, S165001, Box 22, S.C. Dep't of Archives & Hist., contained no slaveholder compensation payments.

59 1744–1745 JOURNAL, *supra* note 58, at 389; *see id.* at 279–80.

60 *Charles-Town*, S.C. GAZETTE, July 30, 1744.

61 1744–1745 JOURNAL, *supra* note 58, at 404.

62 *Id.* at 294.

63 *Id.* at 294–95.

64 *Id.* at 390, 405.

65 JOURNAL OF THE COMMONS HOUSE OF ASSEMBLY: SEPTEMBER 10, 1745–JUNE 17, 1746, at 99 (J.H. Easterby ed., 1956) [hereinafter 1745-1746 JOURNAL].

66 *Id.*

67 *See supra* notes 22 and 27 and accompanying text.

68 Act of Mar. 22, 1745/6, *supra* note 7, para. VI; 1745–1746 JOURNAL, *supra* note 65, at 32.

69 Act of Mar. 22, 1745/6, *supra* note 7, para. VI. Technically, the cap was set at £40 proclamation money. A 1704 proclamation established an exchange rate of £133 local currency to £100 sterling, making the cap equivalent to about £30 sterling. *Notes*, 2 STATUTES, *supra* note 7, at 705, 709; *see* An Act for Ascertaining the Rates of Foreign Coins in Her Majesty's Plantations in America, *reprinted in* 2 STATUTES, *supra* note 7, at 563; Richard M. Jellison, *Antecedent of the South Carolina Currency Acts of 1736 and 1746*, 16 WM. & MARY Q. 556, 559 n.11 (1959); W. ROY SMITH, SOUTH CAROLINA AS A ROYAL PROVINCE: 1719–1776, at 230 n.3, 278–79 (1903). The prevailing exchange rate was generally higher than the proclamation rate. *See* SMITH, *supra*, at 231, 233–34, 274; WEIR, *supra* note 23, at 94–96, 109; Jellison, *supra*, at 556. During the 1740s, the exchange rate was £7 South Carolina currency to £1 sterling, making £30 sterling equivalent to roughly £200 local currency. SMITH, *supra*, at 274, 279; Jellison, *supra*, at 556; *see* EDSON L. WHITNEY, GOVERNMENT OF THE COLONY OF SOUTH CAROLINA 113 (1895); JOURNAL OF THE COMMONS HOUSE OF ASSEMBLY: NOVEMBER 20, 1755–JULY 6, 1757, at 162–63 (Terry W. Lipscomb ed., 1989); JOURNAL OF THE COMMONS HOUSE OF ASSEMBLY: 23 APRIL 1750–31 AUGUST 1751, at 252 (R. Nicholas Olsberg ed., 1974) [hereinafter 1750–1751 JOURNAL].

70 1745–1746 JOURNAL, *supra* note 65, at 144; *see id.* at 74, 148, 160; 1746 Tax-Act, No. 739, sched., S165001, Box 24, S.C. Dep't of Archives & Hist.

71 1745–1746 JOURNAL, *supra* note 65, at 161, 202.

72 *Charles-Town*, S.C. GAZETTE, Apr. 8, 1745.

73 1745–1746 JOURNAL, *supra* note 65, at 120; *see id.* at 96, 128, 139, 158.

74 1744–1745 JOURNAL, *supra* note 58, at 325–26; JOURNALS OF THE SOUTH CAROLINA COUNCIL AND SENATE: MARCH 12–22, 1746, at 36 (LLMC Digital) [hereinafter 1746 COUNCIL JOURNAL].

75 1746 COUNCIL JOURNAL, *supra* note 74, at 36.

76 *Id.* at 35–36; 1745–1746 JOURNAL, *supra* note 65, at 139.

77 1746 COUNCIL JOURNAL, *supra* note 74, at 35.

78 *Id.*

79 *Id.*

80 *Id.*

81 1745–1746 JOURNAL, *supra* note 65, at 128.

82 1747 Tax-Act, No. 755, sched., S165001, Box 24, S.C. Dep't of Archives & Hist.

83 1745–1746 JOURNAL, *supra* note 65, at 141; JOURNAL OF THE COMMONS HOUSE OF ASSEMBLY: SEPTEMBER 10, 1746–JUNE 13, 1747, at 45–46, 139, 146, 364 (J.H. Easterby & Ruth S. Green eds., 1958) [hereinafter 1746–1747 JOURNAL].

84 1746–1747 JOURNAL, *supra* note 83, at 249–50; *see id.* at 370.

85 2 WALTER B. EDGAR & N. LOUISE BAILEY, BIOGRAPHICAL DIRECTORY OF THE SOUTH CAROLINA HOUSE OF REPRESENTATIVES 350 (1977).

86 1746–1747 JOURNAL, *supra* note 83, at 156.

87 *Id.* at 258; *see id.* at 156.

88 *Id.* at 258, 370.

89 1748 Tax-Act, No. 767, sched., S165001, Box 25, S.C. Dep't of Archives & Hist.; 1749 Tax-Act, No. 770, sched., S165001, Box 25, S.C. Dep't of Archives & Hist.

90 JOURNAL OF THE COMMONS HOUSE OF ASSEMBLY: JANUARY 19, 1748–JUNE 29, 1748, at 140 (J.H. Easterby & Ruth S. Green eds., 1961); *see id.* at 107, 131, 142, 155–56, 385; JOURNAL OF THE COMMONS HOUSE OF ASSEMBLY: MARCH 28, 1749–MARCH 19, 1750, at 45, 60, 69, 71, 106, 123, 163, 165, 225, 227 (J.H. Easterby & Ruth S. Green eds., 1962) [hereinafter 1749–1750 JOURNAL].

91 1750 Tax-Act, No. 780, sched., S165001, Box 25, S.C. Dep't of Archives & Hist.

92 1749–1750 JOURNAL, *supra* note 90, at 401; *see* 1750–1751 JOURNAL, *supra* note 69, at 39, 50, 77, 120.

93 1750–1751 JOURNAL, *supra* note 69, at 40; *see id.* at 51, 77, 120; 1749–1750 JOURNAL, *supra* note 90, at 400.

94 1749–1750 JOURNAL, *supra* note 90, at 380, 418, 432; 1750–1751 JOURNAL, *supra* note 69, at 77, 120; *see infra* text accompanying notes 136–46.

95 1749–1750 JOURNAL, *supra* note 90, at 380, 418, 455; 1750–1751 JOURNAL, *supra* note 69, at 120.

96 1749–1750 JOURNAL, *supra* note 90, at 418; *see id.* at 381, 455; 1750–1751 JOURNAL, *supra* note 69, at 77, 120.

97 1749–1750 JOURNAL, *supra* note 90, at 458; *see* 1750 Tax-Act, *supra* note 91, sched.

98 1750–1751 JOURNAL, *supra* note 69, at 42; *see id.* at 53, 78, 120; 1749–1750 JOURNAL, *supra* note 90, at 462.

99 1750–1751 JOURNAL, *supra* note 69, at 42; *see id.* at 53, 78, 120; 1749–1750 JOURNAL, *supra* note 90, at 86–87, 463.

100 1750–1751 JOURNAL, *supra* note 69, at 31; *see id.* at 43, 54, 65, 78, 120.

101 JOURNAL OF HIS MAJESTY'S HONORABLE COUNCIL: DECEMBER 20, 1748–DECEMBER 16, 1749, at 531–36 (LLMC Digital) [hereinafter 1748–1749 COUNCIL JOURNAL]; *see* OLWELL, *supra* note 1, at 83–87.

102 1748–1749 COUNCIL JOURNAL, *supra* note 101, at 532.

103 *Id.*

104 *Id.*

105 *Id.*

106 *Id.* at 532–33.

107 *Id.* at 533.

108 *Id.*

109 *Id.*

110 *Id.*

111 *Id.* at 533–34.

112 *Id.* at 534.

113 *Id.*

114 *Id.*

115 *Id.* at 535; *see* 1740 Slave Code, *supra* note 7, para. XI.

116 1748–1749 COUNCIL JOURNAL, *supra* note 101, at 535.

117 *Id.* at 535–36.

118 *Id.* at 536.

119 1749–1750 JOURNAL, *supra* note 90, at 404.

120 *Id.* at 404–05.

121 *Id.* at 405.

122 *Id.*

123 *Id.* at 422.

124 *Id.* at 422–23.

125 *Id.* at 423.

126 1750–1751 JOURNAL, *supra* note 69, at 34–35.

127 *Id.* at 35.

128 *Id.* at 34–35.

129 *Id.* at 34.

130 *Id.* at 35.

131 *Id.* at 35, 78, 120.

132 1751 Tax-Act, No. 792, sched., S165001, Box 26, S.C. Dep't of Archives & Hist.

133 1750–1751 JOURNAL, *supra* note 69, at 212; *see id.* at 252, 257, 372, 420.

134 *Id.* at 217, 252, 257, 372, 420.

135 *Id.* at 234–35, 309, 373, 420.

136 *Id.* at 211; *see id.* at 251, 256, 372, 419.

137 1748–1749 COUNCIL JOURNAL, *supra* note 101, at 677; *see* OLWELL, *supra* note 1, at 91.

138 1748–1749 COUNCIL JOURNAL, *supra* note 101, at 677.

139 *Id.*

140 *Id.*

141 *Id.*

142 *Id.*

143 *Id.* at 677–78.

144 1750–1751 JOURNAL, *supra* note 69, at 211.

145 *Id.*

146 *See supra* note 94 and accompanying text.

147 1751 Tax-Act, *supra* note 132, sched.

148 1750–1751 JOURNAL, *supra* note 69, at 257; *see id.* at 375, 423, 452.

149 *Id.* at 208.

150 *Id.* at 257; *see id.* at 204, 375.

151 *Id.* at 209.

152 *Id.*

153 *Id.* at 210.

154 *Id.* at 257; *see id.* at 252.

155 *Id.* at 257, 287–88, 293.

156 *E.g.*, 1740 Tax-Act, *supra* note 30, at 1; 1745/6 Tax-Act, *supra* note 58, at 1; 1750 Tax-Act, *supra* note 91, at 2.

157 1740 Slave Code, *supra* note 7, para. XLVI.

158 1740 General Duty Act, No. 669, pmbl., 3 STATUTES, *supra* note 7, at 556, 556–57 (renewed by Act of Apr. 16, 1746, No. 737, para. I, 3 STATUTES, *supra* note 7, at 670, 670).

159 WOOD, *supra* note 1, at 325; *see* 1740 General Duty Act, *supra* note 158, para. I; SMITH, *supra* note 69, at 287.

160 NICHOLAS RADBURN, TRADERS IN MEN: MERCHANTS AND THE TRANS-FORMATION OF THE TRANSATLANTIC SLAVE TRADE 64, 66 (2023).

161 1740 General Duty Act, *supra* note 158, para. I.

162 *Id.* paras. I, XXXVI.

163 *Id.* para. XIV; *see* 1739–1741 JOURNAL, *supra* note 25, at 127.

164 WOOD, *supra* note 1, at 325; *see* DANIEL C. LITTLEFIELD, RICE AND SLAVES: ETHNICITY AND THE SLAVE TRADE IN COLONIAL SOUTH CAROLINA 116 (1981); OLWELL, *supra* note 1, at 28; W. Robert Higgins, The South Carolina Negro Duty Law 76 (1967) (M.A. thesis, University of South Carolina) (on file with Milner Library, Illinois State University).

165 South Carolina, Agencies: Treasurer. Accounts Payable, Receivable and Duties Collected, 1735–1773 (LLMC Digital); *see* S.C. DEP'T OF ARCHIVES & HIST., RECORDS OF THE PUBLIC TREASURERS OF SOUTH CAROLINA, 1725–1776, at 7–10 tbl.1 (1969). All years are based on old-style dating, with the new year starting on March 25.

166 1740 General Duty Act, *supra* note 158, para. VI.

167 *Id.* para. III.

168 *Id.*

169 *Id.* pmbl., para. III; *see* 2 ROYAL INSTRUCTIONS TO BRITISH COLONIAL GOVERNORS, 1670–1776, at 673–74 (1967); Higgins, *supra* note 164, at 23.

170 1740 General Duty Act, *supra* note 158, para. III.

171 *See* APTHEKER, *supra* note 1, at 188–89.

172 1745/6 Tax-Act, *supra* note 58, sched.; *see supra* note 60 and accompanying text.

173 1750 Tax-Act, *supra* note 91, sched.

174 1740 Slave Code, *supra* note 7, para. XXI.

3. THE LATE COLONIAL PERIOD

1 1751 Revised Slave Code, No. 790, 7 STATUTES AT LARGE OF SOUTH CARO-LINA 420 (David J. McCord ed., 1840) [hereinafter STATUTES].

2 *See* PETER H. WOOD, BLACK MAJORITY: NEGROES IN COLONIAL SOUTH CAROLINA FROM 1670 TO THE STONO REBELLION 289–92 (1974).

3 1751 Revised Slave Code, *supra* note 1, para. VII.

4 *Id.* para. VIII.

5 *Id.* para. IX.

6 *Id.* para. X.

7 *Id.*

8 *Id.* paras. XI–XII.

9 *Id.* para. XVIII.

10 *Id.*

11 *Id.* paras. I, XV.

12 *Id.*

13 *Id.* para. III.

14 1752 Tax-Act, sched., *microformed on* S.C. Codes & Session Laws: 1736–1759, ST733, at 3, 22–23, S.C. Dep't of Archives & Hist.

15 JOURNAL OF THE COMMONS HOUSE OF ASSEMBLY: NOVEMBER 14, 1751–OCTOBER 7, 1752, at 120, 175, 191, 241, 308 (Terry W. Lipscomb & R. Nicholas Olsberg eds., 1977) [hereinafter 1751–1752 JOURNAL].

16 *Id.* at 36, 51, 58, 83, 88–89, 99–100, 240–41, 306–07.

17 2 WALTER B. EDGAR & N. LOUISE BAILEY, BIOGRAPHICAL DIRECTORY OF THE SOUTH CAROLINA HOUSE OF REPRESENTATIVES 81–82 (1977).

18 1751–1752 JOURNAL, *supra* note 15, at 60; *see id.* at 59, 90, 101–03, 241, 307–08.

19 *Id.* at 177; *see id.* at 159, 193, 241, 308.

20 1753 Tax-Act, No. 818, sched., S165001, Box 27, S.C. Dep't of Archives & Hist.

21 JOURNAL OF THE COMMONS HOUSE OF ASSEMBLY: NOVEMBER 21, 1752–SEPTEMBER 6, 1754, at 80–81, 93, 195, 230, 282 (Terry W. Lipscomb ed., 1983) [hereinafter 1752–1754 JOURNAL].

22 *Id.* at 97; *see id.* at 112, 121, 196, 231, 283.

23 *Id.* at 96; *see id.* at 112, 120–21, 196, 231, 283.

24 JOURNAL OF HIS MAJESTY'S HONORABLE COUNCIL: DECEMBER 20, 1748–DECEMBER 16, 1749, at 674 (LLMC Digital).

25 *Id.*

26 *Id.* at 675; *see id.* at 674.

27 *See* ROBERT OLWELL, MASTERS, SLAVES, & SUBJECTS: THE CULTURE OF POWER IN THE SOUTH CAROLINA LOW COUNTRY, 1740–1790, at 98 (1998).

28 1752–1754 JOURNAL, *supra* note 21, at 78, 94, 118, 196, 230, 282.

29 JOURNAL OF HIS MAJESTY'S HONORABLE COUNCIL: FEBRUARY 4–NOVEMBER 8, 1752, at 279 (LLMC Digital).

30 *Id.*

31 *Id.* at 279–80.

32 *Id.* at 280.

33 1752–1754 JOURNAL, *supra* note 21, at 98, 108, 112–14, 121, 129, 196–97, 231, 283.

34 *Id.* at 98, 113.

35 *Id.* at 114.

36 *Id.*

37 1754 Tax-Act, No. 829, sched., S165001, Box 27, S.C. Dep't of Archives & Hist.

38 1752–1754 JOURNAL, *supra* note 21, at 324; *see id.* at 357, 365, 456, 507.

39 *Id.* at 316; *see id.* at 457, 508.

40 *Id.* at 358, 378; *see id.* at 323, 366, 418, 428, 457–58, 508–09.

41 1754 Tax-Act, *supra* note 37, sched.; 1752–1754 JOURNAL, *supra* note 21, at 328; *see id.* at 417, 427, 457, 508.

42 1755 Tax-Act, No. 835, sched., S165001, Box 29, S.C. Dep't of Archives & Hist.; JOURNAL OF THE COMMONS HOUSE OF ASSEMBLY: NOVEMBER 12, 1754–SEPTEMBER 23, 1755, at 49, 76 (Terry W. Lipscomb ed., 1986) [hereinafter 1754–1755 JOURNAL]; *see id.* at 83, 176, 201.

43 1754–1755 JOURNAL, *supra* note 42, at 30, 76; *see id.* at 83, 176, 202, 284.

44 *Id.* at 29, 77; *see id.* at 49, 78, 83, 85, 176, 202, 284.

45 *Id.* at 135; *see id.* at 177, 202, 285.

46 *E.g., Advertisements,* S.C. GAZETTE, Apr. 9–16, 1754.

47 1754–1755 JOURNAL, *supra* note 42, at 49, 76, 83, 99, 119–20, 127, 176, 202, 284.

48 *Charles-Town,* S.C. GAZETTE, June 11–20, 1754.

49 *Charles-Town,* S.C. GAZETTE, June 20–27, 1754.

50 1756 Tax-Act, No. 856, sched., S165001, Box 29, S.C. Dep't of Archives & Hist.; JOURNAL OF THE COMMONS HOUSE OF ASSEMBLY: NOVEMBER 20, 1755–JULY 6, 1757, at 52 (Terry W. Lipscomb ed., 1989) [hereinafter 1755–1757 JOURNAL]; *see id.* at 27, 70, 180, 274.

51 1755–1757 JOURNAL, *supra* note 50, at 163; *see id.* at 142, 166, 180, 274.

52 *Id.* at 29; *see id.* at 96, 99, 181, 274.

53 *Id.* at 52–53; *see id.* at 29–30, 180, 274; *see* OLWELL, *supra* note 27, at 91.

54 *Charles-Town,* S.C. GAZETTE, July 18–25, 1754.

55 *Charles-Town,* S.C. GAZETTE, Aug. 8–15, 1754.

56 *Charles-Town,* S.C. GAZETTE, Aug. 22, 1754.

57 *Id.*

58 *Charles-Town,* S.C. GAZETTE, Aug. 29, 1754.

59 *See* NEGLEY K. TEETERS, ". . . HANG BY THE NECK . . .": THE LEGAL USE OF SCAFFOLD AND NOOSE, GIBBET, STAKE, AND FIRING SQUAD FROM COLONIAL TIMES TO THE PRESENT 87–93 (1967).

60 1757 Tax-Act, No. 865, sched., S165001, Box 28, S.C. Dep't of Archives & Hist.; 1755–1757 JOURNAL, *supra* note 50, at 309; *see id.* at 318, 327, 451.

61 1755–1757 JOURNAL, *supra* note 50, at 338; *see id.* at 331, 339, 451.

62 *Id.* at 347; *see id.* at 340, 350, 451.

63 *Id.* at 347; *see id.* at 341, 350, 451.

64 *Id.* at 313, 319; *see id.* at 327, 451.

65 *Id.* at 312; *see id.* at 319, 327, 451.

66 *Id.* at 319.

67 1758 Tax-Act, No. 874, sched., 4 STATUTES, *supra* note 1, at 53, 70.

68 JOURNAL OF THE COMMONS HOUSE OF ASSEMBLY: OCTOBER 6, 1757–JANUARY 24, 1761, at 90 (Terry W. Lipscomb ed., 1996) [hereinafter 1757–1761 JOURNAL] (alteration in original); *see id.* at 64, 111, 214.

69 *Id.* at 72; *see id.* at 214.

70 1759 Tax-Act, No. 888, sched., S165001, Box 28, S.C. Dep't of Archives & Hist.

71 1757–1761 JOURNAL, *supra* note 68, at 311; *see id.* at 269, 336, 389.

72 *Id.* at 271, 279; *see id.* at 302, 330, 334, 389.

73 *Id.* at 299; *see id.* at 268, 312, 327, 336, 389.

74 1760 Tax-Act, No. 898, sched., 4 STATUTES, *supra* note 1, at 128, 141.

75 John Donald Duncan, Servitude and Slavery in Colonial South Carolina, 1670–1776, at 584–85 (1971) (Ph.D. dissertation, Emory University) (ProQuest).

76 *Charles-Town*, S.C. GAZETTE, Mar. 17, 1759.

77 *Brought to the Work-House*, S.C. GAZETTE, Mar. 24–31, 1759.

78 *Charles-Town*, S.C. GAZETTE, Apr. 21, 1759; *Charles-Town*, S.C. GAZETTE, Apr. 21–28, 1759.

79 1757–1761 JOURNAL, *supra* note 68, at 554.

80 *Id.* at 476–77.

81 *Id.* at 519.

82 1760 Tax-Act, *supra* note 74, sched.

83 1761 Tax-Act, No. 909, sched., S165001, Box 31, S.C. Dep't of Archives & Hist.; JOURNALS OF THE GENERAL ASSEMBLY OF SOUTH CAROLINA: MARCH 26–DECEMBER 26, 1761, at 60, S165226, S.C. Dep't of Archives & Hist. [hereinafter 1761 JOURNAL].

84 1761 JOURNAL, *supra* note 83, at 145; *see id.* at 159, 173.

85 *Id.* at 17, 20–21, 87, 93, 96, 98, 173.

86 *Charles-Town*, S.C. GAZETTE, Mar. 1–8, 1760.

87 1761 JOURNAL, *supra* note 83, at 15; *see id.* at 77, 84–85, 173.

88 1762 Tax-Act, No. 925, sched., S165001, Box 31, S.C. Dep't of Archives & Hist.; JOURNALS OF THE GENERAL ASSEMBLY OF SOUTH CAROLINA: FEBRUARY 6–SEPTEMBER 13, 1762, at 13, 15, 33, 35, 171, S165226, S.C. Dep't of Archives & Hist. [hereinafter 1762 JOURNAL].

89 1762 JOURNAL, *supra* note 88, at 15, 36, 171.

90 W. ROY SMITH, SOUTH CAROLINA AS A ROYAL PROVINCE: 1719–1776, at 340–49 (1903).

91 1764 Tax-Act, No. 935, sched., 4 STATUTES, *supra* note 1, at 189, 204; JOURNALS OF THE GENERAL ASSEMBLY: JANUARY 24, 1763–OCTOBER 6, 1764, at 27, 80, 211, S165226, S.C. Dep't of Archives & Hist. [hereinafter 1763–1764 JOURNAL].

92 1763–1764 JOURNAL, *supra* note 91, at 34, 91, 211.

93 Richard Waterhouse, South Carolina's Colonial Elite: A Study in the Social Structure and Political Culture of a Southern Colony, 1670–1760, at 164 (1973) (Ph.D. dissertation, Johns Hopkins University) (ProQuest); *see* NICHOLAS RADBURN,

TRADERS IN MEN: MERCHANTS AND THE TRANSFORMATION OF THE TRANSATLANTIC SLAVE TRADE 135–36 (2023).

94 1763–1764 JOURNAL, *supra* note 91, at 25–27, 33–34, 36, 77, 79–81, 90, 92, 94, 211.

95 1765 Tax-Act, No. 940, sched., 4 STATUTES, *supra* note 1, at 214, 227.

96 1763–1764 JOURNAL, *supra* note 91, at 46.

97 *Charles-Town*, S.C. GAZETTE, Jan. 10–17, 1761; *see* Duncan, *supra* note 75, at 721–22.

98 1766 Tax-Act, No. 951, sched., 4 STATUTES, *supra* note 1, at 238, 252.

99 JOURNALS OF THE COMMONS HOUSE OF ASSEMBLY: OCTOBER 8, 1765–APRIL 12, 1768, at 128, S165226, S.C. Dep't of Archives & Hist. [hereinafter 1765–1768 JOURNAL]; *see id.* at 140, 192.

100 1767 Tax-Act, No. 962, sched., 4 STATUTES, *supra* note 1, at 268, 282.

101 1765–1768 JOURNAL, *supra* note 99, at 260; *see id.* at 329, 337, 424.

102 *Id.* at 263; *see id.* at 333, 337–38, 424 (containing the erroneous designation included in the Tax-Act schedule).

103 *Id.* at 265; *see id.* at 334, 338–39, 424.

104 1767 Tax-Act, *supra* note 100, sched.

105 1765–1768 JOURNAL, *supra* note 99, at 250.

106 *Id.* at 335; *see id.* at 250–51.

107 *Id.* at 339.

108 1768 Tax-Act, No. 979, sched., S165001, Box 32, S.C. Dep't of Archives & Hist.

109 1765–1768 JOURNAL, *supra* note 99, at 500, 574; *see id.* at 601, 669.

110 *See supra* note 13 and accompanying text.

111 1765–1768 JOURNAL, *supra* note 99, at 580–81; *see id.* at 504, 601, 669.

112 1769 Tax-Act, No. 990, sched., S165001, Box 32, S.C. Dep't of Archives & Hist.

113 JOURNALS OF THE COMMONS HOUSE OF ASSEMBLY: MARCH 14–NOVEMBER 7, 1769, at 96, 104, 155, S165226, S.C. Dep't of Archives & Hist.

114 *Charles-Town*, S.C. GAZETTE, Jan. 11–18, 1768.

115 *Charles-Town*, S.C. GAZETTE, Feb. 8–15, 1768; *Charlestown*, S.C. & AM. GEN. GAZETTE, Feb. 12–19, 1768.

116 *Charlestown*, S.C. & AM. GEN. GAZETTE, Mar. 11–18, 1768.

117 SMITH, *supra* note 90, at 370–87; ROBERT M. WEIR, COLONIAL SOUTH CAROLINA: A HISTORY 306–12 (1983); MAURICE A. CROUSE, THE PUBLIC TREASURY OF SOUTH CAROLINA 114–20 (1977); *see* 1 ROYAL INSTRUCTIONS TO BRITISH COLONIAL GOVERNORS, 1670–1776, at 208–09 (Leonard Woods Labaree ed., 1967) [hereinafter ROYAL INSTRUCTIONS]; 10 STATUTES, *supra* note 1, at 99–101.

118 SMITH, *supra* note 90, at 371–75; *see* JOURNAL OF HIS MAJESTY'S HONORABLE COUNCIL: DECEMBER 1, 1772–SEPTEMBER 17, 1773, at 182, index (entry for "Tax Bill") (LLMC Digital).

119 JOURNALS OF THE COMMONS HOUSE OF ASSEMBLY: NOVEMBER 28, 1769–SEPTEMBER 8, 1770, at 254, 256, 259–60, 268–70, 275–76, 329–30, 366, S165226, S.C. Dep't of Archives & Hist.; JOURNALS OF THE COMMONS HOUSE OF ASSEMBLY: JANUARY 15–NOVEMBER 5, 1771, at 527, 529–30, 533, 536–37, 540, 564, S165226, S.C. Dep't of Archives & Hist.; JOURNALS OF THE COMMONS HOUSE OF ASSEMBLY: OCTOBER 8–NOVEMBER 10, 1772, at 19, S165226, S.C. Dep't of Archives & Hist.

120 *Charles-Town*, S.C. GAZETTE, Aug. 1, 1769.

121 *Charles-Town*, S.C. GAZETTE, Aug. 17, 1769.

122 JOURNALS OF THE COMMONS HOUSE OF ASSEMBLY: FEBRUARY 17, 1773–SEPTEMBER 15, 1775, at 121–23, 128, 130–31, 135–36, 141–48, 153–54, S165226, S.C. Dep't of Archives & Hist. [hereinafter 1773–1775 JOURNAL].

123 *Id.* at 15–17, 23, 166–67, 169.

124 *Charles-Town*, S.C. GAZETTE, July 2, 1772.

125 *Charles-Town*, S.C. GAZETTE, July 9, 1772.

126 *Charles-Town*, S.C. GAZETTE, July 30, 1772.

127 1773–1775 JOURNAL, *supra* note 122, at 143.

128 *Id.* at 153, 156.

129 *Id.* at 158; *see id.* at 157.

130 *Id.* at 159.

131 *Id.* at 159–60; S.C. & AM. GEN. GAZETTE, Apr. 29–May 6, 1774.

132 1773–1775 JOURNAL, *supra* note 122, at 162.

133 *Id.* at 163; *see id.* at 163–64; ROYAL INSTRUCTIONS, *supra* note 117, at 210.

134 *In the Commons House of Assembly*, S.C. GAZETTE, Mar. 28, 1774.

135 SMITH, *supra* note 90, at 393–94; CROUSE, *supra* note 117, at 36–37, 128.

136 1773–1775 JOURNAL, *supra* note 122, at 280–85.

137 *Id.* at 197–98, 203, 205–06, 210, 213, 217–18, 221, 223, 247, 251.

138 *Id.* at 158.

139 *Id.* at 158, 213, 223.

140 *Id.* at 247.

141 *Id.* at 235.

142 *Id.* at 247–48.

143 *Id.* at 250.

144 *Id.* at 211.

145 *Id.* at 212.

146 *Id.*

147 *Id.* at 228.

148 *Id.* at 249.

149 *Id.* at 251.

150 *Id.* at 248.

151 *Id.*

152 *Charlestown*, S.C. & AM. GEN. GAZETTE, May 6–13, 1774.

153 1773–1775 JOURNAL, *supra* note 122, at 275–76.

154 *Id.* at 275.

155 *Id.*

156 *Id.* at 247.

157 *Id.*; *see id.* at 250.

158 *Id.* at 275–76.

159 *Id.* at 287.

160 *Id.* at 281.

161 *E.g.*, 1753 Tax-Act, *supra* note 20, at 1; 1765 Tax-Act, *supra* note 95, para. II.

162 1751 General Duty Act, No. 793, paras. I–III, XVI, 3 STATUTES, *supra* note 1, at 739, 739–40, 743 (renewed by Act of May 21, 1757, No. 861, para. II, 4 STATUTES, *supra* note 1, at 38, 39; Act of Apr. 18, 1767, No. 960, para. I, 4 STATUTES, *supra* note 1, at 264, 264; Act of Mar. 4, 1775, No. 1009, para. I, 4 STATUTES, *supra* note 1, at 331, 332); *see* SMITH, *supra* note 90, at 287; W. Robert Higgins, The South Carolina Negro Duty Law 30 (1967) (M.A. thesis, University of South Carolina) (on file with Milner Library, Illinois State University).

163 1751 General Duty Act, *supra* note 162, pmbl.

164 South Carolina, Agencies: Treasurer. Accounts Payable, Receivable and Duties Collected, 1735–1773 (LLMC Digital); *see* S.C. DEP'T OF ARCHIVES & HIST., RECORDS OF THE PUBLIC TREASURERS OF SOUTH CAROLINA, 1725– 1776, at 7–10 tbl.1 (1969). All years are based on old-style dating, with the new year starting on March 25.

165 1751 General Duty Act, *supra* note 162, para. VI; *see id.* para. I.

166 *Id.* para. VI.

167 *Id.* para. VII.

168 *Id.*

169 *Id.* para. VIII.

170 Act of Oct. 7, 1752, No. 809, pmbl., 3 STATUTES, *supra* note 1, at 781, 781.

171 *Id.* para. I.

172 *Id.* para. II; *see* Act of May 21, 1757, *supra* note 162, para. VI.

173 Act of May 11, 1754, No. 826, para. I, 4 STATUTES, *supra* note 1, at 10, 10.

174 Act of July 25, 1761, pmbl., *microformed on* S.C. Codes & Session Laws: 1760–1791, ST734, at 7, 7, S.C. Dep't of Archives & Hist.

175 *Id.*

176 *Id.* para. I.

177 *Id.*; *see* Act of Jan. 23, 1765, No. 936, para. I, 4 STATUTES, *supra* note 1, at 206, 209; Act of Apr. 18, 1767, *supra* note 162, para. I; Act of Mar. 4, 1775, *supra* note 162, para. I.

178 Act of Aug. 25, 1764, No. 933, pmbl., 4 STATUTES, *supra* note 1, at 187, 187.

179 *Id.* pmbl., para. I; *see* A.S. SALLEY, JR., BULLS. OF THE HIST. COMM'N OF S.C. NO. 7, THE METHODS OF RAISING TAXES IN SOUTH CAROLINA PRIOR TO 1868, at 7 (1925).

180 WEIR, *supra* note 117, at 165; *see* Letter from Henry Laurens to Richard Oswald (Oct. 10, 1764), *in* 4 THE PAPERS OF HENRY LAURENS 462, 466–67 (1974) [hereinafter LAURENS PAPERS]; Letter from Henry Laurens to James Penman (Nov. 23, 1767), *in* 5 LAURENS PAPERS, *supra*, at 472, 473–74.

181 *See* Act of Aug. 25, 1764, *supra* note 178, para. V.

182 Higgins, *supra* note 162, at 34–35.

183 Publick's Ledger: Duties and Special Funds, Annual Receipts and Disbursements, 1771–1776, *microformed on* Reel No. 1, Records of the Public Treasurers of South Carolina, 1725–1776, N. Mich. Univ.; *see supra* note 164. In 1768, accounting switched to new-style dating, with years ending in December.

184 RADBURN, *supra* note 93, at 143.

185 3 STATUTES, *supra* note 1, at 574.

186 *See* Darold D. Wax, *The Image of the Negro in the* Maryland Gazette, *1745–75*, 46 JOURNALISM Q. 73, 74–75 (1969).

187 *See, e.g.*, 1751 General Duty Act, *supra* note 162.

188 *See* 4 STATUTES, *supra* note 1, at 365, 413, 487, 528, 627, 689.

189 *See* Higgins, *supra* note 162, at 69.

190 *See id.* at 34–35, 82–83, 111–12.

191 HENNIG COHEN, THE SOUTH CAROLINA GAZETTE: 1732–1775, at 12 (1953).

192 *See* David A. Copeland, The Freshest Advices Foreign and Domestic: The Character and Content of Nonpolitical News in Colonial Newspapers, 1690–1775, at 251–52 (1994) (Ph.D. dissertation, University of North Carolina at Chapel Hill) (on file with Davis Library, University of North Carolina).

193 *Id.* at 253; *see id.* at 227–28, 253–54.

194 *See* John Samuel Harpham, *Two Concepts of a Slave in the South Carolina Law of Slavery*, 39 SLAVERY & ABOLITION 101 (2018). *See generally* Jacob I. Corré, *Thinking Property at Memphis: An Application of Watson*, 68 CHI.-KENT L. REV. 1373 (1993).

195 *See supra* note 81.

196 Higgins, *supra* note 162, at 259–64.

197 This figure does not include the 1721 payment of £1,000 in arrears because it cannot be determined how many enslaved persons this payment related to; however, that payment is included in the total payments mentioned in the text. The 1724/5 payments to Colonel Fenwick and others as part of a blanket authorization are excluded from both the total killed and executed and total payments.

4. THE NORTHERN COLONIES

1 LORENZO JOHNSTON GREENE, THE NEGRO IN COLONIAL NEW ENGLAND, 1620–1776, at 15–20 (1942); MARGARET ELLEN NEWELL, BRETHREN BY NATURE: NEW ENGLAND INDIANS, COLONISTS, AND THE ORIGINS OF AMERICAN SLAVERY 108–30 (2015).

2 WENDY WARREN, NEW ENGLAND BOUND: SLAVERY AND COLONIZA-
  TION IN EARLY AMERICA 74–76, 133, 249 (2016); JARED ROSS HARDESTY,
  BLACK LIVES, NATIVE LANDS, WHITE WORLDS: A HISTORY OF SLAV-
  ERY IN NEW ENGLAND 12–13, 17–23, 28–29 (2019); EDGAR J. MCMANUS,
  BLACK BONDAGE IN THE NORTH 1–2, 9–10 (1973).

3 GREENE, *supra* note 1, at 73–74.

4 PETER H. WOOD, BLACK MAJORITY: NEGROES IN COLONIAL SOUTH
  CAROLINA FROM 1670 TO THE STONO REBELLION 143, 150 (1974).

5 GREENE, *supra* note 1, at 77–78; EVARTS B. GREENE & VIRGINIA D. HAR-
  RINGTON, AMERICAN POPULATION BEFORE THE FEDERAL CENSUS OF
  1790, at 72 (1932).

6 GREENE, *supra* note 1, at 79; *see id.* at 80–81; GREENE & HARRINGTON, *supra*
  note 5, at 17–18.

7 GREENE, *supra* note 1, at 75; *see id.* at 74–75, 89–90; GREENE & HARRINGTON,
  supra note 5, at 49–50.

8 GREENE, *supra* note 1, at 87 tbl.6; *see* GREENE & HARRINGTON, *supra* note 5, at
  17–18, 49–50, 63–64.

9 GREENE & HARRINGTON, *supra* note 5, at 67; ROBERT K. FITTS, INVENT-
  ING NEW ENGLAND'S SLAVE PARADISE: MASTER/SLAVE RELATIONS IN
  EIGHTEENTH-CENTURY NARRAGANSETT, RHODE ISLAND 82 (1998).

10 GREENE, *supra* note 1, at 86; CHRISTY CLARK-PUJARA, DARK WORK: THE
  BUSINESS OF SLAVERY IN RHODE ISLAND 12 (2016).

11 IRA BERLIN, MANY THOUSANDS GONE: THE FIRST TWO CENTURIES OF
  SLAVERY IN NORTH AMERICA 8 (1998); *see id.* at 47; NEWELL, *supra* note 1, at
  159.

12 CLARK-PUJARA, *supra* note 10, at 25; *see id.* at 25–26; FITTS, *supra* note 9, at
  69–103.

13 GREENE, *supra* note 1, at 102–03; *see* Robert E. Desrochers, Jr., *Slave-for-Sale Advertisements and Slavery in Massachusetts, 1704–1781*, 59 WM. & MARY Q. 623,
  630–33 (2002).

14 CLARK-PUJARA, *supra* note 10, at 3; *see id.* at 4.

15 GREENE, *supra* note 1, at 124, 128; A. LEON HIGGINBOTHAM, JR., IN THE
  MATTER OF COLOR: RACE AND THE AMERICAN LEGAL PROCESS: THE
  COLONIAL PERIOD 71, 80–82 (1978); BERLIN, *supra* note 11, at 54; NEWELL,
  supra note 1, at 13, 168; Jody R. Fernald, Slavery in New Hampshire: Profitable
  Godliness to Racial Consciousness 38 (2007) (M.A. thesis, University of New
  Hampshire) (ProQuest); Guocun Yang, From Slavery to Emancipation: The Afri-
  can Americans in Connecticut, 1650s–1820s, at 115–16 (1999) (Ph.D. dissertation,
  University of Connecticut) (ProQuest).

16 *See* GREENE, *supra* note 1, at 124–42, 230–31; CLARK-PUJARA, *supra* note 10,
  at 6; FITTS, *supra* note 9, at 109–13; HARDESTY, *supra* note 2, at 67; NEW-
  ELL, *supra* note 1, at 232–33; BERNARD C. STEINER, HISTORY OF SLAV-
  ERY IN CONNECTICUT 11–17 (1893); RALPH FOSTER WELD, SLAVERY IN

CONNECTICUT 9–10 (1935); Dinah Mayo-Bobee, *Servile Discontents: Slavery and Resistance in Colonial New Hampshire*, 30 SLAVERY & ABOLITION 339 (2009); Yang, *supra* note 15, at 29, 34–55, 133–51.

17 Jared Ross Hardesty, *An Ambiguous Institution: Slavery, the State, and the Law in Colonial Massachusetts*, 3 J. EARLY AM. HIST. 154, 159, 165–67 (2013); HARDESTY, *supra* note 2, at 13–17, 62–63.

18 GREENE, *supra* note 1, at 178–86, 192–202; HIGGINBOTHAM, *supra* note 15, at 72–76. *But cf.* FITTS, *supra* note 9, at 210–11.

19 *E.g.*, ACTS AND LAWS OF HIS MAJESTY'S ENGLISH COLONY OF CONNECTICUT IN NEW-ENGLAND IN AMERICA 40, 130, 185, 229–30 (1774) [hereinafter 1774 CONN. ACTS]; 1 ACTS AND RESOLVES OF THE PROVINCE OF THE MASSACHUSETTS BAY 154, 156, 325, 535, 578 (1869) [hereinafter MASS. ACTS]; 2 LAWS OF NEW HAMPSHIRE 128, 138, 196 (Albert Stillman Batchellor ed., 1913) [hereinafter N.H. LAWS]; 3 *id.* at 29, 30; ACTS AND LAWS OF HIS MAJESTIES COLONY OF RHODE-ISLAND, AND PROVIDENCE-PLANTATIONS IN AMERICA 151, 195, 234 (1767) [hereinafter 1767 R.I. ACTS]; *see* McMANUS, *supra* note 2, at 65.

20 GREENE, *supra* note 1, at 218–19; HIGGINBOTHAM, *supra* note 15, at 72; *see id.* at 222–23; CLARK-PUJARA, *supra* note 10, at 44, 52; BERLIN, *supra* note 11, at 55–59; FITTS, *supra* note 9, at 140–44; HARDESTY, *supra* note 2, at 55–62; McMANUS, *supra* note 2, at 68; WARREN, *supra* note 2, at 117–51.

21 *See* McMANUS, *supra* note 2, at 87; *cf.* 2 RECORDS OF THE COLONY OF RHODE ISLAND AND PROVIDENCE PLANTATIONS IN NEW ENGLAND 549–50 (1856) [hereinafter R.I. RECORDS]; NEWELL, *supra* note 1, at 166. Generally applicable criminal laws did resort to capital punishment; however, given their application to all, those laws do not seem to have given rise to the need to purchase slaveholder cooperation in their enforcement. *See, e.g.*, GREENE, *supra* note 1, at 157, 179, 191, 299.

22 CLARK-PUJARA, *supra* note 10, at 6 (footnote omitted).

23 Act for the Better Preventing of Spurious and Mixt Issue, ch. 10, § 5 (1705), 1 MASS. ACTS, *supra* note 19, at 578, 578 [hereinafter Antimiscegenation Act]; GREENE, *supra* note 1, at 191–201, 210–13; HARDESTY, *supra* note 2, at 94–102; McMANUS, *supra* note 2, at 37–38; Desrochers, *supra* note 13, at 658–59.

24 HARDESTY, *supra* note 2, at 64; *see supra* ch. 3.

25 ALVIN RABUSHKA, TAXATION IN COLONIAL AMERICA 767–68, 777, 782, 788 (2008).

26 *But cf.* Act for Granting a Tax upon Polls and Estates, § 1 (1695), 1 MASS. ACTS, *supra* note 19, at 213, 213.

27 COLONIAL LAWS OF MASSACHUSETTS 22, 23–24 (1887); 1 N.H. LAWS, *supra* note 19, at 184–85, 524–25; 1 DOCUMENTS AND RECORDS RELATING TO THE PROVINCE OF NEW HAMPSHIRE 428 (Nathaniel Bouton ed., 1867) [hereinafter N.H. RECORDS]; *see* GREENE, *supra* note 1, at 169; Maurice H. Robinson, *A His-*

tory of Taxation in New Hampshire, 3 PUBL'NS AM. ECON. ASS'N, No. 3, Aug. 1902, at 23–32.

28 *E.g.*, 1 MASS. ACTS, *supra* note 19, at 91–92, 167, 179, 187, 199, 214, 240, 258, 278, 302, 337, 359, 386, 413, 438, 483, 495, 521, 551, 569, 592, 610, 615, 627, 661, 694, 714, 747; *see* GREENE, *supra* note 1, at 128–39, 169–72; GEORGE H. MOORE, NOTES ON THE HISTORY OF SLAVERY IN MASSACHUSETTS 62–65 (1866).

29 Diary of Samuel Sewall, *in* 7 [Ser. 5] COLLECTIONS OF THE MASSACHUSETTS HISTORICAL SOCIETY 87 (1882) [hereinafter MASS. COLLECTIONS].

30 2 N.H. LAWS, *supra* note 19, at 394–96, 406–07; 3 *id.* at 533, 586; 4 N.H. RE-CORDS, *supra* note 27, at 244–45, 301, 304–05, 308, 450, 497, 499; 6 *id.* at 175, 743, 761; *see* Robinson, *supra* note 27, at 33–41.

31 RABUSHKA, *supra* note 25, at 193; *e.g.*, 1 R.I. RECORDS, *supra* note 21, at 306; 2 *id.* at 510–12; 3 *id.* at 21–22.

32 3 R.I. RECORDS, *supra* note 21, at 308; *see id.* at 344; GREENE, *supra* note 1, at 128–39.

33 ACTS AND LAWS OF HIS MAJESTIES COLONY OF RHODE-ISLAND, AND PROVIDENCE-PLANTATIONS IN AMERICA 295 (1745); ACTS AND LAWS OF HIS MAJESTIES COLONY OF RHODE-ISLAND, AND PROVIDENCE-PLANTATIONS IN AMERICA 32 (1752); 1757–1759 R.I. Sess. Laws 131, 132; 1760–1762 R.I. Sess. Laws 33–34, 78–79.

34 ROBERT J. TAYLOR, COLONIAL CONNECTICUT: A HISTORY 42 (1979).

35 1 PUBLIC RECORDS OF THE COLONY OF CONNECTICUT 548–49 (1850) [hereinafter CONN. RECORDS].

36 3 *id.* at 17–18; *see id.* at 405–07; GREENE, *supra* note 1, at 167–68; WARREN, *supra* note 2, at 32; NEWELL, *supra* note 1, at 12, 108, 160, 163, 165, 203, 211–12, 228.

37 4 CONN. RECORDS, *supra* note 35, at 412.

38 *E.g.*, 6 *id.* at 220–21, 239, 338, 525; 7 *id.* at 143; 8 *id.* at 131–33; 10 *id.* at 424; 11 *id.* at 14, 182, 344; 13 *id.* at 360.

39 1774 CONN. ACTS, *supra* note 19, at 135, 137–38; *see, e.g.*, Guilford List Book for the West Society (1732), Guilford Collection, 1731–1856, N.Y. Hist. Soc'y; *see also* LAWRENCE HENRY GIPSON, CONN. TERCENTENARY COMM'N, CON-NECTICUT TAXATION, 1750–1775, at 1–4 (1933); FREDERICK ROBERTSON JONES, HISTORY OF TAXATION IN CONNECTICUT, 1636–1776, at 15–25 (1896); Diana Ross McCain, "As True as Taxes": An Historian's Guide to Direct Taxation and Tax Records in Connecticut, 1637–1820, at 7–8, 13, 20 (1981) (M.A. thesis, Wesleyan University) (on file with Wesleyan University Library).

40 *See* McMANUS, *supra* note 2, at 10.

41 ROBIN L. EINHORN, AMERICAN TAXATION, AMERICAN SLAVERY 37 (2006).

42 *Id.* at 38.

43 GREENE, *supra* note 1, at 27; *see id.* at 50; WELD, *supra* note 16, at 4–5.

44 4 N.H. RECORDS, *supra* note 27, at 615–16; 2 ROYAL INSTRUCTIONS TO BRITISH COLONIAL GOVERNORS, 1670–1776, at 673–74 (1967).

45 4 N.H. RECORDS, *supra* note 27, at 617; *see id.* at 617–18.

46 Antimiscegenation Act, *supra* note 23, §§ 1–2, 6; 24 CALENDAR OF STATE PAPERS, COLONIAL SERIES: AMERICA AND WEST INDIES 110 (1922).

47 Antimiscegenation Act, *supra* note 23, § 8; W.E.B. DU BOIS, THE SUPPRESSION OF THE AFRICAN SLAVE-TRADE TO THE UNITED STATES OF AMERICA, 1638–1870, at 22 (2007). *Compare* 1703 General Duty Act, No. 204, para. XV, 2 STATUTES AT LARGE OF SOUTH CAROLINA 200, 203–04 (Thomas Cooper ed., 1837) [hereinafter STATUTES], *with* 1716 General Duty Act, No. 359, para. XXII, 2 STATUTES, *supra*, at 649, 656.

48 Antimiscegenation Act, *supra* note 23, § 8; *see* BERLIN, *supra* note 11, at 184–85; MCMANUS, *supra* note 2, at 94–95.

49 Act to Encourage the Importation of White Servants, ch. 11 (1708/9), 1 MASS. ACTS, *supra* note 19, at 634.

50 GREENE, *supra* note 1, at 52, 55–56.

51 MASS. H.R. JOURNAL, May 1718 Sess., at 16 (emphasis omitted); *see* GREENE, *supra* note 1, at 51.

52 Act More Effectually to Secure the Duty on the Importation of Negros, ch. 16, §§ 1–2 (1728), 2 MASS. ACTS, *supra* note 19, at 517, 517; *see* GREENE, *supra* note 1, at 53.

53 Act More Effectually to Secure the Duty on the Importation of Negros, ch. 27 (1738/9), 2 MASS. ACTS, *supra* note 19, at 981; MASS. H.R. JOURNAL, May 1732 Sess., at 7, 15, 17; GREENE, *supra* note 1, at 56–57.

54 MOORE, *supra* note 28, at 60 n.1.

55 4 R.I. RECORDS, *supra* note 21, at 34.

56 Rhode Island, Laws: Proceedings of the General Assembly, Feb. 25, 1708 & May 1710, at 4 (LLMC Digital).

57 *Id.* at 5; 4 R.I. RECORDS, *supra* note 21, at 34.

58 Act for Laying a Duty on Negro Slaves That Shall Be Imported into This Colony (1711/2) [hereinafter 1711/2 Duty Act] (emphasis omitted), ACTS AND LAWS OF HIS MAJESTIES COLONY OF RHODE-ISLAND, AND PROVIDENCE-PLANTATIONS IN AMERICA 64 (1719) [hereinafter 1719 ACTS AND LAWS]; 4 R.I. RECORDS, *supra* note 21, at 131, 133–35, 185–86, 197–98; *see* DU BOIS, *supra* note 47, at 23–24.

59 1711/2 Duty Act, *supra* note 58, at 65; MCMANUS, *supra* note 2, at 31–32.

60 4 R.I. RECORDS, *supra* note 21, at 191–93.

61 *Id.*

62 *Id.* at 193.

63 Act for Disposing of Money Raised in This Colony (1729), ACTS AND LAWS OF HIS MAJESTIES COLONY OF RHODE-ISLAND, AND PROVIDENCE-PLANTATIONS IN AMERICA 183 (1730) [hereinafter 1730 ACTS AND LAWS]; *see* 4 R.I. RECORDS, *supra* note 21, at 424.

64 CLARK-PUJARA, *supra* note 10, at 19; *see* GREENE, *supra* note 1, at 55–56.

65 1730 ACTS AND LAWS, *supra* note 63, at 245; 4 R.I. RECORDS, *supra* note 21, at 471; Letter from the Governor and Company of Rhode Island to the Lords of Trade (Dec. 1, 1735), *in* 1 THE CORRESPONDENCE OF THE COLONIAL GOVERNORS OF RHODE ISLAND, 1723–1775, at 73 (Gertrude Selwyn Kimball ed., 1902); *see* GREENE, *supra* note 1, at 56–57.

66 MOORE, *supra* note 28, at 61–62.

67 Act Prohibiting the Importation or Bringing into This Province Any Indian Servants or Slaves, ch. 3, pmbl. (1712), 1 MASS. ACTS, *supra* note 19, at 698, 698.

68 *Id.* § 1.

69 5 CONN. RECORDS, *supra* note 35, at 516; Act for Prohibiting the Importation or Bringing into This Colony, Any Indian Servants or Slaves (1715), ACTS AND LAWS OF HIS MAJESTY'S ENGLISH COLONY OF CONNECTICUT IN NEW-ENGLAND IN AMERICA 209 (1729); Act Prohibiting the Importation, or Bringing into This Colony, Any Servants or Slaves (1715), 1719 ACTS AND LAWS, *supra* note 58, at 78; 4 R.I. RECORDS, *supra* note 21, at 193–94.

70 Act Prohibiting the Importation or Bringing into This Province Any Indian Servant or Slaves, ch. 28 (1714), 2 N.H. LAWS, *supra* note 19, at 152.

71 *Id.* at 152–53; 19 N.H. RECORDS, *supra* note 27, at 52.

72 *See* J. Douglas Peters, *"Removing the Heathen": Changing Motives for Indian Slavery in New Hampshire*, 58 HIST. N.H. 67, 73 (2003).

73 Act Prohibiting the Importation of Negroes into This Colony (1774), 1772–1775 R.I. Sess. Laws 48 [hereinafter 1774 Act]; 7 R.I. RECORDS, *supra* note 21, at 251–53; CLARK-PUJARA, *supra* note 10, at 64–68, 73–74.

74 1774 Act, *supra* note 73, at 49–50.

75 GREENE, *supra* note 1, at 23–38; CLARK-PUJARA, *supra* note 10, at 70.

76 CLARK-PUJARA, *supra* note 10, at 2; *see id.* at 3; WARREN, *supra* note 2, at 48–81.

77 CLARK-PUJARA, *supra* note 10, at 63 (footnote omitted); *see id.* at 17–19, 24.

78 Act for Prohibiting the Importation of Indian, Negro, or Molatto Slaves (1774), 1774 CONN. ACTS, *supra* note 19, at 403, 403; *see id.* at 404.

79 *Id.* at 403 (emphasis omitted); *see* WELD, *supra* note 16, at 11–13; Yang, *supra* note 15, at 56–60, 248–51.

80 *See* James T. Allegro, *"Increasing and Strengthening the Country": Law, Politics, and the Antislavery Movement in Early-Eighteenth-Century Massachusetts Bay*, 75 NEW ENG. Q. 5, 17–23 (2002).

81 MASS. H.R. JOURNAL, Dec. 1763 Sess., at 170.

82 *Id.* at 263–64.

83 *Id.*, Jan. 1767 Sess., at 353, 358, 387, 390, 393.

84 *Id.* at 408–11, 420; *see* MOORE, *supra* note 28, at 126–28.

85 Act for Imposing a Duty of Impost upon the Importation of Negro and Other Slaves Within This Province, Jan. 1767 Sess. Great & Gen. Ct. (Mass. 1767), Winthrop Family Papers, Mass. Hist. Soc'y.

86 *Id.*; *see* GREENE, *supra* note 1, at 44–45; *The Domestic Sale of Enslaved People*, MASS. HIST. SOC'Y, www.masshist.org (last visited Sept. 28, 2023); JOHN J. MCCUSKER, MONEY AND EXCHANGE IN EUROPE AND AMERICA, 1600–1775, at 142, 149 (1978).

87 MASS. H.R. JOURNAL, Apr. 1771 Sess., at 197, 211, 215, 219, 228, 234, 236, 240, 242–43.

88 Letter from Thomas Hutchinson, Governor of Massachusetts, to Lord Hillsborough, Sec'y of State for the Colonies (May 1771), *in* 27 MASSACHUSETTS ARCHIVES COLLECTION 157, 159 [hereinafter MASS. ARCHIVES], *microformed on* Film No. 2297896, item 1, FAMILYSEARCH, www.familysearch.org; *see* MOORE, *supra* note 28, at 130–32.

89 MASS. H.R. JOURNAL, Jan. 1773 Sess., at 195, 203, 208, 225, 252, 259, 287; *id.*, May 1773 Sess., at 17, 85; 3 [Ser. 5] MASS. COLLECTIONS, *supra* note 29, at 432–35; HARDESTY, *supra* note 2, at 119–30; MOORE, *supra* note 28, at 133–36; Chernoh M. Sesay Jr., *The Revolutionary Black Roots of Slavery's Abolition in Massachusetts*, 87 NEW ENG. Q. 99 (2014).

90 Act to Prevent the Importation of Negroes or Other Persons as Slaves into This Province, Jan.–Mar. 1774 Sess. Great & Gen. Ct. (Mass. 1774), 9 MASS. ARCHIVES, *supra* note 88, at 457, *microformed on* Film No. 2294419, FAMILYSEARCH, www.familysearch.org; Act to Prevent the Importation of Negroes or Other Persons as Slaves into This Province, May–June 1774 Sess. Great & Gen. Ct. (Mass. 1774), 9 MASS. ARCHIVES, *supra* note 88, at 460, *microformed on* Film No. 2294419, FAMILYSEARCH, www.familysearch.org; MASS. H.R. JOURNAL, Jan. 1774 Sess., at 104, 221, 224, 226, 228, 237, 241–43; *id.*, May 1774 Sess., at 27, 41; Minutes of Council: 1770–1776, 86 MASS. ARCHIVES, *supra* note 88, at 329, 332, *microformed on* Film No. 2364053, FAMILYSEARCH, www.familysearch.org; MOORE, *supra* note 28, at 136–43.

91 RABUSHKA, *supra* note 25, at 183, 187–88, 388–89, 477, 599, 777, 781.

5. THE MIDDLE COLONIES

1 EDGAR J. MCMANUS, BLACK BONDAGE IN THE NORTH 2–5 (1973) [hereinafter MCMANUS, BONDAGE]; EDGAR J. MCMANUS, A HISTORY OF NEGRO SLAVERY IN NEW YORK 1–22, 80 (1966) [hereinafter MCMANUS, SLAVERY]; GRAHAM RUSSELL HODGES, ROOT & BRANCH: AFRICAN AMERICANS IN NEW YORK & EAST JERSEY, 1613–1863, at 6–33 (1999); PATIENCE ESSAH, A HOUSE DIVIDED: SLAVERY AND EMANCIPATION IN DELAWARE, 1638–1865, at 9–18 (1996); WILLIAM H. WILLIAMS, SLAVERY AND FREEDOM IN DELAWARE, 1639–1865, at 1–10 (1996); EDWARD R. TURNER, THE NEGRO IN PENNSYLVANIA: SLAVERY—SERVITUDE—FREEDOM, 1639–1861, at 1–3 (Negro Universities Press 1969) (1911); A. LEON HIGGINBOTHAM, JR., IN THE MATTER OF COLOR: RACE AND THE AMERICAN LEGAL PROCESS: THE COLONIAL PERIOD 100–14 (1978). *See*

generally Christopher Moore, *A World of Possibilities: Slavery and Freedom in Dutch New Amsterdam, in* SLAVERY IN NEW YORK 29 (Ira Berlin & Leslie M. Harris eds., 2005).

2 IRA BERLIN, MANY THOUSANDS GONE: THE FIRST TWO CENTURIES OF SLAVERY IN NORTH AMERICA 178–82 (1998); EVARTS B. GREENE & VIRGINIA D. HARRINGTON, AMERICAN POPULATION BEFORE THE FEDERAL CENSUS OF 1790, at 90–91, 106, 114–15 (1932).

3 HIGGINBOTHAM, *supra* note 1, at 100.

4 HODGES, *supra* note 1, at 36, 44; Melissa Amy Maestri, The Atlantic Web of Bondage: Comparing the Slave Trades of New York City and Charleston, South Carolina 37 (2015) (Ph.D. dissertation, University of Delaware) (ProQuest).

5 Act of Aug. 4, 1705, ch. 149, 1 THE COLONIAL LAWS OF NEW YORK FROM THE YEAR 1664 TO THE REVOLUTION 582, 582 (1896) [hereinafter N.Y. LAWS].

6 *Id.* at 583.

7 *Id.* at 584.

8 Act of Oct. 30, 1708, ch. 181, 1 N.Y. LAWS, *supra* note 5, at 631, 631.

9 Letter from Lord Cornbury to the Board of Trade (Feb. 10, 1707/8), *in* 5 DOCUMENTS RELATIVE TO THE COLONIAL HISTORY OF THE STATE OF NEW-YORK 39, 39 (E.B. O'Callaghan ed., 1855) [hereinafter N.Y. DOCUMENTS].

10 *Id.*

11 HODGES, *supra* note 1, at 64.

12 Act of Oct. 30, 1708, *supra* note 8, at 631.

13 *Id.*

14 Act of Oct. 29, 1730, ch. 560, 2 N.Y. LAWS, *supra* note 5, at 679; Letter from Governor Montgomerie to the Lords of Trade (Dec. 21, 1730), *in* 5 N.Y. DOCUMENTS, *supra* note 9, at 903, 905; *see* Jill Lepore, *The Tightening Vise: Slavery and Freedom in British New York, in* SLAVERY IN NEW YORK, *supra* note 1, at 78; Carl Nordstrom, *The New York Slave Code*, 4 AFRO-AMS. IN N.Y. LIFE & HIST., no. 1, Jan. 1980, at 7, 10–17.

15 Act of Oct. 29, 1730, *supra* note 14, at 684–86.

16 *Id.*; *see* Act of July 27, 1721, ch. 412, 2 N.Y. LAWS, *supra* note 5, at 62.

17 Act of May 14, 1745, ch. 790, 3 N.Y. LAWS, *supra* note 5, at 448–49.

18 Act for Regulating Negro, Indian and Mallatto Slaves Within This Province of New-Jersey, ch. 9, 1704 N.J. Sess. Laws 18.

19 24 CALENDAR OF STATE PAPERS, COLONIAL SERIES: AMERICA AND WEST INDIES 484 (1964) [hereinafter CALENDAR]; *see id.* at 488, 503; 22 *id.* at 381, 383; Lepore, *supra* note 14, at 81.

20 N.J. GEN. ASSEMB. JOURNAL, 1703 Sess., at 128; George Fishman, The Struggle for Freedom and Equality: African Americans in New Jersey, 1624–1849/50, at 98 (1990) (Ph.D. dissertation, Temple University) (ProQuest).

21 JOURNAL OF THE GOVERNOR AND COUNCIL: 1682–1714, *reprinted in* 13 DOCUMENTS RELATING TO THE COLONIAL HISTORY OF THE STATE OF NEW JERSEY 439–43, 445, 448 (Frederick W. Ricord & William Nelson eds., 1890) [hereinafter N.J. DOCUMENTS]; JOHN E. POMFRET, COLONIAL NEW JERSEY: A HISTORY 133–34 (1973).

22 Act for Regulating of Slaves, ch. 39 (1713/4), 1713 N.J. Sess. Laws 51, 52–54.

23 *Id.* at 53–54.

24 *Id.* at 54.

25 *Id.*

26 Act to Regulate the Trial of Slaves for Murder and Other Crimes, ch. 475, §§ 1, 4, 1768 N.J. Sess. Laws 37, 37, 39.

27 Act for the Trial of Negroes, ch. 61, § IV (1700), 2 STATUTES AT LARGE OF PENNSYLVANIA FROM 1682 TO 1801, at 77, 79 (James T. Mitchell & Henry Flanders eds., 1896) [hereinafter PA. STAT.]; *see id.* §§ I–III; TURNER, *supra* note 1, at 26.

28 Appendix I, § II, 2 PA. STAT., *supra* note 27, at 449–56, 495; Act for the Trial of Negroes, ch. 143 (1705/6), 2 PA. STAT., *supra* note 27, at 233.

29 Petition of William Righton & Robert Grace to John Evans, Lieutenant Governor of Pa. (1707/8), Logan Family Papers, Box 4, Folder 34, Hist. Soc'y of Pa.

30 2 MINUTES OF THE PROVINCIAL COUNCIL OF PENNSYLVANIA 405–06 (1852) [hereinafter PA. COUNCIL MINUTES]; *see* HIGGINBOTHAM, *supra* note 1, at 290–91.

31 Act for the Better Regulating of Negroes in This Province, ch. 292, pmbl. (1725/6), 4 PA. STAT., *supra* note 27, at 59, 59 [hereinafter 1725/6 Slave Code]; 2 VOTES AND PROCEEDINGS OF THE HOUSE OF REPRESENTATIVES OF THE PROVINCE OF PENNSYLVANIA 467 (1753) [hereinafter PA. HOUSE JOURNAL].

32 1725/6 Slave Code, *supra* note 31, § I; *see* Act for Laying a Duty on Negroes and Mulatto Slaves Imported into This Province, ch. 467, § X (1761), 6 PA. STAT., *supra* note 27, at 104, 109–10 [hereinafter 1761 Duty Act].

33 ROBIN L. EINHORN, AMERICAN TAXATION, AMERICAN SLAVERY 88 (2006); *see id.* at 91–92; JOSEPH E. ILLICK, COLONIAL PENNSYLVANIA: A HISTORY 211–12 (1976).

34 *See* 2 PA. COUNCIL MINUTES, *supra* note 30, at 56, 60, 128–34; JOHN A. MUNROE, COLONIAL DELAWARE: A HISTORY 115–20 (1978).

35 WILLIAMS, *supra* note 1, at 34.

36 Act for the Trial of Negroes, ch. 43(a), §§ 1–3 (1726), 1 LAWS OF THE STATE OF DELAWARE 102, 102–03 (1797) [hereinafter DEL. LAWS]; *see* ESSAH, *supra* note 1, at 34; WILLIAMS, *supra* note 1, at 34.

37 Act for the Trial of Negroes, *supra* note 36, § 3.

38 *Id.*

39 Act for Raising County-Rates and Levies, ch. 102(a), §§ 3–5 (1742), 1 DEL. LAWS, *supra* note 36, at 257, 259–61.

40 Duke of York's Laws (1664/5), 1 N.Y. LAWS, *supra* note 5, at 6, 59–60; *see* MI-
    CHAEL KAMMEN, COLONIAL NEW YORK: A HISTORY 77–78 (1975); *cf.*
    John Christopher Schwab, *History of the New York Property Tax*, 5 PUBL'NS AM.
    ECON. ASS'N, no. 5, Sept. 1890, at 19, 22–31, 36.

41 Duke of York's Laws, *supra* note 40, at 60.

42 Act of Nov. 11, 1692, ch. 29, 1 N.Y. LAWS, *supra* note 5, at 308, 309; *e.g.*, 1 N.Y.
    LAWS, *supra* note 5, at 598; 2 *id.* at 530; 4 *id.* at 398; *see also* ALVIN RABUSHKA,
    TAXATION IN COLONIAL AMERICA 408, 499, 629, 800 (2008).

43 1 JOURNAL OF THE VOTES AND PROCEEDINGS OF THE GENERAL ASSEM-
    BLY OF THE COLONY OF NEW-YORK 37 (1764) [hereinafter N.Y. ASSEMBLY
    JOURNAL]; *see id.* at 38; 1 JOURNAL OF THE LEGISLATIVE COUNCIL OF THE
    COLONY OF NEW-YORK 23 (1861) [hereinafter N.Y. COUNCIL JOURNAL];
    CHARLES W. BAIRD, CHRONICLE OF A BORDER TOWN: HISTORY OF RYE,
    WESTCHESTER COUNTY, NEW YORK: 1660–1870, at 182, 202 & n.1 (1871).

44 1 THE MINUTES OF THE COURT OF SESSIONS (1657–1696), WESTCHES-
    TER COUNTY, NEW YORK 105 (Dixon Ryan Fox ed., 1924); *see id.* at 104–05.

45 *See, e.g.*, 4 N.Y. LAWS, *supra* note 5, at 721, 809, 815, 826, 884; 5 *id.* at 110, 482.

46 Act of Apr. 3, 1775, ch. 1740, 5 N.Y. LAWS, *supra* note 5, at 858, 860.

47 Act of June 19, 1703, ch. 137, 1 N.Y. LAWS, *supra* note 5, at 550, 550–51.

48 Act of Oct. 11, 1709, ch. 199, 1 N.Y. LAWS, *supra* note 5, at 682; Act of Nov. 28,
    1734, ch. 624, 2 N.Y. LAWS, *supra* note 5, at 876.

49 2 N.Y. COUNCIL JOURNAL, *supra* note 43, at 1209.

50 *Id.* at 1308.

51 Act of June 1, 1693, ch. 112, 1 PA. STAT., *supra* note 27, at 213, 214; *see* Law About
    Taxation, ch. 127 (1683), 1 PA. STAT., *supra* note 27, at 90, 91; Law About County
    Levies, ch. 102 (1693), 1 PA. STAT., *supra* note 27, at 204.

52 Act of Feb. 28, 1710/1, ch. 180, § II, 2 PA. STAT., *supra* note 27, at 373, 375; *see* 2 PA.
    STAT., *supra* note 27, at 390; 3 *id.* at 85, 129–30, 179; 4 *id.* at 14; 5 *id.* at 202, 295–96,
    342, 383, 600; 6 *id.* at 11, 349–50, 358.

53 RABUSHKA, *supra* note 42, at 416, 512, 647–48, 815–16.

54 *See* Act for Raising County-Rates and Levies, *supra* note 39, § 5; *see id.* § 7; Act of
    Nov. 1, 1766, ch. 187(a), § 9, 1 DEL. LAWS, *supra* note 36, at 429, 432–33; Constitu-
    tion or System of Government of 1776, art. 24, 1 DEL. LAWS, *supra* note 36, app.
    at 82, 89.

55 DEL. H.R. JOURNAL, Jan. 1796 Sess., at 10.

56 Act for the Valuation of Real and Personal Property Within This State, ch. 98
    (1796), 2 DEL. LAWS, *supra* note 36, at 1247.

57 *Id.* §§ 7–9; DEL. H.R. JOURNAL, Jan. 1796 Sess., at 41, 59, 66, 69, 93, 100–03, 125,
    128, 130, 133; DEL. S. JOURNAL, Jan. 1796 Sess., at 56, 61–63, 67, 70–72.

58 *Compare, e.g.*, Levy List, Mispillion Hundred, Kent County (1795), *microformed
    on* Film No. 6495, item 113, FAMILYSEARCH, www.familysearch.org, *with* Levy
    List, Dover Hundred, Kent County (1797), *microformed on* Film No. 6495, item
    115, FAMILYSEARCH, www.familysearch.org.

59 HODGES, *supra* note 1, at 47; POMFRET, *supra* note 21, at 24–28, 32; EDWIN P. TANNER, THE PROVINCE OF NEW JERSEY, 1664–1738, at 25–27 (1908).

60 THE GRANTS, CONCESSIONS, AND ORIGINAL CONSTITUTIONS OF THE PROVINCE OF NEW JERSEY 118, 125, 130, 269, 306–07, 321, 334–35, 350, 377 (Aaron Leaming & Jacob Spicer eds., 1881) [hereinafter N.J. GRANTS].

61 *Id.* at 436, 493–94, 521–23, 550, 561.

62 *E.g.*, 1704 Tax Act, ch. 3, 1704 N.J. Sess. Laws 1, 2 (disallowed); 1709 Tax Act, ch. 16, 1708/9 N.J. Sess. Laws 9, 11; 1719 Tax Act, ch. 98, 1718/9 N.J. Sess. Laws 79, 81; 1722 Tax Act, ch. 107, 1721/2 N.J. Sess. Laws 123, 125.

63 1711 Tax Act, ch. 35, 1711 N.J. Sess. Laws 49, 50; 1713/4 Tax Act, ch. 58, 1713 N.J. Sess. Laws 29, 32; N.J. GEN. ASSEMB. JOURNAL, 1711 Sess., at 169–71, 177, *microformed on* Records of the States of the United States: Microfilms, 1703–1740 Assembly Minutes, N.J., A.1b, Reel 1a, N.J. State Archives [hereinafter Records of the States]; *id.*, 1713 Sess., at 239–41, 247–50, *microformed on* Records of the States, *supra*.

64 1711 Tax Act, *supra* note 63, at 50.

65 *See* POMFRET, *supra* note 21, at 164–65; RABUSHKA, *supra* note 42, at 648.

66 *E.g.*, 1752 Tax Act, ch. 249, 1752 N.J. Sess. Laws 3, 11.

67 *Compare, e.g.*, 1704 Tax Act, *supra* note 62, at 2, *and* 1709 Tax Act, *supra* note 62, at 11, *with* 1716/7 Tax Act, ch. 81, 1716 N.J. Sess. Laws 113, 118, *and* Act of Dec. 6, 1769, ch. 495, 1769 N.J. Sess. Laws 54, 58.

68 General Impost Act, ch. 85, § II (1700), 2 PA. STAT., *supra* note 27, at 105, 107; Act of Jan. 12, 1705/6, ch. 164, § V, 2 PA. STAT., *supra* note 27, at 280, 285; *see* William Renwick Riddell, *Pre-Revolutionary Pennsylvania and the Slave Trade*, 52 PA. MAG. HIST. & BIOGRAPHY 1, 4 (1928); Darold D. Wax, *Negro Import Duties in Colonial Pennsylvania*, 97 PA. MAG. HIST. & BIOGRAPHY 22, 23, 29 (1973).

69 Act to Prevent the Importation of Negroes and Indians into This Province, ch. 192 (1712), 2 PA. STATUTES, *supra* note 27, at 433 (disallowed) [hereinafter 1712 Duty Act]; Darold D. Wax, The Negro Slave Trade in Colonial Pennsylvania 266–69 (1962) (Ph.D. dissertation, University of Washington) (ProQuest).

70 2 PA. HOUSE JOURNAL, *supra* note 31, at 110; *see* Wax, *supra* note 68, at 30. *Compare* 1712 Duty Act, *supra* note 69, § I, *with* Impost Act, ch. 181 (1710/1), 2 STATUTES, *supra* note 27, § I (disallowed shortly before expiration).

71 TURNER, *supra* note 1, at 70; 2 PA. HOUSE JOURNAL, *supra* note 31, at 110; *see* Wax, *supra* note 69, at 267.

72 App. III, § II, 2 PA. STATUTES, *supra* note 27, at 543–44, 552, 555; HIGGINBOTHAM, *supra* note 1, at 294; Riddell, *supra* note 68, at 9; Wax, *supra* note 68, at 39–40; *see* 1 PA. HOUSE JOURNAL, *supra* note 31, at xix–xx; 2 *id.* at 175.

73 2 PA. HOUSE JOURNAL, *supra* note 31, at 159–60; Act for Laying a Duty on Negroes Imported into This Province, ch. 218, § I (1715), 3 PA. STAT., *supra* note 27, at 117, 117–18 (disallowed after expiration).

74 *Contra* Wax, *supra* note 69, at 269–74.

75 Act for Imposing a Duty on Persons Convicted of Heinous Crimes and Imported into This Province as Servants, ch. 248, pmbl. (1722), 3 Pa. Stat., *supra* note 27, at 264, 264; *see id.* at 264–65; 4 Pa. Stat., *supra* note 27, at 164–65, 360–61; Turner, *supra* note 1, at 8 n.30.

76 *See supra* note 32 and accompanying text.

77 3 Pa. Stat., *supra* note 27, at 159, 238, 275; 4 *id.* at 52; Turner, *supra* note 1, at 4; Wax, *supra* note 68, at 40.

78 1725/6 Slave Code, *supra* note 31.

79 *Id.* § II; *see* Wax, *supra* note 69, at 28–29.

80 Act for Laying a Duty on Negroes Imported into This Province, ch. 304, § I (1729), 4 Pa. Stat., *supra* note 27, at 123, 123; 3 Pa. House Journal, *supra* note 31, at 83, 87.

81 Turner, *supra* note 1, at 8 n.30.

82 1761 Duty Act, *supra* note 32, § XII; Wax, *supra* note 68, at 24, 26–27; Wax, *supra* note 69, at 257–59; *see* 3 Pa. House Journal, *supra* note 31, at 282, 295, 318, 495; 4 *id.* at 17, 47, 62–64, 88–90, 112–14, 147–49, 197–201, 229–32, 266–69, 325–27, 475–79, 613–15, 752–56, 848–51; 5 *id.* at 77–79, 122–25, 183–86, 228.

83 *Compare* Turner, *supra* note 1, at 7–9, 65–77, *with* Wax, *supra* note 68, at 28–39.

84 Wax, *supra* note 68, at 35, 39, 44; Wax, *supra* note 69, at 166–238, 274–81.

85 5 Pa. House Journal, *supra* note 31, at 144; *see* 4 *id.* at 536–37; Turner, *supra* note 1, at 6; Darold D. Wax, *Africans on the Delaware: The Pennsylvania Slave Trade, 1759–1765*, 50 Pa. Hist.: J. Mid-Atl. Stud. 38, 39–40 (1983).

86 1761 Duty Act, *supra* note 32, § I; *see* 5 Pa. House Journal, *supra* note 31, at 146, 165; 8 Pa. Council Minutes, *supra* note 30, at 576, 578, 580–81; Wax, *supra* note 68, at 35–37.

87 Act of Feb. 20, 1768, ch. 572, pmbl., 7 Pa. Stat., *supra* note 27, at 158.

88 6 Pa. House Journal, *supra* note 31, at 428; *see* Wax, *supra* note 68, at 37–38; Letter from Anthony Benezet to Granville Sharp 9 (Feb. 18, 1773), Granville Sharp Collection, N.Y. Hist. Soc'y, https://digitalcollections.nyhistory.org [hereinafter Benezet February Letter].

89 Benezet February Letter, *supra* note 88, at 9–10.

90 *Id.* at 10.

91 *Id.* at 3; 6 Pa. House Journal, *supra* note 31, at 439.

92 Act of Feb. 26, 1773, ch. 681, §§ I–II, 8 Pa. Stat., *supra* note 27, at 330, 330–31.

93 Letter from Anthony Benezet to Granville Sharp 2 (Mar. 29, 1773), Granville Sharp Collection, N.Y. Hist. Soc'y, https://digitalcollections.nyhistory.org [hereinafter Benezet March Letter]; *see* Wax, *supra* note 68, at 38, 43–44; Wax, *supra* note 69, at 287–88.

94 8 Pa. Stat., *supra* note 27, at 332.

95 1761 Duty Act, *supra* note 32, § VI; *e.g.,* 5 Pa. House Journal, *supra* note 31, at 551; 6 *id.* at 136–37, 140–43, 246; *see* Darold D. Wax, *Negro Imports into Pennsylvania, 1720–1766*, 32 Pa. Hist.: J. Mid-Atl. Stud. 254, 256–60 (1965); Wax, *supra* note 69, at 40–48, 252–53, 262–63.

96 WILLIAMS, *supra* note 1, at 31.

97 RABUSHKA, *supra* note 42, at 512, 647–48, 814–16.

98 WILLIAMS, *supra* note 1, at 30–31.

99 *Id.* at 171.

100 MINUTES OF HOUSE OF REPRESENTATIVES OF THE GOVERNMENT OF THE COUNTIES OF NEW CASTLE, KENT AND SUSSEX UPON DELAWARE: 1765–1770, at 114 (1931).

101 *Id.* at 126; *see id.* at 125.

102 *Id.* at 126.

103 *Id.* at 127.

104 *Id.* at 127–28.

105 WILLIAMS, *supra* note 1, at 171 (footnotes omitted).

106 Instructions for Lord Cornbury (1702), N.J. GRANTS, *supra* note 60, at 619, 640.

107 MCMANUS, BONDAGE, *supra* note 1, at 13.

108 *See id.* at 13, 34–35; TURNER, *supra* note 1, at 5 n.20; Maestri, *supra* note 4, at 128.

109 Act for Laying a Duty on Negro, Indian and Mullatto Slaves Imported and Brought into This Province, ch. 50 (1713/4), 1713 N.J. Sess. Laws 81 [hereinafter 1713 Duty Act]; *see* MCMANUS, BONDAGE, *supra* note 1, at 131–32.

110 1713 Duty Act, *supra* note 109, at 82.

111 Letter from Governor Hunter to the Lords of Trade (Aug. 27, 1714), *in* 4 N.J. DOCUMENTS, *supra* note 21, at 195, 196.

112 ACTS OF THE GENERAL ASSEMBLY OF THE PROVINCE OF NEW-JERSEY 31 (Samuel Allinson ed., 1776).

113 N.J. GEN. ASSEMB. JOURNAL, 1738 Sess., at 326, *microformed on* Records of the States, *supra* note 63.

114 JOURNAL OF THE GOVERNOR AND COUNCIL: 1738–1748, *reprinted in* 15 N.J. DOCUMENTS, *supra* note 21, at 30, 50; *see* HENRY SCOFIELD COOLEY, A STUDY OF SLAVERY IN NEW JERSEY 15 n.2 (1896).

115 JOURNAL OF THE GOVERNOR AND COUNCIL, *supra* note 114, at 343.

116 *Id.* at 384; *see id.* at 345, 351.

117 *Id.* at 385.

118 N.J. GEN. ASSEMB. JOURNAL, Mar. 1761 Sess., at 8; *see id.* at 11.

119 Petition of Inhabitants of New Jersey Opposing Importation of Slaves (1761), SEDSL006, Box 1-13, Item 15, N.J. State Archives.

120 N.J. GEN. ASSEMB. JOURNAL, Nov. 1761 Sess., at 9.

121 *Id.* at 14.

122 Letter from Governor Hardy to the Lords of Trade (Jan. 20, 1762), *in* 9 N.J. DOCUMENTS, *supra* note 21, at 345, 346.

123 Act for Laying a Duty upon Negroes and Mulatto Slaves, ch. 369, § 14 (1762), Sept. 1762 N.J. Sess. Laws 18, 23 [hereinafter 1762 Duty Act]; Letter from Governor Hardy to the Lords of Trade (May 2, 1763), *in* 9 N.J. DOCUMENTS, *supra* note 21, at 382, 383.

124 1762 Duty Act, *supra* note 123, § 1.

125 *Id.*; Letter from Governor Hardy, *supra* note 123, at 383.

126 1762 Duty Act, *supra* note 123, § 7.

127 Letter from the Lords of Trade to Governor Franklin (July 13, 1764), *in* 9 N.J. DOCUMENTS, *supra* note 21, at 444, 447.

128 Act for Laying a Duty on the Purchasers of Slaves Imported into This Colony, ch. 463, § 1, 1767 N.J. Sess. Laws 13, 13.

129 *Id.* §§ 2, 4.

130 Act for Laying a Duty on the Purchasers of Slaves Imported into This Colony, ch. 494, §§ 1, 7, 1769 N.J. Sess. Laws 9, 9, 11; N.J. GEN. ASSEMB. JOURNAL, Oct. 1769 Sess., at 10–11, 13.

131 *See* COOLEY, *supra* note 114, at 18; HODGES, *supra* note 1, at 86, 124–25; POMFRET, *supra* note 21, at 214; Fishman, *supra* note 20, at 169–79.

132 N.J. GEN. ASSEMB. JOURNAL, Oct. 1769 Sess., at 40.

133 *Id.*, Nov. 1773 Sess., at 19; *see id.* at 22–26, 29, 59, 69–70, 73, 123.

134 *Id.* at 65, 68.

135 *Compare, e.g.*, Petition of Citizens of Perth Amboy Opposing Slave Manumissions (Jan. 12, 1774), SEDSL006, Box 1-14, Item 16, N.J. State Archives, *and* Petition of Citizens of Middletown Opposing Slave Manumissions (Feb. 2, 1774), SEDSL006, Box 1-14, Item 17, N.J. State Archives, *with* Petition of Inhabitants of Burlington County Advocating the Manumissions of Slaves (c. 1775), SEDSL006, Box 1-19, Item 3, N.J. State Archives, *and* Petition of Inhabitants of Middlesex County Advocating the Manumissions of Slaves (c. 1775), SEDSL006, Box 1-19, Item 28, N.J. State Archives.

136 N.J. GEN. ASSEMB. JOURNAL, Nov. 1773 Sess., at 79, 114, 132, 155, 161–62, 201; *id.*, Jan. 1775 Sess., at 7–8, 14, 22, 26, 30, 40, 46; *id.*, Nov. 1775 Sess., at 7, 13.

137 Act of May 1, 1702, ch. 107, 1 N.Y. LAWS, *supra* note 5, at 476, 479, 484 (disallowed); Act of Sept. 24, 1709, ch. 194, ACTS OF ASSEMBLY: PASSED IN THE PROVINCE OF NEW-YORK, 1691–1718, at 97, 98 (1719); *see* 1 N.Y. LAWS, *supra* note 5, at 714, 736.

138 Act of June 21, 1714, ch. 273, 1 N.Y. LAWS, *supra* note 5, at 801, 803; Act of July 5, 1715, ch. 292, 1 N.Y. LAWS, *supra* note 5, at 847, 848; Act of Sept. 1, 1716, ch. 324, 1 N.Y. LAWS, *supra* note 5, at 898, 899–900; Act of Oct. 16, 1718, ch. 365, 1 N.Y. LAWS, *supra* note 5, at 1010, 1012.

139 *See* HODGES, *supra* note 1, at 74.

140 Maestri, *supra* note 4, at 80–81.

141 *See id.* at 10.

142 Act of June 24, 1719, ch. 366, 1 N.Y. LAWS, *supra* note 5, at 1013, 1014.

143 2 N.Y. LAWS, *supra* note 5, at 18, 255–56, 430, 432, 772, 774, 1048, 1050; 3 *id.* at 88–90, 92, 151, 223, 277, 417, 480, 616, 655, 732, 745, 872, 879, 963, 965, 968–69, 999; 4 *id.* at 9, 159, 183, 279, 359, 471, 549, 625, 689, 765, 846, 908, 951, 1023; 5 *id.* at 9, 133, 265, 450, 603, 714; *see* 42 CALENDAR, *supra* note 19, at 30–31.

144 *See* Letter from Governor Hunter to the Lords of Trade (Nov. 14, 1710), *in* 5 N.Y. DOCUMENTS, *supra* note 9, at 177, 178; Letter from the Council of New-York to

the Lords of Trade (Dec. 13, 1711), *in* 5 N.Y. DOCUMENTS, *supra* note 9, at 292, 293–95.

145 Maestri, *supra* note 4, at 60.

146 Letter from Governor Hunter to the Lords of Trade (July 7, 1718), *in* 5 N.Y. DOCUMENTS, *supra* note 9, at 507, 509; *see* Letter from President Van Dam to the Lords of Trade (Nov. 2, 1731), *in* 5 N.Y. DOCUMENTS, *supra* note 9, at 925, 927–28; MCMANUS, SLAVERY, *supra* note 1, at 35; Darold D. Wax, *Preferences for Slaves in Colonial America*, 58 J. NEGRO HIST. 371, 374–79 (1973).

147 1 N.Y. COUNCIL JOURNAL, *supra* note 43, at 433–34.

148 Lepore, *supra* note 14, at 87–88; *see id.* at 85–87; HODGES, *supra* note 1, at 93, 103–05; MCMANUS, SLAVERY, *supra* note 1, at 28–30; James G. Lydon, *New York and the Slave Trade, 1700 to 1774*, 35 WM. & MARY Q. 375, 383–84, 387 (1978); Maestri, *supra* note 4, at 99–101, 113.

149 *See* 1 N.Y. ASSEMBLY JOURNAL, *supra* note 43, at 806.

150 *See, e.g.*, 1 N.Y. COUNCIL JOURNAL, *supra* note 43, at 631.

151 Editorial, N.Y. WKLY. J., Mar. 28, 1737, supp. at 3; *see* MCMANUS, SLAVERY, *supra* note 1, at 150–51.

152 N.Y. GEN. ASSEMB. JOURNAL, Jan. 1773 Sess., at 21–23, 87–89; *id.*, Jan. 1774 Sess., at 20–22, 26, 43–44; *id.*, Jan. 1775 Sess., at 13, 30–31, 41–42; Benezet March Letter, *supra* note 93, at 2–3.

153 Benezet March Letter, *supra* note 93, at 2.

154 *Id.* at 3; 2 N.Y COUNCIL JOURNAL, *supra* note 43, at 1892.

155 Benezet March Letter, *supra* note 93, at 2; 2 N.Y COUNCIL JOURNAL, *supra* note 43, at 1912, 1974.

6. THE SOUTHERN COLONIES

1 ALLAN KULIKOFF, TOBACCO AND SLAVES: THE DEVELOPMENT OF SOUTHERN CULTURES IN THE CHESAPEAKE, 1680–1800, at 23–44 (1986); EDMUND S. MORGAN, AMERICAN SLAVERY, AMERICAN FREEDOM: THE ORDEAL OF COLONIAL VIRGINIA 298–308 (1975) [hereinafter MORGAN, FREEDOM]; PHILIP D. MORGAN, SLAVE COUNTERPOINT: BLACK CUL-TURE IN THE EIGHTEENTH-CENTURY CHESAPEAKE AND LOWCOUNTRY 1–23 (1998) [hereinafter MORGAN, COUNTERPOINT]; Russell Menard, *From Servants to Slaves: The Transformation of the Chesapeake Labor System, in* 2 THE ATLANTIC SLAVE TRADE 341 (Jeremy Black ed., 2006).

2 Act of Jan. 9, 1734, 1 COLONIAL RECORDS OF THE STATE OF GEORGIA 50, 50–51 (Allen D. Candler ed., 1904) [hereinafter GA. RECORDS]; *see* HAR-OLD E. DAVIS, THE FLEDGLING PROVINCE: SOCIAL AND CULTURAL LIFE IN COLONIAL GEORGIA, 1733–1776, at 3–4, 12–13 (1976); A. LEON HIGGINBOTHAM, JR., IN THE MATTER OF COLOR: RACE AND THE AMERICAN LEGAL PROCESS: THE COLONIAL PERIOD 222–27 (1978); BETTY WOOD, SLAVERY IN COLONIAL GEORGIA, 1730–1775, at 1–11, 16–19 (1984).

3   Act of Aug. 8, 1750, 1 GA. RECORDS, *supra* note 2, at 56; *see* DAVIS, *supra* note 2, at 13, 31–32; HIGGINBOTHAM, *supra* note 2, at 236–49; WOOD, *supra* note 2, at 24–87; Darold D. Wax, *Georgia and the Negro Before the American Revolution*, 51 GA. HIST. Q. 63, 65–75 (1967).

4   MARVIN L. MICHAEL KAY & LORIN LEE CARY, SLAVERY IN NORTH CAROLINA, 1748–1775, at 10–11 (1995). *See generally* MORGAN, COUNTERPOINT, *supra* note 1.

5   KAY & CARY, *supra* note 4, at 22; *see id.* at 10–25.

6   IRA BERLIN, MANY THOUSANDS GONE: THE FIRST TWO CENTURIES OF SLAVERY IN NORTH AMERICA 115 (1998); *see id.* at 115–18, 150; PHILIP J. SCHWARZ, TWICE CONDEMNED: SLAVES AND THE CRIMINAL LAWS OF VIRGINIA, 1705–1865, at 16–23, 61–164 (1988); Alan D. Watson, *North Carolina Slave Courts, 1715–1785*, 60 N.C. HIST. REV. 24, 25 (1983).

7   Act for the Apprehension and Suppression of Runawayes, Negroes and Slaves, ch. 8 (1672) [hereinafter 1672 Act], 2 STATUTES AT LARGE OF VIRGINIA 299, 299 (William Waller Hening ed., 1823) [hereinafter VA. STATUTES]; Act About the Casuall Killing of Slaves, ch. 1 (1669), 2 VA. STATUTES, *supra*, at 270, 270; MORGAN, FREEDOM, *supra* note 1, at 312.

8   1672 Act, *supra* note 7, at 299–300; WILLIAM ZEBINA RIPLEY, THE FINANCIAL HISTORY OF VIRGINIA, 1609–1776, at 110–11 (1893). Around this time, the legislature set the value of a pound of tobacco at 2d for purposes of paying quitrents and 1.2d for other purposes. RIPLEY, *supra*, at 50 n.3, 104; 2 VA. STATUTES, *supra* note 7, at 222, 233–34, 244, 288. At the quitrent rate, the figures in the 1672 Act translate into compensation of £37 10s for enslaved Blacks and £25 for enslaved Native Americans.

9   Act for Preventing Negroes Insurrections, ch. 10 (1680), 2 VA. STATUTES, *supra* note 7, at 481, 481–82.

10 Act for Suppressing Outlying Slaves, ch. 16 (1691), 3 VA. STATUTES, *supra* note 7, at 86, 86; MORGAN, FREEDOM, *supra* note 1, at 330.

11 Act for the Speedy and Easy Prosecution of Slaves, Committing Capital Crimes, ch. 11 (1705), 3 VA. STATUTES, *supra* note 7, at 269, 270; *see* 4 VA. STATUTES, *supra* note 7, at 126–28; 6 *id.* at 107.

12 1705 Slave Code, ch. 49, para. XXXVII, 3 VA. STATUTES, *supra* note 7, at 447, 460; *see* 8 VA. STATUTES, *supra* note 7, at 523.

13 1705 Slave Code, *supra* note 12, para. XXXVII.

14 *Id.* paras. XXXVIII-XXXIX; *see* 6 VA. STATUTES, *supra* note 7, at 111; 8 *id.* at 523.

15 Act Amending the Slave Code, ch. 4, para. XVI (1723), 4 VA. STATUTES, *supra* note 7, at 126, 131; *see id.* at 131–32; 6 VA. STATUTES, *supra* note 7, at 111; HERBERT APTHEKER, AMERICAN NEGRO SLAVE REVOLTS 176–78 (1943).

16 VA. GAZETTE (Purdie & Dixon), May 4, 1769, at 3; *see id.*, Apr. 29, 1773, at 3; *id.*, May 16, 1771, at 3; *id.*, Apr. 11, 1766, at 4.

17 *See* JACK P. GREENE, THE QUEST FOR POWER: THE LOWER HOUSES OF ASSEMBLY IN THE SOUTHERN ROYAL COLONIES, 1689–1776, at 66 (1963);

S.M. Pargellis, *The Procedure of the Virginia House of Burgesses*, 7 WM. & MARY Q. 143–45, 147, 149 (1927); Act Concerning Public Claims ch. 8 (1705), 3 VA. STAT., *supra* note 7, at 261–62; *see* 5 VA. STAT., *supra* note 7, at 377; 7 *id.* at 528; 8 *id.* at 316; *e.g.*, 2 *id.* at 507–08; 2 JOURNALS OF THE HOUSE OF BURGESSES OF VIRGINIA 170–83 (H.R. McIlwaine ed., 1914) [hereinafter BURGESSES JOURNAL].

18 Email from Kenneth Forest, Archives Reference Servs., Libr. of Va., to author (Mar. 15, 2023) (on file with author); *see* 2 BURGESSES JOURNAL, *supra* note 17, at 170 (1682 Book of Public Claims); Abstract of the Report from the Committee of Public Claims (1701), CO 5/1312 (Adam Matthew, Colonial America); Abstract from the Reports of the Committee of Public Claims (1705), CO 5/1340 (Adam Matthew, Colonial America); *see infra* note 19 and accompanying text; *cf.* Copy of the Most Material Part of the Journal of the Committee for Publick Claims (1699), CO 5/1310 (Adam Matthew, Colonial America).

19 Abstract of the Report of the Committee of Public Claims 2–3 (1702), CO 5/1313 (Adam Matthew, Colonial America).

20 *E.g.*, 3 BURGESSES JOURNAL, *supra* note 17, at 125, 214, 351, 388; 4 *id.* at 247; 5 *id.* at 342, 407.

21 *See* 3 LEGISLATIVE JOURNALS OF THE COUNCIL OF COLONIAL VIRGINIA 1596–1600 (H.R. McIlwaine ed., 1919); *e.g.*, 7 BURGESSES JOURNAL, *supra* note 17, at 196, 316, 357, 406; 9 *id.* at 166–67, 178, 206–07, 210; 11 *id.* at 28, 36, 39, 56, 60, 103; 12 *id.* at 90–91, 134, 170–71, 174, 180–81, 313, 317; 13 *id.* at 11, 27, 36, 192, 224–25, 271, 275.

22 29 ARCHIVES OF MARYLAND 160–61 (1909) [hereinafter MD. ARCHIVES]; JEFFREY R. BRACKETT, THE NEGRO IN MARYLAND 117–19 (Negro Universities Press 1969) (1889).

23 Act of June 8, 1717, ch. 13, para. IV, 33 MD. ARCHIVES, *supra* note 22, at 111, 112. In Maryland, at that time, the mixed-race children of White women were born into thirty-one years of servitude. Act Relating to Servants and Slaves (1715), 30 MD. ARCHIVES, *supra* note 22, at 283, 290.

24 36 MD. ARCHIVES, *supra* note 22, at 321.

25 *Id.* at 323.

26 BRACKETT, *supra* note 22, at 119.

27 Act of May 28, 1737, ch. 2, 40 MD. ARCHIVES, *supra* note 22, at 86, 87; Act of May 28, 1737, ch. 7, 40 MD. ARCHIVES, *supra* note 22, at 92, 93–94; *see* 42 MD. ARCHIVES, *supra* note 22, at 142, 612–13; 44 *id.* at 645, 647; 46 *id.* at 619–20.

28 40 MD. ARCHIVES, *supra* note 22, at 319–20.

29 *Id.* at 478, 559.

30 Act for the Relief of John Blandford and Hannah Ratcliffe, ch. 4 (1741), 42 MD. ARCHIVES, *supra* note 22, at 248.

31 44 MD. ARCHIVES, *supra* note 22, at 41, 177; Act for the Relief of Joseph Scott of Worcester County, ch. 11 (1768), 61 MD. ARCHIVES, *supra* note 22, at 439–40;

Act for the Relief of Mary Hindman of Talbot County, ch. 11 (1769), 62 MD. AR-CHIVES, *supra* note 22, at 127.

32 42 MD. ARCHIVES, *supra* note 22, at 452.

33 Act of June 7, 1751, ch. 14, 46 MD. ARCHIVES, *supra* note 22, at 618; 46 MD. AR-CHIVES, *supra* note 22, at 608; 50 *id.* at 567, 570; 55 *id.* at 395–96; 58 *id.* at 181, 183; 59 *id.* at 287, 289; 63 *id.* at 394.

34 Email from Micah Connor, Libr. Assoc., Md. Hist. Soc'y, to author (Feb. 9, 2023) (on file with author); email from Rachel Frazer, Reference Archivist, Md. State Archives, to author (Feb. 9, 2023) (on file with author).

35 28 MD. ARCHIVES, *supra* note 22, at 136–37, 144, 154–55, 161, 181, 257, 431–32, 504, 576; 31 *id.* at 30–32, 34, 58, 69, 79–80, 119, 157, 182; 32 *id.* at 3, 17, 36, 55, 91–92, 96, 114–15, 130, 144, 163, 178–79, 188, 200, 247, 306, 312–13, 333–35; *see* BRACKETT, *supra* note 22, at 130–35.

36 1715 Slave Code, ch. 46, para. XI, 23 STATE RECORDS OF NORTH CAROLINA 62, 64 (Walter Clark ed., 1904) [hereinafter N.C. RECORDS].

37 *Id.*

38 4 N.C. RECORDS, *supra* note 36, at 123–24.

39 *Id.* at 148–49.

40 *Id.* at 530; 1739 Session, General Assembly Session Records, Record ID 66.8.1., N.C. State Archives.

41 1741 Slave Code, ch. 24, paras. XLV, LIII, 23 N.C. RECORDS, *supra* note 36, at 191, 201.

42 *Id.* para. XLVI.

43 *Id.* paras. LIII–LIV.

44 *See* Marvin L. Michael Kay & Lorin Lee Cary, *"The Planters Suffer Little or Nothing": North Carolina Compensations for Executed Slaves, 1748-1772*, 40 SCI. & SOC'Y 288, 292–93 (1976).

45 KAY & CARY, *supra* note 4, at 66; *e.g.*, N.C. GAZETTE, Oct. 6, 1775, at 6; *id.*, Sept. 2, 1774, at 4; N.C. MAG., Jan. 11, 1765, at 8.

46 Act Amending the Slave Code, ch. 6, para. IX (1753), 23 N.C. RECORDS, *supra* note 36, at 388, 390.

47 Act Amending the Slave Code, ch. 7, para. I (1758), 23 N.C. RECORDS, *supra* note 36, at 488, 488 [hereinafter 1758 Act]; *see* Watson, *supra* note 6, at 32.

48 1758 Act, *supra* note 47, paras. II–III.

49 *Id.* paras. IV–V.

50 *Id.* para. VI.

51 Act Amending the Slave Code, ch. 7, paras. II–III (1764), 23 N.C. RECORDS, *supra* note 36, at 656, 656; Kay & Cary, *supra* note 44, at 298–99.

52 KAY & CARY, *supra* note 4, at 90; *see id.* at 31, 89–90.

53 8 N.C. RECORDS, *supra* note 36, at 353, 355–56, 403, 405, 409; 9 *id.* at 406, 418, 516.

54 JOHN SPENCER BASSETT, SLAVERY AND SERVITUDE IN THE COLONY OF NORTH CAROLINA 32 (1896); *see* 8 N.C. RECORDS, *supra* note 36, at 303.

55 1755 Slave Code, 18 GA. RECORDS, *supra* note 2, at 102; *see* 18 GA. RECORDS, *supra* note 2, at 296–97, 621; DAVIS, *supra* note 2, at 127; WOOD, *supra* note 2, at 112; Robert Strudwick Glenn, Jr., Slavery in Georgia, 1733-1793, at 31–34 (1972) (B.A. senior thesis, Princeton University) (on file with Princeton University).

56 1755 Slave Code, *supra* note 55, at 114; *see id.* at 112–14, 119–20.

57 *Id.* at 114; *see id.* at 114–15.

58 *Id.* at 140.

59 1765 Slave Code, 18 GA. RECORDS, *supra* note 2, at 649, 660–63, 665, 669–70; *see* HIGGINBOTHAM, *supra* note 2, at 262–63; WOOD, *supra* note 2, at 124–28.

60 Act Amending the Slave Code (1766), 18 GA. RECORDS, *supra* note 2, at 760, 760–61.

61 *Id.* at 761.

62 *Id.* at 761–62.

63 Order in Council (June 26, 1767), *reprinted in* 28 [pt. 2] GA. RECORDS, *supra* note 2, at 233; PROCEEDINGS AND MINUTES OF THE GOVERNOR AND COUNCIL, *reprinted in* 10 GA. RECORDS, *supra* note 2, at 459; JOURNAL OF THE COMMONS HOUSE OF ASSEMBLY, *reprinted in* 14 GA. RECORDS, *supra* note 2, at 574–75 [hereinafter COMMONS JOURNAL]; JOURNAL OF THE UPPER HOUSE OF ASSEMBLY, *reprinted in* 17 GA. RECORDS, *supra* note 2, at 460 [hereinafter UPPER HOUSE JOURNAL]; Report of Sir Mathew Lamb to the Board of Trade (Oct. 26, 1766), *in* 28 [pt. 2] GA. RECORDS, *supra* note 2, at 172, 173; Glenn, *supra* note 55, at 49–50.

64 1768 Slave Code, para. XI, 2 EARLIEST PRINTED LAWS OF THE PROVINCE OF GEORGIA, 1755-1770, at 183, 187 (John D. Cushing ed., 1978) [hereinafter EARLIEST LAWS]; *see* 2 EARLIEST LAWS, *supra*, at 272, 274; COMMONS JOURNAL, 14 GA. RECORDS, *supra* note 2, at 580; UPPER HOUSE JOURNAL, 17 GA. RECORDS, *supra* note 2, at 426–28, 441–42, 445–46, 452–53; Glenn, *supra* note 55, at 46–48.

65 UPPER HOUSE JOURNAL, 17 GA. RECORDS, *supra* note 2, at 447–48; Letter from James Wright to the Board of Trade (June 8, 1768), *in* 28 [pt. 2] GA. RECORDS, *supra* note 2, at 251, 254–55.

66 1770 Slave Code, para. 18, 19 [pt. 1] GA. RECORDS, *supra* note 2, at 209, 224; *see* Order in Council (Mar. 6, 1769), *reprinted in* 28 [pt. 2] GA. RECORDS, *supra* note 2, at 327; Letter from Richard Jackson to the Board of Trade (Feb. 21, 1771), *in* 28 [pt. 2] GA. RECORDS, *supra* note 2, at 342; Order in Council (June 7, 1771), *reprinted in* 28 [pt. 2] GA. RECORDS, *supra* note 2, at 346; WOOD, *supra* note 2, at 129; Glenn, *supra* note 55, at 50–52.

67 1755 Slave Code, *supra* note 55, at 124; *see id.* at 142–43; 1765 Slave Code, *supra* note 59, at 674–75, 687; 1770 Slave Code, *supra* note 66, paras. 28, 46.

68 1770 Slave Code, *supra* note 66, para. 46.

69 HIGGINBOTHAM, *supra* note 2, at 50–53, 211–12.

70 ROBIN L. EINHORN, AMERICAN TAXATION, AMERICAN SLAVERY 29, 40–44 (2006).

71 1 BURGESSES JOURNAL, *supra* note 17, at 16; *see* Dennis Dryden Forrest, A History of Taxation in Colonial Virginia, 1607–1775, at 14–28 (1931) (M.A. thesis, College of William & Mary) (ProQuest).

72 Act VI (1644), 1 VA. STATUTES, *supra* note 7, at 286, 286; *see* 6 VA. STATUTES, *supra* note 7, at 42.

73 EINHORN, *supra* note 70, at 38.

74 Act I (1642/3), 1 VA. STATUTES, *supra* note 7, at 240, 242; Act VII (1644/5), 1 VA. STATUTES, *supra* note 7, at 292, 292.

75 Northampton County Court Order Book 161 (1652/3), *microformed on* Film No. 32737, FAMILYSEARCH, www.familysearch.org; *see* KATHLEEN M. BROWN, GOOD WIVES, NASTY WENCHES, AND ANXIOUS PATRIARCHS: GENDER, RACE, AND POWER IN COLONIAL VIRGINIA 119 (1996).

76 Joseph Douglas Deal III, Race and Class in Colonial Virginia: Indians, Englishmen, and Africans on the Eastern Shore During the Seventeenth Century 258 (1981) (Ph.D. dissertation, University of Rochester) (ProQuest).

77 Act XLVI (1657/8), 1 VA. STATUTES, *supra* note 7, at 454, 454; *see* Lancaster County Order Book 36 (1657), *microformed on* Film No. 32140, FAMILYSEARCH, www.familysearch.org; BROWN, *supra* note 75, at 119.

78 Act XIII (1662), 2 VA. STATUTES, *supra* note 7, at 170, 170; *see* MORGAN, FREEDOM, *supra* note 1, at 235, 310; MORGAN, COUNTERPOINT, *supra* note 1, at 14–15. *But cf.* BROWN, *supra* note 75, at 120 (viewing this change through a class/gender lens but without adequate support for that interpretation, *see id.* at 85–86, 335).

79 Act VII (1668), 2 VA. STATUTES, *supra* note 7, at 267, 267.

80 Act VII (1680), 2 VA. STATUTES, *supra* note 7, at 479; MORGAN, FREEDOM, *supra* note 1, at 310.

81 BROWN, *supra* note 75, at 122.

82 Act Concerning Tithables, ch. 7 (1705), 3 VA. STATUTES, *supra* note 7, at 258, 258.

83 5 BURGESSES JOURNAL, *supra* note 17, at 369; Act Amending the Slave Code, *supra* note 15, para. XXI; *see* BROWN, *supra* note 75, at 123; MORGAN, FREEDOM, *supra* note 1, at 337.

84 Act for Exempting Free Negro, Mulatto, and Indian Women, from the Payment of Levies, ch. 37, para. I (1769), 8 VA. STATUTES, *supra* note 7, at 393, 393; 11 BURGESSES JOURNAL, *supra* note 17, at 198; *see id.* at 203, 246, 251; 6 EXECUTIVE JOURNALS OF THE COUNCIL OF COLONIAL VIRGINIA 394–95 (H.R. McIlwaine ed., 1930) [hereinafter EXECUTIVE JOURNAL].

85 John A. Kinnaman, The Internal Revenues of Colonial Maryland 59 (1954) (Ph.D. dissertation, Indiana University) (ProQuest); *see id.* at 89–110, 251–86, 389–492; *e.g.*, 1 MD. ARCHIVES, *supra* note 22, at 59–60, 122–24, 292, 296, 298, 302–03, 313, 407, 417.

86 Letter from Governor Horatio Sharpe to Frederick Calvert (Nov. 9, 1757), *in* 9 MD. ARCHIVES, *supra* note 22, at 99, 101; *e.g.*, 1 MD. ARCHIVES, *supra* note 22, at 262, 269; 15 *id.* at 139; 42 *id.* at 659.

87 Acte Concerning Taxable Persons, ch. 15 (1662), 1 MD. ARCHIVES, *supra* note 22, at 449, 449; *see* 1 MD. ARCHIVES, *supra* note 22, at 536–37; 2 *id.* at 150, 216–17, 290–92, 336–38, 399, 464–66.

88 Act for Constables Takeing the Lists of the Taxables, ch. 14 (1676), 2 MD. ARCHIVES, *supra* note 22, at 538, 539; *see* 2 MD. ARCHIVES, *supra* note 22, at 542–47; 7 *id.* at 82–85, 214–16, 245–47, 327–30, 435–38; 13 *id.* at 123–26, 139–42, 211–13, 538–39; 22 *id.* at 362–63, 514–15.

89 7 MD. ARCHIVES, *supra* note 22, at 159; *see id.* at 166–68.

90 Act of Nov. 15, 1712, ch. 15, 38 MD. ARCHIVES, *supra* note 22, at 158, 158; *see* 30 MD. ARCHIVES, *supra* note 22, at 276.

91 Act of Nov. 6, 1725, ch. 4, 35 MD. ARCHIVES, *supra* note 22, at 427, 427.

92 Tax Act, ch. 63, para. II (1715), 23 N.C. RECORDS, *supra* note 36, at 90, 91; *see id.* para. I.

93 Act to Ascertain What Persons Are Tythables, ch. 51, para. III (1715), 23 N.C. RECORDS, *supra* note 36, at 72, 72. For discussion of a racially motivated change to this definition of tithables, see *infra* text accompanying notes 178–84.

94 Act for the Lessening the Pole and Land Tax and Preventing of Concealments, ch. 1, paras. I–IX, XX (1720), 25 N.C. RECORDS, *supra* note 36, at 162, 162–64, 166.

95 *Id.* para. X.

96 Act Issuing Bills of Credit, ch. 2, paras. VI–VII (1722), 25 N.C. RECORDS, *supra* note 36, at 173, 174; *see* 3 N.C. RECORDS, *supra* note 36, at 190.

97 Tax Act, ch. 1, para. V (1758), 25 N.C. RECORDS, *supra* note 36, at 370, 370; *e.g.*, 23 N.C. RECORDS, *supra* note 36, at 122, 151, 255–56, 295, 315, 329, 395, 423, 494, 518, 540–42, 617, 675, 749, 781, 801, 841, 850; *see* Letter from Governor Burrington to the Lords of Trade (May 19, 1733), *in* 3 N.C. RECORDS, *supra* note 36, at 475, 486; CORALIE PARKER, THE HISTORY OF TAXATION IN NORTH CAROLINA DURING THE COLONIAL PERIOD, 1663–1776, at 97–124 (1928); Marvin L. Michael Kay, *The Payment of Provincial and Local Taxes in North Carolina, 1748–1771*, 26 WM. & MARY Q. 218, 220, 223–25 (1969).

98 Petition of Inhabitants of Orange and Rowan Counties, *in* 8 N.C. RECORDS, *supra* note 36, at 81, 83; *see* 8 N.C. RECORDS, *supra* note 36, at 75–84; 23 *id.* at 117; Kay, *supra* note 97, at 221.

99 ALVIN RABUSHKA, TAXATION IN COLONIAL AMERICA 701, 853 (2008); Percy Scott Flippin, *The Royal Government in Georgia, 1752–1776: IV. The Financial System and Administration*, 9 GA. HIST. Q. 187, 187–92 (1925).

100 *See* COMMONS JOURNAL, 13 GA. RECORDS, *supra* note 2, at 517–18, 533–36; *e.g.*, 18 GA. RECORDS, *supra* note 2, at 66, 164, 393.

101 *E.g.*, 1763 Tax Act, para. II, 1 EARLIEST LAWS, *supra* note 64, at 181, 182.

102 COMMONS JOURNAL, 13 GA. RECORDS, *supra* note 2, at 517–18, 534–35; *id.*, 14 GA. RECORDS, *supra* note 2, at 47–48.

103 Acts of May 1695, ch. 9, 38 MD. ARCHIVES, *supra* note 22, at 51, 52; *see* 38 MD. ARCHIVES, *supra* note 22, at 69–70; 19 *id.* at 181, 193, 308; Margaret Shove Morriss, Colonial Trade of Maryland, 1698–1715, at 76–81 (1914) (Ph.D. dissertation, Bryn Mawr College) (Google Books).

104 19 MD. ARCHIVES, *supra* note 22, at 308; Acts of April 1696, ch. 7, 38 MD. ARCHIVES, *supra* note 22, at 80, 81.

105 22 MD. ARCHIVES, *supra* note 22, at 497–98; 26 *id.* at 289; 27 *id.* at 261–62, 334, 371; 30 *id.* at 328; 38 *id.* at 84–86, 165.

106 Act of Oct. 3, 1704, ch. 67, 26 MD. ARCHIVES, *supra* note 22, at 349, 349; *see* 30 MD. ARCHIVES, *supra* note 22, at 330–31.

107 Act of Aug. 10, 1716, ch. 6, 38 MD. ARCHIVES, *supra* note 22, at 198; *see* 30 MD. ARCHIVES, *supra* note 22, at 412, 505.

108 33 MD. ARCHIVES, *supra* note 22, at 5, 18–19, 69; *see* BRACKETT, *supra* note 22, at 43.

109 Act of Oct. 26, 1723, ch. 19, pmbl., 34 MD. ARCHIVES, *supra* note 22, at 740, 740; *see* Act of June 8, 1717, ch. 10, 33 MD. ARCHIVES, *supra* note 22, at 109.

110 Act of Nov. 2, 1728, ch. 8, para. V, 36 MD. ARCHIVES, *supra* note 22, at 281, 282.

111 BRACKETT, *supra* note 22, at 43.

112 Address of the Pennsylvania General Assembly (Feb. 11, 1756), *reprinted in* MD. GAZETTE, Mar. 4, 1756; 31 MD. ARCHIVES, *supra* note 22, at 105–13.

113 Act for His Majesty's Service, ch. 1 (1754), 50 MD. ARCHIVES, *supra* note 22, at 559, 563, 566; Act for His Majesty's Service, ch. 5 (1756), 52 MD. ARCHIVES, *supra* note 22, at 480, 516–17, 520.

114 58 MD. ARCHIVES, *supra* note 22, at 512–13.

115 *Id.* at 263, 265, 345, 377, 379, 381, 384, 388, 415.

116 61 *id.* at 232; 64 *id.* at 217.

117 Act of Nov. 29, 1771, ch. 7, 63 MD. ARCHIVES, *supra* note 22, at 242, 243; *see* 63 MD. ARCHIVES, *supra* note 22, at 20; Letter from Anthony Benezet to John & Henry Gurney (Jan. 10, 1772), *in* GEORGE S. BROOKES, FRIEND ANTHONY BENEZET 283, 286 (1937); Letter from Anthony Benezet to Benjamin Franklin (Apr. 27, 1772), *in* BROOKES, *supra*, at 287, 289; *cf.* 64 MD. ARCHIVES, *supra* note 22, at 59, 62–63, 114, 116, 127–28.

118 Letter from Anthony Benezet to Granville Sharp 3 (Mar. 29, 1773), Granville Sharp Collection, N.Y. HIST. SOC'Y, https://digitalcollections.nyhistory.org.

119 W.E.B. DU BOIS, THE SUPPRESSION OF THE AFRICAN SLAVE-TRADE TO THE UNITED STATES OF AMERICA, 1638–1870, at 9 (2007); RABUSHKA, *supra* note 99, at 840.

120 1699 Duty Act, ch. 12, 3 VA. STATUTES, *supra* note 7, at 193; Darold D. Wax, *Negro Import Duties in Colonial Virginia*, 79 VA. MAG. HIST. & BIOGRAPHY 29, 31 (1971); *cf.* 2 VA. STATUTES, *supra* note 7, at 134–35.

121 1699 Duty Act, *supra* note 120, pmbl.

122 3 VA. STATUTES, *supra* note 7, at 212–13, 225, 233; *see* Wax, *supra* note 120, at 32–33.

123 1710 Duty Act, at 4, 7, Virginia Acts, 1710, CO 5/1385 (Adam Matthew, Colonial America).

124 4 BURGESSES JOURNAL, *supra* note 17, at 281; BROWN, *supra* note 75, at 216–17; Wax, *supra* note 120, at 33–35.

125 4 BURGESSES JOURNAL, *supra* note 17, at 286.

126 Letter from Colonel Spotswood Commenting on Legislation (Mar. 6, 1710/1), CO 5/1316 (Adam Matthew, Colonial America).

127 Letter from Mr. Harris in Relation to an Act of Virginia for Laying a Duty on Liquors and Slaves (Sept. 23, 1723), CO 5/1319 (Adam Matthew, Colonial America); *see* James A. Rawley, *Richard Harris, Slave Trader Spokesman*, 23 ALBION 439, 450 (1991).

128 LAWS OF VIRGINIA: BEING A SUPPLEMENT TO HENING'S THE STATUTES AT LARGE, 1700–1750, at 67, 130 (Waverly K. Winfree ed., 1971) [hereinafter SUPPLEMENT]; 5 BURGESSES JOURNAL, *supra* note 17, at 223; Wax, *supra* note 120, at 31.

129 Wax, *supra* note 120, at 35.

130 VIRGINIA SLAVE-TRADE STATISTICS 1698–1775, at xiii tbls.1 & 2 (Walter Minchinton et al. eds., 1984) [hereinafter MINCHINTON].

131 5 BURGESSES JOURNAL, *supra* note 17, at 339, 388.

132 1723 Duty Act, SUPPLEMENT, *supra* note 128, at 237, 238, 241.

133 5 BURGESSES JOURNAL, *supra* note 17, at 400; 4 EXECUTIVE JOURNAL, *supra* note 84, at 449; *see* 33 CALENDAR OF STATE PAPERS, COLONIAL SERIES: AMERICA AND WEST INDIES 336, 343–44, 383–84, 399 (1934) [hereinafter CALENDAR]; 34 *id.* at 18, 20–21, 84, 99, 319, 381; Rawley, *supra* note 127, at 450–51.

134 1727/8 Duty Act, SUPPLEMENT, *supra* note 128, at 285, 285, 291.

135 Letter from William Gooch (June 8, 1728), CO 5/1321 (Adam Matthew, Colonial America).

136 *Id.*

137 36 CALENDAR, *supra* note 133, at 212–13, 261–62, 390–92, 470; Rawley, *supra* note 127, at 451.

138 4 EXECUTIVE JOURNAL, *supra* note 84, at 265; 6 BURGESSES JOURNAL, *supra* note 17, at 116.

139 6 BURGESSES JOURNAL, *supra* note 17, at 125.

140 *Id.* at 132.

141 1732 Duty Act, ch. 3, paras. I–II, 4 VA. STATUTES, *supra* note 7, at 317, 317–18.

142 Abstract of a Letter from Major Gooch (Oct. 5, 1732), CO 5/1323 (Adam Matthew, Colonial America).

143 4 VA. STATUTES, *supra* note 7, at 394; 5 *id.* at 28–31, 160–61, 318–19; 6 *id.* at 217–21, 353–54; 7 *id.* at 281; 8 *id.* at 190–91, 336–37.

144 5 *id.* at 92–94; 6 *id.* at 419–20, 466–70; 7 *id.* at 81, 282, 363, 383, 639–41; 8 *id.* at 343–44, 348; *see* Wax, *supra* note 120, at 31; 9 BURGESSES JOURNAL, *supra* note 17, at 211, 284–85, 296–97; 6 EXECUTIVE JOURNAL, *supra* note 84, at 149–50.

145 9 BURGESSES JOURNAL, *supra* note 17, at 95–96, 211.

146 Tax Act, ch. 1, para. XI (1760), 7 VA. STATUTES, *supra* note 7, at 357, 363; *see* 6 EXECUTIVE JOURNAL, *supra* note 84, at 149–50; Wax, *supra* note 120, at 37–38.

147 Letter from Lieutenant Governor Fauquier to the Lords of Trade (June 2, 1760), *in* 9 BURGESSES JOURNAL, *supra* note 17, app. at 284–85.

148 1767 Additional Duty Act, ch. 28, 8 VA. STATUTES, *supra* note 7, at 237; 6 EXECUTIVE JOURNAL, *supra* note 84, at 303–04, 617–18.

149 1769 Additional Duty Act, ch. 8, 8 VA. STATUTES, *supra* note 7, at 337; 6 EXECUTIVE JOURNAL, *supra* note 84, at 394–96, 630.

150 *See* MORGAN, FREEDOM, *supra* note 1, at 345–46; RABUSHKA, *supra* note 99, at 429–32, 534–36, 668–75, 835–38, 856–57.

151 *See* Petition of the Merchants of Liverpool (July 1770), *in* 4 DOCUMENTS ILLUSTRATIVE OF THE HISTORY OF THE SLAVE TRADE IN AMERICA 151–52 (Elizabeth Donnan ed., 1935) [hereinafter DOCUMENTS].

152 12 BURGESSES JOURNAL, *supra* note 17, at 256–57.

153 *Id.* at 283–84.

154 Letter from Lord Dunmore to Earl of Hillsborough (May 1, 1772), *in* 4 DOCUMENTS, *supra* note 151, at 153–54.

155 1772 Duty Act, ch. 15, 8 VA. STATUTES, *supra* note 7, at 530; 6 EXECUTIVE JOURNAL, *supra* note 84, at 651–52.

156 12 BURGESSES JOURNAL, *supra* note 17, at 176–78, 240; Pargellis, *supra* note 17, at 145.

157 13 BURGESSES JOURNAL, *supra* note 17, at 278–80.

158 KULIKOFF, *supra* note 1, at 65; *see id.* at 69–76; MORGAN, COUNTERPOINT, *supra* note 1, at 59–62, 84–85, 95.

159 KULIKOFF, *supra* note 1, at 66.

160 MINCHINTON, *supra* note 130, at 65–189.

161 KULIKOFF, *supra* note 1, at 66.

162 Constitution, ch. 2, para. I (1776), 9 VA. STATUTES, *supra* note 7, at 112, 113.

163 Act of Aug. 8, 1750, *supra* note 3, at 61.

164 COMMONS JOURNAL, 13 GA. RECORDS, *supra* note 2, at 460, 463.

165 *Id.* at 524, 531; *see id.* at 520, 523, 582; Letter from James Wright to the Board of Trade (Oct. 1, 1762), *in* 28 [pt. 1] GA. RECORDS, *supra* note 2, at 382, 383.

166 1761 Duty Act, para. IX, 1 EARLIEST LAWS, *supra* note 64, at 117, 118–19.

167 *Id.*

168 *Id.* para. XIII.

169 1767 Duty Act, 2 EARLIEST LAWS, *supra* note 64, at 143; *see* COMMONS JOURNAL, 14 GA. RECORDS, *supra* note 2, at 302–03; Letter from James Wright to the Board of Trade (June 15, 1767), *in* 28 [pt. 2] GA. RECORDS, *supra* note 2, at 226, 230.

170 Act of Dec. 24, 1768, para. VIII, 2 EARLIEST LAWS, *supra* note 64, at 229, 231–32.

171 COMMONS JOURNAL, 15 GA. RECORDS, *supra* note 2, at 74.

172 1773 Duty Act, 19 [pt. 1] GA. RECORDS, *supra* note 2, at 439, 440–41; COMMONS JOURNAL, 15 GA. RECORDS, *supra* note 2, at 141, 148, 157–58, 261, 263–66, 279–80, 287; UPPER HOUSE JOURNAL, 17 GA. RECORDS, *supra* note 2, at 560, 563, 577.

173 1773 Duty Act, *supra* note 172, at 442.

174 Letter from Richard Jackson to the Board of Trade (June 11, 1774), *in* 28 [pt. 2] GA. RECORDS, *supra* note 2, at 394, 394; *see supra* note 99 and accompanying text.

175 Order in Council (Dec. 19, 1774), CO 5/677 (Adam Matthew, Colonial America); *Proclamation*, GA. GAZETTE, Mar. 29, 1775.

176 Darold D. Wax, *Preferences for Slaves in Colonial America*, 58 J. NEGRO HIST. 371, 379 (1973); *see* Letter from Governor Burrington to Duke of Newcastle (July 2, 1731), *in* 3 N.C. RECORDS, *supra* note 36, at 142, 154.

177 Walter E. Minchinton, *The Seaborne Slave Trade of North Carolina*, 71 N.C. HIST. REV. 1 (1994); *see* Letter from Governor Burrington to Commissioners of His Majesty's Customs (July 20, 1736), *in* 4 N.C. RECORDS, *supra* note 36, at 169, 172; KAY & CARY, *supra* note 4, at 19–21; ROSSER HOWARD TAYLOR, SLAVEHOLDING IN NORTH CAROLINA: AN ECONOMIC VIEW 20–22 (Negro Universities Press 1969) (1926).

178 Act for an Additional Tax on all Free Negroes, Mulattoes, and Mustees, ch. 5, paras. I–III (1723), 23 N.C. RECORDS, *supra* note 36, at 106, 106 [hereinafter 1723 Act].

179 *See supra* text accompanying note 93.

180 1715 Slave Code, *supra* note 36, para. XVI; Act Concerning Marriages, ch. 1, para. XIII (1741), 23 N.C. RECORDS, *supra* note 36, at 158, 160; *see* KAY & CARY, *supra* note 4, at 67.

181 Amendment to the Act for Obtaining an Exact List of Taxables, ch. 3, para. II (1749), 23 N.C. RECORDS, *supra* note 36, at 345, 345.

182 1723 Act, *supra* note 178, paras. IV–V.

183 9 N.C. RECORDS, *supra* note 36, at 97; *see id.* at 146–47; 5 *id.* at 295; 6 *id.* at 902, 982; BASSETT, *supra* note 54, at 69.

184 Act for Obtaining an Exact List of Taxables, ch. 2, para. II (1760), 23 N.C. RECORDS, *supra* note 36, at 526.

185 MORGAN, COUNTERPOINT, *supra* note 1, at xvi.

CONCLUSION

1 *See generally* ANTHONY C. INFANTI, OUR SELFISH TAX LAWS: TOWARD TAX REFORM THAT MIRRORS OUR BETTER SELVES (2018).

2 *See* PHILIP D. MORGAN, SLAVE COUNTERPOINT: BLACK CULTURE IN THE EIGHTEENTH-CENTURY CHESAPEAKE AND LOWCOUNTRY 263 (1998).

3 ALL THE PRESIDENT'S MEN (Warner Bros. 1976), *quoted in* THE YALE BOOK OF QUOTATIONS 258 (Fred R. Shapiro ed., 2006).

4 Sheryl Gay Stolberg, *House Democrats Consider Commission on Slavery Reparations*, N.Y. TIMES, June 19, 2019, at A17; *see* WILLIAM A. DARITY JR. & A. KIRSTEN MULLEN, FROM HERE TO EQUALITY: REPARATIONS FOR BLACK AMERICANS IN THE TWENTY-FIRST CENTURY 9–27 (2020); Ta-Nehisi Coates, *The Case for Reparations*, ATL. (May 21, 2014), www.theatlantic. com; Adeel Hassan, *No Easy Answers on Reparations*, N.Y. TIMES (June 21, 2019), www.nytimes.com; *see* ALFRED L. BROPHY, REPARATIONS PRO & CON 19–40, 62–74 (2006); Joe R. Feagin & Eileen O'Brien, *The Growing Movement for Reparations, in* WHEN SORRY ISN'T ENOUGH: THE CONTROVERSY OVER APOLOGIES AND REPARATIONS FOR HUMAN INJUSTICE 341 (Roy L. Brooks ed., 1999) [hereinafter BROOKS].

5 Astead W. Herndon, *For Democrats in 2020: Race-Conscious Policies Could Become a Divide*, N.Y. TIMES, Feb. 22, 2019, at A12; Emma Goldberg, *How Reparations for Slavery Became a 2020 Campaign Issue*, N.Y. TIMES (May 31, 2021), www.nytimes.com; Julian Routh, *Common Ground Aplenty at Forum for U.S. House Democratic Candidates for 12th District, but Differences Arise*, PITT. POST-GAZETTE (Mar. 14, 2022), www.post-gazette.com.

6 Hassan, *supra* note 4; Stolberg, *supra* note 4; H.R. 40, 116th Cong. (2019).

7 H.R. 40, 117th Cong. (2021); Marianna Sotomayor, *House Panel Approves Bill to Create Commission on Slavery Reparations*, WASH. POST (Apr. 14, 2021), www. washingtonpost.com.

8 *E.g.*, Giulia Heyward, *Reparations for Black Residents Are Becoming a Local Issue as Well as a National One*, N.Y. TIMES (Sept. 25, 2021), www.nytimes.com.

9 Emmanuel Felton, *A Chicago Suburb Promised Black Residents Reparations. Few Have Been Paid*, WASH. POST (Jan. 9, 2023), www.washingtonpost.com.

10 Neil Vigdor, *North Carolina City Approves Reparations for Black Residents*, N.Y. TIMES (July 16, 2020), www.nytimes.com; Sarah Honosky, *What Does Reparations Mean? 8 Months into Process, Asheville Still Finding Its Way*, ASHEVILLE CITIZEN TIMES (Dec. 26, 2022), www.citizen-times.com.

11 Act of Sept. 30, 2020, ch. 319, 2020 Cal. Legis. Serv. 319 (West); CA. TASK FORCE TO STUDY & DEV. REPARATIONS PROPOSALS FOR AFR. AMS., FINAL REPORT 39–52 (2023).

12 Alan Blinder, *Mulling Reparations, California Sets Aside $12 Million as a Start*, N.Y. TIMES (June 29, 2024), www.nytimes.com; Emmanuel Felton, *California Budget Includes $12 Million for Reparations for Black Residents*, WASH. POST (June 28, 2024), www.washingtonpost.com.

13 20 ILL. COMP. STAT. 405/405-540 (West, Westlaw through P.A. 103-583 of 2023 Reg. Sess.); Grace Ashford & Luis Ferré-Sadurní, *New York to Consider Reparations for Descendants of Enslaved People*, N.Y. TIMES (Dec. 19, 2023), www. nytimes.com.

14 Emmanuel Felton, *Providence Offers Reparations to Address Racism. White People Can Apply*, WASH. POST (Nov. 29, 2022), www.washingtonpost.com.

15 BROPHY, *supra* note 4, at 147–49; Eric A. Posner & Adrian Vermeule, *Reparations for Slavery and Other Historical Injustices*, 103 COLUM. L. REV. 689, 689, 747 (2003).

16 *See* Felton, *supra* note 9; Debbie-Marie Brown, *One-Year Anniversary of Evanston's Reparations Vote: Reflection, Discussion with Local Newsmakers*, EVANSTON ROUNDTABLE (Mar. 21, 2022), www.evanstonroundtable.com; *Evanston Local Reparations*, CITY OF EVANSTON, www.cityofevanston.org (last visited Oct. 21, 2023) (see FAQs).

17 Felton, *supra* note 9; Estate of H.H. Weinert v. Comm'r, 294 F.2d 750, 755 (5th Cir. 1961); Treas. Reg. § 1.61-1(a) (1957); 35 ILL. COMP. STAT. 5/203(a)(1), (e)(1) (West, Westlaw through P.A. 103-583 of 2023 Reg. Sess.); *see* Andre Smith & Carlton Waterhouse, *No Reparation Without Taxation: Applying the Internal Revenue Code to the Concept of Reparations for Slavery and Segregation*, 7 PITT. TAX REV. 159, 171–85 (2010).

18 Felton, *supra* note 9; Gina Castro, *Two Reparations Recipients Haven't Used the $25,000 Grants, and Expiration Date Looms*, EVANSTON ROUNDTABLE (Jan. 29, 2023), www.evanstonroundtable.com.

19 Felton, *supra* note 9; Castro, *supra* note 18.

20 Felton, *supra* note 9.

21 Gina Castro, *City Council Approves Direct Cash Payment Reparations*, EVANSTON ROUNDTABLE (Mar. 27, 2023), www.evanstonroundtable.com; Carlos D. Williamson, *As Ancestor Payments Wrap Up, Reparations Panel Plans for Direct Descendant Grants*, EVANSTON ROUNDTABLE (Oct. 6, 2023), www.evanstonroundtable.com; *see infra* note 26.

22 *See* Felton, *supra* note 14.

23 *Id.*

24 Teo Armus, *A Chicago Suburb Wants to Give Reparations to Black Residents. Its Funding Source? A Tax on Marijuana*, WASH. POST (Dec. 2, 2019), www.washingtonpost.com; Andy Fies, *Evanston, Illinois, Finds Innovative Solution to Funding Reparations: Marijuana Sales Taxes*, ABCNEWS (July 19, 2020), www.abcnews.go.com.

25 *See* Evanston, Ill., Res. 58-R-19, Commitment to End Structural Racism and Achieve Racial Equity (June 5, 2019). *See generally* MORRIS ROBINSON, JR. & JENNY THOMPSON, EVANSTON POLICIES AND PRACTICES DIRECTLY AFFECTING THE AFRICAN AMERICAN COMMUNITY (2021).

26 Gina Castro, *Reparations Committee Feels Pressure to Disburse Grants to City's Ancestors*, EVANSTON ROUNDTABLE (Oct. 7, 2022), www.evanstonroundtable.com; Bob Seidenberg, *A Reparations Program in Search of a Funding Source*, EVANSTON ROUNDTABLE (Nov. 15, 2022), www.evanstonroundtable.com.

27 *See supra* note 26.

28 *Cf.* Economic Growth and Tax Relief Reconciliation Act of 2001, Pub. L.
No. 107-16, § 803, 115 Stat. 38, 149; *see* Jerome R. Hellerstein & Walter
Hellerstein, State Taxation ¶ 20.02, Westlaw (database updated May
2023).

29 *E.g.,* Brophy, *supra* note 4, at 3–18, 143–50, 169–76; Boris I. Bittker, The
Case for Black Reparations (1973); Darity & Mullen, *supra* note 4.

30 *See* Brandon Hasbrouck, *The Antiracist Constitution*, 102 B.U. L. Rev. 87 (2022);
see also Brophy, *supra* note 4, at 58–62.

31 Brophy, *supra* note 4, at 158–64; Boris I. Bittker & Roy L. Brooks, *The Con-
stitutionality of Black Reparations, in* Brooks, *supra* note 4, at 374; Posner &
Vermeule, *supra* note 15, at 715–21. *See generally* Carlton Waterhouse, *Follow the
Yellow Brick Road: Perusing the Path to Constitutionally Permissible Reparations
for Slavery and Jim Crow Era Governmental Discrimination*, 62 Rutgers L.
Rev. 163 (2009).

32 600 U.S. 181 (2023). *Compare* Bittker, *supra* note 29, at 105–27, *with* Bittker &
Brooks, *supra* note 31, at 381–85.

33 Emmanuel Felton, *City Sued for Paying Hundreds of Black Residents $25,000 in
Reparations*, Wash. Post (June 4, 2024), www.washingtonpost.com.

34 *See* Vincent M. Southerland, *Toward a Just Future: Anticipating and Overcoming
a Sustained Resistance to Reparations*, 45 N.Y.U. Rev. L. & Soc. Change 427,
450–55 (2021); *e.g.,* Dorothy A. Brown, The Whiteness of Wealth:
How the Tax System Impoverishes Black Americans—and How
We Can Fix It 215–22 (2021).

35 Legal creativity of an insidious sort was also displayed in other domains, as when
laws were created to ensure the perpetuation of slavery by having status descend
through the mother rather than the father, as was customary in England. Lorenzo Johnston Greene, The Negro in Colonial New England,
1620–1776, at 126 (1942); A. Leon Higginbotham, Jr., In the Matter
of Color: Race and the American Legal Process: The Colonial Period 43–44 (1978); Thomas D. Morris, Southern Slavery
and the Law, 1619–1680, at 43–49 (1996). *Compare* Act of Sept. 21, 1664, ch.
30, 1 Archives of Maryland 533 (1883), *with* Act of June 3, 1715, ch. 44, 30
Archives of Maryland 283, 289–90 (1910).

36 *See* Mary Ziegler, Dollars for Life: The Anti-abortion Movement and the Fall of the Republican Establishment (2022);
Dobbs v. Jackson Women's Health Org., 597 U.S. 215 (2022).

37 *See* Leadership Conf. on Civ. & Hum. Rts., Persevere: Our On-
going Fight for an Equal Justice Judiciary (2023); Carl Hulse,
Progressives Plan a Nationwide Push to Overhaul the Supreme Court, N.Y. Times,
Apr. 20, 2023, at A18.

38 Jack M. Balkin, *The Reconstruction Power*, 85 N.Y.U. L. Rev. 1801, 1840 (2010);
see id. at 1837, 1839–40; Transcript of Oral Argument at 57–60, Allen v. Milligan,

599 U.S. 1 (2023) (No. 21-1086); William M. Carter, Jr., *The Second Founding and the First Amendment*, 99 TEX. L. REV. 1065, 1081–82 (2021).

39 For a discussion of the broader reworking of the civil rights landscape that such efforts might simultaneously unleash, see Hasbrouck, *supra* note 30, at 153–63.

40 *See generally* ANTHONY C. INFANTI, TAX AND TIME: ON THE USE AND MISUSE OF LEGAL IMAGINATION (2022).

41 I.R.C. §§ 6428–6428B.

42 *See* Jeremy Bearer-Friend, *Paying for Reparations*, 67 HOW. L.J. 1 (2023–2024); Smith & Waterhouse, *supra* note 17, at 186–207, 209.

43 L.G. Sherrod, *Forty Acres and a Mule*, ESSENCE, Apr. 1993, at 124.

44 *20,000 Blacks Seek Tax Refund Based on Vetoed 1866 Measure*, N.Y. TIMES, Oct. 20, 1994, at B12.

45 David Cay Johnston, *I.R.S. Paid Millions in False Claims for Slavery Credit*, N.Y. TIMES, Apr. 14, 2002, § 1, at 22.

46 *See generally* SUZANNE METTLER, THE SUBMERGED STATE: HOW INVISIBLE GOVERNMENT POLICIES UNDERMINE AMERICAN DEMOCRACY (2011).

47 McCulloch v. Maryland, 17 U.S. 316, 431 (1819).

INDEX

Page numbers in italics indicate Boxes, Figures, and Tables.

ABOUT THE AUTHOR

ANTHONY C. INFANTI is the Christopher C. Walthour, Sr. Professor of Law at the University of Pittsburgh. He teaches and writes in the area of tax law, with a particular focus on critical tax theory. Among other works, he is the author of *Our Selfish Tax Laws: Toward Tax Reform That Mirrors Our Better Selves* and *Tax and Time: On the Use and Misuse of Legal Imagination*.